Graceful Women

Graceful Women

Gender and Identity in an
American Sikh Community

Constance Waeber Elsberg

THE UNIVERSITY OF TENNESSEE PRESS
Knoxville

utp

Copyright © 2003 by The University of Tennessee Press / Knoxville.
All Rights Reserved. Manufactured in the United States of America.
First Edition.

All photographs were taken by the author.

This book is printed on acid-free paper.

Library of Congress Cataloging-in-Publication Data

Elsberg, Constance Waeber. 1945–
Graceful women: gender and identity in an American Sikh community /
Constance Waeber Elsberg.
    p. cm.
Includes bibliographical references and index.

ISBN 1-57233-214-X (cl.: alk. paper)

1. Healthy Happy Holy Organization.
2. Religious life—Sikhism.
I. Title.
BL2018.7.H43 E47 2003
294.6'65'0820973—dc21   2002014837

Contents

Illustrations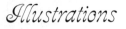

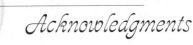

Acknowledgments

I would like to thank my colleagues at Northern Virginia Community College who have encouraged me in this project. I am particularly grateful to the administration of the college for leave time and to Jean Braden for her unstinting support and help in scheduling my courses so that I could pursue this interest.

I would also like to thank those who have commented on drafts of this book, and specially thank two experts on the Sikh experience, Verne A. Dusenbery and W. H. McLeod, for their helpful advice, and Patricia A. Powers for her suggestions and long-term support.

A special thank-you to Jean Reynolds, without whose early computer help this project might never have reached completion, to Kathryn E. King for typing the bibliography, and to my editor, Karin Kaufman.

To Steve and Laura, thank you for being you, and to John, thank you, for everything.

To all of the women (and a few good men) who shared their lives and their thinking about those lives, and to Tara, who opened the doors, my gratitude and affection. Sat Nam.

Setting the Scene

Sadhana (1981)

The days begin early, before dawn. Ideally, they begin with yoga, meditation, and Sikh worship. Ashram residents emerge from suburban homes and make their way to the house where devotions will be held. Their early morning faces are pinched and pale. Their heads are covered with turbans or kerchiefs, and their apparel is predominantly white or blue. Goatskin mats are tucked under arms, and sometimes children are carried as well. There are greetings as people remove their shoes and then enter a dimly lit room. One by one they bow and settle on their mats. Some prepare for yoga by flexing the spine. They sit cross-legged, hands holding their knees, as they alternately bend and straighten their backs.

Morning worship begins with group chanting of a mantra. This is followed by some preliminary exercises and then by physically demanding yoga sets. The room fills with rustles and sighs as devotees begin the "breath-of-fire," a distinctive breathing technique done in association with yoga postures that requires rapid and continuous breaths, using the abdomen to inhale and exhale. After the yoga, there is another period of chanting, and the women's voices, clear and lovely, rise above the men's, the sounds seeming almost to assemble, take shape, and hover in the room. Some people sway as they chant, and slowly they are lifted out of themselves and into a unity of syllables, sounds, and souls.

Then there is just the memory of sound as the participants wrap themselves in blankets and shawls and turn inward for a period of silent meditation. The sun rises and the room lightens as silence gives way to prayers and songs, and finally the sweet, sticky *karah prasad* (a gift, a sacramental food made of sugar, flour, and clarified butter) is passed and received in cupped hands. Now that the morning discipline is over, the tone changes and focused effort gives way to jokes and gossip before people leave for their adjacent homes to have breakfast and to begin the rest of the day's activities.

Those activities are varied because the ashram residents work in a number of different settings. Some work independently, some are involved in "family businesses" run by members of the organization with which they are affiliated. Their hope, whatever they do, is that they have so prepared themselves for the day ahead that they will be able to live it "consciously," attentively, and with a positive attitude. They hope to bring the peace and insights of meditation into the everyday world and to channel the spiritual energy they raise into their daily lives. They hope, above all, to maintain the connection to the Divine that they have established.

Living in contemporary North America, with its postmodern pastiche of styles and social worlds and segmented lives, they aim to become "single-pointed." They assume that there is such a thing as Truth, that lives can follow a coherent plot line, and that they are following a spiritual path that can traverse all terrains, cut through confusion, and skirt temptations. In a time of rapid change they seek anchorage in an ultimate reality existing behind the shifting veils of appearance and illusion. They envision a higher reality that can absorb all contradictions and unite all the seeming oppositions. They embrace discipline and group living as a means of personal and social transformation.

Many have adopted the Sikh religion. Most are affiliated with the Healthy Happy Holy Organization, known familiarly to its members as 3HO. Incorporated in Los Angeles in 1969, 3HO for a brief period existed as a loosely knit group of counterculture youth practicing yoga under the direction of an Indian Sikh named Harbhajan Singh Puri, who soon came to be known as Yogi Bhajan. Bhajan trained these students so that they too could become yoga teachers, and he encouraged them to fan out over the country in order to found ashrams. By 1972 they had succeeded in establishing ninety-four official ashrams, located in North America and abroad.

As the number of members and ashrams grew, and as Yogi Bhajan issued instructions and guidelines for living a spiritual life and began to give legal form to his creations, the organization changed in form and tone. Everyday life was increasingly structured, and, rather than just exploring yoga and meditation, members began to adopt a formal religion. In the early 1970s, with Bhajan's encouragement, they began to take Sikh vows. This change in direction was institutionalized when Bhajan incorporated the Sikh Dharma Brotherhood (later shortened to Sikh Dharma in deference to the feelings of women members) in California in 1973 (Dusenbery 1990b).

Today, 3HO and Sikh Dharma are parallel organizations. As a teaching and outreach organization, 3HO sponsors courses in subjects such as kundalini yoga, meditation, nutrition, and spiritual healing. It also operates preschools, runs a training program for kundalini yoga teachers, puts on a yearly Peace Prayer Day, and sponsors a number of summer training camps for women. Sikh Dharma is the administrative and religious arm of the organization. It consists of an international network of ashrams whose affairs are hierarchically organized under Yogi Bhajan's leadership. Below him are regional directors, an advisory council, and ashram directors. One can participate in 3HO activities without becoming a Sikh, but 3HO and Sikh Dharma are intertwined in many practical ways, which reflects the fact that many members' beliefs are a syncretic mix of Sikhism and yogic traditions (and also incorporate elements of New Age and counter culture thought).

In addition to 3HO and Sikh Dharma, other bodies have been created over the years. These include the Amar Infinity Foundation and nonprofit organizations such as the Kundalini Research Institute and the Guru Ram Das Center for Medicine and Humanology. Members of 3HO have also created numerous businesses. A management team (Khalsa International Industries and Trades) provides strategic planning, market support, and financial help to members' businesses if a director requests these services.

The formal intent of 3HO/Sikh Dharma was clarified early in the organization's history, as this summary of 3HO goals, published in an article written for the journal *Communities* in 1975, suggests: "a growth-enhancing milieu directed towards growth on at least four levels: a healthy body through yoga, diet, and hygiene; a healthy happy mind through meditation, Sikh Dharma . . . and group support; healthy-happy interpersonal relations through a group consciousness and group activities; and a spiritually-oriented attitude of gratitude, a realization of the oneness we all share" (Comeau and Singh 1975, 41). His students assume that Yogi Bhajan designed their mosaic of beliefs and practices specifically to meet their requirements. "He studied us very thoroughly and very intently for the first three years; he was getting a feel for our needs," says a spokeswoman. Members view the resulting life-style as a harmonious whole, an innovative adaptation of diverse traditions. The morning devotions, which combine yoga and Sikhism, dramatize this mix.

The above description of those devotions is based on my first encounter with *sadhana* and my general impression of it. In 3HO/Sikh

Dharma *sadhana* is broadly defined as "any practice of self correction that provides the mind and body with a disciplined channel to express the infinite within one's self" (Gurucharan Singh Khalsa 1978, 14), but it is generally used to refer to the morning ritual. I had attended 3HO-sponsored workshops before I attended *sadhana*, but the workshops had been of a general type that appeal to seekers after personal change and self-knowledge, and they had not really prepared me for what I found. I knew that the woman who conducted the workshops belonged to a spiritually oriented community, but when she invited me to attend *sadhana* as a visitor, I did not realize that she had made religious vows, and I knew almost nothing about Sikhism. Once there, I was impressed by the devotion on many of the faces and entranced by the beautiful Sikh *kirtan*, which, I would soon learn, are the prayers of the Sikh gurus set to music. When I got up to stretch and move around, I was also amused to find several people asleep on sofas in another room; discipline evidently lived side by side with normal human frailty.

Khalsa Women's Training Camp (1983)

Some three hundred women have temporarily left their families, ashrams, and jobs in various parts of the United States and Canada—and some have even come from overseas—to participate in the Khalsa Women's Training Camp. The campsite is located outside of the town of Española, New Mexico, near one of Sikh Dharma's major ashrams. It is intended to provide a setting in which 3HO women, and others who are interested in learning more about the 3HO life-style, can assemble to study aspects of this spiritual path. Courses are offered in subjects such as "Study of the Siri Guru Granth Sahib" (the Sikh sacred scriptures), "Beginning Gurmukhi" (the script in which the scriptures are written), "Conversational Punjabi," and "Yoga and the Spiritual Woman," as well as in practical fields such as "Marriage and Family Counseling," CPR, and homeopathy. For many of the women this is a welcome opportunity to relinquish domestic obligations and spend time with friends. Many also view attendance as a discipline, an opportunity to attend morning *sadhana* more frequently or to intentionally change aspects of the self. Yogi Bhajan teaches that American women have been exploited and rendered so "insecure" that self-esteem and spiritual understanding have been eroded. Here, attendees are supposed to experience purging of unhealthy cultural "programming" and "neuroses" and to fully experience themselves as the spiritual beings that they truly are. They are also expected to overcome personal weaknesses and become strong and "righteous."

This year, Yogi Bhajan teaches a daily yoga class which is enthusiastically received. Participants arrive early to claim choice locations and come casually dressed for a good workout. There is always a buzzing and a tangible excitement; no matter how physically difficult the yoga sets may prove, Bhajan's class is viewed as a special occasion. Bhajan also appears to enjoy himself. He is jolly and expansive and often teases participants, accusing them, perhaps, of getting fat and lazy, or pretending that an exercise has only been in progress for a few seconds when, in fact, long exhausting minutes have passed.

On some days the yoga sets begin immediately without any preface or discussion, but today Yogi Bhajan is talkative. He skips from topic to topic: use of the breath in yoga, a diet he has been on, even hydrotherapy, a healing technique in which, he tells his audience, he was trained when he was younger. Suddenly, he is critical, complaining that people in the West make "messes" and then expect others to clean up after them. He appears to be talking about all kinds of messes: environmental, political, social, emotional. "You create it; you suffer with it. And you have to clean it. If you think somebody from outside will come and take care of you and clean after you, you are very sickly sick and you better wake up." Then he shifts tone again, and, sounding very upbeat, he begins to lead the group in a series of exercises based on yoga postures. At one point he introduces a lion pose: "Tough fingers. Tough fingers, like claws. . . . Just get through this exercise. Come on. Come on. You are invincible woman. Go, go, go, go, go. . . . Breathe, breathe the breath-of-fire. . . . Get wild, get wild, get the anger out now. You can really be a lioness. Last three minutes. Come on, come on. . . . Roar to do it." (The campers obligingly roar and a cacophony ensues.) When the exercise is finished, Bhajan encourages his students to relax and enjoy the rewards of their exertions: "Inhale, exhale, inhale again. . . . Come with me. I will take you where there's nothing but health, beauty, joy, and happiness. It is the domain of the wisdom of God. Come. Come. Come. Relax. Good. See how happy, we are done."

Later, on a hot mid-afternoon, participants are taking a break before Yogi Bhajan addresses the assembled camp. The dirt paths are dusty and comparatively deserted. Women, dressed in their good white clothes, are beginning to gather under a large yellow-and-white-striped canopy. An open tent flap reveals considerable domesticity for so primitive a setting: I spot rugs, clothes hung tidily on hangers, an oscillating fan, and a makeshift altar. Nearby, in a small, open structure, a few women are ironing skirts or dresses in preparation for the lecture. Further down a path, two women are holding the ends of a long, white scarf known as a *chunni*. They have dampened it and now are flapping it in the air so that it will dry wrinkle-free. It will be worn over a turban, falling back over the shoulders like a veil to create the desired graceful effect.

More and more women converge under the canopy, some carrying tape recorders and notebooks to capture important points in the lecture. Most also carry water bottles for relief from the dry July heat. While they wait they chant to "set the vibrations" for Bhajan's appearance. When he arrives he exits from a sleek automobile and is flanked by guests and security guards. Members of the audience stand until he is settled on a stage, where he sits cross-legged under a picture of one of the Sikh gurus. All listen attentively as he talks about the problems that American women encounter and delineates a vision of the ideal, spiritual woman. As they ponder his message, they believe that it is healing just to be near to him. Later, many will comment on his ability to pinpoint the very issues that are troubling them.

These scenes of *sadhana* and of ladies' camp capture aspects of women's lives in 3HO that were well established by the 1980s. The women are by turns both devout Sikhs and energetic yoga students. They are often quiet, reserved, pious, and obedient, but they are also quite likely to be talkative, practical, and assertive. They actively pursue enlightenment, performing demanding physical regimens in order to strengthen mind and body, awaken spiritual energies, "cleanse" the subconscious of past pain and karma, and experience spiritual highs and "group consciousness." In this effort, they can be Yogi Bhajan's enthusiastic, humorous, and self-disciplined confederates, sharing with him in a common effort. At other times they are very much the students, mere neophytes, and relatively passive recipients of the teacher's wisdom. At times they see themselves as part of a cultural vanguard, leading the way into a brighter future. At other times they see themselves as seekers trying to find their way through the maze of Western materialism and false consciousness, receiving instruction so that they may learn the true nature of womanhood and regain their birthright of dignity and grace. They have all turned to a man raised in another culture, expecting that, with his help, they will learn to unearth and polish what he calls "the diamond within."

A Conversation (1995)

"It's a very good story; it's all stories," says Prabhupati Kaur. She and I are sitting at a small table in front of a coffee bar just off the plaza in the Old Town section of Albuquerque on an unseasonably warm November day. We are discussing the history of 3HO/Sikh Dharma.

She is an ex-member (a "graduate," she would say) of 3HO. As we watch the parade of people going by, she reminisces about her days in the organization. She no longer wears the white clothes and turban that she wore every day for years, so there is nothing to distinguish her from other people enjoying the day, although her biography sets her apart. Prabhupati is a writer, so it seems natural to her to view the organization as a fabric of stories. She tells me that, if she were to tell the organizational story, it would be in fictional form. She would create composite characters and mingle actual and imaginary stories. While her preference is for fiction and poetry, she is supportive of my attempt to tell the 3HO/Sikh Dharma story in an ethnographic format.

As we discuss our impressions of women's lives in 3HO/Sikh Dharma, Prabhupati supplies one plot line that she thinks is commonly enacted. Many of the people in the organization are "out of touch with their feelings," she says. They are "so busy being who they should be that they no longer know who they are." She thinks that members repress their emotions and deny whole portions of the self in their efforts to enact their spiritual ideals. This, I know, is an interpretation she attaches to her own experience. She ties her journey out of the organization to a confrontation with repressed experiences and feelings. While it certainly does describe the lives of some of the present and past members of 3HO/Sikh Dharma, I am inclined to think that this is only one of many possible stories that can be extracted from the 3HO experience. In fact, I think that the organization itself often functions as a kind of narrative resource—a source of imagery, metaphor, myth, and plot—and that these symbolic goods make meaningful action possible for many members.

By the time of this conversation I have been contemplating the organization, off and on, since I first encountered it in 1980. Now I am telling Prabhupati something about my efforts to structure my findings. But I admit that my concerns are deeper than structure, really. How can I capture the quality of the 3HO experience? How can I portray the organization's many facets and contradictions: its distinctive mix of humor and earnestness, of the creative and the formulaic, its combination of ebullience and restraint, empowerment and submission? Can my language, or the language of social science for that matter, contain all of this without removing the life, the essence, from it?

She asks if my concerns are shared by other social scientists who write about religious subjects or about women's lives. I assure her that they are, that, in fact, a number of writers are questioning the value of the genre and attempting to reinvent the ethnography (Clifford 1988;

Clifford and Marcus 1986). They have tried new formats, among them confessional ethnographies, forms employing fictional and poetic devices, and collaborative and "messy texts" that incorporate many voices and points of view while privileging none (Van Maanen 1995; Denzin 1997). She nods approvingly, but I tell her that most of these have been severely criticized and some have been marginalized (Denzin 1997, 264).

Van Maanen (1995) notes that "just what is required of ethnography today is by no means clear, and among its producers and consumers alike, restlessness is the norm" (2). As I talk to Prabhupati, I share some of that restlessness. I know that I want to produce an evocative text, one that conveys the flavor of 3HO women's experience. I want the women's voices to be heard. I also want to speak at times in a personal voice rather than hide behind the persona of the value-free social scientist. And it seems to me that a portrait of a changing and complex organization such as 3HO/Sikh Dharma should occasionally employ shifting points of view and stylistic variations in order to convey the quality of the organization itself. But I am not contemplating a form that is particularly experimental or unusual; it seems to be enough that 3HO women's lives are both of these things.

Indeed, I plan to incorporate individual stories and voices into my account, Prabhupati's among them. I am aware of the ethical concerns associated with doing this: the possibility of misrepresenting an individual's views and feelings, of revealing acts and attitudes that a member would prefer to keep private, and the ever-present chance that information revealed in my work will somehow subject an individual to the disapprobation of her peers. I plan to eliminate names and many personal details, and I intend to provide the women I have interviewed with opportunities to review what I have written, but I cannot guarantee that there will be no repercussions for the people I have interviewed. But this still seems the most honest approach—the one most likely to "get at" the nature of women's experiences in 3HO and the one least likely to distort its reality.

As Prabhupati and I talk, we address the issue of how to portray the organization from the insider's perspective—from the point of view of its women members, who tend to see it as an organization that offers opportunities unavailable elsewhere—and how to balance this approach by also looking at it from a distance, recognizing that many ex-members, like Prabhupati, are quite critical of the organization's leadership, and that, like any organization, it can extend some degree of control over minds and bodies (e.g., Foucault 1979, 1980; Shupe 1998).

We both know how difficult it is to be even-handed when analyzing a spiritual organization, especially one that was created in order to offer its membership an alternative to business as usual. Some of the literature on the "new religious movements" runs to extremes. The anti-cult literature (for which Prabhupati feels some affinity) makes unsubstantiated accusations of "brainwashing," while some of the sociological literature seems to overlook abuses of power (Hexham and Poewe 1997, Lewis 1998). I hope to steer a middle course, but it is difficult. After all, there is no final word on the new religions, and our responses to them must inevitably reflect our understandings of spirituality, our hopes and fears about organizations, and our sense of how we should collectively utilize our skills, create and experiment with identities, and give substance to our dreams. Our interpretations reflect our attitudes toward social experimentation, our willingness to make compromises in order to create and retain alternative forms, and our sense of the right relationship between individual and group.

I tell Prabhupati that, throughout the course of my fieldwork, I have been impressed by the calm and careful speech, the creativity, and the abilities of the women who are drawn to 3HO. I have liked most of the women I have met. And I have respected their willingness to break from socially prescribed ways of living. Thus, I will write with considerable sympathy. But I will also write as a social scientist, as a feminist, and as someone who tends to be distrustful of hierarchical organizations.

Prabhupati understands my point of view, although she is less inclined than I am to view the members as spiritual explorers and the new religions as social experiments. She perceives more conformity and less innovation. Perhaps someday she will write her own account. Now, as I write this several years after our conversation, I still find the women's lives absorbing. These are lives that should be documented, and, however imperfect, I am the available narrator.

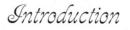

Introduction

The morning worship (*sadhana*) described previously is a central practice of 3HO/Sikh Dharma. A 3HO publication, dating from the early years of organizational life, lays out the aims and the techniques involved. Readers are told that "the yogic scriptures require at least 2½ hours of sadhana before the rising of the sun. You must dedicate at least one-tenth of each day to God" (KRI 1978, 15). They are also told that the morning meditation is a means of "cleaning the subconscious of fears and releasing new reservoirs of consciousness and energy" (15). Once the habit of daily worship is acquired and the subconscious is cleansed, they are told that they can enter a state of "neutrality" in which an individual "never need rely on a finite motivation or structure for the sense of self, for the sense of meaningfulness, or for the power to act creatively" (16). When the devotee is no longer motivated by worldly desires or dependent upon "finite" structures, awareness of the infinite is possible and true enlightenment begins. In time, the devotee may enter "the stage of *prabhupati*," which in 3HO is sometimes described as "atunement to the superconsciousness." Then, she can encounter an encompassing totality where all boundaries cease to exist and the oneness of creation is revealed and, as 3HO members sometimes chant, "God and me, me and God, are one."

When, in the 1960s, Bhajan began teaching at the East-West Cultural Center in Los Angeles, he made a point of saying that he was teaching kundalini yoga, a discipline which, he assured his young students, would lead to enlightenment faster than the hatha yoga that is generally taught in North America. His techniques, he said, were intended to rapidly awaken and raise kundalini energy—a form of divine power incarnate in the body (where it is often visualized as a snake, lying

1

curled at the base of the spine). The upward movement of this energy through several bodily centers, or *chakra*s, is said to lead to liberation for the individual: liberation from the illusion that we all are isolated separate selves, liberation from self-interested actions and perceptions, and liberation from the accumulated weight of past thoughts and deeds. On a somewhat less exalted plane, Bhajan also claimed that the yoga would protect against many physical problems and would provide a different, and desirable, form of the chemical highs which many of his students had previously sought.

The concept of kundalini energy is embedded in Tantric teachings. Texts that are referred to as "Tantras" date back to the ninth century, although the underlying ideas are older (Pintchman 1994). The writings elaborate on doctrines and disciplines that are supposed to lead the individual toward empowerment, well-being, and liberation (Brooks 1990). They typically conceptualize the divine as having both masculine and feminine aspects. The feminine aspect (*shakti*) is often said to provide the energy which actualizes and embodies the divine, while the masculine aspect is tied to spirit and to consciousness. Bhajan teaches that women, as embodiments of *shakti*, represent the creative power of the universe, and he adds that this spiritual power has long been neglected and debased in Western society. I have not encountered any writings or speeches in which Bhajan elaborates upon the philosophical basis of his understanding of *shakti*, and so I am not sure if he draws on a particular school of thought, although it seems reasonable to assume that he has been influenced by Hindu Tantric Saktism (which will be discussed in the next chapter). He most often uses the term *shakti* for practical, rather than philosophical, purposes, using it, for example, in order to explain differences between the sexes. In general, he describes the feminine principle as that which is creative, gives form to the world, and brings about change. Tantra is an entire world view, but the tendency in 3HO is to speak of it primarily in terms of "white Tantric Yoga" and thus refer to it as a practice. (Similarly, 3HO members generally employ the term "kundalini" to refer to kundalini yoga.) Although the concept of kundalini can be found within the traditions of Tantra, Bhajan distinguishes between the two, referring to certain of his classes as kundalini yoga courses and others as Tantric yoga workshops. Tantric yoga in 3HO is an occasional practice said to balance masculine and feminine energies and to provide a rapid means of "cleansing" the psyche. It is said to overcome "blocks" that exist in the subconscious mind. Kundalini yoga, on the other hand, is a daily practice.

Yoga was the first pillar of his organization, but Bhajan's students soon learned about Sikhism as well. Some of Bhajan's first yoga students joined a Sikh study circle when they learned that Bhajan was attending it, and he led a group of devotees to the seat of the Sikh religion, the Golden Temple, in 1971. Shortly after that event he began to formally introduce Sikh rites and beliefs. His students began to adopt Sikh practices, and some "took *amrit*," that is, they were formally initiated into the Khalsa, or Sikh brotherhood. It is not required that a Sikh take this step—there are many Sikhs of Indian background who have not done so—but 3HO members were initiated in large numbers. When they did, they adopted the symbolic markers of Khalsa affiliation, "the Five K's," which are *kesh*, or unshorn hair; the *kangha*, a comb representing tidiness and "orderly spirituality" (Cole and Sambhi 1978, 128); the *kara*, a steel bracelet symbolic of an unbreakable bond with the guru; the *kirpan*, a short sword representing commitment to righteousness and to the Sikh faith; and the *kacch*, a pair of breeches signifying modesty. Over time, 3HO members, whether initiated into the Khalsa or not, also adopted Punjabi names and their own version of Punjabi dress. Like Sikhs in the Punjab, most of the women took the middle name Kaur (princess), while the men adopted Singh (lion). Unlike Indian-born Sikhs, they took Khalsa as their last name. They began to dress primarily in white (this was their own innovation), and both men and women adopted the turban (which is only worn by men in the Punjab). Sikh worship was incorporated into the morning *sadhana*, which had originally centered upon yoga but may have already been based upon the Sikh practice of daily meditation on the divine Name (the *nam*) as a means to achieving mystical union with God (it is recommended to do this in the early, "ambrosial" hours of the day). They embraced other major Sikh ideals and practices, such as regular service to the community, hard work, almsgiving, and active but principled involvement in the world. They came to acknowledge both the Guru Granth Sahib (the Sikh sacred scriptures) and the Sikh community as vessels of the guru, and to appreciate the Sikh vision of God. In a 3HO translation of one of the most frequently read Sikh prayers, Jap Sahib, God is described:

> He is nameless, placeless, casteless
> He is Formless, and has no pre-written destiny
> He is the primal form. . . .
> He is without preference
> He is prevailing here and there, on this side and that side
> He is without attachment to anything. (Kaur 1971, 54)

In Sikhism, God is not to be worshiped in a particular form—not, for example, as Vishnu or Durga or any of the Hindu gods and goddesses—but as the ultimate source transcending all manifestations. One expression of this Sikh view of the sacred is the Sikh teaching that caste is of no consequence in spiritual affairs. The women and men of 3HO/Sikh Dharma are proud of the egalitarian messages that are embedded in this Sikh vision of the godhead and in the teachings of the first Sikh guru, called Nanak, who rejected spiritual distinctions based upon caste and gender.

Bhajan has established administrative bodies and a ministry to which he has appointed both men and women. These Sikh Dharma organizational arrangements do not always parallel Punjabi practices. There is, for example, no appointed ministry in Punjabi Sikhism, although there are *granthi*s, lay people who are responsible for caring for and reading from the Guru Granth Sahib, and there is now a tendency in some ethnic Sikh *gurdwara*s (Sikh places of worship) in the United States for the *granthi* to perform marriages and funerals (Richardson 1985).

In North America there is contact between ethnic Sikhs and the American-born members of Sikh Dharma, and they do attend one another's services and participate together in major observances and celebrations, but the two groups tend to remain essentially separate. Cultural differences partially explain this separation, but it also exists because of differences in religious practices. Several Sikh Dharma/ 3HO practices depart from those of Punjabi Sikhs. Sikhs from the Punjab, for example, do not generally practice yoga, and although 3HO members are vegetarians and drink no wine or caffeine, vegetarianism is not necessarily associated with Sikhism (Dusenbery 1990b). Some ethnic Sikhs are distrustful of the intense loyalty exhibited by Bhajan's devotees, although many are respectful of the knowledge and piety that these American Sikhs exhibit (Singh 1977; Dusenbery 1990b, 346; Melton 1992). American-born Sikhs, in turn, are often critical of the traditional gender roles enacted in Punjabi Sikh communities and have expressed disapproval of those Indian Sikhs who are not particularly strict in their observances. They are also typically impatient with what they refer to as "Sikh politics" (Dusenbery 1990b, 1989b).

Because they have adopted the Sikh identity, the future of the men and women of Sikh Dharma is entangled with the future of Sikhs everywhere, and so it is helpful to know something about Sikhism as a global presence. Until recently, Sikhism was primarily a regional religion, albeit one with a tradition of migration, that was practiced in the Punjab area of northern India (Dusenbery 1989a). The Punjab was annexed by the English in 1849, and the earlier out-migrations tended to be in the direction of areas where the English exerted their influence. In the late 1800s Sikhs migrated to Indonesia, Australia, Fiji and New Zealand, and East Africa. Later, in the 1900s, they traveled to the United States and Canada. In the first decade of the twentieth century approximately five thousand Punjabi immigrants settled in Canada and a like number in the United States (Dusenbery 1989a, 6). The first major migration of South Asians to the United States was actually via Canada when Punjabi farmers fled British Columbia following an anti-Oriental riot in Vancouver in 1907 and settled in California (Williams 2000, 213). Both countries restricted Indian immigration soon after that date, with the result that migrants could not send for extended family members. It was not uncommon for Sikh men to marry outside of the religion because there was a shortage of Sikh women in North America, and, as a result of this, and because of pressures to assimilate, they often were not initiated into the Khalsa, were clean shaven, and did not wear the turban (Richardson 1985; Dusenbery 1990b).

A second wave of migration began after Indian independence and the Second World War. In Canada, this brought working-class immigrants to the lumber industry in British Columbia and business and professional Sikhs to the East and to the Plains. In the United States, Sikh immigrants tended to be professionals, and they gravitated toward the cities (Dusenbery 1989a). In the middle decades of the century, a number of Sikhs came to the United States for higher education and then stayed on (Mann 2000, 260). The majority of South Asians have come since 1965, which was when the Immigration and Nationality Act abolished quotas based on national origins (Williams 2000, 214). Many of the Sikhs who came after the change in the law were professionals holding degrees from Indian universities (Mann 2000, 261). Quite recently, since the 1980s, Sikhs have come in order to flee persecution, which they have experienced in India and elsewhere. Those who came from India left in the aftermath of Sikh-Hindu violence following the assassination of Indira Gandhi and an unsuccessful struggle to create an independent Sikh state. Others have fled political persecution in East Africa and Afghanistan (Mann 2000). Many of the recent migrants advocate strict adherence to the outward symbols of Khalsa identity. This has led to some tension between the more assimilated Sikhs and the newly arrived conservatives. There are also tensions related to region of origin and to caste, income, gender, and politics in this increasingly diverse community (Dusenbery 1989a, Mann 2000).

There are now over one million Sikhs living outside of India (Dusenbery 1989a). Of these, approximately 200,000 are in the United

States, "with distinct concentrations in California, Chicago, Michigan, and the greater New York and Washington, D.C. areas" (Mann 2000, 260). Although major decisions governing Sikh religious practices continue to issue from India, Sikhs residing outside of the Punjab represent a growing and significant constituency, and, as Sikhism becomes a world religion, Sikhs are attempting to shape an appropriate identity (Cole 1988; MacLeod 1989a, 1989c; Dusenbery 1989a, 1989b; Mann 2000). Some favor retaining the traditional Khalsa ways, others advocate a more flexible version of Sikhism that accommodates local variations in language, dress, and values. On issues of gender, Mann finds that "young Sikh women educated in the United States . . . have begun to seek the unequivocal application of the principle of gender equality in both the sacred and mundane domains of Sikh life" (2000, 273). Viewed from a global perspective, 3HO/Sikh Dharma is one new form that Sikhism has taken, one based firmly on the Khalsa way of life but one that has been adapted to a distinctive North American setting. It is one piece in a shifting mosaic, one discourse among many competing interpretations of the Sikh identity.

This Study

From my first acquaintance with 3HO, I wondered about its appeal to American women. Like other academic women with feminist leanings, I was puzzled by women's conversion to the new religions, which, on the surface at least, appeared to be quite patriarchal. Why did these women accept traditional domestic roles at a time when so many other women were defining those roles as oppressive? Many of my informants had been attached to the counterculture of the 1960s and 1970s, which was certainly not an environment friendly to structured and hierarchical organizations like 3HO. Why did they embrace it? And why did they choose a religion with a martial tradition?

My puzzlement led to doctoral research on women's lives in 3HO, with a focus on the Washington *sangat* (congregation). In 1981, when I began, there were approximately fifty adults residing in three Washington area communities, as well as many children and several college-age youth. I attended workshops, which for two years included a monthly women's group; I took Tantric yoga classes when Yogi Bhajan came to teach them in Washington; and I conducted interviews with residents. There were thirty-one women in residence near the end of my research (1988); I had conducted intensive interviews with eighteen of them and shorter interviews with all but four of the others, as well as having interviewed many of the non-Sikh women who attended the women's group. I supplemented the Washington interviews with telephone discussions and letters to 3HO women in other parts of the country when I required information about specific subjects, and I visited the headquarters in Los Angeles. I attended the "ladies camp" (formally called the Khalsa Women's Training Camp) outside of Española, New Mexico, in the summer of 1983. There I followed the daily routine, attending lectures and classes and rising before dawn for yoga and meditation. I also read several years' worth of the organization's official transcriptions of Yogi Bhajan's lectures, which he delivered daily to the assembled camp (these had been collected almost from the camp's inception).

After I completed my dissertation, I remained in regular contact with several of my informants. Six of the women with whom I originally conducted intensive interviews later withdrew from 3HO, and I conducted exit interviews with them, and later another of these women left. I have also attended events that some of these former members have sponsored; these range from yoga classes to women's circles to drumming sessions and parties. I conducted interviews with other ex-members between 1991 and 1995. In addition, I was in contact with a network of ex-members during a brief period when this network existed as a semiformal group of men and women who exchanged writings and ideas. Because I did not want to confine my follow-up to ex-members, I returned to two Virginia communities in 1995–96 in order to talk with five of the Washington women I had originally interviewed and to meet with others who were either new to the ashram or with whom I had not spoken extensively before. I also conducted telephone interviews with 3HO women from different areas of the country about current ashram practices and roles. I would have liked to supplement this qualitative data with an extensive survey, and I requested, but was denied, permission to conduct such a survey at the 1994 women's camp session (the request was denied on the grounds that the camp increasingly attracts non-Sikh women and thus would not provide the type of sample I desired). In 2001 I conducted further interviews with a number of individuals who were knowledgeable about current developments and trends in 3HO/Sikh Dharma.

Ex-members' Narratives

Woven throughout this ethnography are the stories of two women who have left 3HO/Sikh Dharma, the women I met with in Albuquerque. One of these women, Prabhupati Kaur, has essentially separated herself from the organization, although not from the Sikh religion. Simran

Kaur, the other, was at one time a leading figure in the organization, but then left it and was estranged for a long period of time. When I spoke with her she was contemplating a return. Soon after that she did renew her affiliation for a little over a year. Each of these women has, at one time or another, expressed views critical of 3HO/Sikh Dharma, but each also feels that she benefited from her association with the organization. I have included their stories for a number of reasons. Both women have interesting approaches to framing their 3HO experience. They are thoughtful, observant, knowledgeable, and verbally and intellectually gifted. Both have written about their impressions of the organization. Both have maintained a continuing dialogue with their Sikh Dharma experience, and I have had the opportunity to see that dialogue evolve and change. Thus their experience is accessible and readily adapted to the ethnographic format and to a view of 3HO/Sikh Dharma as a narrative resource.

The nature of their experience differs, however. Simran saw 3HO/Sikh Dharma from the top, as it were. Prabhupati Kaur saw it more as an ordinary and, as she describes it, somewhat "fringy" member. Their stories add an extra dimension to my account, but their inclusion should not to be construed as an assertion that their experience is representative of most 3HO women's lives, or as a statement of my agreement with these two women's perspectives. Rather, their voices provide a counterpoint to others. I use pseudonyms, of their choosing, for them. For other women I have simply called them "A.," "B.," "C.," and so on, but a letter is not consistently assigned to the same woman from chapter to chapter.

When I spoke with her in Albuquerque in 1995, it was the first time that I had met Prabhupati Kaur face-to-face, although I had read some of her work. At this point she was no longer in Sikh Dharma and was acting as coordinator for the network of ex-members. This was also the first time that I had met Simran face-to-face, although I had spoken with her when she first left the organization. Now, ten years later, she had reestablished contact with Yogi Bhajan and other 3HO members. Simran was one of Bhajan's early students and a founder of the organization. She was a role model for women in the organization. It was difficult, both for her and for the organization as a whole, when a series of events left her with no choice but to separate from "the dharma." Now, at the time of my visit, she was feeling that her life had come full circle and that it was time to return to what she long ago began. She had come to clarify her own memories and opinions and to act as an author, to add her twists to the plot and to shape the ending. "I wanted to bring it to a place of healing and completion," she told me, "with no expectations, with no needing to go over the past, just go in loving presence. . . . I'd been there in the beginning and I'd been a part of creating all that it was. . . . a big part of me was very attached to seeing this [the story of 3HO] come out right, seeing this have a good ending." She, and some other ex-members, speak of the "shadow side" of the organization. They mean this in a Jungian sense and are referring to repressed, hidden, or negative aspects of organizational life. Simran viewed her return as an opportunity to integrate the light and the dark—to make 3HO, and herself, whole. "And," she added, "for me, spirituality ultimately is about being whole."

Prabhupati Kaur confided that, in her early years in 3HO, she had almost idolized Simran. When I asked her how she remembered Simran from those days, she replied, "I was a million miles away from her. She was very close to Yogi Bhajan and his inner circle. And I lived in a little ashram. . . . She was an icon. . . . Looking back on it, all that was attracting me to 3HO—the devotion, the willingness to work together, the community—was really coming from Simran."

Women in New Religions and in 3HO/Sikh Dharma

There is now a growing body of literature on women's lives in the new religious movements, as well as in conservative Christian groups and in Orthodox Jewish groups. Much of this work explores ways in which these groups appear to offer solutions to problems and dilemmas that surround contemporary gender roles and family life. Thus Stacey describes an informant's conversion to evangelical Christianity as a "strategy for achieving heterosexual intimacy, one facilitated by the surprisingly feminized view of a loving marriage" (1991, 59). Kaufman was told by newly converted Orthodox Jewish women that "orthodoxy put them in touch with their own bodies, in control of their own sexuality, and in a position to value the so-called feminine virtues of nurturance, mutuality, family and motherhood" (1991, 8). Davidman (1991) found women converting to Orthodox Judaism in search of a committed family life, and Jacobs (1990) views the new religions as attempts to create an idealized American family. Palmer has looked at seven of the new religions and finds that part of their appeal lies in the fact that each reduces role overload: "women's role and function is simplified and specialized in each community." Thus, "in none of these communities are women expected to bear the triple (or even quadruple) burden of parenting, breadwinning, and housekeeping . . . and sometimes sexy, attractive wife" (1994, 218). She goes on to suggest that such groups also provide young women with an opportunity to experience a rite of passage which "facilitates the difficult metamorphosis from girlhood to womanhood" (258). Goldman (1999) looks at the lives of women who lived at Rajneeshpuram, in Oregon, between 1981 and 1985. These followers of Bhagwan Shree Rajneesh found a setting in which women's talents were valued and where they could exercise considerable freedom. Devotees were encouraged to have many partners, but not to have children. Like Palmer's devotees, they eliminated role overload, but they did so by avoiding the role of wife and the demands of family life. Her subjects were successful women before they began to follow Bhagwan Shree Rajneesh, but they had found their success ultimately unsatisfying. What they gained in the movement, Goldman says, is acceptance of their talents combined with something they had not previously experienced: "love and gratitude for their work" (28). And these women, who typically did not admire or did not want lives like their own mothers' lives "could become emotionally centered because taking sannyas allowed them to escape any remaining possibilities of being like their mothers," while it protected them "from the routine sacrifices associated with femininity in our culture" (246).

Most of these authors suggest that it can be misleading to classify religions as either patriarchal or feminist. Rather, they try to see the world through their informants' eyes and to find the benefits accruing to women in the groups they study. Jacobs, who focused on "leavers," takes a somewhat different approach and attends to ex-members' accounts of the darker sides of the groups and reports on abuses experienced by a number of women.

My own approach overlaps with that taken by each of the authors cited above, but I look less at family issues and am more concerned with the ways in which 3HO/Sikh Dharma acts as a source of narratives and as a mediating and experimental structure. I see 3HO as a setting where members can reconfigure the cultural tensions that have shaped their experience, where they can mingle Eastern and Western views of selfhood, where they can control the stimuli to which they are exposed, and where they can question and alter dominant cultural codes (Melucci 1989, 1994; Fine 1995). I see it as a place to experiment with individual identities and to reconstrue gender, but also as a setting for the creation of collective identities. I am fascinated by the women's shifting explanations and understandings of their own biographies and settings as these change with time, with circumstances, and with organizational priorities. I want to portray their sense-making, their weaving of narratives, and the construction and reconstruction of meaning at both individual and organizational levels.

While I am as interested in the process as in the whys of affiliation, I, like the other observers I have mentioned, have attempted to enumerate benefits inherent in attachment to 3HO. In order to do so, I have examined members' explicitly stated reasons for persisting in the organization, have looked at common themes in their narratives, and have compared their lives to those of women in other new religions. Thus (as in the cases of Orthodox Judaism and of several fundamentalist and evangelical Christian groups), a stable family life is one of the goods available to 3HO women. Husbands are expected to be involved in family matters and to provide steady financial support to their wives and children. Yogi Bhajan and his wife, Inderjit, have, over time, produced a multitude of prescriptions and suggestions for raising children and for maintaining viable relationships with the opposite sex. These can ease some of the confusion that surrounds contemporary family life and gender roles.

Beyond these benefits, 3HO offers some protection against the buffeting which many women now experience with the rapid spread of global capitalism. If the organization prospers they can expect some financial and emotional support, and they can assume that they will be surrounded by a caring community in old age. One woman I interviewed told me about a discussion in a university course that she was taking. Students were discussing the factors that give rise to homelessness, and the professor asked if the students felt vulnerable. Everyone in the class except for this women could imagine becoming homeless; she was certain that her friends in Sikh Dharma would not allow that to happen.

While 3HO affiliation should be understood in terms of benefits such as these, a real "feel" for 3HO requires a look at the distinctive emphases and characteristic twists that typify members' accounts. The following are among the central, recurrent themes in 3HO women's stories.

A Source of Self-Esteem and Belonging

Many 3HO women clearly believe that the organization's vision of womanhood affords them self-esteem and self-respect. For example, one member, who works as a counselor, told me that she thought the essential 3HO message on gender was that "women are valuable and important . . . and can value themselves greatly just because they are women. . . . I teach that to my family, and in counseling I use it too." Another said she thought Bhajan's teachings contradict the image of women as "second-rate." Rather, Bhajan says, "we're more than first-rate; we're the hand of God." Several said that they agreed with Bhajan's assumption that men and women are essentially different (3HO members often say that "men and women are like two different species"), and that accepting this teaching freed them from a need to compete with men (presumably on male terms). "We should have what they have, but not be them," as one informant put it. These women said that in accepting difference they raised self-esteem. Several appear to accept something close to the Victorian idea of separate gender spheres (Cott 1977; Smith-Rosenberg 1975, 1985; Welter 1966). Most also talk about their delight in finding a community of compatible people who share their values. They mention the ways in which the community functions like an extended family, supporting members in hard times, easing the burdens of child rearing, and offering numerous opportunities to share one's life and grow from that experience.

A Source of Narratives, Symbols, and Embodied Representations

Integration and Praxis

In a detailed description of one young child's acquisition of language and narrative capability, Bruner, who has made an extensive study of the role that narrative plays in individual lives, finds that the youngster was "in search of an integral structure that could encompass what she had done with what she felt with what she believed" (1990, 89). Narrative, he argues, provides that structure, and adults, as well as children, create stories so they can weave into a whole the disparate pieces of self, biography, and society. They can create some kind of a mesh between feelings, beliefs, and actions. The women who join 3HO/Sikh Dharma have a particularly strong need to do this. This is partly a matter of seeking relief from role fragmentation (Bird 1978; Palmer 1994), but it is also more. Many have a hunger for meaning, connection, and praxis. Their actions must be meaningful in a world in which they find many beliefs superficial and where much that people do appears "mechanical." They seek meanings that are applicable to everyday life, and 3HO provides these in the form of a rich array of metaphors, practices, and rituals that infuse daily life with significance. The organization helps its women members to integrate spiritual and material concerns, beliefs and actions, identities and daily routines. Praxis is a central element of Sikh ethics.

Appealing Rituals, Symbols, and Metaphors

Sikhism and Tantra are rich in rituals, symbols, and metaphors, and many of these are sensually appealing and physically grounded. This is true, as well, of Hinduism which was, historically, a major source of Sikh beliefs and practices. Lynch finds that, in Hinduism, emotions are grounded "in nature in the form of food, music, and scent" (1990, 14). A number of writers, both of an academic and of a more activist bent, have argued that women seek and need religious forms that assert the immanence of spirit, forms that are grounded in ordinary experience—a spirituality that is embodied, sensual, at one with all living things (e.g., Christ and Plaskow 1979; Christ 1980; Plaskow and Christ 1989; Eller 1993; Wessinger 1993a; Winter, Lummis, and Stokes 1994). Feminists have for some time criticized religious traditions that favor an abstract spirituality over embodied experience, since these religions so often associate women with a supposedly "lesser" physical realm.

If women often seek a spirituality grounded in the senses, this is to be found in 3HO/Sikh Dharma where much of life is aesthetically and sensually pleasing and where beliefs are often expressed in physical forms. In Sikhism one praises and experiences God through music and poetry, and, in Sikh Dharma, chants and music are woven through the days. In 3HO/Sikh Dharma, one alters the self via physical practices such as yoga, meditation, and diet. One remembers one's ultimate identity by employing physical cues—by wearing the five K's, a turban, and white clothing—and expresses one's grace by wearing a long, flowing *chunni*. Health and physical well-being are central goals, and women try to find time in their schedules for exercise and for preparing and consuming high quality foods. Many are knowledgeable about nutrition and about herbs and massage. Physical surroundings also receive attention. Houses are meant to embody peace and harmony, and are decorated with care. The result is calming and often quite lovely. Many 3HO women seek the same effect in their interpersonal dealings, making a genuine attempt to create interactions that are calm and dignified, and this can give life a gentle, thoughtful flow often lacking in the surrounding world. Members of the organization aim for a life that is "conscious," a daily reality in which every act is intentionally and carefully chosen. While this is a difficult, perhaps impossible, ideal to realize, the attempt often gives life a pace and a depth that are aesthetically satisfying.

The value set on everyday sense experience is reflected in many women's accounts of affiliation. Quite a few women say that the feelings of well-being associated with yoga and meditation first attracted them to 3HO. Many cite the importance of music in the Sikh tradition, and one even told me that it was the Sikh emphasis on *nad*, or sound currents, that brought her into the fold. A few spoke of the Golden Temple as a symbol that embodied all they had sought, a physical manifestation of the spiritual home.

The Sikh view is that the senses and the intellect, the transcendent and the everyday, the moment of mystical union and the everyday struggle to survive in an ethical way are equally important. As one commentator puts it, "acknowledging the spirituality as well as the sensuality of human life, the Sikh existential ideal posits an integration of the two" (Singh 1993, 114). In 3HO/Sikh Dharma, women, as embodiments of *shakti*, are said to be particularly gifted in the art of bringing the two together.

A Source of Balance and a Way of Mediating Stress and Conflict

Centering, Balancing, and Positioning the Self

3HO women talk about the ways in which organizational practices (which they frequently call "the technology") enable them to maintain "clarity" in the face of stress and anxiety. They talk about the ways in which yoga, meditation, and diet have helped them when they faced major personal losses and difficult decisions. They also say that 3HO practices enable them to better balance the different aspects of their personalities. In many cases one also gets the impression that the organization has given them techniques for managing and modifying a traditional feminine ego structure (Chodorow 1974, 1978). They have learned to be less frequently overwhelmed by others' needs and personalities, to better balance individuation and merger, and to maintain a sense of individual autonomy in their interactions.

Thus 3HO seems to offer relief from fragmented identities and from the pressures on women to meet others' needs and expectations. Some beliefs are rather similar to those that Palmer found in a group called the Institute for the Development of the Harmonious Human Being (which she understandably shortened to IDHHB), where women identify "with their 'essence' rather than their bodies or social roles" (1994, 218). The approach is different in 3HO/Sikh Dharma, the self is not simplified by reducing it to an essence, or to one or two major roles, but one is a "spiritual woman" first and foremost, and only secondarily an occupant of roles. Thus there is the one dominant essential meta-role.

Many members, and ex-members, are gifted. They have original ways of seeing things. Many have a knack for symbolic and musical expression. They need a setting where the mind can push at the frontiers of the literal, where it can sparkle, where individuals can experience emotional highs and even aim to experience bliss. Some of these needs can be met by 3HO, as well as by many other new religions or in other cultural niches, but many of these gifted members require not only a setting but also *forms* that can encompass their visions; they need the means to structure creativity, and they need channels for the imagination. It appears that 3HO can answer these needs because it offers a means of both expressing and disciplining the imagination, and it provides opportunities to harness an original point of view to the routines and duties of everyday life. It also teaches techniques for focusing attention and limiting distractions.

Mediating Conflicts in American Culture and in Women's Lives

Several commentators have identified conflicts that permeate American society and impinge upon individual efforts to construct a self and to manage identities. These include a separation between public and private spheres (Berger 1977), between rational and imaginative or between economic and symbolic realms (Matthiessen 1941; Marx 1964; Douglas 1977), and between individualism and commitment to a group (Bellah et al. 1985; Hewitt 1989). There may be further conflicting pulls toward both conformity and rebellion (Hewitt 1989). Shapiro suggests an underlying gender imagery: "[In] the association of men with individualism and women with social relationship. . . . what we see, I think, is our culture's continuing attempt to deal with the conflict between the individual and society, and our ambivalence about the individualism that has been institutionalized and celebrated to such an extraordinary degree in our economic and cultural life. Gender symbolism plays a central role in how we think about all this" (1995, 13).

In addition to these widespread cultural conflicts women must manage additional gender-related dilemmas. There are, for example, particularly powerful and opposing pulls in the directions of career and familial norms, toward self-assertion and self-effacement, and between putting others first and pursuing one's own goals. In general, "the discourses through which the subject position 'woman' is constituted are multiple and contradictory. . . . The contradictory knowing that inevitably results can debilitate women" (Davies 1992).

Stories, myths, narratives, and rituals are means of mediating such contradictions. With their comprehensive view of a reality transcending all dualisms, 3HO/Sikh Dharma and other new religions based on Eastern traditions offer one way to maneuver between conflicting pulls and desires, and sometimes to even mediate and reconstruct these. The 3HO woman imagines herself calm, centered, dignified, able to remain an island of peace and clarity through all stress and conflict. The dharma provides a middle road (a "path") that travels between individualism and a self deeply embedded in social ties, between careerism and traditional domestic roles, between imagination and instrumentality. It offers its women members the role of the spiritual woman who is neither career woman nor housewife, and the ideal of participation in a marriage in which masculine and feminine energies are perfectly balanced. In short, it offers the kinds of imagery, rituals, myths, and stories that many contemporary women seek.

At many points in its relatively brief history the Sikh religion has offered a vision of wholeness, of a place of peace beyond strife. One of the heroines of Sikh literature, Sundari, the protagonist of a popular novel published during the Sikh renaissance of the early twentieth century, but set in the eighteenth century, represents this aspect of the Sikh vision. Here a contemporary commentator describes Sundari's environment and her response: "Her society was divided into different religious and racial factions which were continually at war with one another. Abductions, robberies, and killings abounded. It was a period of strife and conflict. But rather than blame the opponent, Sundari accepts a mutual blindness. She states this at one point: All this suffering is owing to the deviation from the path of the One. . . . Following the One, all human beings become beaded together. . . . Through love we become one force" (Singh 1993, 198). This vision of oneness and unity is a gift that has had considerable meaning to 3HO members, many of whom have experienced "multiple and contradictory" visions of selfhood, and most of whom, having been young in the 1960s and 1970s, were raised in a period of comparable strife.

An Instrument for Managing Cognitive Dissonance

Human beings, says Bruner, "in interacting with one another, form a sense of the canonical and ordinary as a background against which to interpret and give narrative meaning to breaches in and deviations from 'normal' states of the human condition." Narratives account for deviations (1990, 67). Experiencing "breaches" in their lives, 3HO women have actively sought meaning and mediation in the tales and tenets of Sikhism and Tantra.

Many of the original members of 3HO had straddled countercultural and conventional lives. Many were innovative and rebellious in their early years. A number describe themselves as having always been "different," as yearning for things that others never cared for. They know about tears—and rips—in the fabric of meaning.

Prabhupati has an amusing personal story to illustrate this. At loose ends and looking for something to read one night, she picked up a copy of the *I Ching* and settled down with it. The *I Ching* is an ancient Chinese system of divination. To use it, one asks questions and then flips coins. The way that the coins land is translated into patterns of lines, and these, in turn, are combined into groupings of six lines referred to as hexagrams. Each hexagram has a meaning: "That was the beginning of the week I turned religious. It took me no time, of course, to find three pennies and start throwing them around and start reading my fortune and those of others. There was only one problem. Every time I asked about myself I kept coming up with the same answer, Hexagram number 20, over and over, every single time. . . . I soon became completely obsessed with coin tossing. I woke up in the middle of the night and threw those coins, Hexagram 20" (Kamlapati Kaur Khalsa 1994a, 1).

She discovered that hexagram 20 had "something to do with the need for contemplation in one's life." She and her husband discussed her odds-defying results, as well as the dislocations they had experienced since moving from a small town to an urban center, and decided that indeed they needed to find a place of calm. The upshot was a joint decision to take a yoga class, and they came upon one offered by 3HO.

Managing Information Overload

3HO/Sikh Dharma provides schemata for condensing, codifying, and storing information. These reduce the energy output required of an individual when she gathers information from the world and allow her to simplify the choice-making process. At the same time, 3HO members recognize that some forms of information are not readily simplified and categorized, that one must sometimes be open to experience in all of its complexity. It seems to me that 3HO enables members to balance their information processing. They gain frameworks to use in ordering their experience of the world, but, by adopting meditation practices and embracing the ideal of becoming egoless and, by extension, perfectly open to experience, they also retain the possibility of regularly obtaining rich, chaotic, uncompressed and spiritually significant information. 3HO/Sikh Dharma allows them to alternate between openness and simplification, to open and close the doors of perception.

This point of view resembles that taken by the theorists who write about "new social movements." They work from the premise that contemporary movements differ from earlier, more ideological and class-based movements. Rather than seeking instrumental changes in policy and government, their members are likely to be involved in a search for identity, a quest that encompasses previously private and quotidian aspects of life (Johnston, Laraña, and Gusfield 1994).

Melucci argues that this is necessitated by the characteristics of an information-based society:

> [A]ccess to knowledge becomes the terrain where new forms of power, discrimination, and conflict come into being. Simultaneously, the sense of individual experience, that is, the ability to incorporate the increasing quantity of information transmitted and received into an interior principle of unity, becomes increasingly fragile. A split opens between the realm of instrumental knowledge, which efficiently manipulates the symbolic codes that select, order, and direct information, and wisdom as the integration of meaning into personal experience. The result is the search for identity, the quest for self that addresses the fundamental regions of human action: the body, the emotions, the dimensions of experience irreducible to instrumental rationality. . . . Identity must be forever reestablished and renegotiated. (1994, 112–14)

Structure of the Book

This work essentially follows a historical and biographical progression. Thus, the reader will, in a general way, follow the growth of the organization, the experiences of women members, and the flow of my research over the years.

Part I provides an overview of Sikh and Tantric teachings and some historical background to these traditions. It also addresses tensions in American culture which were vividly exposed in the late 1960s and early

1970s when 3HO/Sikh Dharma was taking shape and looks at the counterculture from which many of the original members emerged.

Part II presents 3HO ideas about gender and womanhood. It examines Bhajan's depictions of the ideal woman and describes the Khalsa Women's Training Camp.

Part III consists primarily of individual narratives. In these, members capture their first impressions of yoga and of 3HO. They describe their early acceptance of 3HO disciplines and the gradual process of affiliation. In this section, I also provide a typology covering women's expressed reasons for joining and portray members making concrete efforts to interpret and apply central ideals and beliefs.

Part IV looks at the underside of organizational life: at some of the members' doubts, fears, and struggles, at some organizational crises, at sense-making efforts in the face of these crises, and at the process of disaffiliation.

Part V looks at members' ongoing interpretations and reinterpretations of organizational beliefs and of their own individual biographies. It looks at leavers as they rebuild their lives and at long-term members as they mature and their interpretations of Sikh traditions and 3HO practices evolve.

A Reflexive Note

If one assumes that any ethnographic account, however accurate and well informed, is to some degree a story, a creation, this would suggest that it is not only members of 3HO/Sikh Dharma who are telling stories but also the narrator. What line am I taking? How does it relate to the individual narratives that my informants construct?

Jeffcutt (1993) discerns an "emerging genre of writing in organization studies." He notes an abundance of quest stories. In a "romantic" form of the quest, a researcher or a consultant goes into an organization hoping to increase understanding of organizational problems and help improve the overall tone and functioning of the organization. Then the researcher finds that the organization is restrictive and ridden with obstacles to communication and change. It is difficult to conduct research, but this individual manages to overcome resistance and finds ways to bring insight, harmony, and new ways of thinking into organizational life. Simran viewed her return to 3HO in this light. To return was difficult and painful, but she was hoping that her presence could make 3HO/Sikh Dharma a more open and flexible organization.

Jeffcutt also discovers a reverse version of the romantic quest: the internal obstacles triumph, and the researcher is not welcomed, or her insights are rejected. In this case, "organizational failure is most commonly articulated as cultural rigidity or lack of adaptability" (1993, 31). This is a version of the 3HO experience that one hears from ex-members. Often they will talk about ways in which they tried to introduce new ideas and practices only to find their best intentions rejected.

Finally, there is an "epic" form of the genre in which the researcher "embarks on a process of academic passage towards the interpretation of culture and symbolism in a particular setting. Success in the quest is the achievement of a persuasive account, through the ordeal of being physically and theoretically exposed" (30). This is probably a fair description of the story line that originally motivated me to pursue this kind of qualitative research. I set out to analyze the organization, hopeful that I would attain unique insights into the symbol systems and structure of 3HO. Later I found myself "theoretically exposed" as I began to feel a considerable amount of ambivalence. I experienced a tug of war between a part of me that wanted to celebrate 3HO women's lives and their solutions to contemporary dilemmas and another part which said that these women were far too ready to allow a man to define their womanhood, that they were too pliable and, perhaps, too obedient. I wanted to paint a sympathetic picture of 3HO simply because it is a social experiment, and I felt that, as such, it deserved respect. On the other hand, I often thought that 3HO members weren't being experimental enough, that they were accepting too many ready-made formulas for living. And although I sympathized with the generally appreciative tone taken by sociological researchers who study the new religions, I began to wonder if these sociologists weren't sometimes insufficiently aware of women's vulnerability in these settings. I soon realized that I would have to study my own ambivalence and internal debates. Perhaps some of the conflicts I experienced were even shared by 3HO women. In any case, "duality" was a significant concept in 3HO, and it seemed that in its structure, ideology, and symbols, 3HO/Sikh Dharma not only mediated but also sometimes reproduced conflicts and dichotomies that existed outside its boundaries. I encountered a quotation from Yinger that suggested that I was not entirely off the track: "What seems to me the most crucial aspect of countercultural participation is heightened ambivalence" (1982, 303). Perhaps this ambivalence, and a concomitant desire to transcend it, drew some women into the organization and kept them there, and perhaps a similar motive led me to study a new religion and kept me meditating upon 3HO as if upon a koan.

While many of my reactions have yielded to the passage of time, they have left an impression, and the interplay of quests and narratives—those of women who have remained in the organization, those who have left, and my own—is reflected in the following pages. I have attempted, within that framework, to present a balanced account of the traditions, the biographies, and the twists and turns of everyday culture-building that make up the 3HO story.

PART ONE

Background

CHAPTER 1

Roots and Sources: Sikhism and Tantra

*I*t is not difficult to understand why Bhajan's version of Tantric yoga appealed to young rebellious students in the 1960s. As one writer notes, "Tantra is body-positive and antipuritanical. The Tantric teachers place self-experimentation above social morality, and the texts typically warn the uninitiated and initiate alike that their teachings are radical and dangerous. But they are also insistent that they offer a shortcut to enlightenment in the present age of spiritual and moral decline" (Feuerstein 1998, 235). Tantra seems to have been ready-made for the intelligent counterculture individual who felt that her culture was "uptight" and in decline, that her college classes were too abstract and removed from the great issues of the time, that her parents' lives were too safe and conformist to serve as models, and that she was called to live an adventurous and important life.

Some of the more individualistic principles and sentiments embedded in Tantric thought, however, do not necessarily provide a solid basis for organization building. Over the years, Bhajan and his students have added elements that provide additional structure and direction. These include Sikh beliefs, Hindu practices, and New Age practices, with Sikhism and yoga providing the two philosophical pillars of the organization. Of the two, Sikhism has become the dominant strand in the 3HO pattern. It is the belief system that is most strongly emphasized, but both are of significance in members' lives. This chapter examines these two aspects of organizational life.

Sikhism

Many North Americans have had their view of Sikhism shaped by the dramatic events that unfolded in India when, in 1983, a Sikh activist by the name of Sant Jarnail Bhindranwale occupied the Golden Temple (or, more properly, the administrative center, the Akal Takht). He was eventually evicted by Indira Gandhi's troops, an action which many Sikhs, no matter how they viewed Bhindranwale, experienced as a violation of a sacred place and as an insult to all Sikhs. When Gandhi herself was assassinated by her Sikh bodyguards in 1984, the ensuing mob violence directed against Sikhs was dramatically captured by the media. Images of militancy on both sides, and of atrocities and deep-seated religious hatreds, are not easily forgotten, certainly not by those who lived through this period on the Indian continent, not by the Sikhs living in diaspora around the globe, in fact, not by anyone who closely followed the events. These events can seem far removed from the early years of Sikhism, a religion that originated with the words of Guru Nanak, often depicted as a peaceable mystic and poet.

It is necessary to know something of the history of the Sikh religion, in India and in North America, in order to understand what 3HO members believe, how they construe gender, how the organization establishes its boundaries, and where Sikh Dharma stands in the complex and changing world of Sikhism.

The reader should know, however, that Sikh historiography is contested territory. Western and Sikh historians have often viewed Sikhism from differing vantage points. Western historians have taken the disinterested and "objective" tone expected of them as scholars in a secular tradition. They have examined the social contexts in which Sikhism emerged and evolved. They have uncovered conflicting strands of belief and have tied these to group and class interests. They tell a story of shifts, alterations, and reversals in the Sikh identity and have often attempted to separate cherished folk traditions from documented historical narratives. Some have sought to deconstruct Sikh conceptual categories.

Many Sikh historians have viewed this approach with alarm, or at least with suspicion. They have felt that their religion was being belittled, or that the approach was likely to undermine adherents' faith (Dusenbery 1989b). A few appear to have simply attempted to hold sway over the academic field of Sikh studies (McLeod 1999). Unlike their Western counterparts, a number of Sikh historians are inclined to see a steady unfolding in Sikh teachings, rather than shifting responses to historical conditions. Many emphasize the unique and revelatory aspects of the religion rather than the cultural traditions and social forces that may have shaped it. Some have resented the ways in which Western historians tend to place Sikhism within the broad context of Hinduism and Bhakti religion. As Barrier notes, "[I]n India, one of the main thrusts of recent Sikh scholarship has been to show the distinctiveness of the faith rather than its connections and similarities to other traditions." Describing the concerns of contemporary Sikh commentators, he writes, "[T]hey are concerned to reinforce . . . a sense of historical continuity, a clear differentiation between Sikhism and Hinduism from the time of the first Guru. . . . Most recently, they have shared an insistence that nonviolence has never been a cardinal element within Sikh ideology. They wish to show that the defense of Sikhism through the use of force is a traditional Sikh value" (1993, 13).

Any narrative account of the origins and development of Sikhism is likely to support one version of the Sikh identity over others. Since my study is an attempt to contribute to Western understandings of Sikhism, I have depended primarily upon the sources that are typically cited in North American and British Sikh scholarship. In this process, I have tried to select authors who incorporate or respectfully acknowledge Sikh criticisms of Western work. But I have also turned to writers who are clearly skeptical of any simple rendition of the Sikh story; I have done this on the assumption that this is the best way to avoid some of the more interested interpretations that may intrude on any work of history. My own preference is for historians who treat Sikhism as "an emergent and contested reality" (Dusenbery 1989c, 17) because, first, I think that intellectual and social realities are always complex, multi-faceted, and shifting, and second, because such an approach forces us to render our interpretations of historical events with some humility, remembering that we cannot think, or write, about the past without being influenced by present concerns. But I would not push this approach too far because there is some compelling scholarship suggesting considerable continuity in Sikh identity and practices since the time of Nanak (e.g. Grewal 1997; Mann 2001).

To the extent that Sikhism has received attention in general treatments on world religions, it has typically received brief coverage (Juergensmeyer 1979, 1993). For some time it was treated as a descendant of both Hinduism and Islam, but today the preferred approach among Western academics is to place Sikhism "within the context of fifteenth- and sixteenth-century India, especially the milieu of the medieval *sants*" and to view it as arising primarily within a Hindu milieu while recognizing some Islamic influences (Juergensmeyer 1993, 14; McLeod 1976). This scholarship places Sikhism in the general context of Bhakti religion, which, though it originated earlier, had become popular throughout India by the fifteenth and sixteenth centuries. Bhakti stresses devotion as the route to God (as opposed, for example, to the paths of knowledge or good works). In northern India there are two major variations on the Bhakti theme: *nirguni* and *saguni* (Lorenzon

1995). Those who follow *nirgun* Bhakti are committed to the worship of a single divinity that is without form or attributes. Practitioners of *sagun* Bhakti, on the other hand, direct their devotion to the various embodied manifestations of the Hindu pantheon, to figures such as Vishnu and Shiva. *Saguni* is the dominant form in India, but Sikhism emerged from the *nirguni* strain.

There have been numerous Bhakti sects and cults, and in the period preceding the emergence of Sikhism there were a variety of these. Devotees in each sect (or path, which is perhaps a better term with which to describe one of these groupings) typically worshiped a particular deity or espoused a distinctive theology and form of worship. They usually followed a teacher. Often the groupings were endogamous. Many were reformist, seeking to moderate formalized and hierarchical versions of orthodox Bhakti (Hiltebeitel 1989, 30), and often they "stressed the use of vernacular languages instead of Sanskrit" (Richardson 1985, 106).

The *sant*-singer tradition of northern India was one of the many offshoots from these Bhakti roots and is seen as a direct source of Sikhism. The *sant*s drew upon Tamil poetic conventions, employing landscape imagery and comparing religious devotion and personal experience of the divine to the delights of romantic love. The branch from which Sikhism emerged has been traced back to nondualist interpretations of Vedanta and to the teachings of Adi Sankara (Kushwant Singh 1989, 111). Sankara (788–820) taught that ultimate reality is without qualities but that it can, nonetheless, be grasped through knowledge and direct intuitive experience (Hiltebeitel 1989, 29).

The *sant*-singers criticized *saguni* polytheism and ritualism. They put little value on external forms of worship and piety and "laid firm and unqualified emphasis on the interior nature of spiritual understanding" (McLeod 1997, 91). Liberation was to be attained by meditating upon the internal voice or word of the Divine. The *sant*s also rejected interpretations of the caste system which suggested that an individual's spiritual qualifications were determined by caste standing. Indeed, *nirguni* religion was originally favored by lower castes and classes, and it clearly represented an alternative to the Brahman-dominated *saguni* traditions. Early *nirguni* Bhakti "embodied a fairly direct rejection of the ideology of *varnasramadharma*" (Lorenzen 1995, 20). It can be viewed, as McLeod puts it, as both a "method of spiritual liberation, and as a form of social protest. Both elements are inextricably linked" (1997, 91).

McLeod tells us that the *sant*s' beliefs and practices were influenced by the Nath tradition. This is of particular interest for a study of 3HO/Sikh Dharma because the Naths were yogis, and the Nath path was a "representative of the ancient tantric tradition." The Naths were much respected among the general population in the Punjab and much of northern India at the time (1997, 93).

Sikhs trace their origins to Guru Nanak (1469–1539), a seeker who issued from a high caste Hindu family. Although Sikh historians often treat him as a unique figure, others see him as one of the poet *sant*s. McLeod (1989c) tends to portray him as an inward-looking mystic who rejected external and institutional forms of religion. Other scholars (e.g. Grewal 1990, 1997; Mann 2001) point instead to his creation of an active and on-going community of believers, and they trace the defining Sikh beliefs and practices to this community. Many commentators emphasize the fact that Nanak taught that the only route to God is *nam simran* (meditation on the divine name), and that he advocated daily meditation before dawn. The goal was a personal and mystical experience of God, recognition of dependence on God as the source of all things, and liberation from *haumai*, a term that is rendered as "separation" in 3HO, and sometimes translated as "self-centered pride" (McLeod 1989c, 142), or "self-reliance": "Haumai is a difficult idea to render into English. Perhaps self-reliance is as satisfactory a term as any. . . . Self-reliance is often praised as a great human virtue, but for Guru Nanak it is a condition which blinds man to his dependence upon God" (Cole and Sambhi 1978, 77). Liberation from the cycle of rebirth and from delusion is said to come "by conquering haumai, ceasing to be worldly-minded" and becoming "God-filled." To attain these goals, in turn, requires that one recognize, delight in, and submit to the inner presence of God (ibid., 68).

Nanak and the gurus who followed him composed many poems and hymns, and today Sikhs believe that reciting and singing these, as well as quietly meditating on the divine Name, are routes to illumination. The delusions of the ego, such as pride and self-seeking, are said to be washed away by these practices. As a contemporary guide to Sikhism puts it, "[S]inging the Glory of the Lord, the Mighty King, will help purge the mind of its impurities. By glorifying the Divine, the human mind imbibes divine qualities. . . . By prayer and praise, one's mind comes in touch with Nam and becomes illuminated" (Sikh Missionary Center 1990, 269). The effects of such devotion are said to be heightened in the company of holy and enlightened individuals, and this is one reason that the congregation (*sangat*) is important in Sikhism. Lorenzon captures the Sikh approach when he tells us that, "although *nirguni* literature directs the devotee to worship a formless, universal God, this God does take partial embodiment in the Name of God and in the collective Words (*bani*) and the person of the Guru and the saints" (1995, 2).

Prayer, devotion, and meditation on the divine Name are not the sole touchstones of Sikhism. Sikhs, when asked for a concise rendering of their religious principles, often cite three nouns: *nam, dan,* and *isnan,* which translate as "divine Name," "almsgiving," and "pure living" (McLeod 1989c, 1). These principles go back to Nanak and reflect his concern with both mystical experience and with everyday ethical living. Sikhs will also stress *seva* (service) and honest, hard work.

Nanak criticized those Hindu sects that favored withdrawal from the world, and he taught that there was no need for extremes of asceticism or renunciation. Instead, he advocated the householder role and established a community of householders and worshipers at Kartarpur. Each individual was to "gently" discipline and develop the self; "ascetic austerity, penances, celibacy, and the like, had no place in Nanak's religion" (Singh 1963, 1:46). Nanak also maintained that caste was irrelevant to spiritual growth and established free kitchens in which people of all castes could eat together, a practice that has since been institutionalized in Sikh communities as *langar.* Richardson suggests that one source of Nanak's support was "the commercial classes," so "Nanak denounced beliefs that stressed renouncing the world. . . . Instead, he offered theological support for all vocations" (1985, 107).

As in Hinduism, *maya*—illusion; the material world viewed as illusionary—is an explanation for many human difficulties. The Sikh understanding of *maya,* however, differs somewhat from that found in some Hindu traditions. Thus, Gill (1975) observes that for Sikhs, "the world is not an illusion as assumed by Vedanta. It is very much there although it is phenomenal and it keeps changing every moment" (17). From this point of view, problems arise when people cling to the world's temporary forms and become overly attached to them.

Nanak established a basic Sikh principle, that of balance. As one authority puts it, Sikhism can be viewed as a religion of "equipoise" (Gill 1975). Its practitioners attempt to balance mysticism and practicality, to live in the world but to recognize their dependence on God. The good Sikh is expected to achieve a balance between God-consciousness and practical affairs. Gill suggests that the tradition provides a "four-fold" goal for followers: (1) to possess a healthy body, (2) to possess a healthy mind, (3) to get proper metaphysical knowledge, and (4) to live a life of spirit (1975, 18). This is obviously quite similar to the 3HO aim of creating a "healthy, happy, holy" individual.

Nanak chose a devoted follower, Guru Angad (1504–1552), to succeed him, and Angad in turn was followed by a series of other gurus, through the tenth and last, Guru Gobind Singh (1666–1708). Their writings have been collected, and because these writings represent for Sikhs the voice of God speaking through human representatives, they have long had a sacred quality. One of the distinctive traits of Sikhism is the importance of texts, and it is also notable that "the process of collection began extraordinarily early" (Mann 1993, 144). There is evidence that a volume of Guru Nanak's hymns was compiled during his lifetime. It was expanded by Guru Amar Das and updated by Guru Arjan (Mann 2001). Today it is known as the Adi Granth or the Guru Granth Sahib. It contains writings of the gurus and of medieval Indian poet-saints. It includes the Japji, one of Guru Nanak's compositions, which is recited daily by devout Sikhs (including those in 3HO), as well as other hymns by Gurus Nanak, Ram Das, and Arjan. It is treated with reverence.

There is another major text, of later origin, called the Dasam Granth. Its contents are popularly attributed to the tenth guru, Gobind Singh. It includes the Bachitar Natak and the Zafar-nama which recount events from Gobind Singh's life. Then there are prayers and narratives, with much of the narrative "focusing on legends from the Hindu Puranas and on anecdotes which appear to have little to do with religious belief " (McLeod 1984, 6). There is considerable controversy surrounding their authorship. Many Sikhs attribute the entire work to Gobind Singh, but there are reasons to question that attribution. McLeod summarizes the different views: "The traditional answer to the question of authorship is that the entire collection is the work of Guru Gobind Singh himself. A more cautious view restricts his contribution to the first three sections, attributing the remainder to poets of his entourage; and a rigorous interpretation holds that nothing except the Zafar-nama can be safely attached to the Guru" (1984, 7).

These questions of authorship are complex, and, not surprisingly, historians often disagree about them. A shortage of scholars with the necessary linguistic skills compounds the difficulties. We will return to this issue because one commentator, Harjot Oberoi, raises some interesting questions about gender and about goddess themes in Sikhism.

The Sikh gurus propounded doctrines and practices that modern women converts can appreciate. A recent feminist Sikh commentator (Singh 1993) argues that Nanak's distinctive vision "reveals a significant repatterning of that theological mold which has the male in the center and the female as but subordinate and auxiliary to him" (26). Nanak was critical of avoidances and pollution beliefs surrounding women and asked how a man could view women as impure when he himself was born of a woman—a comment often cited, and repeated, by Yogi Bhajan. Guru Amar Das opposed the practices of sati (immolating a widow on the funeral pyre of her husband) and purdah. Gobind Singh opposed female infanticide. Guru Hargobind, like Nanak, taught that marriage was not an impediment to the spiritual life. All of the gurus directed their teachings to both men and women, and Gobind Singh taught that both sexes were to receive initiation (Shanker 1994).

In addition to the actual teachings of the gurus, one finds imagery in their writings which elevates the feminine, and often does so without creating the disembodied, romanticized, or purely maternal vision of womanhood that one so often finds in religious traditions. Singh finds abundant feminine imagery; in fact, she goes so far as to say that Nanak's poetry "promotes a shift from an androcentric to a feminist construction of the cosmos" (1993, 39). She and another commentator (Shanker 1994) have both noted the extensive incorporation of bridal and marital imagery in the Adi Granth.

Singh compares the works of Nanak and Kabir (who was also one of the writers who composed in the *sant* tradition) and finds Nanak's style far more sympathetic to women, to nature, and to contemporary feminist and womanist concerns. Kabir's approach to his reader is different, she says. He is always "pounding with questions or prodding with riddles," while Nanak's style is free of such devices, a "naturally spontaneous poetry" in "the mode of supreme wonder" (1993, 38). Both poets work with the image of the bride, but she finds "Kabir's opinion of women is contemptuous and derogatory," and she cites other scholars who find his work "misogynist" (114). In general, she argues that "Kabir and the Sants of Northern India generally valued an ascetic life in which women play no significant role" (114), while Nanak was different. In Nanak's poetry, she says, body and mind, as well as male and female principles are united. The bride yearns for her Beloved, but her "devotion doesn't call for renunciation and asceticism; she opens the way to the Transcendent by living fully and authentically" (116).

Singh follows in the footsteps of other Sikh commentators who emphasize the distinctive characteristics of the Sikh tradition; in fact, she questions the derivation of Sikhism from the *sant* tradition given the distinctive qualities she finds in Nanak's style and outlook. But her approach is unique in that she views gender-related attitudes as an original dividing line between Sikhism and its surrounding cultural matrix, even if time has since largely erased that original boundary: "In the original Punjabi the gender of the One is not differentiated, but the translators, interpreters, and commentators have invariably referred to the One as 'he' and kept the male image at the center of their discussions" (1993, 52).

Shanker is less sanguine about early treatments of gender. She finds many conflicting images of women in the Guru Granth Sahib. In many passages, she finds that "the idea that woman is evil, unclean, an impediment is not rejected, as we are often made to think, but endorsed in the Guru Granth" (1994, 209). She concludes that "the precepts of the gurus concerning the amelioration of the situation of women remained just that: precepts" (198).

Just as there are differing views concerning the representation of women in the early years, there are differing views about the clarity of the Sikh identity and the nature of the boundaries separating Sikhs from other religious groupings at this time. Oberoi finds that the Sikh movement "had shown little enthusiasm for distinguishing its constituents from members of other religious traditions and establishing a pan-Indian community" (1995, 38). Grewal (1997) disagrees, finding an early and distinctive identity and no empirical evidence to support Oberoi's position (13). Many Western historians detect a change in Sikhism after the death of Guru Arjan (1606). They point to growing militancy, to Sikh assumption of temporal authority, and to an influx of individuals of Jat background into the ranks of Sikhism. At this time, Sikhs armed themselves in order to resist India's Mughal rulers, and the sword became part of the Sikh way of life, a means of defending the path.

These developments were institutionalized by Guru Gobind Singh, who is known as the originator of the Khalsa. The original Khalsa ideal was the "soldier-saint," who was at once a pious follower of the Guru and a fearless wearer of the sword. According to Sikh tradition, the Khalsa was initiated in a very dramatic way. Accounts vary, but most agree on a set of events. On a day of celebration in 1699 (Baisakhi) many Sikhs had assembled. When Gobind Singh addressed the audience he stunned his listeners by announcing that he required the head of a Sikh as a sacrifice. After a period of silence a devoted follower hesitantly offered himself. He was taken to a nearby tent. This sequence of events was repeated four more times. The assembled Sikhs believed that Gobind Singh was indeed killing the reluctant volunteers, but after the fifth "sacrifice," Gobind Singh called the five forward and they emerged unscathed. Some say that goats, rather than Sikhs, had been slaughtered. Others say that Gobind Singh brought the brave men back to life. Gobind Singh praised the courage and devotion of the heroes (the "cherished five" or *panj piare*) and asked them to drink *amrit*—sweetened water stirred with a two-edged sword. Today Khalsa Sikhs undergo an initiation in memory of that event, and this is the initiation that many 3HO members have undertaken.

Guru Gobind Singh's sons having predeceased him and the Khalsa having been successfully established, he is said to have declared the succession of gurus ended. Henceforth, the spirit and wisdom of the gurus would reside solely in the scriptures and in the Sikh congregations.

McLeod (1976) has suggested that popular histories foreshorten and simplify the founding of the Khalsa. He argues that it actually emerged over time as the Sikh constituency changed. The first Sikh leaders were from Kshatryia families, the second level of the caste system, as were most original followers of the tradition (this is Yogi Bhajan's caste), but by the seventeenth and eighteenth centuries they were being joined by more and more Jats (peasants, now a landholding group in the Punjab). Today the Jats constitute the majority of the Sikh population. They brought to the religion a martial tradition, and this, in combination with changing political realities, contributed, according to McLeod, to a slow change in beliefs which is now encapsulated in the popular mind.

Oberoi (1994, 1995), in his recent rethinking of Sikh history, suggests that the Khalsa identity was elaborated throughout the first three-quarters of the eighteenth century. In making this argument, he disagrees with two other schools of thought: those historians who would argue that the Khalsa only became dominant in the nineteenth century under the British and those who would see it springing directly from the injunctions of Guru Gobind Singh. Rather, Oberoi argues that during the eighteenth century the Khalsa steadily developed distinctive ideas of moral duty (*rahit*) and established life-cycle rites which were readily distinguishable from Hindu customs. Over time, newly instituted taboos further separated Khalsa from non-Khalsa. Hair was not to be shorn. Sikh women were not to marry outside of the religion. Sikhs should not associate with Muslims or with members of a variety of other groups, including "all those who had dared challenge the orthodox line of succession of ten Sikh Gurus" (1995, 50). Amritsar was established as a pilgrimage site and many congregations were established.

In addition, the unique Sikh link to the divine was forged. "In the unsettled conditions of the eighteenth century the Khalsa Sikhs were in desperate need of a cohesive principle that would replace the institution of the living Gurus" (Oberoi 1995, 51). That replacement was found in two principles, both of which could be traced back to the early guru period. First, there was the doctrine of the eternal Guru which holds that *bani*, the words of the gurus, represent the voice of God. As the repository of their words, the Adi Granth became the guru. Second, there was the concept of the Guru Panth, which held that the guru was present wherever Sikhs assembled as a *sangat* (1995, 51).

Gobind Singh battled the Mughal rulers, and so did leaders who came after him. Their bravery brought them allies and converts. The Khalsa grew in numbers and favor throughout the eighteenth century, and "the rural poor, the urban underprivileged and others who persisted on the margins of the Punjabi society readily responded to the Khalsa campaign to turn the existing world upside down" (Oberoi 1995, 52). An invasion from Iran in 1738 "dealt a mortal blow to the Mughal empire" and "disrupted the Mughal administration of the Panjab" (Singh 1999, 18). However, an Afghan ruler took advantage of the weakened Mughals and also made numerous incursions. Sikhs responded by dividing into small groupings called *misl*s, each with its own sphere of operations (Singh 1999). Over time, some of these gained considerable power and control over land, but this led to a general loss of unity among Sikhs. The Khalsa gradually regrouped, particularly under a famous Sikh, Ranjit Singh. He, by virtue of his conquest of yet another Afghan invader, became maharaja of the Punjab in 1801. He made a number of further conquests in his efforts to extend his state. He ruled for almost forty years, and "his success as a ruler was due to the fact that he did not discriminate between his subjects on the basis of religion" (Singh 1999, 23). His government and army were drawn from among Sikhs, Hindus, and Muslims, and he hired foreigners to train his army (Singh 1999). Under his rule *gurdwara*s were placed under the management of an elite (*mahant*s) who were not necessarily Khalsa Sikhs.

Oberoi (1994, 24) says that diversity characterized the Sikh world at this point. He notes that not all Sikhs were initiated into the Khalsa and argues that clean-shaven Sikhs (sahajdharis) were common. Grewal (1997) responds that the sahajdharis were actually limited to one sect, the Udasis, who were arguably outside of the Sikh fold.

Sulakan Singh (1983), who has made a study of the Udasis, sees them as taking a compromise position between Sikhism and Hinduism, and he places them close to the nondualistic Vedantic school of philosophy (95). The Udasis revered Guru Nanak, but they also "believed in a parallel independent line of succession" other than that from Nanak to Gobind Singh (75), which they trace to Nanak's son. Moreover, they rejected the Sikh doctrine that the guruship had been vested in the Adi Granth, and, while consulting the Granth, they also turned to the Hindu sources. While some were householders (particularly in the nineteenth century), most were celibate and ascetic. They also practiced hatha yoga. They were in favor under the reign of Ranjit Singh; indeed, "about 70 per cent of the total Udasi establishments enjoyed state patronage" (Singh 1981, 39).

Such acceptance of the Udasis, says Oberoi, is indicative of the fact that, although "by the second half of the eighteenth century a distinctive Khalsa normative order had emerged" (Oberoi 1995, 50), the lines between Sikhism and Hinduism were not always clear, and Sikhs in this time period still turned to their Hindu roots in their efforts to define an identity.

One sees this tendency in some forms of Sikh literature. It is, for example, sometimes found in the *gur-bilas* literature. As McLeod describes this genre, it was "a treatment which exalted the courage of the Gurus and lauded their skill in battle. Inevitably its exponents concentrated their attentions on the two great warrior Gurus, on Guru Hargobind and preeminently on Guru Gobind Singh. . . . [T]he *gur-bilas* literature is far more important as a testimony to the beliefs of writers and their contemporary circumstances than to the actual lives of the Gurus" (McLeod 1984, 11).

The *gur-bilas* works are also of interest because goddess themes, and the concept of shakti, appear in some of the accounts. Some of the *gur-bilas* that were written in the nineteenth century appear to reflect a Hinduization of Gobind Singh that occurred under the leader Ranjit Singh. Thus in the Gurbilas Patshahi 10, "It was the Goddess (Devi) who asked for the creation of the *Khalsa*. Guru Gobind Singh arranged an elaborate ritual to make the Goddess appear at the Ganges. A sixteen year old girl was sacrificed. The Goddess appeared before the Guru . . . and blessed the Guru with the power 'to rule the world and to destroy the Turks.' (Hans 1981, 50). This account "has the stamp of the times of Maharaja Ranjit Singh. Some kind of equilibrium had to be maintained between the Hindus and the Muslims. The Sikh rulers could present themselves as the leaders of Hinduism by making their Gurus Hindu" (Hans 1984, 104).

The goddess also makes an appearance in the Chaupa Singh Rahit-nama, a code of conduct for the Khalsa, one of several that have been compiled since Gobind Singh's death. It appears to date from between 1740 and 1765 and is attributed to Gobind Singh's tutor, Chaupa Singh Chhibbar. McLeod tells us that "in its extant form it presents considerable difficulties from an orthodox Khalsa point of view. . . . These include . . . its insistence upon traditional deference towards Brahmans . . . and its embarrassing involvement in the Devi cult" (1987, 10). It "relates, as if it were authentic, the notorious story that Guru Gobind Singh was persuaded to seek the blessings of Mata Devi (the goddess Kali or Durga) on his new Panth by celebrating the traditional *hom* or fire ritual" (15).

Such themes also appear in the Dasam Granth. Indeed, "approximately 80 per cent of the collection comprises largely a retelling of Hindu myths," and three of the narratives "graphically depict the goddess Durga or Devi" (McLeod 1997, 177–79). McLeod finds that "the eighteenth-century and early nineteenth-century commentators believed that he [Gobind Singh] was involved with Durga worship and in consequence practically all of the major works of that period (together with portions of the Dasam Granth) deal with this as what they imagined to be a definite fact. The *gur-bilas* literature, for example, has frequent references to Durga and to shakti" (1999, personal communication).

This theme also interests Nikky-Guninder Kaur Singh (1993), who draws our attention to stories about the goddess Durga that are included in the Dasam Granth. These stories are reworkings of the old epics in which Durga represents the kind of courage which is more often associated with male warriors. She attacks enemies, stands up for her principles, and cuts away all things false and hypocritical. Her symbol is the sword. Thus Singh suggests that the sword symbolism associated with the Khalsa may originally have had a female component, which has since been omitted in the retellings. She attributes these writings to Gobind Singh, but views them not as evidence of goddess worship but as a form of myth making. She suggests that Gobind Singh singled out Durga "as a model of moral force and martial prowess for both men and women" (1993, 127). In fact, she maintains that one could even say that he was "remythologizing, which entails the retelling of stories and myths from the past from the female point of view" (142), and that "Guru Gobind Singh's choice of Durga means unequivocal acknowledgment of woman's power in society" (126).

Whether Gobind Singh was "remythologizing," or whether he himself was being mythologized, the presence of these themes suggests that such syncretic beliefs and practices have a history in Sikhism. Even Bhajan's emphasis on shakti, and his appropriation of elements of Tantrism, are similar to processes that have occurred before, if often at the margins of the community.

According to Oberoi, diversity within the Sikh path continued into the early nineteenth century when Khalsa hegemony was temporarily eclipsed by the Sanatan Sikh tradition, a new form which "resulted from the conceptual and strategic rapprochement between the Khalsa and *Sahajdhari* identities" (1994, 93). Sanatan was a priestly tradition which drew freely upon the Vedas and the Mahabharata. It was disseminated by members of elite families and by holy men, as well as by members of a number of religious orders. Among these orders were ascetic groups like the Udasi and Nirmalis.

Oberoi finds an appreciation for feminine principles in the Sanatan tradition. At this juncture in Sikh history he tells us that the Dasam Granth held equal status with the Adi Granth, and in the Dasam Granth, the tales based on the Puranas (the ancient Hindu scriptures which incorporate popular tales, many about Krishna) "add a maternal dimension to Sikh understandings of Ultimate Reality" (1994, 97). This is not a generally shared view, however. Mann (2001, 21–22) would disagree about the stature of the Dasam Granth. He finds that contemporary sources indicate that it was always treated as a secondary text. Singh, in her feminist reading of Sikh history, is critical of the Sanatan tradition. Because the Udasis and the Nirmalas "were essentially reared on classical Indian exegesis," she argues that their analyses eclipsed the Sikh view of the transcendent, replacing it with "the Hindu *Zeitgeist.*" She goes on to say that her "contention is that until the symbolic value of Sikh literature is truly understood and its difference from the neighboring traditions is acknowledged, Guru Nanak's and his successor Gurus' aim of uplifting the role and status of women cannot be fulfilled" (1993, 255).

While the priestly Sanatan tradition was thriving among the elite, the folk traditions of rural Punjab were simultaneously shaping Sikhism, although "official Sikh historiography has always maintained a stony silence on Sikh participation in popular religion" (Oberoi 1994, 139). Indeed, many of the distinctive traits of contemporary Sikhism grew out of official repudiations and reconstructions of this popular religion. This process may be of considerable importance for understanding how womanhood has been construed and the feminine experience shaped within the Sikh tradition.

Oberoi finds that in the rural Punjab, Hindu and Sikh practices often overlapped. Sikhs participated in the worship of the goddess Devi in her forms as Durga and Kali. They expressed their devotion at Hindu shrines and fairs and even belonged to religious orders dedicated to this goddess. Sitala Devi, the goddess associated with smallpox (she could both inflict and cure the disease) was worshiped by elites and non-elites alike. One Sikh ruler built a temple to this goddess in her form as Mansa Devi, and many ordinary Sikhs undertook pilgrimages and participated in cults dedicated to her. Both Sikhs and Hindus made offerings to Dharti Mata (Mother Earth), and "a common belief was that every month Mother Earth slept for seven days, and during those days no digging, ploughing or sowing should be performed" (Oberoi 1994, 168).

Some women were also cast as witches (*dains*) whose powers were attained by "control over a spirit through certain formulae and incantations" (Oberoi 1994, 171). A *dain* was feared, and it was believed that she could "find anything on earth, patch up or open the sky, restore life, set fire to water, turn stone into wax, torment lovers and transform powerful people into sheep or monkeys" (ibid.). Women evidently were often possessed by spirits as well, an event which, as Oberoi suggests, may have been an oblique way for "a powerless sector of society to voice its dissent and articulate needs normally suppressed" (159).

Such folk observances came to be viewed by the Sikh hierarchy as superstitious and inappropriate, but judging by the way some of these traditions echo through contemporary accounts, Sikh participation continued in spite of opposition, and it continues into the present. Thus, in an ethnographic account of Punjabi symbols and rituals pertaining to women which was published in the 1970s, Hershman (1977) found that goddess worship was flourishing among both Sikhs and Hindus.

Similarly, Erndl finds that "the Hindu Goddess has become more and more popular throughout the ages, coexisting with male Gods and in many cases making them superfluous" (1997, 20). In a recent study of a goddess cult in northwestern India she finds that "[t]he worship of Devi (the Goddess) is one of the most vigorous and visible of religious phenomena in northwest India today. Her cult is a regional variant of the pan-Hindu worship of the Great Goddess. . . . In the greater Panjab region . . . she is most commonly called by the nickname Seranvali (Lion Rider) or simply Mata (Mother). Her cult is one in which esoteric Tantric elements mingle with popular devotional (*bhakti*) worship" (Erndl 1993, 3–4). She also tells us that the "eclectic and nonsectarian quality of the popular religion extends beyond Hinduism to embrace Sikhism. . . . Many Sikhs are enthusiastic participants in the Goddess cult, in spite of the fact that Sikh religious leaders are at pains to distinguish Sikhism from Hinduism and that present political tensions have driven the wedge even further" (ibid., 9). She finds that both men and women are involved in the cult, although it is often women who are possessed by the goddess (1997, 21).

The reign of Ranjit Singh was followed by less-glorious years for Sikhs. Although they successfully resisted English conquest for some time, they were defeated in two Anglo-Sikh wars, and the British annexed the Punjab in 1849. Under the British, Sikhs formed a series of Singh *sabha*s (societies created to strengthen and reform Sikhism) which contributed significantly to the current form of Sikh practice.

Encountering a "colonial state which aimed at codifying everything" (Oberoi 1994, 236), the Sanatans created the first Singh *sabha* to record and preserve Sikh customs, rituals, and history. This first organization was to give rise to the Singh Sabha movement, which was ultimately removed from the control of the Sanatan Sikhs. But in the early years Oberoi claims that the *sabhas* inscribed the Sanatan version of Sikhism, an inclusive version that incorporated Hindu sources, folk traditions, rituals rooted in clan and lineage observances, and the beliefs and practices of diverse groupings that clustered around living gurus. Oberoi describes it as "carnavalesque" (1994, 256).

This version was soon to be replaced, as "in colonial Punjab, during the second half of the nineteenth century, there emerged a restless new elite that cut across kin ties, neighbourhood networks and even caste affiliations" (Oberoi 1994 265). This "new elite," in its struggle to formulate a culture that was viable and productive in the contexts of modernization and British rule, dipped freely into the ideas of the European Enlightenment. The elite also appears to have responded to perceived threats from other religions (Grewal 1990, 145), threats seemingly emanating from Christian missionaries and from the Arya Samaj (originally a movement to purify Hinduism via a return to the Vedas, which later gave rise to a variety of organizations, some of which were militantly pro-Hindu), as well as growing militancy among Muslims in the years leading up to Partition in 1947. Like their Hindu counterparts in the Arya Samaj, they attempted to rationalize their religion and to purge it of "superstition." They sought to institute standard practices and to create a religious community that transcended the usual divisions based on locale, teacher, caste, and lineage (Oberoi 1994, McLeod 1989c). Maintaining that Sikhism had met with a decline, they "preached reform and regeneration of the Khalsa" (McLeod 1989c, 62) and were referred to as the Tat Khalsa or "pure Sikhs." They opposed worship of living gurus (still a practice among some Sikhs at that time) and of popular saints. They sought to end Sikh participation in rural festivals and to replace "Rabelaisian features with puritanism, asceticism and restraint" (Oberoi 1994, 313). Oberoi adds that "reformers among the new elites were unhappy with the fusion of gaiety, abandonment and occasional ritual inversions through female speech which they saw as being aimed at male domination" (313). Now "conceptions of the divine in feminine terms were no longer permissible" (320).

The British, Oberoi argues, brought Western conceptions of religion with them to India and expected a religious tradition to have clearcut boundaries and creeds. The new Khalsa-oriented versions of

Sikhism met their preconceptions. Moreover, Khalsa initiates, with their distinctive dress, were physically recognizable. Soon Khalsa Sikhs developed a reputation as courageous and loyal soldiers. Unable or unwilling to incorporate the many strands of Sikh identity in a single category, the British favored this distinctive and visible Tat Khalsa version (Oberoi 1994).

The Tat Khalsa emerged as the dominant form of Sikh identity, and "by the turn of the century the exponents of Tat Khalsa theory had asserted an effective claim to interpret the nature of tradition and to enunciate the approved pattern" of Sikh behavior (McLeod 1989c, 71). The *sabha*s were consolidated under a coordinating organization called the Chief Khalsa Diwan, which, over time, attempted to clarify the nature of Sikh identity, publishing in 1917 a "comprehensive code" (now the Rehat Maryada) for Sikh rites (Grewal 1990, 147).

Oberoi's interpretation seems to be intended to challenge claims that Khalsa hegmony and the Rehat Maryada are based on long historical tradition. Instead, he associates them with colonial rule, and with rigidity, puritanism, and male domination. This is, naturally, an unwelcome point of view in many circles, and one that can be countered by a number of arguments, but even if one sees in it a distortion of the historical record, this approach raises issues that should continue to be addressed, particularly, perhaps, by women scholars.

In 1919 Sikhs established a political party, the Central Sikh League, whose goals were to enhance Sikh control over religious and cultural institutions and to encourage Sikhs to join the struggle for Indian independence. In 1920 a group of Sikhs met to create an elected body to manage *gurdwara*s (seeking to remove Udasis, among others, from positions of oversight) (Juergensmeyer 2000). A more activist political arm, the Shiromani Akali Dal, was also created at that time, and it launched a nonviolent campaign for control of the *gurdwara*s. After years of marches and demonstrations the goal was attained, and in 1925 the British acceded and established a managing body, the Shiromani Gurdwara Prabandhak Committee (the Central Gurdwara Management Committee, or SGPC). The SGPC has been a major force in Sikh affairs ever since. The Akali Dal subsequently joined Mahatma Gandhi in civil disobedience. Members were involved in planning for independence and received much respect from their fellow Sikhs when they opposed Ramsey McDonald's proposals for a Punjab Legislative Council on the grounds that his version did not provide sufficiently for Sikh representation. Today, the Akali Dal is still a force in Punjabi politics, but is more frequently challenged than in the past.

Throughout the 1940s, Indian religious groups jockeyed for administrative arrangements that would benefit their constituencies. Often their policies and actions were motivated by fear of becoming a disadvantaged minority in a particular region. The Muslim League actively campaigned for an independent state. Official Sikh bodies opposed the creation of Pakistan and also made it clear that, if such a state were created, they would not be subject to a Muslim majority.

In the months leading up to independence, growing religious violence convinced Nehru that Pakistan was a necessity (Grewal 1990). The resulting Partition of August 1947 divided the Punjab. Sikhs had to completely evacuate the western portion, in the process losing claim to Nanak's birthplace and many other sacred sites, as well as to considerable agricultural and mineral assets (Pettigrew 1975). Twelve million people were displaced in the Punjab (Mann 1993, 155). While the suffering was massive, the one arguable benefit to Sikhs was that it concentrated the population so that Sikhs were no longer a small minority population in the Punjab (McLeod 1989b, 110).

Since Nehru had at one time considered reorganizing Indian provinces according to languages spoken, many Sikhs had hopes for a Punjabi-speaking province and for official recognition of Gurmukhi, the Punjabi script in which the Guru Granth Sahib is written. Akali Dal leaders began to press for a Punjabi-language state. Various promising formulas were devised and compromises fashioned, but, for a variety of reasons, none of these was implemented. Refusing to give up, the Akalis sponsored the Punjabi Suba movement in an effort to achieve their goal. Many Hindus were distrustful of this movement, interpreting it as a scarcely veiled effort to create a Sikh majority state (Gupte 1985).

The movement generated demonstrations, fasts, and violence, and, finally, the Indian government's decision in 1966 to divide the Punjab into three states. One of these was called Punjab and was 52 percent Sikh (Gupte 1985, 123). The Sikhs were, at last, a majority somewhere, and the new alignment was followed by a period of Sikh flowering, with much celebration of Sikh traditions and extensive publications in the field of Sikh studies. But the settlement also left a residue of problems that continue to complicate Indian politics. Under Indira Gandhi the Akalis demanded that the new state boundaries be readjusted so that the Punjab included Punjabi-speaking areas of the neighboring states. They also protested the way in which the central government allocated water rights and industrial licenses. The Punjab prospered in the 1970s, and Sikhs began looking to invest their wealth. Under these circumstances "many Sikhs came to see the Indian government's policy of controlling all industrial licensing from New Delhi and steering investment to poorer but more populous and vote-rich provinces in the Hindi heartland as an obstacle to these aspirations" (quoted in Gupte 1985, 123).

The Akali Dal initiated a *dharm yudh* (righteous war) to push for the desired reforms, which had been codified as the Anandpur Sahib Resolution. This led to confrontations and to some violence. The party was also at loggerheads with Indira Gandhi and supported her rival, Jaya Prakah Narayan. Members of the Akali Dal participated in a rally in New Delhi where there were calls for civil disobedience in order to unseat her (Grewal 1990, 213). Gandhi responded with emergency rule in October 1983. The Akalis, in turn, led mass actions, such as an attempt to block all Punjabi roads.

The Punjab was becoming increasingly divided. There were the relatively long-term divisions between castes, between wealthy landowners and the less fortunate, between adherents of the Congress and Akali parties, between strict and more permissive followers of the religion. There was also now a proliferation of sects and increasing opposition to the two traditionally powerful political parties, the Akali Dal and the Congress Party. Grewal describes "increasing militancy and sectarian polarization" (1990, 218).

Over the years, various leaders had advocated the creation of Khalistan—a separate Sikh state—but agitation for this goal now increased. Among the advocates, Sant Jarnail Bhindranwale was the best known. Originally a religious teacher in the countryside, he became entangled in Punjabi politics as an advocate for Sikh orthodoxy. He was particularly incensed by the activities of the Sant Nirankari sect, a group which clings to the idea that the words of the ten gurus are not the final revelations of Sikhism, believing instead that they are today following a living guru. When this guru (Baba Gurbachan Singh) led a congregation in worship at Amritsar, Bhindranwale and others urged action against them and tried to stop the proceedings. This led to a violent clash and several deaths (Grewal 1990). Later, Baba Gurbachan was murdered and Bhindranwale was suspected, as he was in a later death as well, but he remained free. Bhindranwale was adamant in his support of the Anandpur Sahib Resolution and rejected an Akali search for compromise. He occupied the Akal Takht on December 15, 1983.

Tensions came to a head at this point. In June, Indira Gandhi sent troops to dislodge him, and "Sikhs around the world were outraged" by this intrusion (Gupte 1985, 126). Her subsequent assassination by two Sikh body guards on October 31, 1984, was followed by the massacre of thousands of Sikhs by Hindu mobs. Sikhs and Hindus continued to clash, and the Sikh independence movement burgeoned: "During its heyday, from 1981 to 1994, thousands of young men and perhaps a few hundred women joined the movement. They were initiated into the secret fraternities of various rival radical organizations. . . . By 1988, more than a hundred people a month were killed. . . . Accompanying the increase in violence was a general collapse of law and order, especially in rural areas of the state near the Pakistan border" (Juergensmeyer 2000, 89–90). At the time, 3HO/Sikh Dharma officially decried Bhindranwale's actions, and Yogi Bhajan did not support the more militant Sikh efforts. Today, the level of violence has decreased.

Yoga

There is, as we have seen, some historical precedent for combining yoga with Sikhism, although this is not the accepted approach today. There is also a certain logic to the 3HO version of this marriage. Like Sikhism, Tantra is not world-rejecting. Also like Sikhism, it did not originate with the Brahman elite, but rather has appealed to ordinary people. And both Sikhism and Tantric yoga are intended to inform everyday life but are also said to open the individual to numinous experiences of unity with the divine.

Nonetheless, Bhajan's merger of yoga and Sikhism troubled Punjabi-born Sikhs in the early years, and this was a divisive issue that sometimes separated American and ethnic Sikhs, although today it appears to have faded in significance (e.g., G. Khalsa 1993). One early pamphlet (Trilochan Singh 1977) was highly critical of Bhajan's incorporation of Tantric beliefs (and of Yogi Bhajan in general). The author argued that the Tantric yogin is pantheistic, whereas Sikhism portrays an "absolute and supreme God" (1977, 10). He was troubled by the potential importation of Tantric sexual imagery as well. As a Sikh, one does not so much discover God in the self as learn that one exists in God (Cole and Sambhi 1978). Members of 3HO render this as becoming a "channel" for God's will. There is a difference between the individual empowerment that is a goal of the white Tantric yoga that Bhajan teaches and the handing over of the self to God which Nanak urged. This inconsistency is not a glaring feature of 3HO/Sikh Dharma, but it is present.

When they first attended his classes, Bhajan's early students encountered a large, bearded charismatic teacher. He told them that he had studied yoga under two masters of the discipline, and that he had received the title mahan Tantric, which made him the only person entitled to teach white Tantric yoga classes. He also made much of the fact that he had studied under Sant Hazara Singh. Trilochan Singh, however, disputed these claims (1977, 108).

Bhajan's version of yoga addressed many counterculture goals and concerns. He offered a vision of life in which acquiring property, positions, or status could matter, but would also be secondary to more important concerns. Thus, he sympathized with countercultural critiques of American materialism but kept the door open for practical accommodation to what counterculture people called "the system." Enlightenment, liberation, and the creation of a better society were the goals, he said, and his students would be in the forefront of change, members of an elect whose spiritual practices would usher in the New Age. They would prepare and strengthen themselves through the practice of yoga. Yogananda, in *Autobiography of a Yogi*, a book recommended by Bhajan, says, "the deeper the Self-realization of a man, the more he influences the whole universe by his subtle spiritual vibrations, and the less he himself is affected by the phenomenal flux" (1946, 193). This is the assumption in 3HO; however marginal and disempowered they had previously felt, Bhajan was giving 3HO men and women the techniques they needed in order to attain influence and change the world.

Bhajan's approach was eclectic. He combined "aspects of Karma Yoga, Hatha Yoga, Bhakto [*sic*] Yoga, Mantra Yoga, and Laya Yoga" (Dusenbery 1975, 19). He also appears to have combined elements of Buddhist and Hindu versions of Tantra. He encouraged his students to learn about the different types of yoga. In particular, they were encouraged to read Patanjali's *Yoga Sutras*.

Patanjali is usually cited as a source for hatha, rather than kundalini, yoga. Patanjali compiled and systematized ideas that can be found in the Upanishads, in Vedanta, and in the Mahabharata. His classical yoga is a distillation of these and is essentially dualist (Eliade 1969), as it separates matter and spirit. Patanjali is assumed to have lived in the second century B.C.E., but yogic practices may date back to early civilization in the Indus Valley (Melton 1990, 501). Patanjali's version assumes that suffering is due to mental states, to the human tendency to mistakenly identify the true self with the mind and its thoughts. The mind, he argues, is an aspect of matter (*pakriti*) rather than of spirit (*parusha*). Spirit is without attributes, and this presents problems and paradoxes. How can the mind know spirit? How can the soul, which resides within matter, be freed? The answer is that there is within the person an intelligence (*buddhi*) which, while it is not spirit, does reflect the glory of spirit, much as the moon reflects the sun (Eliade 1969). This intelligence can be enhanced and utilized by the seeker. This is done by employing a variety of disciplines or yogas. The novice learns a series of steps by means of which the body can be subjugated and the senses mastered until they are under the direction of the mind. This is a necessary first step so that the entire body can be used to focus on spirit.

Equally important is the control of thoughts and attachments. As long as the individual identifies with the ego and continues to form attachments and aversions there will be no liberation. Willing, feeling, thinking, desiring, all of these leave accumulated, subliminal traces (*vasanas*) which shape future actions and entrap the individual in the world of matter. Classical yoga teaches techniques for transcending these attachments and provides means by which the individual can cease to identify with the distracting and mechanistic mind which produces them (Feuerstein 1991, Varenne 1976). "The task that yoga sets itself," notes Varenne, "is to destroy *vasanas* without producing new ones" (1976, 89). Techniques include self-restraint, the use of specific postures and meditative techniques, and various forms of breath control and mental concentration. Yoga practitioners also may experiment with states of consciousness and experience ecstatic states that transcend the small self (Feuerstein 1991). They slowly learn to still the mind and body, to break "the subconscious-conscious circuit" (Eliade 1969, 57).

It is understood that this does not happen without a fierce struggle. The subconscious (to use modern psychological terminology, which 3HO members employ) resists "any act of renunciation and asceticism, every action the effect of which might be the emancipation of the self." Each act of self-denial represents a threat that "the mass of yet unmanifested latencies might be deprived of its destiny" (Eliade 1969, 58). Moreover, as the practitioner reduces the activity of mind and body, the stored-up contents of the mind demand attention: "we find descriptions in all the texts of the terrible mental phantasmogoria that explodes at the moment when the adept attains meditative nonactivity" (Varenne 1976, 89). The belief is that, if the yogi can hold firm through this and many other trials, pure intelligence will finally be freed to apprehend God in moments of intuitive understanding and joy, even to experience union with divinity (*samadhi*).

Many of Bhajan's teachings can be viewed as extensions of Patanjali's sutras. Not only does he teach the physical disciplines, but in his talks he dramatizes the struggles involved in the spiritual life, warning his students to beware of a psychic backlash. He assures his followers that they will learn to "fry" the subconscious and its contents. He differs most clearly in his rejection of asceticism, but he does teach that the ego must be subdued and uses the image of self as chariot, an image that derives from the Upanishads:

> The body is like a chariot
> of which the soul is the owner;
> the intelligence is its driver,
> the mind plays the part of the reins;
> as for the horses, those are the senses;
> the world is their arena.
>
> (From Katha Upanishad,
> quoted in Varenne 1976, 84)

Members of 3HO add elements of Tantric yoga to this base. While they commonly talk about "kundalini" and "Tantra" as two separate forms of yoga practice, Tantra is the broader term, and kundalini yoga is one of the disciplines embraced by Tantric practitioners. Having said that, however, we must admit that it is difficult to define Tantrism. The term embraces several different schools of thought. One authority notes:

> The chronology and history of early Tantric literature are obscure. Scholars not only argue about dates, but they even disagree on what exactly the term "Tantra," "Tantrism," "Tantric literature," and so forth designate. It is difficult to distinguish clearly between Tantric elements and Tantrism as a fully developed ritual and doctrinal system. . . . Although texts identifying themselves as "Tantras" began to appear only in approximately the ninth century, the seeds of the "Tantric tradition" were clearly sown prior to this period. . . . In Tantra, some of the various strands . . . present in the mainstream Vedic-Brahmanical tradition are woven together with others that probably sprang originally from various non-Vedic, popular traditions. (Pintchman 1994, 108–9)

One of the conceptual inspirations is found in the early Upanishads. This is the idea that there are only two principles at work in the universe: consciousness and inert nature. Mookerjee (1977) hypothesizes that this idea evolved and blended with early Indian goddess worship. Infinite, formless consciousness was associated with a male principle, and the natural world of objects and change with the feminine principle, or *shakti*. *Shakti* was said to take the form of creation, destruction, or maintenance, her function being to "veil, limit or finitise pure infinite formless Consciousness so as to produce form" (Woodroffe 1929, 10). By creating form, *shakti* produces the impression that all objects are separate and bounded when, in fact, all phenomena are one.

In Shaiva (worship of Shiva) and Vaishnava (worship of Vishnu) Hinduism, the male deities are paired with female consorts. Within these divine couples it is the female figures who are the source of *shakti* or dynamism, but this active principle works through the male figure. There is an implied separation between matter (female) and spirit (male). Similarly, one finds that "in Tantra generally the Absolute, although singular in essence at the highest level, is understood to be essentially polarized into female and male aspects. . . . The male aspect of God cannot act alone but only through his energy, his *sakti*, with whom he is inseparably united and who is hypostatized as a goddess" (Pintchman 1994, 110). In some traditions the god is considered supreme, and the associated goddess is subordinate, but in Shakta Tantrism the goddess associated with *shakti* is elevated. And Pintchman finds that "many forms of Tantra propose the existence of a divine power or *sakti* that is described as supreme in both cosmogonic and cosmological contexts and is clearly identified as feminine" (1994, 110). Where the goddess alone is worshiped (Shaktism) it is *shakti* "identified with the Great Goddess" that is "the ultimate reality itself and the totality of all being." The tendency in this case is to assume that "matter itself, while always changing, is sacred and is not different from spirit" (Erndle 1997, 21).

It is, perhaps, its practices that define Tantrism as much as its doctrine. Thus Brooks finds that "Tantrism entails specific forms of *sadhana* or spiritual discipline. . . . In the most general sense, a Tantric spiritual discipline . . . is defined as a systematic quest for worldly prosperity, empowerment, and final liberation by esoteric means. . . . It requires both correct understanding . . . and active ritual participation leading the aspirant to experiential knowledge" (1990, 48–49).

He notes that "Tantra" is literally "a loom" in Sanskrit, and Tantras "weave together concepts and prescriptions for action to create distinctive, synthetic types of spiritual discipline" (1990, 5). It is largely the form of this discipline, and, in Shakta Tantra, the primacy of *shakti*, that makes the Tantric practitioner unique.

The Tantric practitioner works upon the stage of the human body, or, more accurately, the "subtle body." The subtle body is not visible but nonetheless real, a model for the physical body. It is said to have a variety of channels and nodes (*chakras*). Tantric yoga is said to work on this subtle body, and Tantric practices are intended to pierce illusion and create an experience of the ultimate unity. Tantra teaches that in order to experience this unity the individual must realize that the body is a microcosm of the universe and that the primal energy and the cosmic consciousness lie within the self. The goal "is not the discovery of the unknown but the realization of the known, for 'What is here, is elsewhere. What is not here, is nowhere'" (Mookerjee and Khanna, 9). The essential relation is between "the adept as a microcosmic divine self (*atman*) and the macrocosmic reality of Sakti and Siva as the Absolute Brahman" (Brooks 1990, 59). This is where the concept of kundalini energy, sometimes said to be an internal manifestation of *shakti* residing at the base of the spine, is central. Believers say that, in an awakened individual, the kundalini rises up the spinal cord and is united with pure consciousness (see Bharati 1965; Krishna 1971, 1974; White 1979; Woodruffe 1964). Microcosm and macrocosm are then united.

There are dramatic accounts of this event in the literature on kundalini yoga. The following, describing an awakening during a meditation led by Yogi Amrit Desai, the founder of Kripalu, another of the new religions, is representative: "The first thing I noticed was a wave of euphoria softly permeating my being. I felt intensely happy. . . . Suddenly surges of energy—like electric charges—streaked up my spine. These gradually evolved into a steady current of hot energy flowing from the tip of my spine to the top of my head. . . . Brilliant colors swirled inside my head; I thought I would burst with happiness" (Butler 1979, 185).

Yogis say that this type of experience is rare. It is more common "for tiny bits of this energy to be released through various means. One then experiences breakthroughs, bursts of energy and enthusiasm, peak experiences, a sense of well-being, and similar changes in consciousness" (Rama 1979, 33). Like other practitioners, 3HO members assume that their practices will raise the kundalini energy. They acknowledge that it may take years of effort to slowly release and raise it, and they equate its rise with progress along the spiritual path. With time, they believe, the energy will unite with the universal consciousness. Then, as a 3HO member put it, "you can be one with God, with the essence of consciousness; you can tune in and know everything."

In the 3HO version of kundalini yoga, breath control (*pranyam*), mantra recitations, and yoga postures are often followed by meditation, which is to be enjoyed for the peace and clarity it brings but also has practical applications. In a meditative state the individual is supposed to be able to calmly identify and face the fears and anxieties that ordinarily limit her behavioral and emotional repertoire. Over time these can be "neutralized" until "the mind is cleared of the clouds of fear and begins to see the light and power of creative consciousness" (Khalsa 1978, 15–16). Regular yoga and meditation are also said to broaden the range of everyday awareness. The meditator becomes aware not only of her feelings but of others' reactions and perspectives, more "sensitive" in 3HO parlance.

Tantra became a popular philosophy across India as early as the sixth century and was combined, in some cases, with Buddhism in northern India. There are accounts of accomplished women practitioners working within this tradition between the eight and twelfth centuries A.D. While the number of female Tantric practitioners never approached the numbers of their male counterparts, women did become noted disciples and teachers. A belief that "masculine" and "feminine" traits are to be found in each individual probably contributed to the acceptance of these women disciples (Ray 1989).

Tantric Buddhism made its way to Tibet via northern India. In Tibet it became a distinctive tradition which depends heavily upon symbolism, visualization, and sound currents. Rituals are intended to enable the practitioner to experience the ultimate unity. By means of these rituals, or *sadhana*s, duality is said to be overcome and the channels and *chakra*s cleansed. The *sadhana*s incorporate *mudra*s (positions and gestures), mantras, *bij-mantra*s ("seed" syllables or sounds), and extensive visualizations based on deities and mandalas (e.g., Blofeld 1992). Devotees are urged to harness all experience in the service of realization (Guenther 1975). In the end, all categories can be eliminated so that, as in other Buddhist traditions, reality is perceived clearly, without boundaries and cognitive mediation.

As in the Tibetan tradition, 3HO members perform a daily *sadhana*, and they employ many of the same techniques and have a similar practical view of the process. They use *mudra*s, *bij-mantra*s (*Sat Nam*, taken from Sikhism) and visualizations, and they place considerable emphasis upon "sound currents." They speak of the practices as particularly powerful, even dangerous, and of the need for the guidance of a guru when one first attempts them. This, it appears, is a widely shared view of Tantric practice. Brooks finds it in a Hindu version as well. "Srividya adepts," he writes, warn that "one who is ill-equipped or not properly trained in *kundalini* yoga can expect life-threatening consequences, including disease and insanity" (1990, 58). Bhajan's warnings are similar. Brooks also emphasizes the role of the guru among Tantrics. They place, he says, "an extraordinary emphasis on the authority of the teacher. . . . Tantrics understand the guru as the vital link to the ultimately inherent power that pervades the universe and resides within the individual" (64–65). This view of the guru conflicts with the Sikh understanding of the teacher's role, and Bhajan appears to situate, or attempt to situate, himself between the two.

Brooks also tells us that "the word 'Tantra' in contemporary vernacular Indian languages, such as Tamil or Hindi, is frequently used to conjure notions of effective black magic, illicit sexuality, and immoral behavior" (1990, 5). In part, the Tantric reputation is due to the incorporation of the "five m's" by some Tantric practitioners. These include the drinking of wine (*madya*) and performance of ritual sexual intercourse (*maithuna*) (Kelly 1990). Bhajan is therefore careful to tell his students, and other audiences, that he teaches "white Tantric yoga," which he contrasts to the "left-handed" sexual form.

Many of his interpretations have a concrete, technical, and scientific tone. A mantra becomes "a technical device for regulating the mind." Specific sounds are said to have particular effects, and sounds "are exact keys which you touch to telegraph your message to the infinite self. Your entire system is played by these sounds. Each sound vibrates and integrates a different chakra to its full radiance within the aura" (KRI 1978, 37). Yoga sets are said to affect particular bodily organs and glands. Even kundalini energy is associated with the pineal gland: "All you have to do is uncoil that energy and make a functional connection with your pineal gland. Once that master gland, that seat of the soul, has started secreting, it will give you the power to reach your self-realization in relationship to the total universal awareness" (KRI 1978, 11).

Bhajan claims to be the only person in the world entitled to teach white Tantric yoga. White Tantric sessions have been offered at solstice gatherings, and, in addition to these sessions, Yogi Bhajan has traveled around the United States and Canada teaching courses in a number of cities. The yoga appears to be similar to the kundalini yoga that he teaches, except that most exercises are done by a male and female together. Partners are lined up opposite each other during the sessions. The lines, they are told, must be perfectly straight so as not to interfere with the "magnetic field." According to one informant, the Tantric courses were originally much more demanding than they are today because "when we first started doing Tantric, white Tantric yoga had not been practiced on this planet for fifty or one hundred years, something like that, and we had to burn a place for us in the universe. . . . Once white Tantric energy had established itself in the universe . . . we just had to maintain that energy." Tantric energy is thus said to be generated by the group and serves as a symbol of its emerging identity and power.

Bhajan plays a more central role than in kundalini yoga. In a rather remarkable passage, one of Bhajan's spokeswomen describes this role:

> He encompasses everyone with his aura and you get cleaned out, and in an hour or two you do what would take you ten years. . . . So he physically suffers a lot from those courses. . . . His spine gets very hot. . . . It's a very real thing, and those who can see auras can see it. He waits until the aura turns a certain, proper, color, then he has to separate the male from the female polarities. That's why you cannot practice any of those exercises unless he's there, because you could get merged with the other person's aura and you might not be able to separate it again. (S. Khalsa 1983)

In this description Bhajan and his followers are symbolically united in a colorful flow of auras. Yogi Bhajan takes on the struggles and sufferings of the entire membership as Tantric participants are merged in group energy and consciousness. Indeed, in 3HO, Tantric imagery is frequently employed to symbolically celebrate the group, its unity, its potential power, and Bhajan's special role within it. Members' auras flow together in an image symbolic of an emerging collective identity.

This organizational function of the imagery is understandable since the 3HO adaptation of Bhajan's version of Indian and Tibetan Tantra emerged in conjunction with the elaboration of a collective identity. The boundaries of group and self were defined in the imagery and language of Tantra, and kundalini energy came to represent a form of power which did not emanate from the social or political order but issued instead from a spiritual source, via the spiritual teacher. It was a nonpersonal energy, waiting to be tapped, available to whomsoever was willing to learn about it, practice the disciplines, and remain within the organization, where special knowledge and skills were available.

It is easy to imagine that, for refugees from the counterculture, these were valuable concepts that resonated with countercultural and New Left demands for empowerment. For those literally seeking the energy and the justification they needed to enact personal visions, here was a reserve. For those who saw the social order as immoral, unstable, and rapidly changing, an alternative, and secure, grounding was available. One woman summed up the appeal this way: "I guess when you relate to that thing that's higher than you but within you, you feel like nothing can really bother you. You don't have to rely on other people and things like that so you can have more security."

Looked at from the point of view of organizational dynamics, Bhajan's combination of Tantric and Sikh traditions is a promising one. The Tantric tradition provides shared imagery and ritual. It creates an expectation of empowerment for individuals and for the organization as a whole and offers a powerful vision of the unity of all beings and of all of creation. Further, it celebrates the feminine principle. Sikhism adds structure, discipline, identity, and models for everyday living. It offers men a longstanding, ethical, and dramatic version of manhood. The next chapter looks more closely at the distinctive form that 3HO/ Sikh Dharma has taken.

Drawing on the Sikh and Tantric Traditions

Prabhupati, who is inclined to organize her life around symbols, provides some excellent examples of 3HO-inspired syncretism at work. Even though she has not been affiliated with 3HO for years, she employs her own idiosyncratic mix of imagery drawn from both the Tantric and the Sikh traditions.

In this first passage, taken from a letter, she begins by upbraiding me for asking if she takes the idea of kundalini energy literally or if she thinks it is "just symbolic":

> You said that cursed of all phrases, "just symbolic"! Yes, I too believe that Tantra is "just symbolic," but I don't believe that that is merely a mere thing. Our whole psyche revolves around symbols. . . . When we start seeing patterns in our lives that reflect or resonate with the archetypical faerytales, myths and sacred stories of our ancestors, or the ancestors of others, deep spiritual and cultural meaning arises for us. . . . For me the symbols, metaphors and stories of the Tantric traditions of India and Tibet have been molding me for some time now. They resonate with my story, or maybe it is the other way around.

She concludes, "[J]ust follow the path whose symbols give you the most juice."

Here, in another letter, she employs Sikh warrior imagery to explain some of the decisions she made when she was associated with 3HO/Sikh Dharma:

> I notice that everyone has certain events in his or her life that I call "Warrior Acts." These are the stands that we take as individuals that authentically express some deep sense of purpose and independence. These acts give us a sense of identity and when we think back on our lives we tend to remember those power acts against the background of "life as usual." . . . Joining 3HO in the first place was a Warrior Act. . . . For me becoming a Sikh was totally counter-culture and my joining facilitated a couple of fundamental Warrior Acts. The most important was that my life became much more geared toward exploration and mastery of the inner realms rather than the outer realm. I also got to explore the 60s idea of communal living and joining the Ashram expressed my hope that there is more to life than "life as usual" as documented by the T.V. News. . . . Birthing my children at home has been a major stand in my life where I have made doctors serve me and my babies rather than letting myself passively agree to make the doctors comfortable! Not cutting my hair has ultimately had little to do with Sikhdom but it has served as a stand against the whole beauty industry. I do not allow "experts" to dictate how I present myself and 3HO has given me the strength to face the world, make-up and mask free.

CHAPTER 2

Clearing a Path,
Building Bridges

*M*any new religious movements and organizations emerged in the early 1970s. As they created and joined these organizations, devotees had to attend to more than their spiritual lives: they faced the tasks of fashioning collective identities and nurturing feelings of solidarity (Gamson 1992). In 3HO, as in similar movements, they employed any number of strategies in this endeavor. I discuss several in this chapter, focusing particularly upon ways in which the young adults who became affiliated with 3HO set about interpreting and combining various relevant belief systems. In the early years, 3HO members sought to synthesize elements of their dual cultural inheritance. They accepted and rejected aspects of American and Punjabi culture (as they interpreted and defined these). They enthusiastically embraced the Khalsa tradition and positioned themselves vis-à-vis ethnic Sikhs. They retained, reframed, and jettisoned various countercultural beliefs and practices. They elaborated images and metaphors as they created new versions of old traditions. As they did these things, they sometimes looked to the New Age and Human Potential movements, as well as to other expanding new religions and to the burgeoning women's movement, for ideas and examples.

They had some leeway in creating new cultural combinations, and could, in a sense, mix and match likely pieces of different traditions. There were factors limiting their creativity, however. They were constrained by beliefs and values once they adopted them. After they had embraced Sikhism, for example, the behavior of women in 3HO was compared to that of ethnic Sikh women. Once they were "on a spiritual path," as they phrased it, 3HO members were committed to appropriate forms of discourse and to ongoing communication with other religious groups. They had entered a new world where they were actively engaged in both "culture-making" (Hart 1996) and systematic efforts to embrace and conform to unfamiliar traditions and codes.

Sociocultural Tensions

I would hypothesize that, in part, the impetus to create new cultural combinations and embrace unfamiliar traditions was generated by the women's experience of cultural tensions and discontinuities. Originating as it did in the counterculture of the late 1960s and early 1970s, 3HO/Sikh Dharma was born in a time of change and conflict. Most of 3HO's early adherents appear to have had at least some experience of hip life (Bailey 1974, Tobey 1976). They also matured along with the intense political and ethnic divisions of the late 1960s; they set sail on rising tides of both anger and idealism.

Divisions and contradictions marked the society in which they came of age. They were exposed to the American ideology of individualism but also grew up in a world of large organizations and mass movements. Growing up as the global and service economies took shape and expanded, they were positioned between old and new economic orders. From the time that they were students, they encountered bureaucratic expectations that they learn specialized bits of information, compete with other students, and prepare themselves to fit into clearly delimited, utilitarian roles (Tipton 1982) in other large organizations when they graduated. They were encouraged to create bounded, goal-oriented identities. On the other hand, they faced pressures to develop a form of selfhood that functions well in a service economy and in a rapidly changing, increasingly diverse and relativistic culture: a self with many faces, capable of understanding the perspectives and assumptions of different groups and cultures, a self able to transcend boundaries and specialties, a self that could attune itself to changing currents of thought and adapt to new situations. They experienced alternating pressures to individuate and to empathize, to "be true to themselves" and to "fit in," to set boundaries around the self and to extend the self. They experienced pressures both to "find themselves" and to "be popular," to cultivate unique personal qualities and to develop the "other directed" (Riesman [1950] 1973) personalities that can work successfully with others in large organizations.

Representatives of the first television generation, as they were so often called, they had also been exposed to the juxtapositions which the mass media produce so freely. They saw wrenching pictures of poverty followed by advertisements geared to the affluent consumer. The daily news skipped from developed countries to third world cities. They were accustomed to the confrontation of imaginative worlds and hard realities and to the juxtaposition of the great and the small, the personal and the impersonal.

The women members were likely to have encountered some additional and distinctive double messages. Women were expected to conform to the bureaucratic ideals but also to prepare themselves for lives of familial self-extension. They were to prepare for both domesticity and lives of public achievement. They were expected to succeed in competitive academic settings, but too often they were expected to do so without appearing to compete with males or to anticipate rewards equivalent to those that their male counterparts could anticipate in the future.

Many of the social critics who wrote during this period emphasized the ideas of conflict, paradox, or dilemma. This was particularly true of writers who influenced the counterculture and the New Left, both of which, in turn, shaped the thinking of many 3HO members. Norman Mailer, for example, described a kind of generalized American schizophrenia: "We call it hypocrisy, but it is schizophrenia, a modest ranchhouse life with Draconian military adventures; a land of equal opportunity where a white culture sits upon a Black . . . [A] land of family, a land of illicit heat; a politics of principle, a politics of property; a nation of mental hygiene with movies and TV reminiscent of a mental pigpen" (1968, 136).

Similarly, when they drafted a manifesto for their emerging leftist movement, the New Left authors of the *Port Huron Statement* (1962) criticized the United States as a land of "disturbing paradoxes" and rampant hypocrisy. Reminiscing about the early years of Students for a Democratic Society and the drafting of this document, Todd Gitlin writes, "There was a longing to 'unite the fragmented parts of personal history,' as The *Port Huron Statement* put it—to transcend the multiplicity and confusion of roles that become normal in a rationalized society: the rifts between work and family, between public and private, between strategic, calculating reason and spontaneous, expressive emotion" (1987, 107).

Soon, variations on this theme were to be elaborated in feminist writings. Feminists took aim at dualistic modes of thought that opposed nature and culture, emotion and reason, and body and mind—all dualities which permeate Western thinking and tend to carry gendered freight, with women regularly being associated with the less-valued poles (e.g., Glennon 1979, Ortner 1974).

The conflicts that flared in the 1960s and early 1970s represented an intensification, or magnification, of the tensions and paradoxes already inherent in American society. Raised in the midst of these conflicts, 3HO members were structurally placed to experience them personally and to interpret and filter that experience through the theories of the counterculture and the New Left.

While it is limited, there is a sociological and anthropological literature concerning the impact of conflict, paradox, and ambivalence. A number of cultural commentators, for example, have adopted a perspective that treats culture as a series of opposing values or competing goals (Berger 1977, Erikson 1976, Bellah et al. 1985). Hewitt (1989) finds that American culture poses a series of dilemmas. "Culture," he writes,

> does not landscape the human world smoothly or harmoniously, but presents broken surfaces. Its objects, as often as not, invite opposite forms of conduct, both facilitating and interfering with any particular course the person might chart. . . . This is true of any culture, but it is especially true of American culture, which confronts its inhabitants with sharply and visibly opposed objects. . . . The result is that American culture fosters a considerable fund of ambivalence—cognitive, conative, and affective—that underlies and shapes the construction of self. (235)

Such an approach provides a useful perspective from which to regard the new religions that flourished in the 1970s. It would seem likely that some of these groups proved appealing because they contributed to, or appeared to resolve, the cultural tensions and dialogues in a distinctive way. The Eastern-oriented movements, in particular, emphasize the unity of all experience while employing dualistic concepts and paradoxes as a mode of teaching. They can encompass contradictions within a single, broad spiritual perspective and can ease devotees' ambivalence and offer solutions to their internal conflicts. Thus Sikhism offered to North Americans in the 1970s what it had provided in Guru Nanak's day: "[T]o a society torn by conflict, he brought a vision of common humanity—a vision which transcended all barriers of caste, race and country" (Harbans Singh quoted in Singh 1993, 28).

Similarly, Tantra is a tradition rich in imagery and techniques intended to enable the practitioner to experience the ultimate oneness underlying all forms and dualities.

By generating mediating imagery and structures, 3HO enables members to move beyond personal, social, and national conflicts. It provides members with opportunities to transcend cultural tensions, gendered polarities, and internalized ambivalence. But it not only eases and mediates tensions, it sometimes reflects and reproduces tensions that are embedded in the dominant culture (See Hall's 1987 treatment of aspects of life in Jonestown as expressions of more widespread social trends and Lopez 1981, 1992).

The women who joined 3HO had a special need for structures that might enable them to mediate tensions and move forward. The women's movement was growing when they were in their teen years, but not when they were younger, so their gender socialization spanned both old and new visions of the ideal female biography. Rubin describes the kinds of internalized divisions that can accompany maturation along such gender fault lines: "Parental and social ambivalence leaves its mark, producing women who are cleft in two—torn between the intellectual and intuitive parts of self, between the need to achieve in the larger world and the need for human relatedness" (quoted in Weigert 1991, 49). By the time they encountered 3HO, many of the women members had also adapted to countercultural versions of womanhood. These added to the complexity of their self-images. The contradictory messages encountered in the course of their maturation, when combined with those already embedded in American culture and in modern conditions, were formidable in their number and array.

Weigert suggests that ambivalence is a central fact of modern social life. "Modern culture," he finds, "generates deep ambivalences that need to be balanced, synthesized, or overcome. To be modern is to be a sundered and opposing self " (1991, 180). When faced with this modern malady, there *are* advantages that women often bring to the task of easing the conflicts: a tendency to share their experience with one another, a respect for intuitive and wholistic ways of knowing, and a wisdom born of generations of contested and contradictory demands on the self. Women also have the experiential knowledge that "'masculine' and 'feminine' can be encompassed in one being" (Davies 1992, 59). In the new religions, and in the women's spirituality movement, women have been particularly creative in their efforts to forge new narratives and to find rituals and symbols that can ease personal pain and ambivalence. They have had to do this, though, along with the other tasks entailed in membership in one of the new religions, and we now take a quick look at the nature of these tasks.

Reframing Cultural Experience
From Counterculture to Spiritual Technology, from Ideology to Imagery

For many of the women who encountered 3HO in its early years, the study of yoga and of Eastern religions seemed to be a natural extension of their countercultural life-style. Others viewed these old traditions as antidotes to aspects of countercultural and political ways of being in the world. A small portion were in real pain as a result of their experimentation outside of the "straight" world and were in immediate need of new ways to interpret and shape their experience. Since many seemed unable to embrace the formal education that family and friends expected of them, they did not have access to the bridge into adulthood that was typically employed by their cohort of intelligent and questioning middle-class women. They needed a way to move forward without abandoning all of the values and visions that had animated their lives thus far. They required a direction, a foothold, or some time and peace in which to think about and formulate a future.

At a time when the new religions were still relatively new on the social scene, Robbins, Anthony, and Curtis suggested that many of them served an integrative function, "reconciling and adapting alienated young persons to dominant social institutions" (1975, 49). One way in which these authors saw this happening was in the development of meaning systems that could "combine or synthesize countercultural values with traditional or mainstream orientations" (51).

Taking a somewhat different approach, Kent (2001; 1988) suggests that the "religiously ideological movements" of the 1970s represented a new stage in the social movements of the 1960s. Disillusioned with the results of political action and countercultural innovations, the young gave up on the old means toward revolution but did not abandon the goal. They "adopted new means to their goal by taking personalized religious or psychotherapeutic action against themselves. For the new religious movement, the revolution still would come, but its arrival would be heralded by a personal transformation of purified individuals, and its appearance would (have to) be a divinely orchestrated event" (1988, 113).

Both approaches are directly applicable to the 3HO experience, and each speaks to devotees' efforts to devise livable combinations out of various pieces of the cultural worlds around them. But 3HO women could not settle for just any synthesis. Rapprochement with dominant institutions was not the sole, or major, motivation for joining. They required an overriding purpose in life and congruence where there had been disorder.

One way to approach the transformation of these countercultural youth into spiritual young adults is to examine some of the ways in which they and their leaders have framed and reframed their experience. This approach facilitates an appreciation of the ways in which members of groups such as 3HO combine different cultural traditions, how they mediate cultural contradictions, how they make sense of life on a day-to-day basis, and how they forge connections between self and group.

Frame Alignment

Framing refers to a process found within social movements. It is "the conscious strategic efforts of movement groups to fashion meaningful accounts of themselves and the issues at hand in order to motivate and legitimate their efforts" (McAdam 1996, 339). It can be difficult to create frames that are collectively shared, and movement actors may employ frame alignment strategies in their efforts to do so. Intended to align individual and collective identities or to reconcile seemingly incompatible cognitive orientations (McAdam 1994; Hunt, Benford, and Snow 1994), these strategies include "efforts by which organizers seek to join the cognitive orientations of individuals with those of social movement organizations" (McAdam 1994, 37). While frame alignment strategies have been described primarily in the context of secular social movements, they are readily observed in alternative religions, such as 3HO/Sikh Dharma, as well. Using these strategies, actors "seek to affect various audiences' interpretations regarding the extent to which [an organization's] ideology and goals are congruent with targeted individuals' interests, values and beliefs" (Hunt, Bedford, and Snow 1994, 191).

Examples of these processes are readily found in the early history of 3HO, when Bhajan was actively fashioning a belief system that would prove meaningful and appealing to the young people who sought out his yoga classes and his new organization. "Frame bridging" is one form that frame alignment may take. It involves connecting frames from different but "ideologically congruent" settings (Snow et al. 1986, 467). Thus Bhajan took the concept of community, which was a frame of great importance in counterculture life, and linked it to the Sikh *sangat* and the Hindu ashram. Similarly, Bhajan told his followers that it was their task to usher in the age of Aquarius. The idea of an approaching age of Aquarius was already embedded in New Age and countercultural circles. He readily combined this frame with his own spiritual teachings.

Bhajan's descriptions of the New Age are often more impressionistic than they are detailed, but they do provide a general picture of a desired future and rationales for action in the present. In the 1970s and 1980s he depicted the waning age of Pisces as a period of social inequality during which *maya* reigned and social structures were materialistic and exploitive. People acted out of insecurity and greed. Now he teaches that the world is actually in the midst of the transition to the Aquarian age: "November 11, 1991, we entered into twenty-one years of transition into the Aquarian Age, which comes into full force in the year 2013. The twenty-one years are divided into three 7-year periods of increasing intensity" (Khalsa 1996, 307).

Selections from a commemorative volume, compiled on the occasion of Bhajan's fiftieth birthday (1979) and consisting primarily of tributes and articles written by 3HO members, exhibit the frequently critical tone then directed toward the Piscean arrangements—and toward other aspects of American culture. In it, one writer describes America as "one of the most irreverent, hedonistic societies in the world" (L. Khalsa 1979, 344). Another laments, "Social existence in the corporations, on the street and within the subcultures is chaotic and hostile, a war against all which has spread to all facets of society. For most, the social landscape is at best bleak and the prospects of the future so disheartening that hints of catastrophe haunt our times" (W. Khalsa 1979, 335). The note sounded is similar to the countercultural and New Left critiques that were widespread at the time: the social structure is exploitive and the culture distorted; the current reality is in its death throes, and the world finds itself on the "cusp" of a new age.

Much is made in early 3HO rhetoric of the sacrifices endured by participants in the counterculture, and 3HO members are sometimes depicted as part of a small, surviving elite who are trying to establish the new reality: "It is the Aquarian Age to which we look, for which we suffered, for which we left home. . . . It is a tragedy that many of us, being the people of love, are rotting in hospitals and half of those left are in jails" (Bhajan 1973d).

In contrast to the present arrangements, 3HO members are told that the coming Aquarian age will be based upon experiential knowledge, and this knowledge will be fairly distributed among all people. Each individual will follow his or her own trail and "seek his own soul in the way he likes" (Bhajan 1973d, 10). This does not mean that people will become self-absorbed, however. They will develop an awareness of their connectedness to one another. The "vibrations" will change and spiritual awareness will be widespread.

Although he talks about the future, Bhajan often directs his attention to the transition stage, rather than to the final state. The transition is depicted as a difficult time requiring all of the skills, knowledge, and spirituality that 3HO members can muster. The difficulties will be partly attributable to the changes in "vibrations." The next generation will be extraordinarily sensitive to these, and "[t]he new race which we are going to have on this planet will be subject to some funny things; that is, that everybody will feel everything about everybody, without figuring out why they feel it or where they feel, but they do feel it and this is going to make people very crazy. . . . It will be normal on this Earth that ninety percent of the people will be crazy" (Bhajan 1979c, 349).

Before the transition is accomplished the society will be inundated by "tidal waves of insanity." Everyday behavior and ordinary understandings of reality will be insufficient to meet the challenge. Individual concerns and desires will pale before the enormity of the change: "Your little families, your little world, your little home, your little money, your little ego—man, you are just talking like idiots! Your dead bodies will lie on these roads, your children will be orphans and people will eat them alive. That is the time we are going to face. There will be tremendous insanity" (Bhajan 1974b, 8).

In the early years of 3HO's development these coming conditions provided a motivational framework (Hunt et al. 1986). They required that members align their personal lives with 3HO priorities. Bhajan told his students that they must elevate and toughen themselves in order to meet the coming challenges. Each individual was to fortify her nervous system through yoga and meditation in order to sustain the new vibrations. He told his students that they must become extraordinarily strong, singleminded, and disciplined. They must be able to endure hardship. They had entered 3HO/Sikh Dharma as plain carbon, but they must emerge as diamonds.

He also said that they should ready themselves to comfort people outside of the organization and to help ordinary people to channel the new mental energy. By practicing spiritual disciplines they could ease the transition for others: "One white-clad follower of the life to be healthy, happy and holy should be enough to take away the loneliness, the sickness from the whole locality" (Bhajan 1974b, 8).

They were also to try to exemplify the New Age life-style in the present. Tobey, an early observer of 3HO, encountered this theme and refers to it as "exemplary prophecy": "By manifesting and enjoying proleptically (before the time of widespread fruition) what one expects the future to bring, one hopes to influence society and bring nearer the time of fulfillment or ease the transition" (1976, 27). Bhajan told his followers that they should strive to make themselves "so beautiful, so loving, so enchanting, that God should find them" (1973c, 331). They should become "the real flower children" who would change the world.

Because Bhajan locates the source of change in an invisible realm of energy "vibrations," he suggests that present and future problems are not essentially political or social, although they can take those forms. The changes and the cures lie in physical, spiritual, and psychological realms. The countercultural desire to confront and change basic social and cultural arrangements is retained, but it is framed in new metaphorical, spiritual, and personal terms, with Bhajan's students among the few people in the world who will attain the expertise required to understand and manage the dramatic changes to come.

Similarly, social and cultural tensions appear to have been reframed in the language of psychic energies and physical properties. In fact, Dusenbery found that in the 3HO of 1975, "nearly one's entire range of possible behaviors, one's entire relationship to all aspects of everyday life, can be evaluated in terms of positive or negative energy received" (1975, 20). Positive and negative energy, he found, were derived from social sources, as well as from "celestial bodies, air, water, minerals, food-stuffs," and other people's emanations. The yoga student could produce and influence positive energy flows via breath and body control, by choosing a sound diet and proper grooming and clothing, by maintaining a regular yoga practice, and by controlling thoughts, words, and actions. All of these helpful practices came to be called "the technology." The wrong practices—drinking alcohol, thinking negative thoughts, acting thoughtlessly, or failing to practice yoga and *sadhana*, for example—were potentially destructive and could produce negative energy (ibid., 23).

Maple, in a more recent ethnographic description of the Los Angeles Sikh Dharma *sangat*, describes the technology as both "a tool to be used to dissolve the obstructions which stand in the way of maintaining god-consciousness" (1991, 52) and "an interpretive mechanism for the minute problems, euphorias and understandings of daily life" (47). The technology is a means to re-render everyday codes and assumptions (Melucci 1989) and to gain control over many facets of everyday life.

As they employ it, 3HO members are engaged in efforts to forge new social identities, to alter their thought processes and motivations, and to manage physiological processes.

In the course of their efforts to embrace the technology and to reframe their experience, 3HO members have regularly transformed ideologies and intuitions into imagery, as in the previous example in which they create a world of subtle and pervasive energies. Members' beliefs depict a reality in which physical, mental, emotional, social, and spiritual realities interpenetrate, and their convergence is readily depicted in images associated with energy. This imagery also resonates with frames used before members joined 3HO. If American society was often criticized by counterculture adherents for being segmented, artificial, and out of balance, and if counterculture youth often longed for a unified world, then 3HO created an alternative and wholistic—if often invisible— world readily understood in terms of energy streams and forces.

When people are creating a new organization out of many cultural pieces there are times when it is difficult to align frames. The frames that one would wish to connect are dissimilar, or even contradictory, and it would appear unlikely that they can be unified. Then it is necessary to "transform" a frame, as when Bhajan transforms old political concerns into spiritual and metaphorical forms. Or one may encompass a frame within a larger, global frame (Snow et al. 1986, 473–74). Bhajan frequently did this in the course of his efforts to introduce Sikh ethics and gender ideals to his students. His insistence that students abandon the use of all drugs and alcohol, for example, clearly contradicted the countercultural preference for experimentation with mind-altering drugs. He had to substitute a new and broader understanding of consciousness and provide new means of attaining highs. Bhajan's expectations regarding feminine modesty were similarly out of step with previous frames. Women, he said, were not to wear short or revealing clothing; they were not to appear unclothed in front of acquaintances or strangers (as they might, say, in a health club changing room); they were not even to nurse babies in public. This was in opposition to some of the countercultural attitudes toward the body, which tended to favor "being natural," defying traditional codes of modesty, and celebrating the body. Bhajan substituted the idea of the graceful woman, whose clothing and demeanor expressed a hitherto unrecognized spiritual beauty. Bhajan's expressed preference for traditional family and work life also came into conflict with previous frames—particularly with the countercultural distrust of social institutions such as marriage. Bhajan transformed marriage into a yoga, making it a spiritual discipline rather than another middle-class convention. And further, by arranging marriages himself and by saying that he did this on the basis of the partners' auras, he took advantage of the transformative power of imagery. He turned marriage into a matter of obedience to the spiritual teacher, and, in an interesting way, made it a form of self-actualization since he claimed that the auras indicated that the partners needed one another to complete their work on Earth. When Bhajan transformed frames, the new values and procedures were often justified on both spiritual and pragmatic grounds. He said that they are not only right, but that they will work. They will lead to success in personal endeavors, to better relationships, to greater happiness.

3HO and Counterculture Values

In their attempts to both maintain some countercultural values and accommodate to mainstream ethics, Bhajan and his students often employed "frame amplification," as certain mainstream or countercultural values were highlighted and adopted, and "motivational framing," when frames were chosen because they provided a rationale for action. It is worth looking more closely at these processes in 3HO. The works of Steven Tipton (1982) and Timothy Miller (1991) are helpful in this regard. Tipton finds that counterculture morality is based upon three underlying preferences: (1) for situational and expressive ethics, (2) for wholism (which is accompanied by a distrust of bureaucratic specialization), and (3) a stance of acceptance rather than a desire to change the world. Tipton contrasts this countercultural ethic with a "utilitarian" style of evaluation. The utilitarian looks not to an immediate situation but to the future and asks whether an action will lead to maximization of desired consequences. This utilitarian assessment is a comparatively "normless" approach, and it is one that favors specialized roles, practical exchanges, and "analytic discrimination." It is an approach that regards life as a series of problems to be solved and nature as a resource to this end. Elements of both ethical approaches are incorporated into 3HO.

Situational and Expressive Ethics

A situational approach to ethics is valued in 3HO. Ideally, a member should bring full awareness and "God-consciousness" to every moment and to every situation. If she does this she can become a "clear channel" for God's will and can judge any situation clearly and fairly and can then act appropriately. But 3HO has evolved a form of moral pragmatism which blends the utilitarian's future-oriented cost-benefit type of analysis with situational ethics. The 3HO woman seeks to be attuned to the nuances of a situation and to live fully in the here and now, but within that framework, effective self-presentation and pragmatic planning are encouraged.

Several of the women I have interviewed claim that, after years of practicing yoga, they find that they have developed their intuitive capacities. This follows from the belief that the "third eye" (or sixth *chakra*) is the seat of intuition. As the kundalini energy is raised, this faculty is said to be activated. They say that they use this strength when they judge the nature of situations and the reliability of people's statements. They trust their own awareness of situational energies.

But this use of intuition and the application of situational ethics is limited by various organizational teachings and expectations. It is assumed that the devotee is not always attuned to higher forces, nor is her kundalini energy always at the higher *chakra*s. So there are guidelines for behavior in various situations and numerous warnings about the possibility of mistaking self-interest for intuition. There is, as well, the option of checking one's perceptions and plans with Yogi Bhajan himself or with the head of one's ashram.

Much of the value that the counterculture placed on expressivity has been abandoned. This is not to say that the counterculture desire for honest communication has been eliminated; to the contrary, it is valued highly. But self-expression has been curtailed and disciplined. Now motivational framing dominates, and expression is tied to individual effectiveness and to organizational motives. Members believe that an individual should say what is appropriate to a situation, what is likely to lead to goal attainment, and what is comprehensible to the listener. One should be attuned to time and place and style, and one should always use speech in a positive manner.

Bhajan has much to say on this topic and submitted a dissertation to the University for Humanistic Studies titled "Communication: Liberation or Condemnation" (1980). He teaches that all communication should serve a positive purpose: it should impart information, raise consciousness, or spread happiness and love. It should always be directed toward the best qualities in each of the communicators, and it should never be intended "to force a person to agree, accept or reject what you're saying" (Bhajan 1983a).

As one might gather from the above, the emphasis on positive communication can curtail expressions of anger, fear, and the like. Indeed, in 3HO emotionality is often suspect. Women are sometimes criticized for being overly emotional, and one hears the phrase "emotional-commotional" used to denote an undesirable state. Impulse control is enjoined because emotions and drives can disturb the ideal balance which the much-valued "neutral mind" should achieve. Maple (1991) found that both positive and negative emotions could be suspect: "Allowing positive emotions to reign creates a mirage of perfection which dulls the motivations for personal growth. Negative emotions invite condemnation and hopelessness and blunt the acceptance of a limitless self. . . . Extravagant displays of positive or negative sentiments are rare and at least a few informants have voiced concern that the emphasis on emotional control in the community has reached an extreme" (70).

I have heard the same concern expressed, although only by those, like Prabhupati, who have left 3HO. It is often one of their major points of criticism. When I have interviewed women who remain in 3HO, they have typically maintained the desired persona, speaking calmly and evenly and revealing no extremes of feeling. I have received the desired impression of grace—theirs is often a calm and pleasing style—and of a carefully considered approach to the issue at hand.

I have suggested that 3HO/Sikh Dharma represents a kind of fulcrum, a middle way, for members who are trying to mediate the cultural conflicts and tensions that have surrounded, shaped—and, sometimes, misshaped—their lives. The preference for moderation makes sense in this context, but it is interesting to find 3HO women maintaining an emphasis on balance and "neutrality" at a time when women in many other traditions are questioning such control over feelings and emotions. There are, clearly, potential ironies here if the balance that was originally such an organizational attraction becomes confining. But I do not want to overstate this point, particularly because 3HO women *do* talk about appreciating their distinctive womanly traits—and sometimes emotionality is considered a desirable feminine quality. Thus, I recently heard the following statement from a woman who has been a Sikh for over twenty years, and if her comment is at all indicative of current thinking among the women, they may be altering their assessment of the emotions. She was talking about the power of women, and I had asked how she was using or realizing that power: "For me, it's realizing the fact that I'm different from my husband, like the fact that I might be emotional, or whatever, can be very strong. It can be a contribution instead of just something to be ashamed of." While his advice can be adapted to individual needs and circumstances, it is clear that Bhajan advocates forms of self-expression that will enhance the organization's image in the outside world, that will minimize internal conflict and criticism, and that will allow for flexibility as 3HO meets changing circumstances, but it is equally clear that women members seek out satisfying forms of self-expression. At the meeting point of these motivations, identity is constructed.

Wholism

We have seen that much 3HO imagery is wholistic. At the individual level Bhajan's students seek the experience of unity by trying to become entirely imbued with the divine. Each Sikh should remember that she is an individual expression of a transpersonal whole and strive for "serviceful" and God-conscious performance. She aims to feel "centered" and to act in accordance with the promptings of her soul. But the countercultural conceptualization of wholism is also adapted for pragmatic purposes so that the 3HO approach does not preclude role playing, specialization, and concern with self-presentation. When these are required by the organization they are endorsed, and the old countercultural opposition to bureaucratic action is suspended—after all, 3HO is bureaucratically organized.

Sikh Dharma discussions of women's nature and role reveal a distinctive twist on the wholism theme. Bhajan teaches that a woman should remember that she is first and foremost a spiritual being, that she is, by nature, more spiritual than a man. She should never allow any single role to lead her to lose sight of this central reality. "You are a spiritual woman first," says Bhajan, and he teaches that this spirituality should come before career, wifehood, or motherhood.

Acceptance

Members are told that "all things come from God and all things go to God," and they try to believe this from the very core of their being. The corollary of this belief is that people on the spiritual path should accept hardship, service, and obedience as willingly as they welcome joy, wealth, and autonomy. A devotee should believe that whatever exists has purpose, meaning, and worth—however unfair or unsatisfying it may appear from a limited human perspective. Submission to God's will and to the spiritual teacher is the path to liberation.

Sikhs also believe, however, that one should actively fight injustice, and, as we have seen, theirs is a rather martial view of sainthood. In 3HO/Sikh Dharma this takes the form of beliefs that one should stand up for truth, defend the Dharma, and do internal battle with any urges to slack off in ones commitments. Ideals of acceptance and activism coexist. These somewhat contradictory ideals were also part and parcel of the settings from which 3HO emerged. The counterculture espoused an appreciation for things as they are, a willingness to "groove" and enjoy, but also embedded in the counterculture, and in more activist, politically oriented circles, was a commitment to undermining or changing the status quo. In 3HO, both tendencies were harnessed, although it is important to remember that, while acceptance and activism are expected of both sexes, it is men who are expected to be the braver and more assertive sex. Still, both are supposed to be proactive in a spiritual sense, always striving to improve themselves and the world around them.

Generally speaking, 3HO blends some of the linearity and pragmatism of the utilitarian perspective with the intuition and wholism of the countercultural ethos. It is easy to imagine ways in which women benefit from the freedom to maneuver between these two approaches. One can argue that women have traditionally been raised to value merger with others (Chodorow 1974), and that women have often been ready to trust intuitive modes of decision making. These are retained and held in high esteem in 3HO, but they are placed within a context that allows for practical accommodation to modern circumstances. Women members have an opportunity to place themselves on a continuum of values—to seek out a point between mainstream and alternative ethics, between doing and being, between traditionally feminine and more contemporary modes of decision making—although there are limits to that freedom and a number of constraints embedded in the new codes they have adopted (Hart 1996).

Science

Tipton does not discuss attitudes toward science, but criticisms of Western science and, more generally, of positivism, were part of the countercultural and New Left climate in which 3HO matured. Science was frequently viewed as a dehumanizing force whose products were put to use by the world's major powers in their efforts to dominate lesser nations and to maintain control within their own national borders as well. Science divided the world into segments for the purpose of study; it reduced the complex and mysterious to formulas; it fit life into mechanical models. Such critiques were further developed by women writers such as Evelyn Fox-Keller (1989) and Sandra Harding (1991, 1986). In retrospect, the feminist critiques seem to have been almost inevitable given the role that formal science has played in the creation, elaboration, and reification of dichotomies that have been culturally marked by gender: dichotomies such as mind versus nature, reason versus emotion, objectivity versus subjectivity, and detachment versus social commitment, with the "feminine" poles typically devalued. Feminist readings of the history of science find numerous examples of early scientists equating nature with women—and sounding all too eager to subdue both.

Dusenbery (1975, 37) suggests that Bhajan and his students originally viewed kundalini yoga as a replacement for Western science and notes that they referred to it as an "ancient science." Western science was viewed as materialistic, a lower form of knowledge than that finally achieved via meditation and kundalini yoga. One of the West's master frames was thus reduced in stature and encompassed by a supposedly higher and superior framework.

It may be that 3HO wholism, energy symbolism, and "science" offer women members, at least superficially, an alternative epistemology seemingly divorced from some of the categories imposed by traditional science and from the "masculine project" of subduing nature. It is also a way of viewing the world in keeping with the counterculture's efforts to re-enchant the world and re-create broken connections. Members are thus not out of tune with various writers of countercultural and, later, feminist and postmodern bents who have championed a new version of science (e.g., Bleier 1986; Fox-Keller 1985, 1989; Griffin 1988; Harding 1986, 1991; Merchant 1980; Roszak 1969, 1972; Toulmin 1982; Tuana 1989).

Other Counterculture Themes

Miller (1991), and earlier commentators (e.g., Cox 1968, Roszak 1969), discerned a strong religious element in the counterculture. As Miller points out, "[T]he counterculture was a movement of seekers of meaning and value, a movement which thus embodied the historic quest of any religion" (17). "New religions," he finds, "were part of the countercultural matrix" (94). Thus to move from counterculture activities and friendships into a yoga-centered organization was a natural enough development, an almost predictable bridging of frames.

In his book *The Hippies and American Values*, Miller devotes chapters to "the ethics of dope, sex, rock, community, and cultural opposition," thus listing many of the causes that the counterculture embraced and themes that 3HO has addressed. Dope gave way to yoga and meditation. Rock music gave way to Sikh *kirtan* (hymns), but the focus on music was retained, and many an interviewee has told me how important music is in her life and in Sikh Dharma. The hip desire to establish meaningful community was essentially retained, but community was defined in a highly structured way. The cultural opposition and criticism that were so much a part of the hip and New Left mindsets remained constants in 3HO, but they were moderated. Miller also makes another interesting and less commonly heard point. The counterculture, he says, criticized and opposed American individualism: "The counterculture opted for collectivism. In the realms of both possessions and the self, self-denial for the community was the order of the day. . . . So far from individualism was the counterculture that the exercise of the ego itself was regarded as needing tight limits" (1991, 100). This was another value that was readily carried into 3HO/Sikh Dharma (although it is not quite so strong today).

The counterculture critique of the social order did not often extend to women's issues. Miller admits that "[t]he heyday of hip came before the widespread dissemination of contemporary feminist thought, and hip writing on sex looks, a quarter-century later, distinctly unenlightened. . . . [A]nd when feminist ideas first began to be raised in progressive circles, around 1968, many male hippies turned out to be as disinclined to give women equal rights and privileges as males elsewhere in society" (1991, 53).

A number of the women I interviewed would agree with this assessment, and would say that hip culture was in many ways demeaning to women. As one longtime member put it, "At that time, in the hippie movement, there was a lot of self-negation for women. I felt like you had to be like one of the guys to be accepted. It was pretty chauvinistic. Because there was no marriage. There was no commitment. . . . [B]asically the guys could go around and do whatever they wanted, and the women had to pay the price."

Bhajan clearly found the hip term "chick" offensive and announced that 3HO women were "ladies" and were to be treated as such. They deserved dignity, respect, and support. He portrayed marriage as a way to provide the security that, he said, all women require in order to thrive. This emphasis on women's dignity was one source of 3HO's appeal to the women who joined in the early years. For some, membership represented an opportunity to discard counterculture gender roles and get on with the business of raising a family with a reasonable degree of support and stability. Others, inoculated with the counterculture distrust of marriage, were not immediately impressed. Whatever the individual's stand on such issues, it was clear that hip sexual ethics were to be rejected in favor of monogamy and restraint. Sexual energy was to be channeled into spiritual forms.

Sikhism as a Dominant Frame

When 3HO members began to convert to Sikhism, Bhajan extended Sikh frameworks so as to encompass aspects of kundalini yoga, New Age thought, and counterculture perspectives. Although he stretched Sikhism to include yoga, he also shifted his emphasis and began to find some flaws in the practice of kundalini by itself. He began to tell students that the disciplines of Sikhism would balance the potential egotism fostered by the yoga. As this was phrased in a 3HO manual, "It is possible that the experience of expansion can lead to a great spiritual ego which is less curable than cancer. The Sikh humility and respect for the one Creator blocks that. The House of Guru Ram Das [one of the Sikh gurus] puts the ideals of self-sacrifice, service, and humility into daily practice" (Khalsa 1978, 18).

Bhajan probably had a number of reasons for combining some of the more self-empowering messages of his version of kundalini/Tantra with the more disciplined, group-oriented, and pious traditions of Sikhism. This step strengthened the connection of the individual to the group, thus fostering the development of a collective identity. Also, Bhajan was severely criticized by some of his Sikh opponents for teaching Tantric practices. By shifting emphasis he could respond to their criticisms while positioning himself for a leadership position in the world of North American Sikhism. He could also encourage discipline and respect on the part of his students; indeed, he explicitly told them that Sikh dharma and ashram living were intended to foster humility. The following brief history of Sikh Dharma should further demonstrate the ways in which Sikhism has been employed and has contributed to a collective identity.

The Evolution of Sikh Dharma

As the story has been recounted to me by members who joined 3HO in the late 1960s and early 1970s, some of Bhajan's students began to attend a Sikh study circle in 1969–70 with their teacher. Conversion to the religion began within this small group in Los Angeles. The first follower to become a Sikh—a woman—did so in 1970. When Bhajan led a group of his students on a trip to India in December 1970, they visited the Golden Temple at Amritsar, and some took *amrit* there. Bhajan met with leaders of such major Sikh organizations as the Shiromani Akali Dal and the Shiromani Gurdwara Parbandhak Committee (SGPC). He returned to the United States using the title "Siri Singh Sahib," a term of respect, which was extended to him by the president of the SGPC. Later, further honorifics were added, and 3HO/Sikh Dharma members now render his title as "Chief Religious and Administrative Authority of Sikh Dharma of the Western Hemisphere." Ethnic Sikhs, it should be noted, generally recognize this title as relevant only to Bhajan's organization, not to all Sikhs in the Western Hemisphere.

A short history written for the commemorative volume suggests that Bhajan was initially cautious about introducing formal religion to his following:

> Returning to the States, the Siri Singh Sahib remained simply 'Yogiji' to his students, and few of them ever thought of him as a 'religious' leader in the traditional sense. He knew that to build a Dharma strong enough to last thousands of years he would have to start with a broad and deep foundation. So he continued to teach about Sikh Dharma in an indirect way, molding the character of his students through yoga and meditation, developing in them the traits which would eventually be necessary for the formation of the Khalsa. (S. Khalsa and G. Khalsa 1979, 119–20)

But if he had doubts, he did not hesitate for long. While the adoption of the religion appears to have been a spontaneous decision by several individuals, it rapidly became an organizational norm, and Bhajan was quick to encourage, legitimate, and integrate Sikh traditions into 3HO life.

The first American Sikh *gurdwara* was inaugurated on November 26, 1972, at Guru Ram Dass Ashram in Los Angeles. *Beads of Truth* (an organizational newsletter) reported that members had been learning the language of the scriptures (S. Khalsa 1973) and now "students who have learned to read fluently in Gurmukhi" were reading from the Sikh scriptures and were generally "responsible and knowledgeable on all aspects of serving and taking instruction from the Guru" (ibid., 10).

By 1972–73 Sikh prayers were added to morning devotions and Sikhism was spreading throughout the membership. Bhajan ordained the first Western-born male ministers in January 1972 and the first Sikh women ministers in June of that year. As previously mentioned, Punjabi Sikh services are not led by ministers. There is the role of *granthi*, or lay caretaker of the Guru Granth Sahib, and this position is sometimes expanded in North American *sangat*s (Richardson 1985, 136). Bhajan incorporated the Sikh Dharma Brotherhood as a religious organization in April 1973. By then, translations of the Guru Granth Sahib had been distributed to all ashrams, and Western Sikhs were learning to sing the Sikh *kirtan*.

Conversion to Sikhism offered new identities, for both Bhajan and his students. For Bhajan, it provided a position in the world of international Sikhism and in interfaith organizations in the U.S.; for members, it meant affiliation with the Khalsa, immersion in a new culture, the possibility of becoming a minister, and connection with a worldwide community. Soon 3HO members were engaging in Sikh rituals, decorating their houses with pictures of the Sikh gurus and of the Golden Temple, taking vows, donning turbans and the five K's, changing their surnames to Khalsa, and receiving new Sikh first names from Yogi Bhajan.

Each individual was free to accept or reject Sikhism, but people took vows in numbers and were clearly encouraged to embrace the religion. The following quotation from a 1972 issue of *Beads of Truth* captures the thinking at that time: "You cannot take half or a part of any of this, using only as much as you choose to and still expect to arrive safely at the destination. The ocean of life is too wide to cross, there is too much maya to delude you, unless you heed all the words of your Guru and follow this true Sikh way of life" (Pond, 7).

Such exhortations paid off. Gardner (a social scientist who studied several of the communal groups that arose in the 1960s and 1970s) noted a change in an early southwestern 3HO ashram (Maharaj) over a three-year period: "In 1970 the members of Maharaj retained their English names and did not wear turbans or the other symbols of Sikh identity, but by 1973 . . . the movement traced its lineage to Guru Nanak . . . and had by then adopted the Sikh costume, saints, ceremonies, texts, and life-style virtually in their entirety. Most devotees had also taken new Sikh names" (1978, 130).

Bailey (who wrote a doctoral dissertation based upon participant observation in several 3HO ashrams) reported that, as of December 1972, Bhajan had ordained sixty-five ministers with authority "to initiate persons into the Sikh Dharma or Sikh way of life, to perform marriages and to perform funerals" (1974, 111). Ministers did not, and still do not, have the right to administer *amrit*. A major function was to perform the general 3HO/Sikh Dharma initiation in which participants take a set of vows designed by Bhajan. Initiates agree to earn their livelihood in an honest fashion, to rise before dawn and "chant and meditate on the Nam," to share their earnings, to "live in service," to "stand up in defense of the weak or oppressed," to embrace the Granth Sahib as sole guru, to avoid narcotics, alcohol, and tobacco, to eat a vegetarian diet, to refrain from cutting the hair and to cover it in public, and, aside from relations with a mate, to live as brothers and sisters (Dusenbery 1975, Bailey 1974). This initiation is a 3HO innovation, quite separate from *amrit*, although clearly reflective of Sikh principles. Bailey remarks that, although the initiation was not required, "in my experience with selected ashrams, most residents had been initiated" (1974, 112).

The dietary rules, the uncut hair, and the morning practice had been in place from 3HO's inception. Now these were combined with more explicitly Sikh practices. Since members had a limited knowledge of Sikhism, vows taken in these early years did not have the clarity and formality that they now have, and some people took on new roles with little understanding and preparation. A woman who took her vows in 1971 remembers: "Sikhism then, our knowledge of it, wasn't what our knowledge of it is now. . . . The teacher who administered my Sikh vows was saying that this was a commitment to be a seeker of truth. It was very vague. You were making a commitment to pursue a spiritual life-style."

Bhajan told his students that embracing Sikhism was a natural extension of their study of kundalini yoga. Sikhism would provide a means of channeling kundalini energy. It would further the development of "group consciousness." Thus in the March 1973 *Beads* Bhajan is quoted as saying that a Sikh temple "is a symbol of group-consciousness" (1973b, 9). And Gardner found that Bhajan was teaching that "the route to God-consciousness is first through individual consciousness and then through group consciousness" (1978, 131). Kundalini had developed the individual consciousness and some sense of group identity; now Sikhism would further prepare the way for first group, and then universal consciousness.

Bhajan also found ways to tie Sikhism to New Age thinking and to members' countercultural and political concerns. The Aquarian age was to be an age of God-consciousness. Drug-induced problems and the confusions of countercultural life were "the price which man is paying in bringing God on Earth" (Bhajan 1973d, 10). As they gave birth to the new era, 3HO members would enact their dreams of reforming society. In time, as members of the Khalsa, they could even gain control of institutions, not by seeking to take them over by force or by political intrigue but by virtue of hard work and God-consciousness: "We will run the factories and establishments. . . . So just relax and feel good, and let us not be aggressive or destructive. . . . Are you going to break the glass windows of our universities which we are going to run tomorrow? . . . So calmly and quietly assure your future, work hard, sweat and build and live up to it. You must. Time has given you a call and you must match it" (Bhajan 1972b, 33).

One appeal that Sikhism can hold for counterculture and New Age sensibilities is that it is, in many respects, an experiential religion, and Bhajan portrayed himself as a middleman whose role was to pass on the Sikh experience of the divine: "I simply feel that God has blessed me to have some knowledge, and if I can share with my brothers and sisters in faith, and they can enjoy the same ecstasy of consciousness, we all can enjoy the same joy" (Bhajan 1974a, 2).

Initially, Bhajan gave voice to a powerful vision, both of what his young hip followers could become and of the Sikh movement that he might forge. He expressed some of his hopes for the young in an early talk, quoted in a 1973 *Bead*: "When I came to this country . . . I saw the coziness of the family was lost and the ego and shallowness rules, then a hope came to me, that if these people, out of this pain, can look to the Infinite and realize it, there shall be a new generation born with new faith" (1973b, 11).

As early as 1972 he spoke of a Western Khalsa-to-be: "We will have our own industries, our own businesses, and we will provide our own jobs and our own culture. We will grow to be a nation of 960,000,000 Sikhs in fulfillment of the prophecy of Guru Gobind Singh" (Khalsa 1972, 343). People who participated in New Age and countercultural activities often had a sense that it was their calling to bring about the new order, or that drastic change was inevitable. Bhajan attached this sense of destiny or calling to the Khalsa.

Throughout the 1970s Bhajan employed New Age and countercultural rhetoric, but he increasingly balanced these with the language of piety and organizational loyalty. The new watchwords were 'discipline,' 'grace,' 'courage,' 'righteousness,' and 'commitment.' Bhajan's style was changing as he cast himself in his formal role as religious leader. He now had new audiences to consider as he sought to establish his organization within the contexts of North American and Indian Sikhism. If his students were to be recognized as practicing Sikhs, and if he was to be the respected leader of Western Sikhism, then he would have to shape his motley following into a disciplined religious body.

Predictably, older Sikh organizations questioned Bhajan's interpretations of the religion. The editor of the magazine of the Sikh Foundation (centered in Stockton, California), Narinder Singh Kapany, and others, criticized his approach (Melton 1986, 185; Singh 1977). Others approved. The director of the Department of History and Punjab Historical Studies at Punjabi University wrote approvingly of Bhajan's innovations, suggesting that Bhajan had breathed life into old yogic systems and had, in fact, "so modified the yoga system as to make it answer to the spiritual, humanistic and theological demands of Sikhism" (F. Singh 1979, 409).

In 1972 Bhajan announced that he was going to become a more demanding leader. For three years, he said, he had "hugged" his students. Now he would "bug" them (Bailey 1974, 104–5). They would be tested and pushed along the spiritual path. If the discipline was too much, people were welcome to leave. Sounding rather like a Marine recruiter, he announced that his mission was to find a few, pure souls who could become "ten times greater than I am." But he also declared that the role of demanding leader was only one aspect of his personality. "There are three in me," he said. There was the Siri Singh Sahib: "He'll find everything wrong with you, analyze you like anything, shatter you like you are nobody." But there was also Yogi Bhajan, the yoga teacher, who was compassionate and nondirective, inclined to say, "[I]t is up to you, son or daughter, do whatever you want." And then there was Harbhajan, the private individual, inclined to avoid discipline, enjoy God's creation and say, "[T]here is no problem in the world, everything is all right" (Bhajan 1979b, 15).

All three of those personas could appeal to his students. Each could meet different needs, speak to a particular value set, or be incorporated into a follower's personality. By claiming each, Bhajan could play a variety of roles in his devotees' lives and offer a model for linking aspects of personal and social identities. The Siri Singh Sahib could function as a leading figure in a major faith and as a spiritual guide. As a critic he could mesh with the superego and could spur the individual to ever greater effort. The yogi could serve as a representation of the realized human being, as a connection to cosmic energy forces and to esoteric traditions, and as an appreciative guide who encouraged the individual devotee to design a personally appropriate path. The private, less responsible figure could offer acceptance of individuals and circumstances as they were. All three personas shaped the organization, but with the advent of Sikhism it was the disciplined, and disciplining, face that was more frequently presented.

What there had been of exuberance and hip style appears to have waned as the organization was formalized. Bailey produced a content analysis of the issues of *Beads of Truth* published between 1970 and 1972. He notes a decline in humor. There had been a "cosmic comic" starring the Kundalini Kid, as well as various humorous articles, but by 1972 these seemed to have been "almost eliminated" (1974, 94). One notes a similar trend in 3HO music, an area of considerable creativity. Songs like "Long, Tall Yogi" were composed in the early years but later were replaced by Sikh *kirtan* and lyrics expressive of a more conventional piety. Today there is still a tongue-in-cheek quality to many of Bhajan's lectures and to much of 3HO life, but this stream of humor runs alongside of, rather than being integral to, the formal organizational culture.

It appears that in the 1970s self-expression was also muted in favor of "positive communication." In a content analysis Bailey looks at regional newsletters and finds that "the news is almost always positive, and there is no mention of such news as a marriage dissolving, a teacher leaving 3HO or an ashram closing" (1974, 94). In 1974 Bhajan even published a general letter informing all students in 3HO that "[i]n case a teacher expresses any doubt about the teachings or about his own personality to any student, immediately a call may be made to me" (reprinted in P. and S. Khalsa 1979, 80).

At the same time, the students were settling down to married life. Bhajan explained to his followers that Sikhism was a religion of householders, and he arranged marriages for many of his young devotees. Bailey estimates that forty marriages were conducted at "3HO festivals" in 1972, and that half of those were arranged.

As the years progressed the Sikh organizational structure was further elaborated. In October 1974 Bhajan established the Khalsa Council as the central administrative body for the Sikh Dharma. In January 1976 he submitted the Articles of Organization for the Sikh Dharma Brotherhood, and these evidently were approved in Amritsar, as well as within 3HO (see P. and S. Khalsa 1979, 132–35).

In 1974 LaBrack described Yogi Bhajan's development: "His teachings evolved into a hard-line, Khalsa-oriented Sikhism with residual, but strong, emphasis on yoga" (1974, 7). But he found that Bhajan's teachings were distinctive, for "grafted on to the historically traditional Sikh practices are some which are associated more with the Hindu Renaissance, such as vegetarianism and a tendency to puritanism; or with the Hindu social system, such as submitting to 'arranged marriages' with other 3-HO members and a definite division of secular statuses and roles along sex lines" (1974, 3–8).

Once he introduced Sikhism Bhajan had new audiences to satisfy in addition to his youthful following. Dusenbery (1990b) found that the original reaction to Sikh Dharma from India was quite positive, but that ethnic Sikhs in North America were from the beginning more restrained in their response. He believes that "the conservative leadership of the

S.G.P.C." were probably more "comfortable" with Bhajan's group than they were with many of the Indian American groups who were either very activist or quite ready to adapt and assimilate (1975, 53). Thus Bhajan faced considerable criticism within North America. Many of 3HO's more idiosyncratic practices were questioned. Chief among these, as we have seen, was the practice of yoga. Bhajan also instituted a variety of titles not employed in the Punjab and gave his organization a hierarchical form, unlike typical Punjabi arrangements. This again has met with disapproval, because, as "the Guru is the only channel between God and devotee, Sikh worship has generally remained free of an elaborate hierarchy of religious functionaries" (Dusenbery 1989c, 80).

Bhajan was also criticized from within the Sikh community by those who felt that he encouraged student adulation. There were also complaints about the sometimes unkempt appearance of 3HO members and about the assertive behavior of some 3HO women. One leadership response was to concentrate upon appearance. Women were encouraged to be "graceful" in demeanor and appearance, and newsletter articles and workshops featured instructions for attractive dressing and appropriate self-presentation. An ex-member who played a leading role in creating the image of the graceful 3HO woman, offering advice on dress, hairstyles and manners, says that this effort was inspired by the need to present a favorable image to outside audiences.

Throughout the 1970s and 1980s ethnic Sikhs and Sikhs associated with 3HO/Sikh Dharma regularly interacted, but they tended to go their separate ways. "Sikhs who come in contact with Sikh Dharma are frequently perplexed by it," McLeod noted, "not knowing whether to embrace its followers as unusually devout or to avoid them as perversely unorthodox. . . . The answer appears to be to let them live their life of obedience, and Punjabis will live another, seldom the twain meeting in any meaningful way. They are accepted as Sikhs provided they maintain a separate existence" (1989c, 118–19).

As they positioned themselves in the international Sikh arena, some 3HO members became quite assertive. They were particularly critical of ethnic Sikhs who had adapted to American ways to the point of cutting their hair or choosing not to follow the practices of the most observant Khalsa Sikhs. As they enthusiastically embraced the Khalsa identity, they sometimes even claimed a superior status. Their criticism was not voiced solely within the 3HO/Sikh Dharma fold. Premka, general secretary of Sikh Dharma, "in a series of letters to influential English-language Sikh journals . . . castigated the Punjabi Sikhs in North America for perceived deviations from proper Sikh practices" (Dusenbery 1989c, 53).

Dusenbery also found that in Vancouver, Gora (white) Sikhs' "sensitivity to 'the intrusion of politics into religion' and to 'caste-consciousness' and the 'subordination of women'" led to breaches with the local Punjabi Sikh community (1989c, 56). He also found Gora Sikhs pushing "for an expanded role for women in the Sikh gurdwaras (e.g., as officiants and participants in Sikh services and as members of the management committees of the temple societies)" (1989c, 169). (Dusenbery borrows the term *gora*, or "white," which is often used by ethnic Sikhs to refer to people in Sikh Dharma. It does simplify discussion when one wants to distinguish between the two categories of Sikh, but some members of Sikh Dharma view it as a disparaging term. I only employ it here when referring to Dusenbery's work.)

Fenton, describing 3HO-Punjabi interaction in Atlanta, describes a similar situation, finding that "the American Sikhs came into conflict with Indian Sikhs on practical and theological issues and stopped participating. The Americans complained that Indians allowed people to worship with them who did not observe the five K's, they allowed non-Sikhs into the fellowship, they served meat and beer at *langar* . . . and in the Americans' judgement, Indians emphasized the social character of the event more than the religious" (1988, 148). In their turn, "[l]ocal Indian Sikhs consider the American 3HO people to be more strictly observant, but they also regard them as too fanatic. . . . Questions have also been raised about whether or not they are following a living guru" (ibid.).

At the same time that they were defining an identity vis-à-vis ethnic Sikhs, 3HO members were adopting a number of distinctive customs and boundary maintenance mechanisms. Bhajan's adherents were leaving behind their hippie styles in favor of turbans, Indian garb, and all-white clothing. Naming practices were institutionalized. Punjabi Sikhs living in North America have adopted the practice of using their clan names as surnames, but members of Sikh Dharma objected to this on the grounds that it speaks of "caste consciousness." Their response was to appropriate "Khalsa" as a last name (Dusenbery 1989c). Bhajan also gave instructions on how and when to sleep and awaken, on how to greet others or answer a telephone. All parts of the body took on new significance. One member, for example, told Maple that "each internal organ of the body had an affinity for, and a vulnerability to, the influence of a specific emotion" (1991, 103). Food and drink became a preoccupation as women learned to prepare vegetarian meals and Bhajan equated specific foods with particular bodily needs and functions. He introduced a variety of "mono-diets" which required that an individual eat only one food for a prolonged period of time in order to improve a bodily function or to heal an illness. Suggestions for managing day-to-day interactions multiplied, as did prescriptions for the enactment of gender. Everyday life became the canvas on which a new identity was drawn. Snow et al. find that typical frame transformation activities include the alteration of "domain-specific interpretive frames" such as group members' ways of thinking about food, the body, and everyday routines (1986, 474) or rendering problematic that which is usually taken for granted (475). Such processes were constant in the early years.

Some customs were adopted because the leadership suggested them, or because members of an ashram discussed a practice and decided to follow it. Some, like clothing customs, began spontaneously and were later institutionalized. This process followed a pattern that has been frequently reenacted in the organization. At first there was an element of play and experimentation with styles. Then respected members of the community adopted them. Bhajan saw and approved some innovations and provided a variety of justifications for those he favored. Thus the turban was said to protect the pituitary and pineal glands. It kept the individual "centered." Once a custom was approved, ashram directors and their wives enthusiastically took it on, and they were imitated by many devotees. Others hung back or resisted and were given time to find their own way to conformity, although those who resisted too long or too hard often found that pressure was applied.

Underlying these visible changes were larger concerns. Members of 3HO were interpreting Sikh ideals in ways that were congruent with their cultural presuppositions (Dusenbery 1989b, 1989c, 1990b). They were also encountering and making sense of distinctive Sikh and Indian assumptions about groupings, identity, and personhood, and about the connection between thought, senses, and emotion, and the nature of the mind-body connection.

Dusenbery maintains that Gora Sikhs often view Sikhism in ways that are unfamiliar to many Punjabi Sikhs. Thus the 3HO Sikhs distinguish between religious and ethnic traits, believing that they are adopting the pure Sikh religion minus Punjabi practices based on regional, familial, *zat*, and gender distinctions: "They hold that religious identity is essentially spiritual and personal, achieved through a full and conscious doctrinal choice (e.g., through spiritual rebirth, confirmation, conversion) rather than ascribed as a fact of natural birth. And they regard religious norms as universal, absolute and inviolable, entailing faithful adherence to some moral code of conduct equally enjoined on all believers and . . . they hold it incumbent on all would-be Sikhs in all places and at all times consistently to manifest their Sikh identity by maintaining identical Sikh religious practices" (1990b, 350–51). This approach is based upon the American understanding of religion as an autonomous institution and a culture-transcending practice. It also legitimates members' own claim to be Sikhs, even if some ethnic Sikhs view affiliation as a matter of birth and custom.

Dusenbery convincingly argues that ethnic and Gora Sikhs also have different ideas about "the nature of persons and groups" (1990b, 335). Dusenbery suggests that "Punjabi Sikhs do not find it problematic to assert their similarities as Sikhs while simultaneously maintaining other diversities and dissimilarities among themselves as Punjabi persons" (1990b, 337). This contrasts, he believes, with the North Americans who adopt a stance of "radical egalitarianism" and regard distinctions based on caste and class as inequitable. My own reading suggests that, in the Punjab, equality takes on a different meaning than it does in North America. Pettigrew, for example, found that, among Jat Sikh males, equality was equated with independence and with maintaining honor (*izzat*) rather than with formal statuses (1975, 18–19).

Although 3HO women appear to have mostly retained American views of equality, in at least one crucial arena they have modified their thinking. They assume, in the case of gender, that individuals can be different and equal. Men and women can hold different statuses and can have distinctly different talents based upon gender, but none of this implies superiority or inferiority. This approach only stretches so far, however, before it breaks. Women in 3HO have not abandoned the American concern with rights and opportunity, and they expect their rights as women to be respected.

It is my understanding that many Punjabi Sikhs do not necessarily think of their religious affiliation as an all-or-nothing matter. Rather, there are degrees of Sikhism, and these, Dusenbery suggests (leaning on the work of McKim Marriott; see Marriott 1976), are tied to an association of Sikhism with the incorporation of "biomoral" substances. Thus "a variety of divine substances constitute the gifts or 'leavings' (*prasád*) of God. These include the words of God (*sabád*), the sounds of God (*bānī*), the name of God (*Nām*), the nectar of God (*amrit*), the sight of God (*darsán*). Such divine gifts are the most refined and transformative of all substances" (1989c, 66). Those Sikhs who have incorporated all of these represent one type of Sikh person, the initiated *amritdhari*. Others have not taken *amrit* but have taken in the sacred sounds, shared in the *sangat*, and received the edible offerings of God (Dusenbery 1990b, 338). People in Sikh Dharma tend not to make these distinctions.

They do, however, appreciate this approach to the divine—via words, sounds, tastes, and sight. Recent work suggests that "in much of India there is no real distinction between mind and body, cognitions and emotion, and asceticism and eroticism." The senses evoke emotions, including religious emotions, and a variety of "modalities for understanding and expressing emotion create a synaesthetic sense of emotion whose experiences, nuances, and elaborations make those of the West seem impoverished" (Lynch 1990, 23).

As we have seen, Bhajan and his followers do make distinctions between cognition and emotion, but they also adopt many of the Indian modalities of experience and much of the Indian approach to divinity. Thus, 3HO members have accepted a new approach to language. They speak of the "sound current" generated when chanting or reading Gurmukhi as a material reality and as an aspect of the guru. They readily merge spiritual and physical practices, assuming that there are spiritual effects and identity alterations following from their choice of clothing and food or their decision to don a turban. They assume that they can alter themselves—their personalities, cognitive styles, capacities—via bodily disciplines. They gain an enriched world where senses, actions, thoughts, and feelings entwine in new ways.

Identity and Metaphor

As they participated in the creation of their version of Sikhism and spirituality, 3HO women employed a variety of images and metaphors. The role of such symbolic material is not addressed frequently in discussions of the new religious movements, but it is a crucial aspect of individual and collective identity formation in 3HO/Sikh Dharma.

In the 1950s, 1960s, and 1970s, when Eastern religions enjoyed a resurgence of interest in the United States, several cultural critics were commenting upon the paucity or inferior quality of American symbolic and spiritual life. Several of the critics who spurred the rise of the counterculture portrayed America as a barren technological wasteland. Theodore Roszak (1969, 1972), in particular, could evoke this vision when he described the ever-expanding "technocracy" that was overwhelming intuitive and mythic approaches to life. He saw it inexorably removing the magic and the depth from life and providing no better substitute than the premise that "the vital needs of man are . . . purely technical in character" (1969, 10). The technocracy, he warned, was becoming as "pervasive as the air we breathe" and "seems capable of anabolizing every form of discontent into its system" (1969, 14).

The spread of Eastern-oriented spiritual movements in the late 1960s and early 1970s seemed to constitute a response to such criticisms. Roszak hoped for a new approach to revolution, an approach that attacked the foundations of the "technocratic citadel" and resurrected communities that shared in a "visionary imagination." With their communalism, their rich imagery, and their emphasis on charisma, intuition, ritual, and transcendence, the new religions appeared to represent an opportunity to undermine "the technocracy" and replace it with an alternative reality grounded in imagery and experience of the sacred.

The Image of the Spiritual Path

One of the images that early 3HO members embraced came ready-made. As previously mentioned, Sikhs sometimes use the term *panth*. It implies shared belief or practice, but without the formality or the boundaries suggested by the words "denomination" and "sect" (Dusenbery 1989c, 174). Members seem to have combined this usage with another that was popular among North Americans who converted to Asian religions or adopted New Age life-styles: they were "on a spiritual path." By choosing this image they could emphasize seeking rather than arriving, the route rather than the destination. The term suggested new possibilities opening up before devotees and so offered hope and an evolving sense of purpose.

The image of the spiritual path appears to have had a special appeal to women. A number of the women who joined 3HO in the early years were uncomfortable with the oppositional political identities that were available in the 1960s and 1970s, particularly where these involved "ripping off the status quo," as one 3HO woman put it. Many describe themselves as having been selectively involved in political action and in the counterculture. Their dispute with contemporary life and their desire for change was associated with a dislike for superficiality, materialism, and, as one informant phrased it, "objectifying social relations." A spiritual orientation could address these concerns, just as the counterculture had done, but it could speak to conventional feminine concerns as well, particularly when it was undergirded by the image of religious group as family (Jacobs 1984, 1990).

The spiritual path, as Sikh Dharma members define it in its broadest sense, is any serious, disciplined effort to obtain enlightenment. The following definition, offered by a young devotee, hints at the elements that are of particular significance for many American Sikh women: clear rules that are to be applied in everyday life, positive thinking, continual effort, and continuous recognition of the divine in self and in others: "It is any kind of thing where people have guidelines in their life and they follow those guidelines . . . being a positive person . . . relating to the God inside them. . . . [T]he thing is to relate to that and realize it's there, realize it's in everybody, and keep working towards always thinking about that, always believing that way."

One member gave me a very succinct definition of the spiritual path: "dedicating myself to living in my higher consciousness on a day-to-day basis." Many similarly emphasized the daily, continual nature of the path. As one woman put it, "[I]f you have a discipline in your life where you do something every day for yourself, for your soul, to uplift yourself, you notice it works. It actually makes a difference." Some also emphasized the many techniques available and the necessity for discipline and service to others. A few made the point that a path implies a goal. The aim is to achieve liberation, or at least to make considerable spiritual progress. As one woman pointed out, they believe that "it is possible for a human being to become a saint through practices and service."

Several women also spoke of their path as one that transcends this lifetime. The following quotation is typical: "Being a Sikh, I feel like it's a soul-level thing, not just this lifetime. . . . I feel like my path has always been with these gurus. . . . For me, it's very, very deep. It's not, 'this works for me in this time and this age.'"

Hewitt (1989) distinguishes between social identity and personal identity. The social identity is formed vis-à-vis a distinct community or setting. It is "the individual's sense or feeling of integration, continuity, identification, and differentiation in relation to community and culture" (1989, 170). Thus social identity would refer to a 3HO woman's identity in relation to other members of 3HO. The personal identity, on the other hand, is formed in a more abstract realm. It locates the person "on the larger and more abstract stage of society, rather than the more enclosed and concrete stage of community" (179). It would refer to a 3HO woman's sense of herself in relation to American, or even global, society. Hewitt suggests that we tend to privilege one of these identities over the other, but which identity is privileged may change over the course of the biography. Part of the value of the path image is that it is applicable to both social and personal identities. The term is sufficiently flexible that members can employ it to speak as lone individuals pursuing personal visions, as members of a spiritual community on a shared quest, or as participants in the larger society.

Members speak of their relief at having found this path and of knowing that it is right for them. But if members feel relief at having found this route, they also speak of the difficulties associated with it.

Many 3HO members are apt to speak of their chosen path as a particularly demanding one which requires constant, visible commitment. They point out that their turbans and white clothing can call forth mockery and misunderstanding. They admit that it is difficult to rise before dawn for *sadhana*. They often struggle to adapt to the everyday strains and demands of ashram living. They know that life on the path challenges commonsense approaches to biography and necessity, that it requires that seekers periodically discard ordinary realities, study their own thought processes, and question their emotional patterns.

The 3HO image of the path can also incorporate an element of anxiety, for there is always the danger of losing one's way. Yogi Bhajan warns that those who follow the path will inevitably be tested. They are warned particularly about *shaktipod*, a term that, as he uses it, refers to a time of doubt and rebellion when a personal desire or a character flaw emerges and threatens to negate the individual's spiritual advances. Then the seeker must struggle against "negativity" and mistrust. The person who maintains her commitment and turns to the spiritual teacher in this time of trouble, 3HO members believe, can triumph and even emerge with renewed faith and a deeper appreciation of life. But many will lose their way at this point and desert the path. The cost then is high, for Bhajan has assured his students that they have spent thousands of lifetimes in search of their path and their spiritual teacher and that, having finally found him, they should not squander this chance to break the cycles of karma (P. and S. Khalsa 1979, 55).

In a similar vein, members are also told that all of their worst traits and "neuroses" will surface if they leave the organization. Devotees anticipate a loss of mental clarity and emotional balance if they cease to attend daily *sadhana*. Many 3HO members also share the feeling that much of American culture is banal. They suggest that everyday social interaction is frequently unimaginative and mechanistic (Shakti Pawhat Kaur 1996, Parsons 1974). They feel that they are striving to become "conscious" while many other people are simply content to live unreflective lives, to respond on the basis of their socialization. To step off of the path is to return to such a trivial and "lower consciousness" way of being.

To step off the path is also viewed a failure of spiritual discipline. Commitment, Bhajan teaches, is the key to a spiritual life. Members must retain their commitment to Sikhism and to group life. Bhajan criticizes Americans for an inability to persevere in difficult circumstances. He tells his students that they must be different from the American average. Rather than give up, they should find ways to improve conditions when social life is rocky, financial pressures loom, or a marriage is unsatisfying. They should be ready to struggle against personal weaknesses and cultural programming, and be prepared to face a variety of difficulties and temptations while engaged in this struggle.

When discussing the struggles encountered on the spiritual path, 3HO members may use martial imagery, and they often speak about the effort to "keep up." Here a woman defines "keeping up": "[I]t's fighting in your everyday life—the blocks in your consciousness. Anything that needs to be done you do it, and you never become overtaken by negativity. . . . The battles you have to fight inside your mind are definitely there."

Thus the path is understood to be both a route to delight and to require the exercise of the will. It is said to offer techniques that will eventually enable serious seekers to "surf on the waves of life," as Bhajan puts it. Organizational practices are expected to free devotees from the limitations of the ego and to finally result in liberation. But seekers are said to come to the organization with many personal and cultural limitations. They will be tempted to distrust the teacher, to abandon the techniques, and to lose faith in the goal. Vigilance and obedience must precede liberation.

Imagery, Organizational History, and Collective Identity

Summarizing his findings on the communal movement of the 1960s and 1970s, Gardner notes that "in the prosperous early years of the movement, the most successful communes were the more open and unstructured ones. . . . In the harder times following 1970, however, it became apparent that the more rigorously organized groups were more likely to survive in the long run" (1978, 219).

In the 1970s, communes were challenged by a national recession, the decline of the student movement, and by the press coverage of the Manson murders. Those that survived what Gardner considers to be the crucial years between 1970 and 1973 tended to employ many commitment mechanisms (Kanter 1972), such as sacrifice and renunciation. Although it was never the type of anarchistic and individualistic organization that Gardner found successful in the 1960s, 3HO did have its more freewheeling ashrams in the early years, and it started as a more loosely knit and individualistically inclined movement. It certainly appears to have moved rapidly in the direction delineated by Gardner.

This trajectory is captured in organizational imagery: in the early years each aspiring yogi took to a spiritual path and attempted to raise the kundalini energy and strengthen her aura; as the organization began to coalesce, it came to resemble a fused or praxis group (Sartre 1976; Hayim 1980). Shared need brought people together, and in their unity they perceived the possibility of freedom, and came to experience "the discovery of one's Self in the Other" (Hayim 1980, 90). The imagery associated with the original practices of Tantra and kundalini expresses characteristics of the fused group as well as of the empowered individual. Sometimes, during Tantric yoga, members are merged in group energy and consciousness. In their unity, their auras are entwined and they are protected from the "negative energy" that may extend from the world beyond. Their identities are merged and recreated in the symbolic caldron of Tantric yoga.

Soon, as 3HO became a religious and a formal organization, clear group boundaries were established. Defining and defending the organization became increasingly important to the membership. Now members defined themselves as Sikhs, adopted the five K's, and took on positions as ministers and regional directors. Wearing the *bana* was increasingly important. The self became a "channel" as much as it was a source of energy. Now members were warrior-saints, and they spoke of the tests and obstacles they expected to encounter as they traversed their path. They struggled to "keep up" and to "overcome blocks" as they encountered difficulties imposed by cultural conditioning, social structure, personal weakness, and karma. At the same time, the women sought a graceful look: their hair up, turbans on, and flowing *chunni*s for special occasions.

As the years passed, members pursued academic degrees, sought jobs that would pay reasonably well, and established families. Entrepreneurship flourished, and 3HO adopted a more world-accommodating stance (Wallis 1984). The self became a balancing act, neither worldly nor ascetic. It was to be "neutral" and humble. It was to mediate between God and society, and between extraordinary and everyday worlds. Like the organization, it was poised between possible stances, seeking balance.

This imagery, which carries so much organizational history and resonance, may also have been shaped by, and may mirror, trends that have occurred in the broader society. The maturation of 3HO members coincided with the emergence of a global society—a vast society which coexists alongside of the demands, rewards, and realities of circumscribed life-worlds. Imagery drawn from both Tantric and Sikh traditions expresses the belief that contingent and higher realities can exist concurrently, and that an individual can move creatively from one to the other. The 3HO image of God as a form of energy which the individual can tap parallels the reality of the worldwide system of social organization and electronic communications which has come to exist.

Such imagery can abet members' efforts to unite disparate aspects of their biographies, to bind personal and social, private and collective identities. It is a tool with which to bridge the various religious traditions, ideologies, and world views that they have embraced at different stages of their lives. It is imagery which can relate different levels of experience: personal, group, organizational, national, and global. On an organizational level, such symbols and images unite various frameworks into a meaningful whole.

But once they are an integral part of organizational life, these symbolic resources are not likely to function solely as links between the individual and the organization, or as an armature upon which members can sculpt a shared consciousness. Metaphors, with their multiple referents, their encoded contradictions, and their capacity to link ideas to feelings (Turner 1967, 1974) can be employed to reify and sanctify what is or to transcend and comment upon the status quo. They are embodiments of accreted history and structure, but they can also change the everyday landscape, including the organizational landscape. The imagery, beliefs, and practices of 3HO reflect shared history and a collective identity, but they also have the potential to destabilize that identity. The organization not only reproduces cultural themes but also provides the symbolic means with which to improvise upon them and even upon the organization's arrangement of them. The group's imagery and beliefs encourage conformity in the name of the collective good while furnishing the wherewithal for individual creativity and dissent. These rich symbolic resources can be applied to cultural innovation, to continuation of the organization in its current form, and to its future transformation.

Attending 1980s Workshops

I have been attending a series of workshops offered by a Sikh woman (a trained therapist) for the public. The attendees are women, and most are spiritual and psychological samplers who have tried other New Age or Human Potential offerings. The goal is personal growth, and the leader's vision of her role in this process is taken from Sikhism, Eastern philosophies, and transpersonal psychology. She says that she wants to help participants

> reconnect with their own inner being, and that means helping them get in touch with those resources or those qualities that are really a part of their more high or evolved consciousness. . . . [A]ll change really is remembering or reconnecting with that highest aspect of yourself. Everybody's got a sequence, steps, that they end up going through uncovering who they are and experiencing it fully. . . . But the thing that runs through all people, the common thread, is that all beings in the long run want to experience an unconditional love and experience a unity or a sense of connectedness with the universe.

In order to achieve this goal she borrows eclectically from different fields. From the Human Potential movement she takes the premise the "we all have infinite, unlimited potential" but our thought processes are self-limiting. She employs yoga and meditation to still the mind, to open the participant to her higher self, and to enable the individual to break repetitive patterns of thought and feeling. From psychosynthesis she takes the related idea that we are not our feelings, or our desires, or our streams of consciousness; rather, we have a separate higher self that we can contact and utilize in order to intentionally unify the personality (see Ferrucci 1982). From neurolinguistic programming she takes specific techniques for identifying problem behaviors and for going back into the past to "change history" and create "positive outcomes" for past situations (see Cameron-Bandler 1978).

The format of a workshop generally requires that participants identify a persistent feeling or behavior that they wish to change. Next, participants imaginatively re-experience a difficult situation when they fell into the undesirable behavior or feeling, and then, after yoga and meditation, when all are in a calm and relaxed state, the workshop leader has each participant ask herself what personal traits or needs impeded successful resolution of that past situation. Such personal obstacles are then "reframed" by looking for their "positive intent." Thus, what one participant saw as a tendency to be overly argumentative and aggressive was reframed as a desire to ensure that her talents and insights were noticed and put to use. Once the positive intent of seemingly undesirable traits is recognized and accepted, the participant is

(Cont'd. from page 91)

asked how she might alternatively fulfill this intent and what resources she would need in order to do this. Then she returns to a meditative state and imagines herself in a situation where she does indeed have the necessary resources, or she remembers a situation in which she did have them. She may then imaginatively re-experience a negative experience, changing it to the desired outcome.

The psychologies employed are essentially optimistic. They place considerable faith in the human capacity to manage self and circumstance, and they assume that humans are essentially good and loving and creative. They tend to focus on cognition, will, and the use of imagery. They are congruent with the more world-affirming aspects of 3HO, and it is understandable that they would appeal to middle-class women in managerial and service occupations, and to women who seek to be creative in their work and in their personal lives. Those who attend are mostly employed in the knowledge and service fields. Thus, one recent workshop included a project manager working for the federal government, a vice president of a small publishing business, the owner of a bookstore, a journalist, a policewoman, a social worker, and myself. Another included most of this group as well as a successful poet and a doctor.

Over time, members of this group have gotten to know one another's concerns and patterns of thinking. Themes have emerged. It seems to me that one common theme is that of a valued, but somewhat threatened, self. We all seem to have a strong sense of self, and we possess knowledge about our strengths, tastes, rhythms, needs, conflicts, and inconsistencies. But we all seem to feel that the self is struggling for expression, or is in danger of being ignored, or going into eclipse, or in some way being violated. We are working to embed it more firmly in its environment, to protect it, to strengthen it further, to root it more deeply. Most of us also want to maintain some of the traditionally female values, but we also want to participate meaningfully in the economic system and to gain greater personal autonomy. In the workshops we are attempting to create—or maintain—a safe and special kind of women's place while we participate in a world that is not particularly friendly or benign but, nonetheless, is, in many ways, appealing.

There is little talk of social change in the group. Members do not seem to want to create a world that is friendlier to our kinds of values and selves—instead they focus primarily on strengthening and altering the self and on finding direction and sustenance in the spiritual realm. The social structure seems to be taken as a given. This is probably where I most differ from other participants, and I periodically want to speak up and suggest making some changes in the outer, rather than the internal, world. But I also know that the workshop leader thinks that this is the way to change things: one individual at a time.

PART TWO

Gender

Khalsa Women's Training Camp 1:
Selections from Journal/Memory

A Sikh informant has told me that if I really want to understand what it means to be a 3HO woman, I should attend the Khalsa Women's Training Camp. She has given me only a brief description of the camp, saying that there will be daily classes and *sadhana*, and that it is an opportunity for spiritual development. She enthuses about the setting: there are lovely cottonwood trees; it is in the countryside near Española, New Mexico. She has tapped into a romantic streak of mine. I have always wanted to visit the Southwest. I think of the Hopi mesas, of the art galleries, of the vistas. Having little to go on, I develop my own fantasy picture of what the camp will be like. It will be surrounded by mountains. There, I will find a peaceful retreat where I can relax, learn more about Sikhism, meditate, meet a range of 3HO people, and still have time to take long solitary hikes in the hills.

I have made a snap decision to go. I have purchased costly airline tickets and have made arrangements to be picked up and taken to the camp. I have borrowed a tent and spent the evening learning to set it up. My son has decided to spend the night in the tent, but he is basically skeptical about my undertaking. "Why do you want to go there?" he asks with twelve-year-old directness. My husband is less straightforward with his doubts. He has just grown quiet and reserved. He raises his eyebrow periodically when I discuss plans. He says little, but I guess that is because he worries about me being attracted to the organization, or perhaps because he, like the husbands of all the attendees, is being left with extra responsibilities.

By the time I'm at the airport and waiting for the plane, nerves have hit me. I have absolutely no idea what this will be like. What have I gotten into? It's difficult to concentrate on reading or on planning interviews. How should I approach this? Should I just be another yoga student? Or should I be an avowed social scientist who arranges formal interviews? Will Yogi Bhajan quiz me on my intentions? How will I manage to get up before dawn? How will I do without my morning coffee?

On the plane I spot a turbaned woman. She must be going to the camp too. I introduce myself and find that we do indeed share the same destination. I ask for more information about the camp and about hiking possibilities in the area. My early fantasies are soon shot down. The camp, she says, is quite crowded, and it isn't possible to go off hiking alone because the residents of Española are not very well disposed toward the Sikhs. In fact, women have been harassed by men from Española who occasionally drive by the camp at night and drunkenly shout at the residents. Because of these incidents the women in the camp are asked always to go places in pairs, and excursions are discouraged. The woman does not seem to be overjoyed to

(Cont'd. from page 95)

meet someone else who is on the way to Española. In fact, she seems generally annoyed at the world and keeps glaring at a small noisy child in a nearby row. Clearly, no child of hers would carry on like that. I return to my seat somewhat disheartened.

When we arrive at Albuquerque, the Sikh woman hurriedly disappears in search of whoever is going to meet her and drive her to the camp. I have paid for transportation from Santa Fe to the campsite and so must travel to Santa Fe. Once there, I settle in to wait at the pick-up point and, when no one appears, make several calls to the camp. Each time I call I receive reassurances that a van will arrive, but it doesn't. It finally becomes clear that it won't, and the voice on the phone provides the name of a cheap hotel in Santa Fe. By now, I am tired, dubious about the whole undertaking, and actually relieved to have unexpected time to myself and an opportunity to explore Santa Fe.

The next day, arriving early to wait for the van, I meet some other would-be campers. The story is different this time. The women are friendly. One of them, like me, is not a Sikh, and we gravitate toward each other. We all go out to lunch together and then ride into camp. When we arrive we find that nearly three hundred women have already set up their tents. The tents are two to three feet apart, and it looks pretty much like a commercial campground. There are a few permanent structures: a small concrete building housing the camp office, another building, referred to as "the carport," used for classes, and a shower room. In the center of the camp there is a large gold-and-white-striped canvas canopy known to all as "the big top." Tents, it seems, are arranged by region. Old pros know where to find the high ground and the shaded areas in their section, while others worry about flooding and hot quarters during the day.

The front entrance of the camp opens onto a rural road, and across that road are miles of rolling brown hills spotted with clumps of desert green. On another side, the camp is bounded by private houses. Just above the campsite is the Española ashram, a collection of trailers and adobe houses. Further beyond, I am told, is Yogi Bhajan's ranch, where those who signed up early enough for swimming lessons can cool off in his pool. Several miles from this site, in the hills, is the primitive site where winter solstice gatherings are held and where the children's summer camp is now located.

I check in and register for classes. My new friend helps me to erect my tent, and we begin to settle in. I am surprised to discover that no meals will be served until lunch the next day. I go to bed tired and rather hungry and wondering if I will be able to wake at four in the morning.

CHAPTER 3

Gender Constructions: "The Grace of God"

The Sikh household into which I was born was part of a Punjabi society that brought together diverse traditions in which the status of women was as dubious as it was crucial. I saw them exalted and I saw them downgraded.

—Nikky-Guninder Kaur Singh, 1993

Early Gender Ideology and the "Grace of God" Movement

A number of ethnographers described 3HO in the early formative years, and each of these (male) observers was struck by the traditionally sex-typed roles he encountered in 3HO ashrams. In the ashrams that Bailey (1974) visited, the women were responsible for all kitchen work, child care, and laundry. Indeed, one woman prepared and served all of the food at the Hartford ashram, and Bailey clearly felt that she was overworked. He only encountered one woman who was teaching yoga classes (that is certainly not the case today—women are as likely or more likely to be teachers than men). All ashram heads he encountered were male, and the men were responsible for ashram maintenance as well as for ashram businesses and classes (106). Gardner, whose observations were made somewhat later, was told that Maharaj ashram (one of the very first, located in New Mexico) had folded because the wife of the ashram head was discontented and would not remain, and Gardner clearly assumes that she had solid reasons for her discontent (1978, 132).

Bailey quotes at length from an early 3HO packet for women which puts forth Bhajan's rules for a successful marriage. Some of these

97

read like an advice column in a 1950s woman's magazine, complete with injunctions for a woman to "stand by her husband's side, come what may," to spread "positive vibrations by always keeping cheerful, positive, healthy, and bright," and to "inspire him always . . . encourage, assist . . . but never . . . lead" (1974, 108). Dusenbery (1975) found 3HO members talking about "natural" sex roles, and discovered that organizationally preferred gender roles were interpreted as expressions of biological differences. Many female characteristics were seen as extensions of women's capacity to bear children, and Bhajan taught that these traits particularly suited women to the domestic sphere. Men, on the other hand, being the larger and stronger sex, were meant to be protectors and to act in the public world. Dusenbery encountered an assumption that "pressuring women into participation in the public sphere rather than encouraging women to excel in the domestic sphere is to doom mankind to lives of insecurity and misery" (44).

Such traditional attitudes surprised these early observers who had reason to expect something quite different. After all, many of the youth who joined these groups had prided themselves on being in the forefront of cultural change and were aware of the rising tide of feminism. Bailey, rather bemusedly, commented that 3HO "seems a long way from the women's liberation movement" (1974, 112). But as more scholars published descriptions of similar communal and Eastern-oriented sects, it became evident that such approaches to gender were common within these groups (e.g., Aidala 1985; Jacobs 1984, 1990; Rochford 1985; Wagner 1982). Traditional approaches to gender were imported by many of the new religious leaders and accepted by their adherents.

Certainly the women's movement posed a potential threat to the leadership pretensions of any male leader of hip women in the early 1970s. Bhajan reacted against much of the rhetoric of the movement, describing feminism as an attempt to deny gender differences and to turn women into "imitation men" (a point that 3HO women may still make today). He portrayed the anger that the movement released as "tantrums" and "ungraceful behavior." He asked his women students, "[W]hat will equal rights give you?" and answered his own rhetorical question: "It is not going to give you protection, but it will make you work to build roads and run heavy machinery. Just to create a showpiece, they will give a few women some prestigious jobs" (Bhajan 1978a, 198).

But the movement and the issues it raised could not be ignored. It became evident that his women students expected Bhajan to speak to women's issues and to recognize distinctively feminine experience. It is to his credit that Bhajan did try to do this, even if his teachings fell within a safe range of ideas that bolstered his authority and allowed him to retain many of his cultural predispositions. He appears to have been genuinely concerned when his women followers expressed a lack of self-esteem and autonomy. Many women tell stories of his empathy for their problems and of his insistence that they learn first and foremost to respect themselves. One of his responses to the women's needs and to the growing pressure to address gender issues was to encourage 3HO women to develop their own movement, albeit within a framework of his own devising. Ever the pragmatist and innovator, Bhajan focused on some of the issues that were addressed by the women's movement in the 1970s, linked these issues to a variety of traditions, and, where they had been originally treated as political issues, he gave most of them a spiritual twist. He built upon an uneven but viable foundation: the goddess traditions associated with Tantra and Hinduism; the more confining provisions of purdah, *stridharma*, and the Code of Manu; the reformist messages of the Sikh gurus; and his criticisms of American culture.

Goddess Traditions

It is almost an article of faith among many spiritual feminists that some of the earliest civilizations were matriarchies and that goddess worship was widespread before patriarchal religions were instituted. The early evidence, however, is often sketchy. In the case of India there are suggestive but inconclusive finds. Excavations in the Indus Valley reveal ancient female figurines. These may well have been goddess figures; they have some of the characteristics later associated with Hindu goddesses (e.g., Hiltebeitel 1989, 4). A number of commentators have argued that cults involving a goddess were absorbed into the beliefs of Aryan invaders who are thought, by some, to have descended upon the valley between about 2000 and 1000 B.C.E. (e.g., Zimmer 1946).

Proponents of an early goddess tradition would argue that, as the Aryans imposed their myths and the Brahmans established their rule, the native matriarchal society was replaced by a hierarchical and rigid patriarchal order (e.g., Carroll 1983, Eller 1993). This is not an assumption that I have heard 3HO members discuss, although they do point to the rich goddess traditions that are woven into Hinduism (and quite a few ex-members might well concur with the feminist rendition).

While the earlier history may be disputed, it is clear that by around 500 B.C.E. a precipitate was forming out of the Indian cultural mix. Priests and Vedic scholars were formalizing and synthesizing what we now call classical Hinduism, and while the emerging precepts and rewards were strongly weighted toward the male gender, the feminine principle had not been entirely vanquished. By the time that the major epics were written down, each aspect of the godhead had a feminine expression. Vishnu had his consort, Lakshmi; Brahma had Saraswati; and, perhaps most important in the present context, Vishnu had the Mahadevi.

The Mahadevi has come to subsume multiple and complex images of the feminine. She is depicted as loving and fearsome, gentle and courageous, self-effacing and powerful, nurturing and destructive. She is the incarnation of *shakti*—of potency and energy—and has come to be worshiped as Parvati, as Durga, and as Kali. As Parvati she is gentle, devoted, and loving, while as Durga/Kali she is a courageous moral warrior who readily destroys illusion, ego, and falsehood. In the Markandeya Purana both Durga and Kali perform prodigious feats as they combat and overcome the forces of evil. These images of the goddess influence Indian life today. Some also appear in Yogi Bhajan's presentations and—in all their beauty, power, ambiguity, and suggestive qualities—are incorporated into 3HO gender ideology.

The Code of Manu and Stridharma

With time, social divisions in India became more rigid as caste and marriage rules were solidified. The priestly schools codified beliefs and practices in the form of *dharmashastra*s. The best known of these, the Code of Manu, has played a major role in defining women's place in Hindu society. The author approved child marriage, curtailed women's rights to own property and to engage in paid employment, and declared marriage indissoluble. Men's spiritual development was extensively discussed in the code, while women's spiritual and intellectual growth were essentially neglected (Carroll 1983, 23). The code rendered men's obligations to their wives secondary to their duties to dharma, caste, and natal family (Mitter 1991, 105). While the code also offered protection to women, it essentially confined them to the domestic sphere—a setting from which place they were to render willing service, devotion, and loyalty. One piece of advice to women is much quoted: "Though he be uncouth and prone to pleasure, though he have no good points at all, the virtuous wife should ever worship her lord as a god" (quoted in Mitter 1991, 105). While Bhajan does not go quite this far, he occasionally comes close when he urges women to see that which is godlike in their husbands and to express devotion and loyalty to a mate's higher self, no matter what his failings may be.

The *dharmashastra*s, as well as the tales recounted in the epics, and centuries of accumulated custom all contribute to the Hindu concept of *stridharma*, which defines the traditional duties and calling of the ideal woman. It calls for her to exhibit modesty, piety, forbearance, and a gentle nature, and to shoulder her burdens with grace and philosophical acceptance. It enjoins devotion and loyalty to family.

While many of these virtues are not much appreciated by Western women today, and obviously can be viewed as means by which women are controlled, one can argue that, at crucial points in Indian history, they have been enlisted in the service of national survival. Thus, Young finds that through *stridharma*, "especially her chastity and loyalty to her husband, her role as mother, her telling of exemplary epic stories, her fasts for the welfare of all, and her deep piety," the Hindu woman "has given the family its social and cosmic mooring." This, Young believes, was "especially important in helping Hinduism survive under Muslim and then British domination" (1994b, 77). Many of the ideals of *stridharma* have found their way into Sikhism as well, where they have probably served a similar function. Quite a few find their way as well into Bhajan's descriptions of the graceful woman, and he appears to assume that women, in their familial roles, represent the bulwark of the organization. It is women who will keep it alive through thick and thin.

Purdah

In northern India, gender roles bear the additional imprint of the provisions associated with purdah. The impact has been particularly strong upon rural Jat Sikhs, but all Punjabi Sikhs have been exposed to this influence. Mandelbaum provides a good general definition of purdah: "beliefs and values about the behavior of women, the restrictions on their movements outside the household and the requirements for their respectful and deferential demeanor within the home" (1988, 2). In a more dramatic vein, he writes of each woman sending forth "within her own household, an unremitting stream of signals, day-long, life-long, affirming her subordination, restating her modesty" (9).

As late as the mid-1960s Pettigrew found that "one of the most immediately noticeable features of rural Jat Sikh society is the separation of the sexes" (1975, 48). Women, she found, were expected to separate themselves by "not sitting with men, not talking to men, not eating with men" (50). The practice of veiling was not extensive, and indeed it was gradually disappearing, but this was "not an indication that purdah has vanished from the mind and feeling." Rather, "the expressions of it are now more subtle and discrete" (50). Family honor (*izzat*) was (and is) inextricably tied to women's reputations. Underlying the practice is an assumption that women's sexual allure is always difficult for men to resist. Women are therefore "expected to view male strangers as possibly predatory, presumptively untrustworthy, and potentially aggressive" (Mandelbaum 1988, 72). The provisions of purdah are supposed to safeguard women, and thus the family honor. These provisions also serve to keep young wives in the background of family affairs as there is a fear that wives might threaten the unity of the idealized joint family by undermining their husbands' loyalty to that unit (ibid., 120).

This is not to suggest that women in northern India have been seen only as potential liabilities. Particularly today, women can also bring honor to the household through educational and occupational attainments. Indeed, for middle-class women the external accouterments of purdah are not considered so important, but "studies of the educated urban middle class . . . indicate that among most of them the traditional demure behavior and other purdah values are still well regarded" (Mandelbaum 1988, 42).

As a native of Pakistan and then as a resident of the Indian Punjab, Bhajan grew up in the world of purdah, albeit not in the environment of village Jat Sikhs since he was of middle-class and Kshatriya background. His talks and pronouncements suggest that he takes feminine demeanor very seriously, although experience has taught him that there are limits to what he can expect from American women. His background shows most clearly in his criticisms of his female students. He regularly accuses them of being disrespectful, and, in general, of behaving in ungraceful ways. On special occasions he expects them to wear a long gauze *chunni* over their turbans—essentially the 3HO version of veiling. He recounts exemplary tales of long-suffering wives and mothers who rise above all difficulties with a calm and self-contained mien. In 1995 (at the women's camp) a student asked Bhajan what was behind the Indian practice of killing female infants, and he replied with *izzat* clearly in mind: "Because you are known for your sensuality and public embarrassment to the parents" (Notes 1995, 113).

There is a genre of psychological interpretation which suggests that aspects of the Indian family system often render Indian men insecure, "emotionally fragile, mistrustful, and jealous" (Mitter 1991, 87; Kakar 1981). Mitter suggests that "not only does a girl learn to bear cheerfully and without complaint all kinds of discomfort, injustice, and misfortune, but she also deduces that one does not defy, berate, or expect too much of men" (1991, 87). This message is echoed in Bhajan's talks to 3HO women. He tells them that they should not make too many demands upon men, that they must not expect too much of them, that often men are not to be trusted. He describes men as "reactive" and in need of women's inspiration and prodding. He also admonishes 3HO women not to argue with husbands but to humor their moods.

Whatever their reservations about the demeanor of traditional Indian women (one 3HO member described it to me as "door-mattey"), or about aspects of graceful womanhood as propounded by Bhajan, most 3HO women can find things to admire in the image of the devoted, composed, unselfish, yet strong, woman. One woman I met at the women's camp, for example, told me a story of her recent visit to India. She and several other Sikhs were scheduled to take dinner with an Indian Sikh woman. It so happened that this woman was struck by a family tragedy on that day. Rather than cancel the engagement, she cooked an elaborate meal, graciously welcomed her guests, and served everyone. I was, frankly, horrified by what seemed like excessive self-sacrifice, and by the willingness of the guests to accept the woman's hospitality under such circumstances. But the narrator spoke with unmitigated admiration; she was telling me the story in order to illustrate her vision of the ideal graceful woman. Another woman I met at the camp was engaged to an Indian Sikh and was devoting her time at camp to a study of appropriate wifely behavior in the Punjab. She was expecting to keep her eyes averted in the company of most men and to walk several paces behind her husband. She was not delighted at the prospect, but she saw such behavior as a necessary cultural adjustment.

Tantra and Sikhism

Of course, Bhajan and 3HO women have not simply drawn upon the traditions of *stridharma*. As we have seen, both Tantra and Sikhism offer some very different ideas. Tantra incorporates the idea that masculine and feminine traits exist in each individual and that *shakti* is available to the disciplined yogi regardless of gender. Nanak's respect for womanhood and his rejection of many patriarchal attitudes has already been discussed. 3HO/Sikh Dharma draws freely on the empowering aspects of these different belief systems.

Power Contained

Mitter, a journalist who has written vividly about Indian women's lives, highlights themes which I have found in 3HO approaches to gender. Like so many commentators, she finds contradictions in Hindu constructions of gender (and many of those can be found in the other major religious traditions as well). Women are assigned goddess-like powers and can ascend, like Indira Gandhi, to the highest positions. But women are also viewed as dangerous, anarchic, and ideally subordinate. The women of the epics, she finds, "broadcast a message that is both tonic and intimidating. It credits a girl/woman with a sense of her own vivid potential and worth. And it enjoins her—as a cosmic responsibility—to channel this force within fixed, inviolable bounds" (1991, 80). Women are depicted as vessels of power, but this power, it seems, must be controlled and contained. Just such a mixed message pervades Bhajan's pronouncements on the subject of gender.

Formulation and Dissemination of Gender Ideals

Gender ideology in 3HO includes descriptions of the feminine nature, guidelines for appropriate womanly behavior, explanations for feminine discontent, and visions of ideal relationships between the sexes. This ideology has been articulated at length by Bhajan, who has for years been giving formal talks on the subject of spiritual womanhood. Many gender axioms were originally propounded at the Khalsa Women's Training Camp. Others were formally elaborated in a variety of publications and presentations, or emerged more informally as the wives of ashram heads became role models and 3HO women began to imitate them, or as 3HO women encountered native Sikh customs and learned more and more about Sikh and Indian traditions.

In 1970 Bhajan taught a few of the 3HO women a mantra, "I am Grace of God," with accompanying instructions for daily recitations. (The article 'the' is usually omitted; presumably this began because Bhajan failed to use it.) He also initiated the 3HO women's movement and gave it a cumbersome title: the "Grace of God Movement of the Women of America." Its goal was to disseminate the Grace of God mantra and to teach women that they were by nature divine, noble, and meant to inspire and "uplift humanity" (S. S. Khalsa 1979). Special packets of information for women were produced under the auspices of the Grace of God movement, and a "Grace of God course" was offered in Tucson in 1972. The winter *Beads of Truth* for 1973 reported that the wife of the Washington ashram director had joined with Yogi Bhajan's wife to teach the first Grace of God course on the East Coast with an "emphasis on some fundamentals of feminine grace, feminine attitudes and aptitudes in the areas of home, family, community and personal appearance" (Khalsa 1971, 6).

In the early years, Bhajan's formal instructions on gender were spread and interpreted by leading women members. These women included his wife, Inderjit; Shakti Parwha Kaur, one of Bhajan's first students;

and Premka, then the secretary general. Two other women members—
Shanti Shanti Kaur and Krishna Kaur—were very active in the Grace
of God movement. Both were very articulate spokeswomen, and each
contributed substantially to thinking in this area.

These women have, or had, a widespread audience in 3HO. Bhajan's
wife (known as Bibiji), who holds a master's degree in psychology, coun-
sels some of the women and is becoming increasingly active in public
affairs. Shakti Parwha Kaur brought with her an extensive history as a
seeker when she encountered Yogi Bhajan. She had already studied
Vedanta and metaphysics, followed Meher Baba, and practiced Sufi
chanting. She was interested in Indian mythology and had crafted
mosaics of Indian goddesses for the East-West Cultural Center. (Khalsa
and Khalsa 1983). She brought a knowledge of goddess themes to the
organization. Premka acted as an advisor to 3HO women on such issues
as appearance, graceful behavior, and child rearing. Shanti-Shanti Kaur
wrote extensively on women's issues and tied 3HO teachings to her previous experience in the women's movement, and Krishna has long been
close to Bhajan and has been much admired and imitated.

As one might expect, many 3HO gender ideals are interpreted,
negotiated, and constructed in the contexts of everyday life—in ashram
settings, at workshops, within marriages, in decisions about careers,
and in efforts to balance work, family, and leisure. Women teach courses
on women's spirituality and related issues, and they adapt Bhajan's
teachings to the needs and perspectives of their audiences. In this chapter, however, we go to the source and examine formal prescriptions for
women's behavior and definitions of women's nature as these have been
put forth and elaborated at the Khalsa Women's Training Camp and in
the shorter-lived Grace of God movement. While the emphasis is upon
the earlier constructions, I have also drawn from recent transcripts of
Bhajan's talks at the camp so that the reader has a sense of the continuities and shifting emphases in his rhetoric.

The Feminine Nature

Portions of the following summary are based on a course, "Yoga and
the Spiritual Woman," offered at the 1983 women's camp, but all of the
principles are widely repeated by 3HO women and many can be found
in Bhajan's lectures and in articles in *Beads of Truth*. As we have seen, a
central teaching, in the early 1970s and now, is that women, as embodiments of *shakti*, have extensive spiritual resources. Women's creative
powers are infinite. Bhajan calls women the "highest incarnation of
planet earth," a phrase I have heard repeated numerous times by 3HO

women. In a 1992 address at the camp he told his female audience, "You are the *Adi Shakti*. . . . You are the Kundalini in every man. You are the universe" (Notes 1992, 57).

One of the more distinctive aspects of Bhajan's portrayal of gender differences is his tendency to quantify these. Thus, women are said to be sixteen times more patient and tolerant than men. Women have sixteen times more "emotional power" and sensitivity than men (e.g., Khalsa and Khalsa 1983). A woman has the capacity to be "very, very compassionate, absolutely sober and very firm. . . . [H]er stamina is sixteen times greater than the man's, she is thirty-two times more firm in her ideas, and sixty-four times more intuitive" (Notes 1979, 157).

Women are frequently portrayed as the more self-sufficient sex. A man needs to center his life on a woman, working for her, loving her, even trying to control her, while a woman "can complete her own circle" (Bhajan 1983b). Infinity resides within the woman; she contains all possibilities. She is often unaware, or unmindful, of her potential, however—and this is the source of many of her problems. Thus, women keep looking outwards: to men for happiness and approval, to worldly statuses for self-definition, to authorities for answers, to the popular culture for its formulations of beauty and romance. These are dead ends that obscure a woman's sacred qualities and lead to disappointment and even misery. Always, says Bhajan, "woman has a solution within herself" (Notes 1986, 38). Thus, 3HO women are supposed to set aside time to look within the self and to appreciate and nurture the special spiritual qualities they uncover there.

Not only are women complete within themselves, but they also are said to be more resilient than men and better able to observe and mend their own foibles: "[M]en are like mirrors; they are unable to repair themselves. Once they get an emotional crack in their minds, they live with it. Two things men do *not* have as a basic quality that women do have: the ability to repair themselves and the ability to see their ego-centric approach" (Bhajan, in P. and S. Khalsa 1979, 217).

Given the limitations of men and the needs of children, women are expected to be a source of inspiration. The woman should be a light, a spiritual presence in the home. Men will sometimes forget spiritual values, but women must hold to these values and gently remind their men of them. Women are also supposed to be better-equipped than men to understand the emotional dynamics of a household and to enrich familial interaction. In the earlier years, particularly, they were admonished to maintain peaceful, tidy, "cozy" homes so that family life could flourish. It is understood, however, that women's sphere can extend beyond the home. A woman can transform the world through gentle, nurturing, creative action.

Although their gifts are extraordinary, women are said to have certain limitations and vulnerabilities. Thus, in spite of their capacity to "complete themselves," women are said to be easily influenced by others' feelings and thoughts. A woman's aura is said to take impressions like a roll of film. This means that she can take on a man's "negativity" and is particularly vulnerable after a sexual encounter. A woman should avoid emotional involvement with more than one man at a time; if she does not, her aura will be "like Swiss cheese" (Bhajan 1983a). This assumption, which I encountered at the camp in 1983, was also prevalent when Maple (1991) was doing research for her ethnographic account of Sikh Dharma in Los Angeles. She found that the Sikhs there believed that any close relationship will affect an individual's aura—whether the individual is male or female—but it is women who tend to carry the mark permanently, and they may pay a price for this: "A woman who has had several partners carries the imprint of each of them, a distracting effect that the Siri Singh Sahib described as like walking around with several voices clamoring inside. It is only through years of celibacy and meditation that the woman can cleanse her aura of another's reverberation" (Maple 1991, 84).

Women are also said to be the more emotional and changeable sex. Almost from the inception of the organization women members have been told that they must learn to "channel emotion into devotion" (Khalsa 1972). They are also told that they should be able to depend upon the corrective steadiness of a man. A man who was once a 3HO counselor (he has since left the organization) nicely captured this vision of the interaction of male and female: "[I]t can be a very beautiful thing— this interplay between his simple ego and steadiness and her many facets of energy and expression" (Khalsa 1977, 236).

Bhajan warns that women can lose touch with the essence of their spirituality. If a woman tries to compete with a man she narrows herself and "loses her vastness" (Khalsa 1983). A woman may fill a variety of roles—mother, wife, employee, ashram member, minister—but she must not become overly embroiled in any one of these nor come to believe that any single role encompasses her true identity. 'Woman' is a spiritual category that subsumes all others, and no woman should, as Bhajan put it at the camp, become "woman with a modifier." If she does this she will become "shallow."

Women also do a variety of stupid, thoughtless, or self-indulgent things that obscure their essential nature and lead to suffering for themselves and others. They may manipulate men or "play games." They may behave ungracefully (enact "dramas and traumas," have "tantrums"), succumb to sensuality, malign themselves, or "sell themselves." These failings appear regularly in Bhajan's lectures over the years.

In the early years Bhajan also made a point of saying that a woman can become alienated from her sacred, core self if she experiences too much "penetrating stress" or "insecurity," and he found insecurity rampant in modern America. In this country a woman could not count on receiving the respect she deserved, nor could she count on a man's loyalty and support. Worse, women were routinely exploited: "Woman is used as a tool of the advertising industry. . . . [T]he most graceful being on this planet is treated disgracefully as a playmate, a sexual toy. When we treat the mother of our next generation in such a lowly negative manner, how can we expect the human condition to improve?" (Notes 1976, 14). Women's spiritual essence, he said, lay buried under America's false images. American society, even members' own families, had reduced woman "from a divine mother to a whore" (Notes 1979, 119).

Bhajan's proposed remedies were not those of the reform and radical feminist movements which were so visible when 3HO gender ideology was formulated—although his solutions are not too distant from those advocated by spiritual and cultural feminists. Relief, he implied, lay in recognizing, accepting, and celebrating the differences between the sexes. The woman who realized her inherently spiritual nature, and the power associated with it, could not help but respect and honor herself and, in turn, receive respect, admiration, even devotion, from men.

Bhajan expressed the hope that the Grace of God movement would raise women's spiritual consciousness and restore women to the place of reverence they rightfully should hold in society. In the context of the movement, Bhajan taught a variety of yoga sets and meditations intended to strengthen women. As an early and enthusiastic proponent of the movement, Shanti Shanti Kaur defined some of the goals associated with the practices. Here she writes about the central mantra: "The Grace of God mantra gives each woman the technology to look deep within her innermost being to heal herself, to regain the positive image of her infinite potential and to restore her rightful place in society. . . . The fears, limitations and the debilitating concepts that an exploitive society has placed on her can then be lifted" (S. S. Khalsa 1979, 42).

As the movement developed, personal appearance became more important. The secretary general couched this new concern in religious terms: "[I]t is most important to work on getting our physical scene together, and when it is done with the right motivation, to become attractive and pleasing to attract God and His creation, to live in a higher consciousness and in a more pure vibration, then that is the key. Then you can be beautiful without being trapped into vanity, then you can be attractive without being seductive. . . . [O]ur attractiveness can be a kind of selfless service, to attract human beings to live the life of a saint" (P. Khalsa 1973, 6).

As we have seen, after they received official recognition from India the American Sikhs were no longer free simply to please themselves in a number of matters. This included their grooming. The hip look was no longer appropriate. In order to legitimate the organization and fos-ter the image of the graceful woman, a new look was created. I asked one of the early leaders about the progression from the hip look to the graceful Indian style. As she remembered events, Bhajan's early students created quite a reaction at the East-West Cultural Center. They were viewed as both unkempt and undisciplined. Over the years, she thinks, Bhajan kept looking for an appropriate style of dress. He reinforced some patterns of dress adopted by the women students who were close to him, and he asked them to consider their image when guests visited 3HO headquarters. He began to sponsor feasts and special events attended by the public and encouraged 3HO people to dress up for these. When women toured with him they had to devise a more dignified way of dressing than in their accustomed miniskirts. In time, said my informant, "having an image as sophisticated, graceful, spiri-tual was somehow my job. I don't think he said it—I just knew it." On their first visit to India "he had me buy a whole bunch of *kirta*s and *churidar*s and *chunni*s in all colors." In general, "he kept designing the look and the impression and the impact he wanted," and various women worked with him in the effort.

While this concern with graceful and feminine styles of dress was out of step with the North American women's movement as it was evolv-ing at the time, there are parallels between that movement and the Grace of God movement. In each, we find an emphasis on the histori-cal exploitation of women. Empowerment, autonomy, and self-esteem are treated as core goals and virtues. Women are encouraged to become the perceivers as well as the objects of perception and are told not to accept externally imposed identities but to look within to find out who they are and how they should live. There is considerable discussion of media portrayals of women as sex objects, and the movement espouses the same ideas of feminine moral superiority that are found in some strands of feminism and that have been important in Indian society since Gandhi spoke of *stree shakti* (Chitnis 1988, 87).

Yet Bhajan appears to have adroitly incorporated those feminist ideas which allow him to appear as liberator and champion while absolving him, as a male leader, of any responsibility for women's unhappiness. He tends to uncover the roots of women's oppression in the soil of American culture, not in the very nature of male-female relations. Or, when he does blame patriarchal arrangements, he declares that he has progressed beyond gender. He can agree with his women students when they claim that they have been damaged by the attitudes of American society and the behavior of American men while insisting that they should serve and treat him (and their husbands) with respect and obedience. This approach also fits into his broader critique of American culture and permits him to cast himself as a leader in the forefront of a struggle against the more oppressive aspects of American life. It is also worth noting that he places feminine identity safely in the spiritual realm, in an arena where he can provide leadership.

Bhajan has amplified some of the values of the women's movement, employed some of the cultural critiques that resonated with disaffected young people in the 1960s and 1970s, and aligned these with some of the teachings of Sikhism and Tantra in such a way as to produce a framework that supports his leadership, answers some of the objections of his Sikh critics, fosters stability in the organization, and meets some of the women members' needs for a meaningful, and proactive, gender identity.

The Khalsa Women's Training Camp

For many of the women involved in 3HO/Sikh Dharma in the early years, summer solstice activities were followed by attendance at the annual Khalsa Women's Training Camp near the solstice site and adjacent to the Española ashram. Accounts of the camp's genesis vary. Most of the women interviewed agreed, however, that the first camp grew out of an impromptu gathering held after the 1975 solstice celebration and that it was formalized the following summer. One account holds that the camp was the dream and project of a 3HO woman, another that it was established at Yogi Bhajan's instigation. Like many other 3HO innovations, it was created ad hoc, was formalized, took on a variety of functions, and has continued to evolve. I attended the 1983 camp session, and I include some description of that year's activities so that the reader can get a close-up picture of the construction of gender roles and gender relations at that stage in the history of 3HO/Sikh Dharma.

In the mid-1970s both the physical conditions at the camp and the camp's program were challenging. Over the years the site has been improved and the daily demands have diminished. The clientele has also changed, tilting toward yoga students rather than longtime members. Attendance has declined, so that in 1992 Bhajan complained that "this is the smallest number attending the woman's training camp we have ever had" (Notes 1990, 9). From 1990 on Bhajan has waxed nostalgic about the old days. "I wish it should have been the Ladies Camp as I started it," he mused in one 1992 lecture (1992, 11). Now, he complained, it has become too comfortable, and "it has become a very fashionable ladies camp and it is ladylike. There are so many complaints about food that finally it has become a cuisine. . . . We used to put you through a hell of a hell, so that no hell can be hell for you. That was our formula" (10).

When I was preparing to attend I was told repeatedly that "ladies' camp" was a "fantastic" experience. When I first arrived, however, I thought that many of the women there seemed subdued or less than happy. It took me a while to realize that many of the women were working hard to change or discipline themselves in some way, or were striving to adapt 3HO teachings and techniques to their lives. They weren't necessarily at camp to have fun. Participants also kept telling me that it was extraordinary for women to have such an opportunity to gather together. They seemed to think that 3HO was unique in its emphasis on the special qualities of women and in its provision for women to leave other concerns behind and simply spend time together. Apparently, they had no knowledge of the many women's groups outside of 3HO/Sikh Dharma at the time, much less of exciting developments in the country as a woman-identified culture emerged.

The women camped in tents at the site. They attended a variety of classes, made a special effort to rise for daily *sadhana*, and convened every evening to hear Yogi Bhajan's address on issues of special concern to women.

Camp days began slightly before 4:00 A.M., when the members of the group on "wake-up duty" fanned out through the tents. Soprano voices chanted a mantra or simply sang, "Wake up, wake up" to the accompaniment of a guitar. Tent flaps were unzipped, sleeping bags rustled. Women in long white bathrobes padded along dirt paths on the way to the shower rooms. There was little talking; a contemplative silence is recommended in preparation for *sadhana*, and it was in any case rather early for conversation. In the shower room, several women took the cold showers that Bhajan prescribes, and there was the occasional sharp intake of breath, or, rarely, the exclamation, "Wahe Guru" issuing from behind the shower curtains. (This is an exclamation that is difficult to translate, though people in 3HO sometimes translate it as "God is Great." The women had been advised to make this response to the shock of the cold water, if they had to say something.) After their showers, most of the women dressed in white exercise clothing, tucked a blanket or mat under their arms, and began to assemble for *sadhana*.

Morning worship began with yoga, and as the leader introduced a yoga set, one could hear sighs, controlled breathing, and bodies sliding on mats as the women, barely visible in the near-dark, exercised and the leader issued instructions. Some women worked very hard, others more slowly; here and there someone was peacefully asleep. Soon the pace picked up, the exercises became vigorous, and breathing grew loud and labored until it was time to begin a meditation period. Then people carefully wrapped themselves in blankets or sleeping bags or shawls. Many of the women at camp had brought oriental or Mexican blankets and wraps, typically white with gold or royal blue embroidery. When they donned these they looked regal; in the predawn shadows they became archetypal shapes, very still and self-contained.

The sun rose, *sadhana* ended, and there was a brief break. Then there was a change of tempo as exercise sessions began with a choice of jogging, walking, or "yogaerobics." In 1983, leaders were assigned to both the jogging and walking contingents. They guided us to safe routes through the nearby hills, but they were also supposed to foster "group consciousness," urging us, for example, to jog in unison rather than each at a separate pace. Aerobics consisted of kundalini yoga exercises cleverly set to music. In place of the pop music favored in secular health spas, there were the more peaceful styles favored in 3HO. One could find white-clad Sikhs doing jumping jacks to the "Hallelujah Chorus" of Handel's *Messiah* and leg lifts to a song titled "You've Got to Serve Somebody."

The camp was divided into functional groups, or *jatha*s, which rotated various responsibilities such as serving meals, planning and directing morning *sadhana*, waking the camp, cleaning the site, and assisting the cooks. Registrants paid a fee to attend, and there were guards and cooks and teachers to be paid and food to be purchased, but much of the camp maintenance was done by the participants, an approach that reflects the 3HO emphasis upon service and personal responsibility. Members are told that they should act on their commitments and do the spade work necessary to maintain them.

At 8:00 A.M. breakfast was served to campers, who arrived carrying bowls, plates, and mats and arranged themselves in several long parallel lines under a canopy. Members of the serving *jatha* walked up and down the lines with offerings of cereal and fruit and milk, with seconds for everybody and special portions for nursing and pregnant mothers.

Classes were offered for the remainder of the morning. The variety of topics was impressive: "dharmic education" (including Punjabi and Gurmukhi classes and "The Life and Writings of Guru Gobind Singh"); "health and healing" (including such topics as ayurvedic medicine, homeopathy, CPR, and the use of a line of beauty products then being marketed by 3HO); "arts" (calligraphy, classical dance of India, drawing, and photography); and "humanology" (including courses such as "Yoga and the Spiritual Woman"; "Marriage and Family Counseling," taught by Bhajan's wife; and "How to Serve the Siri Singh Sahib"). There were also courses in "personal protection" (this included "defensive pistol shooting"), "prosperity consciousness," and various sports.

Morning classes were followed by lunch and another class period from 1:00 to 3:00 P.M. From 3:00 to 4:30 was "siesta time," an opportunity to rest, write home, attend to course homework, or iron clothes in preparation for the afternoon lecture. The time between 4:30 and approximately 6:00 was set aside for meditation and Yogi Bhajan's daily lecture. The lectures varied in length and might begin anywhere between 4:30 and 5:30.

Bhajan addressed the assembled camp from a dais located outdoors under a large canopy (there is now a building on this site). He was supplied with rugs and cushions, a fan, and a drink. He often wore colorful outfits—an orange turban and a multicolored shirt, for example—which contrasted with the white worn by his listeners. Lectures were preceded by chanting, which was intended to "set the vibrations" for Bhajan. Much was made of his electromagnetic field and his sensitivity to vibrations. He became very angry one day when the public address system malfunctioned and later explained his anger by saying that this had disturbed his energy field.

Many of the women taped his talks or took notes during them. The lectures were the centerpiece of each day, a time apart, as well as a time of relative formality, immobility, and receptivity in the midst of a very active schedule. All of the women were expected to attend, to show respect, and to dress carefully for the event. The format not only affirmed

Bhajan's leadership and charisma but also reinforced the image of the graceful, spiritual, and devoted woman.

After the lecture, there was some free time, if one did not have chores, and dinner. Bedtime was early, although there was some coming and going and whispering fairly late into the night. Weekends were usually free, with optional planned trips to places such as Taos or Santa Fe. Schedules were subject to change, however. One weekend Bhajan suddenly announced that everyone was expected to stay in camp in order to clean his compound. All trips were canceled. Attendees were supposed to view such events as opportunities to overcome the desires of the ego and to serve the spiritual teacher, but however much such techniques are an accepted part of the repertoire of many Eastern spiritual leaders, they obviously can take on distinctive hues when viewed through the lens of American culture. Several campers who were not Sikhs cynically conjectured that this might be a way of deploying free labor. I, being equally uncharitable, wondered if it was not an arbitrary means of enforcing leadership.

I tried to monitor my personal responses to such events. One excerpt from my journal, written on a different but similar occasion, catches an angry response:

> We wait for the lecture. Yogi Bhajan is late and we are being asked to fill the time with chanting. I am hot and tired and rapidly getting annoyed. My back hurts from all the unsupported sitting we do here. The wood chips that cover the ground under the "big top" are rough and keep sticking to me. . . . I am convinced that this is an intentional delay, an instructional technique, and I resent it. . . . I am aware that being kept waiting like this may be a method of breaking down the ego, and I know I am supposed to study my own anger. And I am quite willing to admit that my response may be an indication that I take myself and my time too seriously, and that I have become too accustomed to constant activity and don't know how to slow down. But there is such a thing as common courtesy. How can Bhajan call himself their teacher and then treat these women so shabbily, expecting them to bedeck themselves and then wait in this heat?

Within 3HO such a tendency to distrust Bhajan's motives and to respond angrily might be construed as a manifestation of my ego and my "insecurities." The camp would then be an opportunity to confront these response patterns and to convert them from negative to positive. "This camp," says Bhajan, "represents nothing but the behavior in which you relate to your consciousness" (Notes 1981, 122).

Over the years the camp has accumulated layers of goals and functions. Bhajan has referred to several different goals, and participants, of course, arrive with their own priorities and needs. Early on, Bhajan described the camp as a setting where 3HO members could transcend cultural and psychological limitations and prepare for the trials that the future would bring. Here, women were supposed to challenge themselves and overcome personal and spiritual weaknesses. They were to prepare for a leadership role in the time of transition: "I am very merciless because I believe if I am merciful, time will be very merciless to you. . . . You must eliminate your weaknesses. That is the training of this camp. . . . We want to build a fundamental righteousness and we know that woman is the guardian of righteousness. That is why we have this course for women only" (Notes 1976, 195–96). There is less emphasis today on preparing for the hard times ahead, but Bhajan still anticipates hardship, and in 1992 he was telling his listeners that the most important thing for a woman to learn is "how to survive through calamity" (Notes 1992, 10).

In some of his earlier lectures Bhajan criticized campers for even leaving the confines of the camp, suggesting that simply staying there is a discipline and an accomplishment. He explicitly referred to the camp as a pressure cooker (a description that is also applied to solstice gatherings and to ashram life) and clearly would have preferred fewer cars and independent excursions (e.g., Notes 1979, 225). Roll was called every morning after *sadhana* so truants could be identified, and campers practiced military drill daily.

By the time I attended, the most demanding activities had been eliminated, but things were still not easy. We were camping out of doors in the heat of a southwestern summer. Tents could be little infernos during the day, and those days were long and strenuous. Participants without automobiles were essentially stranded during the week, separated from everyday life and most conveniences. The only available store was a small ashram-run shop. We had access to only one public phone, and to use that required a bit of a hike and a wait in line (this was well before the days of cellular phones).

Bhajan's yoga classes were laced with admonishments to "keep up," to "just get through this exercise," and to "keep going." The day after a particularly difficult session, which probably resulted in many stiff muscles, very few people appeared for class. Bhajan sent some of the women out to find the laggards, and then he began to lecture. It is exactly at this point, when things are getting difficult and painful, that one must "push through," he said. One must break through lethargy and neuroses. People think they cannot do this, but the imposition of such beliefs represents a form of cultural exploitation. One must learn to "confront life and come through. . . . This is not the place for your neurotic, idiotic behavior. You work. I will not allow you to use your excuses. . . . You are feeling the pain. Feel the achievement" (Bhajan 1983c).

The same philosophy was applied on an individual basis. I met a young Buddhist woman who had been hired to teach dance at the camp. She was unhappy there and had told Bhajan that she wanted to leave before the official end of the camp. His response was to tell her that she always tried to solve her problems by running from them, and he recommended that she stay so as to break this pattern. When I spoke with her she had reluctantly decided that Bhajan was right and said, in resigned tones, that she had just canceled her arrangements to leave. She had been crying.

Bhajan's admonitions to "keep up" and be "crystallized" by the pressure do not indicate an entirely joyless approach to personal growth, however, and another, more jovial, side to his persona frequently surfaced. The daily yoga classes were a good example. In spite of their difficulty, attendees approached these classes in a cheerful and enthusiastic spirit, far different from the more subdued atmosphere of the afternoon lectures. Bhajan also approached the class with enthusiasm and seemed to enjoy himself throughout. On one occasion he told all of his older students that they were "hopeless" and asked the young girls' *jatha* to come up on stage and show their mothers how to do it right—much to the girls' delight. There was much laughter, and some groaning, during the classes, but when it was time to work, everyone did. The classes were a unified and exhilarating group effort, a shared experience of "breaking through" physical and psychological limitations.

Closely related to the early view of the camp as challenge and pressure cooker is the sense of it as a place to "eliminate neuroses," cleanse the subconscious, and recognize personal defense mechanisms. In fact, the theme of the 1983 summer session was "personal neuroses" and recognition of the unmet needs of the "hidden child" within each adult woman. Participants were required to write an essay in response to the questions, "What are your neuroses?" and "How do you handle them?" Later, individual lists of neuroses were symbolically burned on a fire.

The structure of the camp was intended to enhance self-examination. The lectures encouraged self-questioning and cast a problematic shadow on whole areas of life. Everyday life was bracketed as participants' lifestyles, marriages, and patterns of thinking were held up for examination and criticism. Thus, at the 1983 session Bhajan talked about feelings of emptiness, "a lack of psychological confidence that . . . you are a person," and warned participants against establishing relationships in order to fill such a void, particularly relationships in which men "catered" to them. This was not the only time that he addressed issues of ego strength and ego boundaries or spoke of young women's difficulties in establishing a cohesive sense of self. He attributed such difficulties to insecurity, to an absence of unconditional love in American experience, or to the pressures on women to be pretty, charming, and "a fake." He also said that he was convinced that women too frequently ignored their own intuitions. "You know your tomorrow," he said (Bhajan 1983d, 1983e). Years later he is still urging women to ignore external identities and to be honest, and he is still criticizing them for being playing games or seeming "cheap."

The camp participants devoted a considerable amount of time to discussing and interpreting Bhajan's teachings. They also analyzed their own experience at camp and assigned meanings to events. One interpretation, for example, concerned the "purging" effects of the camp. A woman in a tent adjoining mine told me that the camp "vibrations," the meditations, and the yoga all combined to relieve the "hurt and anger" that burden women. This seemed to be a widely shared idea. One day during and after *sadhana* many women cried, a phenomenon several women attributed to cleansing of the subconscious and release of accumulated pain and anger. One of the leaders of the 3HO women's movement told me something similar about the Grace of God meditation and the 3HO approach in general. She had participated in consciousness-raising groups at her university, she said, but these did not tell her what to do with the anger and grief she uncovered in these sessions. On the other hand, 3HO offered techniques for releasing the feelings of anger, sorrow, and betrayal that she had experienced, enabling her to move on to accomplish something. Indeed, the ultimate goal of all this separation and cleansing is for the women to reconnect with their essential spirituality. Here, at the camp, they are not subject to domestic and occupational obligations and are free to see to their own needs: "You come here to learn, you come here to get rid of obligations, get rid of emotions, get rid of all that and be here relaxed to improve your own consciousness" (Notes 1981, 123).

Thus, although they are told that it is a challenge, campers are also told that the camp represents an opportunity to relax and unwind. There is time for entertainment in the process of self-change. In fact, one of my most vivid memories of the camp is of one of the leisure activities. At one of the yoga classes Yogi Bhajan suddenly announced his intention to take us to a movie. That evening about fifty of us gathered at the camp entrance and piled into the camp van and several personal cars. The organizer told us that she had called the theater earlier in hopes of reserving seats but was told that this could not be done. So, she said, with eyes flashing, clearly enjoying herself as she planned to storm the theater, "I need someone to buy fifty tickets, someone to hand them out, someone to order the popcorn, and two ladies to hurry in and save seats." There was a holiday mood in the air (and, probably, pleasure in being a majority since Sikhs are so often a minority). The people working at the concession stand were amused by an order for fifty bags of popcorn and laughed as they produced them. A Sikh woman proceeded to reserve places by draping toilet paper around a block of seats, thereby reserving them in style. Yogi Bhajan, some Indian Sikh friends, and a member of the Sikh security force sat in the back row. He talked with his friends, but few of our party went back to talk with him. Shakti Parwha moved from row to row, greeting people and joking to turbaned friends, "Would you mind removing your hat, please" and "Could you tell me why you're all dressed in white, please; are you a nun?"

Since the camp was presented as both a rest and a challenge, a retreat and a microcosm of life, participants had considerable latitude in constructing interpretations of the experience. Each woman could bring her own perspectives and priorities to the camp. All brought varying degrees of dedication, insight, interest, and suggestibility to bear. Some said that they attended primarily for a break from routine and an opportunity to see friends from other parts of the country. Others came to gain particular skills—to learn the language of the Sikh scriptures or alternative medical techniques, for example. Some professionals aimed to ply their trades at the camp and in the process build up their individual practices—as massage therapists or homeopathic practitioners and the like. Still other participants were actively "working on" themselves, seeking personal growth and self-change.

It was difficult, whatever one's intent, to entirely avoid self-examination. In the childlike role of summer camper, a participant might find that childhood conflicts, memories, and dependency are reactivated (I certainly encountered this phenomenon). Separated from families and accustomed identities it became easier for participants to entertain new self-descriptions and to question the quality of their lives outside of the camp. Ordinary modes of organizing life and protecting the self lost some of their necessary and taken-for-granted quality.

Lecture Themes

After I attended the 1983 camp session I wanted to compare what I had heard there to Bhajan's talks in earlier years. I read the transcribed speeches for 1976, 1979, and 1981 and attempted to isolate the major themes relating to gender. Much later I compared these to the transcriptions for 1986, 1987, 1990, 1992, and 1995.

When I read the first series (1976–83) I found that the teachings regarding gender, as presented in the lectures, clustered around several themes: (1) security, grace, and service; (2) "projection" (self-presentation) and communication; (3) self-discipline and "control over environments"; and (4) relationships between men and women. When I looked at the more recent lectures I found considerable consistency over the years but some change in emphasis.

Earlier Lectures: 1976–1983

Bhajan often defines gender concepts by their opposites. Thus, security and grace are contrasted with "neurotic," exploitive, unpleasant, and even degrading behavior; service is contrasted to egotism; exerting the will and practicing self-discipline and neutrality is contrasted to behaving in culturally programmed, dependent, and overly "emotional-commotional" ways; and controlling one's "environment" is contrasted with being "reactive."

Security, Grace, and Service

One of the stated goals of 3HO/Sikh Dharma is to efface the trials and sufferings that are attributed to members' early lives and to instill a new sense of security. The American environment, says Yogi Bhajan, creates the one condition that women cannot transcend: "In the total life of a woman there is one word; if that does not exist, you exist. You will only fight, you will only destroy yourself, you will only destroy the relationship when you are insecure" (Notes 1981, 24).

Security is a term that is more often employed than defined in the lectures, but it is possible to gain a general sense of its meanings and uses. It implies self-esteem based on a woman's knowledge of her own divinity and spiritual powers, and on her awareness that she is different in nature from men and hence does not need to compete with or imitate them. It is rooted in a sense of safety and acceptance. In more practical terms, it means that a woman is assured of support if she has children, and that she need only take jobs in which she receives a reasonable level of respect from her male co-workers. It excludes exposure to "destructive" levels of competition, insensitivity, stress, or physical strain, or to too much "ungraceful" language. It implies that a woman should not be "narrowed" by over-investment in occupational norms and competition or by masculine single-mindedness (men are said to only be able to concentrate on one thing at a time, while women can entertain many plans and ideas at once). The term also implies trusting, caring, and respectful sexual relationships: "You must not exploit, or live on any kind of exploitation, and you must not live in any situation where you have to attempt to attain security. You must not enter into any kind of physical, mental, social or domestic relationship until you have security and a guarantee that in every facet of your life, your reproductive faculty and your delicacy is protected" (Notes 1976, 42).

As the above quotation suggests, Bhajan tapped into many of the concerns facing women at the time: changing sexual mores, single parenthood, and the difficulties of competing in a male-dominated workplace. His first reaction (he has made some adjustments since) was to resist many of the changes that were occurring and to argue that they would do violence to women's basic nature or, at least, render women even more insecure than they already were. And the insecurity would, in turn, make women unpleasant and neurotic; women would lose what was left of their essential sense of self and become competitive, nagging, confrontational, and self-destructive. Insecurity would further blur appropriate gender roles: "Whenever you use male language or male technique you are absolutely a failure as a woman. . . . What has gone wrong in America is that the American woman has become a male. She has been asked to use the technology of the male, and she uses it very overwhelmingly. . . . Pusher, rapper, trapper; all these are men's qualities, they are not your features" (Notes 1979, 157).

He wanted to see such traits replaced by the qualities of the graceful woman (in this case, clearly suggestive of *stridharma*): "You are supposed to be simple, graceful, mellow, sweet, charming, firm, truthful, straightforward and serviceful" (Notes 1979, 157). His use of the term "grace" also indicates that grace implies honesty, commitment, and service—including service to men: "Grace means when you worship a man of truth or a situation of truth. Any identity, space and time where truth is served is called grace" (Notes 1981, 97). A woman is said to have several routes to liberation: she can become a woman of God, she can serve a man of God, she can give birth to a man of God, or she can marry and serve a godly husband. A man, on the other hand, has only the one route to follow: he must become a man of God. A wife is expected to bolster her husband's ego and anticipate his needs as he seeks to fulfill this destiny. She should serve, but with dignity, realizing that she is serving the guru in her mate, not his every whim. A wife should "uplift" a husband and create a secure and loving home. Similarly, a follower should support and aid a spiritual leader, surrounding him with peace, comfort, and respect.

Grace also embraces qualities such as serenity, poise, emotional control, and "equilibrium." The graceful woman does not fight, shout, or allow herself to become entangled in emotional quagmires. She is calm and dignified and certain of her own worth, knowing that "[y]our security lies in your spiritual realm, in your spiritual consciousness 'I am, I am, I am the Grace of God.' A woman's solution comes from within" (Notes 1981, 24). She is able to remain centered, to act upon her insights, and to imprint her spiritual nature upon her surroundings.

It should be noted that grace and security are not only held up as ideals but also sanctioned by various threats:

> Ladies who are very good at laying tantrums, and obnoxious in their behaviors and have unpredictable public and social behavior get cysts in their fallopian tubes and ovaries. (Notes 1976, 39)

> Your behavior as a woman has to be congenial, social, and domestic. . . . Anytime you are crude, rude or insecure, you affect your reproductive organs and you totally imbalance the secretion of the glandular system, especially estrogen. (Notes 1976, 40)

> When a man leans on you and you don't give him support, you can go to hell, he doesn't care. That is when you tell him to find it from somebody else; it is *you* who teach the man to cheat, it is *you* who teach the man to lie, it is *you* who sends the man to another woman. (Notes 1979, 217)

Projection

This term refers to the individual's self-presentation and covers behavior, clothing, associates, and choice of words and tone. Projection is a means of meeting the requirements of a particular situation, but it is also a technique for changing the self. Yogi Bhajan teaches that by projecting an ideal self, one can become that self: "It is very wonderful to let you understand that you are what you project. You are not what you are. You are what you project" (Notes 1981, 36).

Bana, the 3HO clothing, becomes a way of presenting the self as modest, pure, and spiritual. The white clothing is intended to remind the individual throughout the day that she is committed to purity and to the inner guru, and to tell members of the public that this is somebody who will help in times of distress. Many members told me that they felt more "centered" when wearing a turban, "less scattered, more meditative and calm," as one woman put it. She said she began by wearing her turban only one day a week, then slowly built up to wearing it regularly. Later she progressed to wearing the *chunni*, which, she said, made her feel more "feminine, graceful and protected." This informant, and several others, mentioned a growing "sensitivity" to moods and atmospheres as they became involved in yoga and meditation. This sensitivity was not always comfortable—it could leave the individual feeling overly exposed to others' feelings—but they felt that the new sensitivity could be counteracted, at least to some degree, by wearing *bana*.

Similarly, language is considered a significant tool for changing one's self, expressing one's essential divinity, and bringing out the best in others. As previously mentioned, 3HO's publishing and research arm, the Kundalini Research Institute, has published a dissertation by Yogi Bhajan. The central thesis is that Eastern perspectives on communication can be usefully combined with Western research, and that communication style is a basic source of both misery and uplift: "The power of the word is indeed the power of the divine. . . . We were not created to suffer in this world. Our suffering is self-imposed through our own ignorance and self-abusing language. Yet, what is the purpose of life if it is not to praise the Creator through His creatures in creation" (H. Khalsa 1980, 67).

Women in 3HO are exhorted to practice "comparative, comprehensive communication" as a way to project and spread their spirituality and as a way to protect themselves from "ungraceful" encounters and situations. They are told that they should not speak on the spur of the moment or in anger; they should not "whine" and complain. All communications should be considered, considerate, adapted to the hearer and the circumstances, and should remind the hearer of higher things.

Further, a woman should avoid ungraceful communications from others. In this regard, some basic, and stringent, rules set out at women's camp are

1. entertain no rude words;
2. entertain no words which do not have as their objective to sponsor you as a woman;
3. answer no coarse communicative dialogue;
4. avoid gross language; we call it truck drivers' language; it's the privilege of men, not you;
5. communicate with absolute manners;
6. receive communication with absolute manners;
7. use graceful words and graceful tones in your communication; and
8. when the communication is not graceful, leave.
   (Notes 1979, 19)

Projection has its negative side as well. Unsuitable clothing and language and poor choice of associates, occupations, and environments project a negative image and may cause trouble and suffering. A woman must constantly strive to convey an image of grace, purity, and dignity in order to protect herself. And self-protection is important since the threat of rape, it seems, is always present. Bhajan's lectures and stories frequently focus on this threat, as well as on the supposed promiscuity of Americans. Listeners are warned to avoid dangerous situations and follow orders—or they will pay the price.

Controlling One's Environment/Self-Discipline

One of the goals of projection is increased control over circumstances. Because so many women have been exploited and have lived programmed and "reactive" lives, it is necessary that they learn to shape or "mold" their circumstances. Fortunately, this is a woman's special power: "Mental degradation is at the highest point in the American woman today because she has not discovered one thing very essential to her: the power to mold her environment and circumstances. It exists only in woman, not in man, just as she can mold a spermatozoa into a human being" (Notes 1981, 13).

Bhajan attributes this capacity to modify her surroundings to a generalized creativity associated with a woman's biological role as mother and to her nature as *shakti*—the source of all forms. A woman can shape reality and overcome any obstacles she may encounter in the process: "The basic quality of every woman is that she can change every negative thing around her to be positive" (Notes 1979, 211).

This gift is essential since they are told that 3HO represents North America's only real hope for a spiritual rebirth. These children of the counterculture "paid a tremendous sacrifice in deaths and overdoses that this new nation might be born. It is not a small situation, don't misunderstand, please. . . . Out of those twenty million people came one thing only, and that's 3HO, which is positive and alive. Out of the Woodstock Nation we became the Steel Nation" (Notes 1979, 167). Now the people of the Steel Nation must strengthen themselves in order to save others from the degradation and deprivation they have experienced. They are to become beacons of light in a world of darkness. Each member must exercise her will in an effort at self-transformation and character building. Women must overcome past exploitation and leave the past behind: "[Y]ou say, 'My mother did it. My father did it.' . . . You are a Jewish princess. . . . You stole, you shoplifted, you cheated, you lied. Great. Stop it now. Now you are you. Now you control the environments; environments do not control you" (Bhajan 1983b).

A woman must learn to push herself beyond what she conceives of as her mental and emotional limits. Participants encountered a metaphor for this process at one of the first women's camps: "That first summer I grew so much from it, just from the obstacle course: climbing the wall. . . . It was a BIG wall and you had to climb it with two other women. The two of them could help you get over it. . . . You had to figure out a way to do it; no one tells you how. And then once you're on the other side you have to jump."

Relations between the Sexes

Bhajan tells his students that marriage should be considered a spiritual union and that it should not be based primarily upon emotion or attraction. Chastity before, and fidelity within, marriage are enjoined, and divorce is discouraged, although it is an option.

If a marriage flounders, he suggests that it is probably due to a failure in the woman's "technology." This technology involves yet another form of molding environments: the molding of male character. According to Yogi Bhajan, men respond to suggestion: "The greatest weapon of a woman is indirect suggestion so gracefully laid down that a man will be attracted to that idea" (Notes 1976, 38). Men must be nudged, supported, and encouraged, not confronted. Competition with men (or other women) is undesirable: "Women should never compete, instead they should always mold" (Notes 1981, 16).

In fact, women are the source of male energy and potency, and men are drawn to women as sources of energy. "[H]e is into anything which can give him energy," Bhajan declares. "Food, ego, direction, territory, anything which is good or bad, which can give this apparatus energy to live on. Then this slob can move" (Notes 1976, 408). Further, "Because the apparatus (man) is still, all she has to do is to give a cue and it starts operating in harmony to her suggestion. . . . Men always react; man is an apparatus" (ibid., 38).

Given the nature of the masculine personality, a woman cannot expect constant emotional partnership: "Man's nervous system needs to be fed, smoothed, and consoled. The brain structure of a man is not designed to give continuous support. Woman, on the other hand, is complete in this area" (Notes 1976, 17). Do not, he says, count on a man "to comfort you when you need it." Nor should a woman share her fears and her weaknesses, and certainly not her anger, with a husband: "[W]hen you have a weakness, talk to your spiritual teacher, never to your man, because you are feeding his negativity" (Notes 1979, 10). In fact, a woman has cause to be on guard with men, for men react to women by either revering or degrading and manipulating them, and male fidelity is always in question.

Clearly, relationships between the sexes are uncertain, and marriage is work for a woman. Men are not asked to work as hard, but they are told that they should respect women's intuition, sensitivity, and spirituality, and that they should provide a secure environment for the family. Their role as fathers is emphasized. An individual is said to have four gurus in a lifetime: (1) the mother, who leaves an almost indelible imprint in the first three years of life; (2) the father, whose influence reigns from ages three to seven; (3) relatives, schoolmates, and friends, whose influence is primary from seven to puberty; and (4) the spiritual teacher. A father's presence and involvement is thus considered crucial.

Later Lectures: 1986–1995

Themes That Have Declined in Importance

By 1986 several themes that were prominent in the early years have faded into the background. There is little discussion of the term "insecurity" and few references to women's need for unqualified love or for family stability. This probably reflects the greater maturity of 3HO members. They are now less interested in assessing their families of origin and have accomplished the task of creating viable family units. Identities are more securely established. The women have also accepted, in general at least, the model of the graceful woman, and therefore are probably behaving less frequently in ways that Bhajan construes as insecure and ungraceful. Another term that ceases to reappear with any regularity is "projection."

There is still some discussion of honest communication and considerable attention to demeanor, but the basics of *bana* and feminine behavior are in place.

The camp is no longer described as an intentionally created pressure cooker and there are no admonitions to toughen oneself and become "like steel." The idea of "working on" the self and striving for excellence is, however, retained. The tone is simply less demanding. Members are older, the new Khalsa has been forged, many nonmembers are now in attendance, and the camp has become a more comfortable and less demanding part of 3HO life.

The idea of the camp as a place to purge the self of conflicts, neuroses, anger, and the pain accumulated over the years is now rarely discussed, and there is less attention directed to the subconscious, although there are some self-evaluation exercises. In general, there seems to be less concern with analyzing and altering the self and a greater emphasis on making life work and on improving the self and the surrounding world.

Continuing Themes

Women's essential nature and her ideal traits remain very much the same, with perhaps the addition of references to her "artistic" nature and to living with some "elegance." In 1986, Bhajan describes women's nature much as he did in the past: "[Y]ou are a living tranquility, peace, harmony, grace and sophistication. . . . [Y]ou are a living sacredness" (Notes 1986, 30). He still maintains that a woman's modes of action should be indirect. Thus in 1992 Bhajan reminds his listeners that a woman's "tools" are elegance, body language, image, kindness, compassion, and "words that penetrate" (Notes 1992, 106). He continues to remind women that they are complete within themselves, and from this position he advises women not to ask three rather feminist questions: (1) "What about me?" (2) "Am I in control?" and (3) "Where is my security?" These he views as needy, demanding questions that one can only ask if one has forgotten that God resides within the self.

Women continue to be criticized for the same old faults in recent lectures. They still are said to deny their nature, play games, seek romance, manipulate, waste energy on externals, and cheapen themselves. Men are still undependable and in need of womanly inspiration. "[T]o handle a man is the most difficult, obnoxious job," Bhajan says. "And mostly the net result is not as good as you expect" (17). Nevertheless, women still must mold and manage men.

Bhajan continues to describe marriage as a sacred union and a form of spiritual training. He makes this quite clear in 1986: "Now this is how I look at marriage. If you cannot merge with each other, one unit of a human being to another unit of a human being, how can you merge with God?" (42) Marriage is not about "body, emotions and feelings," (44) and a man looks to a woman not for sexual gratification but for her spirituality, the trust he experiences with her, and the security and communication he can share with her.

Bhajan is still very much opposed to androgynous models of the sexes. Women must be women: "Woman with her pinky can build heavens; man with his cannons cannot destroy it. Provided that you are a woman. There is a proviso" (56). Further, "You give to the world creative values. You are born to give the world its reality. Man is supposed to protect it. That was the relationship between a man and a woman. And today what have we created? We have created tomboys, tomgirls, transvestites. Girls are dressed as men, men are dressed as women—mentally" (107).

Themes That Have Gained in Importance or Metamorphosed

The most dramatic shift followed in the wake of a lawsuit brought in 1986 by two female ex-members who accused Bhajan and other officers of Sikh Dharma of assault and battery, false arrest and imprisonment, fraud and deceit, infliction of emotional distress, racketeering, violation of the federal fair labor standards act, and involuntary servitude (*S. Premka Kaur Khalsa v. Harbhajan Singh Khalsa Yoiji et al.*, Civil Action No. 86-0838, and *Katherine Felt v. Harbhajan Singh Khalsa Yogiji et al.*, Civil Action 86-0839 [1986], U.S. District Court, Albuquerque, N.M.). Bhajan moved to have the case dismissed, basing much of his argument on First Amendment rights. In pretrial consideration, the judge granted the request to dismiss the complaints that seemed to require findings about Bhajan's honesty, legitimacy, and sincerity. These were the claims for fraud and deceit and for RICO violations. He did not dismiss the claims for assault and battery, false imprisonment, violation of the Fair Labor Standards Act, and intentional infliction of emotional distress (No. 86-838-M Civil Consolidated with No. 86-839-HB Civil, Memorandum Opinion and Order, Oct. 22, 1987, U.S. District Court, Albuquerque, N.M.). It is my understanding, based on the word of reliable sources, that the case was finally settled out of court.

In his talks at this time, Bhajan seeks to rally the troops and to reinforce the collective identity. He does this primarily by framing those who leave the organization, or, worse, litigate against it, as enemies, thus creating an "antagonist identity field" in opposition to which 3HO members define themselves (Hunt, Benford, and Snow 1994, 198). After the suit is filed, Bhajan talks much less about individuals overcoming trials and personal blocks and much more about shared adversity. He admonishes the audience to view adversity as a blessing, to remember that everything has a light and a dark side, that the Khalsa has always been persecuted and has always endured. Hardship, he says, can become a means to "develop the mind to the point that in utmost adversity you don't forget God" (Notes 1986, 123).

He maintains that it is not only himself but the entire organization that has been attacked: "Not a single one of you have been spared. None. They have not attacked a person, they have attacked the very identity of the Dharma" (Notes 1986, 4). He speaks frequently about betrayal. Those who leave, he declares, never cease to seek the destruction of 3HO/Sikh Dharma: "[B]y leaving you don't leave, you just feel sorry. And then it becomes a vengeance, it becomes a vendetta" (ibid., 2). He periodically suggests that his hardships are due to having championed women, as when he muses that "my trouble didn't start until I started GGMWA, the Grace of God Movement of the Women of America."

But if he indulges in a good bit of self-justification and in efforts to strengthen group solidarity, he also seems more aware of the need to please his women followers. In the later lectures, for example, he emphasizes women's power and creativity more than previously. It also seems that recently Bhajan has used more explicit goddess imagery: "Your personality is pure pregnancy. What you touch flourishes. What you destroy never exists. What you inspire shall always win. . . . There is no power in God's kingdom which does not come through you. . . . You see that Goddess with eight hands? That's what you are" (Notes 1992, 54–56).

Bhajan also begins to address the issue of abuse and frames it within the context of woman as *shakti*. He says that a woman in full possession of her powers should be beyond any form of harm or degradation. He often asserts that women in some way are responsible for their troubles, but there also seems to be increasing emphasis on the idea that women are not born to suffer.

Further, there is some softening on the issue of women's lives outside of the home. Over the years Bhajan has become more accepting of contemporary realities and has encouraged women to get the training they need in order to support themselves or contribute significantly to the family income, but he has adjusted reluctantly, as one can see in the following quotations: "This situation which you are confronting here, that every woman should be a tomboy, a hero; should hit hard and get even, is out of pure frustration. It is because the family structure has broken. The man used to go and earn and provide and the woman used to maintain and contain the family. That was the basic balance. Now that balance does not exist, neither can it come back. Mostly men and women have to work to keep life going. I understand that."

Bhajan remains convinced that women's forms of expression must differ from those employed by men: "With all the process of time I have gone through, my idea has not changed. . . . I still believe kindness, compassion, forgiveness and beautiful behavior are the basic gestures of the female" (Notes 1986, 10).

Contradictions, Rhetorical Style, and the Functions of Gender Ideology

One finds contradictory and sometimes disturbing content in Bhajan's discussions of gender. He often employs gender concepts to encourage and to exalt women, but just as frequently he uses them to exhort and deride. If his women listeners are told that they are the highest of beings, they are also criticized for their willingness to neglect or deny their spiritual identities. Bhajan alternately portrays women as strong and as in need of protection, as infinitely capable and as beings who are endlessly at risk. He shifts between messages of empowerment and teachings that will evoke obedience and dependency in his women followers. He praises and then he threatens.

These contradictions are particularly dramatic in his discussions of abuse and hardship. Here opposing frameworks clash and are not readily aligned. Ways of viewing gender and social life that are based upon the traditions of purdah come up against Western feminism. Bhajan's teachings about *shakti* conflict with American understandings of women as victims of abuse.

Sometimes Bhajan is very sympathetic and insightful about the sources of women's pain. At other times he is harshly critical or accusatory. Even when he is relatively sympathetic he tends to attach some blame to women. Thus he attributes most of a woman's problems to "transaggression," which is "aggressiveness she picks up. It is not her. It is what has been done to her or what she feels has been done to her. She feels neglected, rejected, used, abused, misused, and the worst thing is that the majority of the time she participates with it, initiates it, creates it, and then punishes herself with it for the rest of her life" (Notes 1986, 47).

In his harsher voice he tells his listeners that they choose "to be physically beautiful, very sexy and sensual." The typical woman takes "an antique china plate from the Ming dynasty, puts gold leaf on it and very systematically poops on it. . . . You have your Ming plate, that's your physical body. You have the most beautiful gold leaf on it; that's your soul. Then you put the mental poop on it. That's what you want to live with" (Notes 1986, 139).

He frequently poses and probes a paradox in his lectures: If every woman is the creatrix, if each is the embodiment of *shakti*, if a woman knows all and is "the solution" to all of the world's problems, if, in short, she is the power that makes manifest the universe, then why is she so frequently abused? Why do women suffer so?

Most of Bhajan's answers come down either to the nature of the mind and the senses or to women's own responsibility for their pain. Women "forget God," they forget who they really are, they think wrongly, they are seduced by sensuality and do the forgetful things that lead to pain. In the final accounting, "every woman among you creates her own suffering" (Notes 1987, 13). But he admits that, in addition to all the things that women do wrong, there is the problem posed by men. Men, he warns, are "not graceful." They try to degrade women, at the same time hoping that women will not succumb. They try to undermine women's sacred nature, encouraging women to become emotional, sensual, and self-seeking, for men need women and want to bring them down into the male realm. Indeed, he now suggests that much of women's forgetting is due to patri-archal subversion of women's nature: "Within the realm of shallowness he approached you to make you commotional. . . . [H]e subjected you to his will and thus you became subjective. As the centuries have passed this has become your song and dance. Your children, men, families and you are not happy" (Notes 1990, 107).

Paradoxes proliferate when Bhajan talks about physical abuse. Men in his lexicon are essentially "reactive." They require the *shakti* energy in order to do anything; they are impotent without it. If this is so, then how can they rape women unless women are somehow complicit in the act? In some sense they must be: "A woman stimulates rape. A woman stimulates insult. I don't want to blame women, but there is nothing which a woman does not initiate" (Notes 1979, 207).

But if the woman in some way initiates abuse, then somewhere in her being the woman has the potential power to stop the rapist or abuser. Thus, in a 1990 lecture, Bhajan tells a story. He describes a large and powerful man attempting to rape a woman. Bhajan stood ready to come to her defense, but "[t]he woman stood up like a cobra. Her eyes became bigger and bigger. She started looking and he started proceed-ing and finally he stopped, turned and ran. . . . She looked like Death, so determined, so grounded, in her high heels she was totally rooted into planet earth. Perhaps the guy thought she had a black belt in karate or some weapon. When she never moved he understood that one more step and he would be dead. That's how determined she was" (Notes 1990, 107). He seems to suggest that every woman who truly knows her identity and recognizes her power ought to be able to summon such a spiritual defense system. Evidently this assumption, and the implication that women are responsible for abuse, has led to probing questions from some of the women members, for Bhajan's wife felt the need to elaborate on this theme in 1995, explaining that women ought to be very cautious and leave any situation that feels unsafe, but that women are not to blame for rape, rather it may be that a woman "doesn't have the self-esteem or whatever it is to protect herself. . . . I would say it's not a blame or guilt thing but a subconscious patterning that she hasn't had control over but can develop control over through developing the arc line and the aura" (Notes 1995, 170).

In the course of a 1987 lecture a woman in the audience spoke of her impending divorce and the abuse she had suffered at the hands of her husband. Bhajan's reply: "Do you know what has happened? A little peanut has become a mountain. All you need is to smile a little more. . . . If you would have shown your teeth to him he would have never dared to offend you" (Notes 1987, 110). He suggests that men will cool down and all sources of conflict will evaporate if a woman handles things correctly. She should agree with anything a man says when he is angry, refuse to be drawn into conflict, and remain calm and poised. Soon the man will get over his anger, will recognize the woman's wisdom, and all will be well.

I do not know if the woman who raised the issue at camp saw any value in this formula or whether she was simply angered by the way Bhajan minimized her suffering. It is clear that Bhajan has had to formulate a position on this issue; he has been confronted with the growing public concern about abuse. He also seems to be aware that his response is not in keeping with the tenor of the times. In fact, in several talks he makes surprising comments such as "I know that most of you don't like me," suggesting that he often finds himself at odds with the opinions of his female students.

If Bhajan's assumption that women have the potential spiritual power to evade all abuse seems unrealistic to some, the way that his lectures are peppered with tales of rape, as well as of abuse and sexual excess, seems particularly so to me. The following quotations from different years reveal this preoccupation with rape and seem to be intended to frighten his audience:

I was not going to send them into a dangerous situation. They started whining, like hot bitches when people go near their puppies. . . . Finally I said, "I am not going to allow these girls to go on this trail. Period. I'll cancel it." There was one girl who was crying, "yeeeeeyey yeh yeh." She looked ferocious. I asked her, "Have you hiked these Pecos trails?" She said, "Yes." I said, "How many times were you raped?" She said, "Twice." (Notes 1979, 121)

I remember that unfortunate day when there was a phone call and I went to the hospital. What happened was that some guys followed her all the way to her apartment. At night they broke into the apartment and physically molested her. It was an unbearable scene. They not only raped her, they injured her also. And then they shaved her hair, they shaved her head. (Notes 1981, 127)

There was a mother who was a Sikh. . . . When her daughter turned sixteen, the mother divorced her husband. She went to India, picked up her daughter from the school, and brought her back to the United States. Then she asked her boyfriend to rape her. I called her and I said, "Why did you do this?" She said, "You do not know what I went through. I want my daughter to have a taste of the same so she may not say she is superior to me." (Notes 1995, 12)

To read Bhajan's speeches is to encounter the very tendency to either glorify or degrade women which he attributes to all men and to which Nikky-Guninder Kaur Singh alludes in the epigraph at the beginning of this chapter. Bhajan's ambivalence seems to leap from many pages. Sometimes he is empathic and perceptive, and at other times he is cruelly condemning. One can see epitomized in his lectures the contradictory role that religion has so often played in Sikhism and in many of the major world religions. At one moment religion is the powerful enabler, at the next it enjoins submission. Bhajan seems to move back and forth between the two possibilities, depending on his purposes and his feelings. He shifts frames and pits one against the other. Sometimes he views women's issues through a contemporary, liberal, Western lens, but often one encounters many of the assumptions that underlie purdah.

It is not easy to grasp Bhajan's point of view. His view of woman-hood is difficult to decipher, not only because of the contradictory statements he makes, but because of his style of teaching. There are reasons to be cautious about taking Bhajan's lectures at face value since he uses insults and provocative statements as instructional devices. He made this explicit in a 1992 talk when he brought a young girl up on stage to teach the older generation. At one point he began to tell her what it means to be a teacher and instructed her in the art of giving a Bhajan-style speech: "[P]oke, provoke, confront and elevate. Divide your lecture on those terms. . . . Attack everybody. . . . Slaughter them on the spot."

Here Bhajan lays out his lecture format in a revealing and often humorous bit of byplay. He also provides an interesting insight into his approach to the burdens and responsibilities of leadership. It seems that he passes these burdens on to Guru Ram Das and imagines him-self as an egoless conduit for his special guru. Thus, he goes on to tell the girl that when she becomes a teacher, "[w]hat is left of you from this minute onward is nothing but the teacher. You will not judge anything as a female, anything as a male, anything as a person. . . . You will only teach for the benefit, elevation and truth, success and excellence of another person. . . . [Y]ou are a pipe. Water comes through it. . . . Wis-dom comes through you. At stake is Guru Ram Das, not you. Let him look foolish. Push it on. Let dirty water come. . . . It is his problem, not yours. You are never a problem now."

The formula that I find in his talks is similar to that which he describes, except that he starts not by "poking and provoking" but by holding out an ideal. He begins by establishing a topic and assuring his students that they have extraordinary potential. He tells the women, for example, that they are the source of all, the creative spirit. Then he goes on the attack, telling them that they are wasting their potential, living unconsciously, behaving stupidly, and squandering their spiritual assets: "Your psyche is sixteen percent more than a man. Your intelli-gence is sixteen percent more than a man. God gave you everything six-teen percent more because you are going to be a mother. . . . Why are you not sixteen times closer to God than anybody? . . . Why are you dishonest with your own creation? . . . Why the hell are you always on sale?" (Notes 1992, 53).

He typically goes on in this vein for some time, citing shortcomings and failures. He may also contrast the women's performance with the superior behavior of an exemplary character in a story. Finally, in the end, he may introduce a meditation or a prayer or a bit of yoga intended to uplift and alter his audience.

When he told the young teacher in the camp that he intended to "poke and provoke" he was not saying anything that he had not told his students previously. In 1984, an informant told me that this is his approach and suggested that Bhajan begins the summer camp "by breaking down defenses. He challenges, says provocative things that unlock fears and open the unconscious." He gives these tactics time to work, and then, in the final two weeks, "he starts to reintegrate and provides tools to work with the issues he evokes."

Bhajan warns that he is a "Cancer teacher" who is rough on his students. "I cater to no student," he says. "If I love somebody I skin them alive and put red chiles [*sic*] on it. . . . Because what is the relationship between a teacher and student? Hammer and chisel on a stone. What does it create? Sparks" (Notes 1992, 39).

Bhajan presents himself as a teacher whose techniques are intended only for the good of his students. His harsh words and his disciplines are necessary in order to banish ego and break repetitive cognitive patterns so that his students may emerge from *maya* into enlightenment. One may question the ethics of that approach, and the ease with which it can be used to justify insensitivity (I would), but it is only fair to note that his words cannot always be taken literally and that they often should be understood in the light of the teaching and rhetorical devices that Bhajan employs.

Bhajan would claim that gender plays no role in shaping his approach or his attitudes—he has become the conduit, the pipe for the waters of knowledge, a teacher whose goals transcend gender. But to an observer like myself his imagery seems anything but genderless. At one point he even compares teaching to the sexual act: "[Y]ou have to inject. Penis has to go into the uterus and has to move in order to ejaculate. . . . And then the race begins. Many spermatozoa die, one makes it into the egg. . . . Out of all these people and many millions which will come, one will become a student and one becomes a Master" (Notes 1992, 199).

I see his teachings expressing his own ambivalence, placing moral responsibility on women's shoulders (not his own), but also expressing his yearning for purity, union, excellence, and transcendence. I see them, sometimes, as a real effort to liberate the women who listen to him, but they are also strongly influenced by tradition, self-interest, and the desire to stabilize the organization and his own leadership.

Indeed, if one looks at the functions of gender ideology, and of "ladies' camp," in a fairly simple and straightforward way, one finds that many of the gender ideals can function to bind women to their leader and to the organization. Confinement to the camp and separation from home and family undercut all loyalties except those to the Dharma. The attractions of the outside world are further diminished as worldly statuses are devalued and participants' pasts are denigrated or defined as periods of suffering and cultural programming. By insisting on graceful and ladylike behavior, Bhajan effectively cuts off rebellion and feminist ideology. By warning against stressful occupations he may limit women's earning power and hence their capacity to leave the organization. By picturing the outside world as dangerous and exploitive he suggests that women can only be truly valued within the 3HO fold.

The women members, of course, do not tend to view Bhajan's teachings in the skeptical light in which I have presented them. They stress his praise of women, not his criticisms. When they do address his fault-finding they often assume that it is meant to spur growth. From their perspective, the teachings and camp life simply undercut ego and *maya* and serve to remind participants that external rewards and circumstances are undependable. No possession, occupation, human tie, or self-image will last, and none will satisfy the higher aspects of the self. The only lasting reality is the individual's tie to "God and guru." It is the spiritual teacher's duty to foster this awareness, even if he must be temporarily sharp or unkind.

Clearly, gender ideology in 3HO has multiple strands and purposes. It reflects Bhajan's background, culture, and personality, as well as his strategies as a teacher and his students' concerns and needs at different stages of life. It changes along with organizational priorities and with events that impact upon 3HO at different points in the organization's history. Many of the teachings about women, and gender in general, appear to condense, dramatize, epitomize, and institutionalize some core organizational themes and values. They provide gender-specific renderings of otherwise abstract principles such as purity, selflessness, and devotion. They are also employed to foster a collective identity as women are treated as a unit or an archetype. Gender norms and teachings are also used to signal external audiences. The norms concerning women's clothing styles and self-presentation, for example, indicate propriety, legitimacy, and a respect for tradition to the non-3HO Sikh population.

And although Bhajan gives official pronouncements on the subject, gender ideology is a collective product. Women members use it to display their loyalty and to indicate that they understand and hold the expected beliefs and attitudes, but the ideology is constantly adapted and modified by individual members as they apply it to their lives and teach it to their students. The women typically develop their personal interpretations of gender and of graceful behavior. In everyday situations they apply those teachings that they find helpful and ignore some of the others.

They use the teachings to maneuver in a changing society and to manage their family and work lives. Some use the teachings to mark the boundaries of desire and imagination, telling themselves, in essence, "want this, but do not expect that. Cope with this form of stress, but do not expose yourself to that. Put up with this, but draw a line there. Participate in the wider world, but judge yourself primarily by spiritual standards, not by the yardsticks of material success and occupational prestige by which men tend to come out ahead." The following chapters follow women as they sift through, interpret, and apply 3HO gender ideals.

Khalsa Women's Training Camp 2: Edited Journal Entries

I spend my days at camp like everybody else. I mostly manage to get up for *sadhana*. I am taking classes (the counseling class I am taking is excellent and I look forward to it) and have joined a jogging group. I do some chores. I attend the daily yoga classes and lectures. I interview during the quiet times of day: rest time, meals, after dinner. When I need to "go backstage" I talk with my two friends who are not Sikhs, with a Sikh woman who is a university professor and understands my academic perspective, or with the non-Sikh sister of a Sikh friend.

My two non-Sikh friends and I share gossip and discuss our reactions to camp life. We repeat what others have told us about the camp and its purposes, and we share our experiences. K. is involved in many activities; she helps with the young girls, for example. She is also a sampler of the spiritual wares. She recently went to a healer who told her that her kundalini energy was blocked because she had broken a karmic law and that she must find out what law this was. No sooner had she told us about this, and said that she hadn't the faintest idea what it might mean, than Yogi Bhajan called to inquire after her well-being. Was she "freaking out at ladies camp?" he asked. She assured him that she wasn't, but by then she was beginning to wonder if she really had a problem, so she did mention that she was concerned about a personal relationship. When she asked around she was told that such a call was not very common—she should feel honored that Bhajan had called her.

I decided to get a concrete sense of 3HO counseling by bringing a personal issue to Bibiji. She told me to make a list of affirmations about myself, she gave me a visualization to do, and she advised me to create an altar and use it regularly for meditation and visualization. I did my homework and compiled the list of affirmations, and I have been doing the visualization, but I find myself drawing the line when it comes to an altar. The altar feels wrong, perhaps because that would be crossing the line between participant observation and actually being a devotee. I wonder, though, if I should do it as a way of getting closer to 3HO women's experience.

We sometimes share our moments of skepticism. S., for example, was convinced that we were overcharged when we went to the movies (the money was collected at camp and was supposed to cover movie and transportation). I can't imagine the leaders being that petty, but I give voice to my major complaint: I dislike Bhajan's temper and his criticisms of 3HO women. S. responds that these are often warranted because he offers the women so many insights and techniques, and then they are not utilized. All three of us wonder about his centrality in this organization, but K. tempers her doubts by saying that Bhajan has given her some very good advice and that she regards him as her spiritual teacher. S. asks me if I don't think that

(Cont'd. from page 137)

Bhajan "essentially wants to help people." "Well," I say, rather surprising myself, "yes I do, actually." I think he really is trying to help his students work through subconscious conflicts, raise their self-esteem, widen their worlds beyond the realm of the ego, and improve their health. But I also tell her that I have numerous reservations.

Judging from the snippets of conversation I overhear, what we are doing in our discussions and our sampling is typical of what the other non-Sikh yoga students are also doing here. They are trying to understand Bhajan's teachings, assess his motives, learn about Sikhism, and try out the "technologies." This is probably pretty typical of people who have some degree of attachment to 3HO and are trying to decide whether they want to maintain the tie, whether they should strengthen it, and what place 3HO/Sikh Dharma should play in their lives.

K. has her car here, and she occasionally offers us rides. We drove into Santa Fe one night for dinner and enjoyed all the forbiddens: wine, meat (not me, actually; I couldn't bring myself to eat it), coffee. K. kept saying how nice it was to hear a male voice.

S. is an astrologist, an interest she shares with Yogi Bhajan and many of the women here. Many of the Sikhs are also perfectly happy to believe that Bhajan's spirit travels and visits them, and that he can see and interpret their auras. All of this is fascinating from an ethnographic point of view. What a range of realities is here. So many belief systems, almost spread out cafeteria style. But I must admit that, personally, it sometimes leaves me feeling isolated. It's funny. At home, in my own circles, I often feel that I am more right-brained than many of the people I work with, even a bit on the spiritual edge: a little more willing to believe in spiritual possibilities, to trust to intuition, to believe that life is a mystery than my colleagues. I sometimes struggle to be as linear and as focused as academia requires. But all things are relative, and here I feel that I must be the most scientific, doubting, logical, "secular humanist" extant.

I also sometimes feel outsized and exposed. I am well covered and dressed in white, but I am not wearing *bana*, and it's noticeable. The other day a little girl pointed at me and said, "Look, mother, she cut her hair!" I also feel as if I were lacking in grace, much too direct. Actually, I'm not large, nor am I particularly outspoken or assertive, but in this setting I feel that way—so many of these women (though certainly not all) are so petite and soft-spoken and feminine.

The other day a Sikh woman came up to me and said that I have "another kind of women's strength." We talked for a bit after that, but I never asked her what she meant. I thought I knew; I assumed that she was saying that I am a more direct professional type. But now I am kicking myself for making that assumption and not asking her to elaborate. Here I am studying what it means to be a woman in 3HO, someone comes up to me offering basic insights, and I fail to really take her up on her conversational gambit. I have a feeling that I missed a real opportunity for understanding.

My time at the camp is over. I felt quite torn in leaving. Eager to do some sightseeing in the Southwest, to be on my own for awhile. But also that I shouldn't be leaving events in midstream, suddenly stopping the process of living like a Sikh. It seems too sudden, too soon.

On my last full day in camp I managed to wake up for the final yoga sets and for a lovely *gurdwara*. I suddenly began to cry, without really knowing why, although I thought about my mother's illness and aging and about the difficulties of picking up my life again, and of relinquishing the peace of early morning chants.

Later in the day, a camp acquaintance told me that she too had wept her way through the yoga, and the woman in the tent next to mine said that she had cried through *sadhana* over such things as missing her daughter (who is at the children's camp) and wanting to do "summer things" with her. Another woman said that she had been crying most of the day. One of the Sikh women told me that this is called "cleansing," and that it is part of the camp process: the hurt and anger that are so much a part of women's lives are slowly eliminated in this fashion.

The next day I got a ride into town. It felt odd to be alone in a hotel, a stranger, after so much intensive interaction. Throughout the day I found that I was rather self-conscious, aware of myself making plans and re-creating my independence. The process and effort of being a lone individual stood out in sharp relief: I watched myself decide what to do next, where to eat, what to eat, which art galleries to enter in Santa Fe (just about all of them), what pottery to like. It all seemed at once necessary and contrived, free and lonely. I was somewhat anxious, too, about sightseeing on my own, driving off with no one knowing where I was and what I was doing. It felt awkward, lonely, even dangerous, after so much time spent in group living.

But I loved being in an air-conditioned car. I turned on the radio and heard news for the first time, and found an oldies station to drive along with. I sang along to oldies, but when I drove past the camp, the "We Are the Khalsa" song starting going through my head. I made a trip to San Ildefonso, Puye Cliffs, Santa Clara Pueblo, and Chimayó. I actually spent time with members of the Naranjo family, and they showed me some of their pottery. A special day, but I kept wondering what was going on in camp and how various individual stories would turn out. I'm glad that S. and K. are coming in to meet me for dinner tonight. I'll get some gossip, feel a bit more anchored. I have one more day to look around—Taos tomorrow—and then it's back to home, back to routine, to being me, whatever that means.

PART THREE

Beginnings

CHAPTER 4

Affiliation

his chapter moves from the national to the local level, and from the Southwest to the East Coast. It introduces women who have lived in the Washington, D.C., community, one of the older and larger 3HO ashrams. Many of the Washington residents have been in 3HO since the earliest years, so their biographies reflect many of the transformations that 3HO as a whole has experienced. Of course, each ashram has its own distinctive characteristics (Washington, for example, is said to have a family orientation), so there are idiosyncratic elements to the Washington accounts.

The women's accounts are an important source of information concerning organizational history, and their stories provide insights into the original nature and appeal of 3HO life. But it is important to remember that these are after-the-fact accounts, and it would be naïve to assume that they have not been shaped by subsequent events and by current concerns and organizational priorities. They are part of a work in progress, part of the ongoing elaboration of identity.

The reader should know that several of the women whose stories appear here have left 3HO since their original interviews. While the factual content of their accounts would not change, some of their interpretations certainly would if they were reinterviewed today. Nonetheless, I have chosen to retain their original responses as accounts of affiliation told from a member's vantage point. I want to capture a way of thinking and a point in time and sensibility rather than overlay the original accounts with years of experience and reinterpretation. Instead, the altered voices of the leavers will be heard in a later chapter.

The Washington ashram was founded in 1969. From the beginning there was a structure to everyday life, but the tone of things was relatively informal in the first years. Residents assembled for yoga and meditation early in the morning, followed by a light breakfast and housework, then they left for their daily jobs. In the evening there was another vegetarian meal and a yoga class. The class was open to the public, and it expanded as people brought their friends and house mates. "It was, I think, one thing that really made people feel that they were a part of a community growing," one woman remembered. "The class ended at about 7:45, but the last person sometimes didn't go home until 9:30. We all used to just hang out and talk or sing. A local band that was really well-known came to a lot of the classes" (personal communication, Sept. 5, 1985).

By 1972 the Ahimsa Ashram in the Dupont Circle area was quite crowded, with thirty to thirty-five people in residence, the women housed upstairs and the men in the basement. A room that was later converted into a comfortable book-lined office then housed six women, and each of them was assigned half of a chest of drawers, a small bookcase, and one level of a bunk bed. There were jokes about people getting married to escape the crowded conditions. But although people had few belongings and little space, most residents recall the early days fondly, nostalgically remembering camaraderie and pleasure in the new life-style. In time there were five 3HO houses in the Dupont Circle area.

In 1972, the community opened a vegetarian restaurant called the Golden Temple. The men of the ashram did all of the work necessary to convert what had been a shop into a restaurant, and it opened in May. Legally, it was a partnership of about ten couples. It paid for workers' rent and for day-to-day needs. Emotionally, it was a home away from home and an important site for the elaboration of a collective identity. Almost all of the ashram residents were employed there, some working very long hours. Many have happy memories of that time, as does this woman: "Oh, it was just delightful. . . . Most of the people who moved in at that time were about my age—we were in our early twenties or very late teens. So we were young and energetic and lively, and we really centered our life around that restaurant. . . . [T]he work was hard, but we made it into fun. You were with your friends all the time."

Another woman mentioned the opportunities to learn job skills, as well as the cohesiveness fostered by shared work: "I did everything. I was a hostess. I was a waitress. I worked on the cash register. You know, if you were together enough to handle anything you got to do it. . . . It was great. Though I don't think we always realized it, it really brought us so close together; it really made us a family."

Not everybody worked at the restaurant, or at another "family business" such as the Shakti Shoe Corporation. A few people pursued separate careers, but in the early years they were clearly swimming against the tide. Here one woman describes what it was like to maintain a more separate existence: "They would ask me, 'How can you stand to work out there?' And it was kind of like everybody in the outside world had horns and claws and they were out to get me. And there was a lot of peer pressure, that kind of thing: 'Isn't it awful? Don't you miss being with us? We miss having you here.'"

Throughout this early period, much energy was devoted to mastering meditation, yoga, vegetarian cooking, and, soon, Sikhism. Ashram life was absorbing, and it usually overlapped with employment. People were young and enthusiastic about their new lives.

The Members

Backgrounds

The women reported family backgrounds consistent with the profiles of other devotees who joined the Eastern new religions. They were from predominantly white, middle-class families, mostly intact. Their parents were disproportionately Jewish (see Richardson 1986; Goldman 1999), and many were Catholic. In 1968, on the eve of 3HO's founding, 2.9 percent of the United States population was Jewish (Glazer 1972, 161). By 1985, when I had completed my first series of interviews, only 2 percent of the U.S. population was Jewish (Roof and McKinney 1987, 16), while 27 percent of my sample reported that their background was Jewish. Given that the ashram is on the East Coast and that a contingent of residents had moved to Washington from New York, one might reasonably expect a higher Jewish representation than in other parts of the country, but in New York state in 1983 the Jewish population was only 10.6 percent (Feldstein 1984), so the 3HO percentage is still double what one might expect. One-third of the sample reported that they came from Roman Catholic families. This too is somewhat above the national norm, but not dramatically so. In 1965, 25 percent of the nation was Roman Catholic (Greeley 1990, 309), and in 1985, close to the time of the interviews, 28 percent of the population was Catholic (Roof and McKinney 1987, 16). Goldman (1999) reports similar findings, with 20 percent of the sannyansins who followed Bhagwan Shree Rajneesh reporting (in 1983) a Jewish background and

27 percent reporting a Catholic background. As Goldman notes, mainline religions were losing young members at the time that the new religions arose and grew. Reform and conservative Jewish congregations were experiencing losses. While Roman Catholics increased in overall numbers at this time, the increase was due to birth rates and immigration, and there was some loss of members and a decrease in involvement (1999, 228). The new religions were among the recipients of disaffected young people, and these groups were evidently able to deliver a more satisfying form of spirituality than the religions that converts encountered in their childhood homes.

Most of the women reported that they had some college education, approximately 40 percent having completed two years of college and 26 percent having completed four years. There were, in addition, two nursing degrees and two graduate degrees. This is above the national average in the 1970s. A good source of comparative data, although the cohort is somewhat younger than the founding members of 3HO, is a longitudinal study of the high school class of 1972. In that class, 50.5 percent of white females enrolled in college, but by 1976, only 17.6 percent of white females had a bachelor of arts degree and 12.4 percent were current undergraduates (Eckland and Henderson 1981). By 1979, 23 percent had a baccalaureate degree, and 15 percent had two or more years of college (Burkheimer and Novak 1981).

Their average age at affiliation (either moving into an ashram or deciding to make 3H0/Sikh Dharma a way of life) was twenty-four. Members were typically single upon entry. Their involvement was likely to begin with attendance at a yoga class, and that class came to their attention through public advertising or via a friend or sibling already involved in 3HO life. The yoga classes were typically sponsored by the continuing education division of a college, by an "open university," or by a 3HO ashram.

I conducted an extensive series of interviews between 1984 and 1986, and most of the women appearing in this chapter were first interviewed during that time period. Since then, seven of the women interviewed have exited 3HO/Sikh Dharma, and one has formalized her vows. I conducted follow-up interviews with most of the original subjects, and with additional women members, between 1994 and 1996.

Over two-thirds of the women reported that they had at least some involvement with the counterculture during the 1960s and 1970s. Most said that they had not been politically active, although they may have been critical of particular social institutions and of American involvement in Vietnam. While many followed rock groups and smoked marijuana, they made it clear that reading about and considering alternative life-styles and world views was equally important to them. "[W]e were definitely hippies," said one woman, describing herself and her high school friends, "but we were definitely *smart* hippies. We knew where it was at. . . . [We] read all the books." Another characterized herself as a "productive hippie," pointing out that she was usefully employed while she experimented with the hip life-style.

While many had experimented with hallucinatory drugs, only a minority (six) of the women cited the inspiration of a psychedelic vision or a drug-induced restructuring of their cognitive worlds when asked about reasons for joining 3HO. For that minority, however, these experiences were pivotal. The following is a nice rendering of one such event, an LSD-inspired vision which one informant wrote out for me: "I remember experiencing visually the energies of time and space. But my own being or consciousness, I felt, was boxed in into one small cube of massive energy, as if consciousness itself . . . was a massive warehouse of boxes of energies and I was enclosed within one of them. It felt very constraining. Time and space were moving forces, pictured somewhat like the color streams of a vivid rainbow, and I wanted so badly to push out of my box onto those etheric streams." 3HO technology became her means of breaking free and diving into those streams.

Reasons for Joining

Ashram residents are happy to recount their 3HO histories and to recall the early years of their involvement. Their narratives typically mingle shared collective explanations for involvement and affiliation with more personalized accounts. Among the shared elements are these frequently occurring themes.

The Appeal of Sadhana and of Kundalini Yoga

The transformative power of *sadhana* and of Kundalini yoga is a given in 3HO. Even the occasional woman who admits to not much liking yoga will assign it a significant place in her biography. Yoga and meditation are viewed as the grounding for a clearer sense of self and as the starting point in a new way of life. Many women say that early yoga classes and solstice celebrations induced a crystallized awareness of self—moments of clarity and joy when depressions, preoccupations, and habitual affect were altered. Others emphasize an intuition that yoga and meditation could provide a way of gaining greater control over their thoughts, emotions, and patterns of behavior:

I remember my first couple of yoga classes, being really awed that by doing a couple of hours of yoga and meditation my whole sense of reality was altered. Things that had seemed important seemed very lightweight. My sense of confidence was enhanced. My sense of my own depth was much more clear. I mean changes began right away, and they continue.

It was very hard. I was in terrible shape and it was terribly painful. But there was something. I began to fall asleep in all my [college] classes. I got kicked out of a bunch of classes. But one day I was walking to school and I realized, "My God I've been singing out loud at the top of my lungs and I didn't realize it. I'm happy."

Practicing a Spiritual Discipline and Living One's Convictions

Several women spoke of this discipline as the natural next step after experiencing the effects of yoga:

Respondent A: I decided to attend a big yoga festival, the summer solstice, and I went to that, and that convinced me that spending my time learning how to do the disciplines that affected my consciousness and my awareness and my sense of self and the universe was the most important priority I had. So I decided to join a community where that was the main focus. . . . The most rewarding thing has been committing myself to a discipline that is designed to awaken the consciousness, clear the mind.

Respondent B: At first you're interested by the yoga and the power it has and the way it makes you feel, and the kundalini yoga develops the spiritual side in you. . . . [T]hen you become very interested in the meditation and the diets . . . and after that you can get into the Gurmukhi, the prayers . . . you realize that all the tools are very useful. . . . [I]t's following a certain discipline.

Perhaps this theme is best summarized in the following quotation:

I like the community support. . . . I like the family aspect of it. I feel like the members of the community are like-minded to me. They're interested in growth. They're interested in living a clean life. They're interested in spirituality. . . . I like the steadiness of the community, having spiritual practices every day. . . . There's a happiness and freedom that comes with this: the freedom of making a choice to be this way, and a freedom to be able to delve into spiritual life and knowing that it's always there, available.

The Aesthetic Appeal and Its Congruence with Previous Interests

Respondent A: I was interested in language and music. Music has always been what I studied. Those two things are a lot integrated into this way of life.

Respondent B: You get to a point where you want to take those vows. It's like a marriage. It's that beautiful. . . . I was always looking for beauty in life, and now I've found it.

Respondent C: I got into Sikh Dharma through sound. I'm very auditory. . . . [T]he sound current, the beauty of the reading, . . . I love the poetry. I love to hear it. . . . I'd hear *gurbani*, I'd hear the *kirtan*, I'd be able to sing. And it was just like, this is it, this is where I belong.

Escaping a Hypocritical, Unhealthy, or Unsatisfying Way of Life

Respondent A: Somehow I reached the end of my hippie drug phase. I thought I was going to go crazy if I didn't get away or get a change from that. . . . I picked up the phone book and I looked up "yoga" and happened to call "3HO Integrative Yoga" and their hours fitted my schedule.

Respondent B: I just sort of didn't like what I was seeing. . . . [P]eople weren't honest, they weren't direct, and they were lower consciousness. Their motives weren't pure.

Respondent C: Very early I was very disappointed by what I would see in society. . . . [A] lot of lies and cheating and hypocrisy and all that. . . . It's almost like I couldn't believe in that society, . . . and I didn't want to become like what I would see.

Gender Issues Figure in the Women's Accounts, but Are Not Often Prominent

Quite a few of the women mentioned predatory sexual relations outside of 3HO and the relief they experienced on escaping these when they joined the organization. Thus the woman quoted directly above continued: "Basically, when you met men the motives were just to get you. I'm sure it wasn't one hundred per cent that way, but that was what I was experiencing."

Another woman told a harsher tale: "I was married to a very sick man and he used to beat me and stuff. . . . I wanted to be celibate after I left him because I'd been so abused. . . . I was really looking for something that related from the heart and that's what I felt like living in the ashram—there was so much love there."

It is notable that approximately one-quarter of the women interviewed mentioned that at the time of their affiliation they were dissolving, or had recently exited from, significant relationships. Thus 3HO offered them a haven, companionship, and a new approach to gender relations.

Many of my interviewees mentioned Bhajan's teachings on women and how important these were to them, but the teachings are not often mentioned as a reason for affiliation. This may be partly a matter of history. Organizational gender ideology was not in place when the earliest recruits joined 3HO. It was elaborated throughout the 1970s and became central with the establishment of the Khalsa Women's Training Camp in 1975–76.

If one takes them at face value, my findings contrast somewhat with studies of women choosing to join Orthodox Jewish, as well as fundamentalist and charismatic Christian, communities. Those studies indicate that much of the appeal of such groups to women lies in their support of strong families and traditional gender roles which, given the feminization of poverty, the high divorce rate, and the isolation of many single women, is perceived as advantageous by the women members (Ammerman 1987, Davidman 1990, Rose 1987). These things certainly matter to 3HO women, but they are seldom cited as primary or conscious reasons for affiliation.

And my results are not quite congruent with those of Aidala (1985) who found that women in religious communes tend to be "confused and uncertain about traditional gender identities," and that the extensive instructions on gender role performance that these groups provide for their members is a major source of their appeal. Again, such things matter to 3HO members, but they do not seem to inspire affiliation. I think one of my informants expressed a not uncommon point of view when I asked her directly about the role of gender issues in her decision to live in an ashram: "I think it's [gender] just one piece of a larger discontentment . . . people treating each other in disrespectful, degrading, and objectifying ways. . . . [T]hat's what I wanted to get out of."

A Continuum

Members' original motivations and explanations for joining appear to fall along a continuum. At one end are accounts that emphasize alienation from American society and its conventions. Members presenting these accounts stress a youthful feeling that their lives were circumscribed and mundane, and they describe a parallel yearning for beauty and transcendence. They are likely to emphasize the experiential aspects of their awakening: drug experiences, the effects of meditation, their feelings and intuitions. Often they describe identity confusion or uncertainty, and affiliation with 3HO is tied to identity transformation. They may mention the aesthetic appeal of organizational practices.

At the other end of the continuum are accounts emphasizing practical reasons for becoming involved with 3HO, such as career considerations, housing requirements, or financial problems. There is less emphasis on previous pain and discontent and more on the positive benefits anticipated.

Expressive and Pragmatic Reasons for Affiliation

In placing these accounts on such a continuum I am borrowing from Tipton's (1982) comparison of the "expressive" ethic of the counterculture to more conventional, rational, and "utilitarian" modes of evaluating action.

The expressive ethic corresponds to the counterculture ethos which has already been discussed (chapter 2). The person who employs the expressive style values ecstatic experience, whether derived from drugs, music, or meditation. This individual assumes that knowledge is, in the final analysis, experiential and intuitive. She favors an accepting stance toward people and nature; they are there to be appreciated, not to be used or improved upon. The expressive individual favors a holistic approach to the world and to the self. Relationships, ideally, are not fragmented or role-bound.

The utilitarian, on the other hand, favors the use of technical reason to know and to manipulate the world, depending upon such strategies as standardization, sequencing, establishing jurisdiction, and instituting routine procedures. The utilitarian perspective emphasizes "analytic discrimination," and the utilitarian tends to view the world as a place of discontinuous social settings and partial relationships. She accepts these discontinuities and meets the world with the stance of "problem-solving activism."

The responses at one end of the 3HO continuum correspond roughly to Tipton's expressive style, those at the other end to the utilitarian. Thus, at one end, there are accounts emphasizing intuitive experience, the appeal of meditation and the "highs" it produces, and an intense desire to ease a tension between the self and society. At the other end are accounts emphasizing the individual's problem-solving approach to her own needs, the role of practical reasoning in her decision to affiliate, and a step-by-step approach to membership. Personal and career goals, individualism, and the appeal of yoga as a "technology" are more frequently mentioned.

As one might expect, given members' backgrounds, more accounts fall at the expressive end of the continuum than at the utilitarian pole, but as 3HO encourages a balance between the two approaches and appeals to both ways of thinking, both are well represented. Based on this continuum, I have divided the members' accounts into three groups: (1) intense seekers and intuitive joiners, (2) pragmatic seekers, and (3) convenience joiners (see table).

Intense Seekers and Intuitive Joiners

For the intense seekers, affiliation was proceeded by a period of deep longing and much discomfort. The women in this category experienced themselves as different from their families and their peers, as more

MEMBERS CATEGORIZED BY REASONS FOR AFfiLIATING WITH 3HO/SIKH DHARMA		
Intense Seekers/ Intuitive Joiners	Pragmatic Seekers	Convenience Joiners
Expressive Accounts	Utilitarian Accounts	
Express longing, discomfort, alienation from conventional ways of living	Emphasize practical considerations	
Decision making is often intuitive	Speak more about personal volition and planning	
Refer to the individual's path	Often talk about roles in 3HO and about career plans	

SOURCE: Based on Tipton 1982.

intense, thoughtful, and needy. Their accounts suggest an emergent self which was set against the social structure as it was experienced at home, at school, and through the media. This self could not, or would not, be poured into available social roles and secular terms, and there was a sense that it should not have to participate in the antics of self-presentation or accept routinization as an inevitable aspect of life. There was a hunger for transcendence or for expression of the emergent self—for a way of defining it, a path for it to pursue, even for knowledge of the terms that a dialectic between this self and the social world might entail. Several of these women were looking for a new start. The following quotations are typical:

> *Respondent A:* I was very different from other people in my family. I was just different; I felt very different. And I had a tremendous longing and a tremendous emptiness that other people around me didn't feel the need to fill.

> *Respondent B:* I was so ardently longing for something, and I'd already tried all sorts of things to satisfy the longing and they hadn't worked. You know, I'd tried diving into certain political activities and relationships and this and that. . . . I can translate it in various forms throughout my life as always playing hard, working hard, trying hard—hard, hard, hard. Always wanting to get the most out of things, always concerned that I'd be missing out on something—that kind of personality.

Similar, but more experimental and more free-spirited, is a subgroup that I will call "intuitives." They too may have been searching for something, but they seem to have taken almost as much pleasure in the search as in the finding. When they settled upon 3HO it was often because the community and the yoga "felt right." They appear to have been motivated less by a need for channeled self-expression than by a desire to find an accepting, caring community. They emphasize their attraction to the people in the ashram, as well as the good feelings associated with yoga and meditation. The emphasis is on the positive things they found, even on the surprise of this, rather than on their previous longing:

> I was basically looking for a community of people who I could share ideals with and live with in a way that was more meaningful to me. . . . I wasn't looking for *this* necessarily—I was pretty open to whatever came my

way. . . . I was real happy and I'd been happy. I always felt like my growing up years were happy. . . . [T]he whole hippie movement started and it seemed like those people had something that I didn't have. That was the first time I ever thought of myself as missing out on something, that there was something more. . . . [S]o then I started reading. . . . [I]t was a consciousness, and an understanding of what God meant.

These women are particularly likely to attribute their affiliation to destiny and to speak of having found "my place" and "my teacher," as in the following quotation: "I feel like it was my destiny to meet my spiritual teacher in this lifetime and be on a spiritual path in a hundred per cent committed way, and it made me different. . . . I feel like this is my destiny and I can't abandon it now that I know it."

Pragmatic Seekers

Midway between the intense seekers and the convenience joiners are the pragmatic seekers. They approached 3HO, or other Eastern disciplines, more slowly, proceeding stage by stage and becoming in this process further estranged from the "straight" world. Many of the women who fall into this category felt that the life-styles they encountered at college or at work were too impersonal or unhealthy, and that the people they met were too callous or self-indulgent. Several had done some spiritual shopping and had explored various forms of diet, yoga, and alternative beliefs. They assessed 3HO in fairly practical terms, asking how it could further their personal goals. The following are typical comments from this group:

> *Respondent A:* I used to go upstate a lot with my parents and we'd always see these people driving around with deer on their hoods. . . . I just thought about it a lot and eventually turned vegetarian. . . . I went to college. . . . There was a lot of hanging out in bars. I just didn't like what people were into and so I found the ashram—people doing yoga, and I was already vegetarian.

> *Respondent B:* I started reading these health books. . . . [A]t the same time I started, you know, thinking about what I was doing in the hospital. I didn't like it anymore: giving out pills, giving shots, having people have surgery. . . . So anyway, I took my summer vacation

and went to the homeopathic school. . . . [A]nd when I got there there were two Sikhs taking the course. . . . And before this I had also been reading books a little bit on communes and things like that, like *Twin Oaks* was one, so I was thinking about things like that. . . . So I saw the two Sikhs and went up and said "hello," and they said they were camping out and were going to do yoga every morning. And I said, "Well, I do yoga." . . . [S]o I camped out with them and did what they did.

Convenience Joiners

Finally, there are the convenience joiners. They emphasize considerations such as needing a place to live, taking advantage of business opportunities, or joining because a spouse joined. Convenience joiners, in many cases, had contact with the counterculture or with esoteric disciplines but probably would not have joined 3HO if it weren't for practical considerations or for Yogi Bhajan's special efforts to recruit them. The following are two comments from this group:

> *Respondent A:* I was not looking for anything. . . . I would have been a yuppie. I was into [my husband] being a professional and working in this company that was based in London so we got to go to London for conferences and stuff, and the kids going to private schools. . . . But I also was aware of the fact that something was amiss, and what was amiss was my husband. There was something that wasn't clicking right with him. . . . [A]nd when I saw that [3HO] was working . . . and he felt so strongly about it, and since I didn't feel strongly about it one way or another, I decided, "why not."

> *Respondent B:* He [Bhajan] asked me to work with him: "I'll make you a good businesswoman. I want to be proud of you. I want strong women and graceful women." . . . So I just said "OK." I agreed to it. It's pretty hard to disagree with the Siri Singh Sahib.

These three explanatory modes not only inform members' accounts of affiliation but also tend to persist in individuals' descriptions of the later stages of their lives. Throughout their spiritual lives, the intense seekers and intuitive joiners continue to talk about feelings and intuitions, as well as about their path or their destiny. They often focus on end states such becoming a saint, experiencing transcendence, or, as one woman put it, "going into the bliss." The women who fall closer to the middle point on the continuum appear to be more present and task-oriented. They focus on the satisfactions of their family, community, and work lives and speak less of emotional ups and downs. They mention concrete aspects of personal growth and evolution, mentioning such 3HO-endorsed accomplishments as learning how to better live with and help others, becoming more "centered," confident, or mature, and gaining specific skills. They speak of their spirituality as one among many aspects of their lives, and they sometimes separate the stages of their spiritual evolution from the unfolding of their careers or from the biological and parental stages they have encountered.

The pragmatists are particularly likely to report that they have selectively experimented with 3HO practices and beliefs and have consciously decided which aspects of organizational life to embrace and which to downplay or avoid. They have looked for points of contact where their beliefs and interests intersect with those of the collective. Where they find these points they readily embrace disciplines and concepts. When they cannot find a shared perspective they may try out ("stand under") various practices. They will then decide whether a belief or practice "works" or is potentially useful. They seem to make a conscious effort to believe and behave in ways that enable them to belong and to participate in the common discourse, but they may also hold back in some ways.

The remainder of this chapter consists of individual narratives. They exemplify the themes and categories discussed so far, and they should add life to the bare bones of the analytic categories.

Examples: Members' Accounts of Affiliation
Intense Seekers and Intuitive Joiners

A.'s living room has the usual off-white sofa and carpeting, but her personal imprint is everywhere: in touches of lavender, pink, and purple, in floral arrangements, and in softly colored cushions. The room speaks of beauty and peace, and she belongs within it, a calm, pretty, soft-spoken and gentle woman, but a person with presence and will. She was previously quoted as saying that she had always looked for beauty in life and had generally been disappointed. She is young, married, and of Catholic background: "So, very early I had that pure side in me and I wanted to cultivate that pure side. . . . I suffered very much for it, from feeling different and not finding what I was looking for, not being able to totally mingle with society. I've always been a kind person, but I was also a fighter. . . . I was ready to really go all the way to find what I was looking for, to fight against all the conventions so that I could really find the truth."

She had hippie friends, and some of them shared the counterculture's fascination with the East. At twenty she had the opportunity to travel there:

> The first place I arrived in India was Amritsar, and I'd never heard of the Sikhs. . . . But the first place I went in Amritsar was the Golden Temple, and it was very beautiful. So I stayed there about a week to ten days, and every day I would go there and I would do what the Indians did. I would follow and do the same thing: wash your feet, wash your hands, drink some of the holy water and go to the Siri Guru Granth Sahib. . . . I found myself praying there and I was very surprised. . . . [I]t was when I became aware of my faith. So that was the beginning. But then after that I kept going through changes, and I kept traveling in India for four months and I was not particularly religious; I just went on with my normal life. And after four months, it's like I became spiritual[,] . . . totally imbued with God. . . . [T]hen I knew that what I wanted in life was to lead a spiritual way of life and be with spiritual people. Then I went back home, . . . and I went through a hard winter because nobody could really understand me anymore. . . . I was very lonely, and I didn't have a specific path either.

She prayed for guidance or a sign. "[A] few minutes later," she remembers, "I went in the underground, the subway, and in the middle of the crowd I saw like a light and it was a lady. She was wearing white, and she had a turban, and she was very radiant, that's why I saw her like a light. . . . It was like I knew right away she was the answer to my prayer."

She approached the woman, who was a member of 3HO. The woman was happy to talk with her and, in fact, invited her to participate in spiritual activities. Soon A. was doing yoga with a group of 3HO members: "As soon as I started this yoga it was amazing. It was like all the tensions were going away. It was like I experienced a new life with them. And then more and more there was nowhere else to be. . . . So

that's how it started. The nicest thing is that I've found my answers. . . .
I thought what I had in my head was a dream, this dream of beauty and
goodness. It is possible, you know. You have to work on it, but it does
exist and there are a lot of beautiful souls. I've found my way; I've found
my answers."

B. is older than the previous speaker and has left the group since
this interview. She is the product of an upper to upper-middle-class
home, and she, like the previous woman, found her family's life-style
unsatisfactory. She reads the biographies of mystics, being herself
inclined toward mysticism. Motherhood has been one of her greatest
satisfactions:

> My parents were very intellectual, and they often
> talked about other people in a kind of gossipy way, and
> very into politics. I remember, as a child, at the dining
> room table I was just not interested, and I would look
> out the window and go off in my own mind, watching
> the squirrels, the wind in the trees. . . . I always felt that
> I was supposed to play their game, and I tried for
> awhile. I tried to do everything I could to get the emo-
> tional strokes I needed—until I was seventeen. I was
> Dean's List at a small girls' private school, and had
> early admissions at Vassar. . . . [A]nd I was miserable.

When she started college she began to deviate from the route that
had been laid out for her. She could not make herself care about obtaining high grades or pursing any particular intellectual discipline,
although she did care, and deeply, about finding truth. She began to use
marijuana, and later she experimented with LSD. She used both in
order to explore the nature of consciousness:

> I found it fascinating. I didn't use it socially or frivo-
> lously; I used it to go into my own head. I was very
> interested that there was a whole world in there and
> that I had access to it. . . . It was sometimes like being
> in the center of the universe and seeing creation unfold
> before my eyes. . . . It was like going to the source
> where every idea and every form and shape and color is
> stored. . . . [I]t was total bliss. I would just sit with my
> spine absolutely straight, having these visions, feeling
> just immersed in what years later I would call God—at
> the time I never used the word God because "God" was

associated with all the hypocrisy and exclusiveness of the church. We used the term "white light." . . . [I]t was a sense of feeling cared for, and love, absolute love.

She married and dropped out of college. Then she also left the United States because her husband actively opposed the Vietnam War and risked jail if he remained. Together they continued to use drugs experimentally; in fact, her husband founded a group based on the use of LSD. She used LSD as a catalyst for religious experience. Soon she was expecting a child, and pregnancy and childbirth heightened her emerging awareness of a spiritual order:

> I was just beginning to get an awareness that there was something that understood what was going on, and *that* was the energy that was making this baby grow and was going to carry me through the birth. . . . I realized how absolutely immaculate a baby is, and I realized how every single thing I thought made a difference. . . . I mean every vibration—infants are so absorbent. I thought, "If I don't clear up the confusion and neuroses in my mind, my child's going to suffer the way I have." . . . So I became very directed towards finding a spiritual path.

Her husband did not share her spiritual preoccupations, however:

> So I started spending more and more time by myself. . . . It was as though I'd walked through a veil, and I kept thinking he would come along because we'd been through so much together, but he didn't. We returned to this country to check out the whole hippie communal thing and got a VW van. I lay in the back reading *The Aquarian Gospel of Jesus the Christ* and taking care of our child while he drove. . . . We visited a lot of communes—I was ready to settle in everywhere, but he wasn't, and we ended up buying some land and trying to start our own thing.

She happened to attend a 3HO-sponsored yoga class near their property and became convinced that "all the beautiful experiences of drugs were available through this technique." This soon led to participation in a 3HO solstice ceremony and the crystallization and confirmation of a new identity:

> [B]y the end of that solstice . . . I realized that I was divorced from my husband—not legally, but energetically. I really wept a lot. It was just as though the past had just gone, and the only identity that I could relate to was that I was the daughter of Yogi Bhajan. And I really trusted him. I talked with him during that solstice. . . . He just talked to me about how if a mother doesn't respect herself she'll destroy her child, no matter how much she thinks she loves him. If she doesn't respect herself and he comes through her, how can he respect himself? I felt that he heard what I was saying, he understood, and he gave me practical advice. Plus he saw beauty and nobility in me that I didn't even know existed, but he did, and I trusted him.

She moved back to her family home and attended 3HO events in that area. One day, she says, "I asked Yogiji if I should go to India with him—he was leading a group over to India that winter—and he said, "Why not?" And I couldn't think of 'why not,' so I went and I started living in the ashram. I ended out sending off legal papers for divorce from my husband the day my son and I left for India."

C. also tells of an unhappy childhood, although her origins were less affluent and her troubles and her responsibilities were greater. Like the two previous speakers, she came to 3HO at a time of identity change. Like other intuitive joiners she was actively looking for a community and a path that would affirm her emerging sense of self. The appeal of a caring community was central to her decision:

> I was the oldest of five. My mother was mentally ill. My father was really weird. So I just wanted to get out as quickly as I could, and I got involved with some very wild people, and I started doing drugs when I was very young. . . . I just did psychedelics and smoking and stuff, but for me when I did trip it was like I was looking. I always knew there was something that I was looking for, and I remember when I was little I used to pray a lot, and I always felt really close to Jesus and Mary and some of the saints, and I used to just pray and pray.

She practically raised her younger brothers and sisters single-handedly. Then, in her eagerness to get away from home, she became a singer in a rock band and became involved with the band's drummer, a decision she soon regretted because he proved abusive. She found help through a feminist women's clinic: "I lived in the middle of downtown. . . . We were very poor; we didn't have any money or anything. I used to go up there and talk to the women, and they really supported me a lot. They supported me and they told me I could leave him, and they really helped me to figure out how to do it." When her son was a year old she left her husband and returned to her parents' home. Soon after this she became disillusioned with the women's movement: "I was very involved in the women's movement, and I was very disillusioned with it. I felt like everyone, all the women around me, were turning gay. It was like I just couldn't relate to it at all."

Asked to describe herself as she was then, she replied, "I wasn't very strong, and I didn't know who I was because I could be influenced very easily. I was longing to belong, and I was tired. I was really looking for something. . . . I was really looking for something that related from the heart."

A friend invited her to attend 3HO yoga classes, and she was instantly attracted by what she saw:

> The people were so beautiful. . . . Something inside me clicked, and I started going every night. I remember walking around the ashram that night, and my friend was showing me all the different rooms, and not many people were living there. I was in this one room and said, "Oh wow, I'm going to be living in this room," . . . and by January I had moved into the ashram. . . . I felt like living in the ashram there was so much love there. It was genuine, giving, and that's what really kept me there. . . . Right away it affected my self-esteem; plus doing the yoga twice a day I started feeling so much stronger in myself that I just kept growing really quickly.

Pragmatic Seekers

D. is a nurse. Her choice of 3HO membership was entwined from the beginning with her career and her determination to pursue alternative medicine. She has now left 3HO/Sikh Dharma, but she has persevered in her occupational choice. She was previously introduced; she is the woman who first encountered Sikhs when she attended a course on homeopathic healing: "I was a registered nurse, . . . and I started reading alternative health books. . . . [A]nd I started changing my life-style and going off to the health food store. . . . Now when we would go to a bar I'd get an orange juice and a grilled cheese . . . just because of my health. I was still doing drugs and things like that that were just the normal cultural thing. I did marijuana mainly, and, every so often, hash. I started doing drugs around sixteen or seventeen."

She befriended the Sikhs she met at the homeopathy course and began to take yoga classes with them. At the same time, she decided to resign her hospital job, and following her resignation, she lived on unemployment benefits for awhile. She decided she liked the Sikhs and their way of life and asked to move into the ashram. After the waiting period that 3HO often imposes, she did. She worked in the restaurant

> 'cause I didn't want to work in a hospital anymore and I didn't know anywhere else to work. But I kept in touch with these [homeopathic] doctors that I had met and would go to their office and sit-in on their patients every so often. . . . Someone within the ashram was already doing homeopathy for the people, and that person was just about to leave for India, so I kind of stepped into his place. I liked the way they raised their children, and I was already doing yoga and meditation, so it was just more of that same thing. And Yogi Bhajan, the teacher, really had very little to do with my entrance.

E. combines elements of intuitive and pragmatic seeking. Her progress along a spiritual path has been gradual and progressive. She left college with no particular interest in things spiritual and began a professional life as an information specialist. She lived with other young professionals who were also quite secular in orientation. She was a political activist and, looking back, says that, until she developed her interest in Eastern religions, politics "had kind of been my religion."

Her life began to change when she became quite serious about a male friend and the two set up housekeeping together. Unlike her previous house mates, he was apolitical and had an interest in yoga and Eastern teachings. Now she began to explore these things as well. A friend signed her up for a yoga class at a city university, and the teacher happened to be from 3HO. She liked the class, and soon her interests expended. She began to read the yoga sutras and became curious about t'ai chi.

At this point Ronald Reagan was elected president, and both she and her partner disliked the new conservative atmosphere (her politics were left wing). They decided to leave the country for awhile and "ended up in Taiwan because I wanted to study t'ai chi. I got really interested in that all of a sudden." By the time they returned a year later she described herself as a yogi and was also immersed in the Bahagavad Gita. She reconnected with 3HO and even helped to establish a Kundalini yoga center. She met more 3HO people and "each year I got a little further in." She still had no intention of converting, however, and explored other religions as well.

She moved to the Washington area in the mid-1980s. The apartment she found was not immediately available, and so she lived at the Ahimsa Ashram while waiting for it. Bit by bit she became involved in the *sangat*, but she had no desire to live where most of her Sikh friends lived. Her work life and her interest in international affairs continued, and she attended graduate school; spirituality was one aspect of a busy life.

But her life began to change, and at this point in her narration she begins to sound more like an intuitive joiner as she stresses the experiential aspects of Sikh Dharma. After graduate school she found herself underemployed. Things were not going well with her boyfriend and, in general, she says, "I had some very very painful times." Following a Sikh Dharma practice she prayed to Guru Ram Dass and "found I could get stabilized just by calling on his energy."

At this point the *sangat* happened to do an intensive reading from the Granth Sahib and asked her to take part. The experience, she says, affected her. "I was really upset with my boyfriend, and it was so relevant to what I was reading. She was also touched by "the beauty of the reading, and of the sound current." She delved more deeply into the *nad* (sound current) and found great delight in it, in Gurmukhi, and in "the visuals" and the poetry of Sikh devotion. She has previously been quoted as saying that she came into 3HO "through sound," but actually the auditory and aesthetic experiences, although deeply satisfying, probably would not have been sufficient to induce her to make a formal commitment. The final push came when a friend in Florida called "out of the blue" to invite her to do *seva* (service) for Yogi Bhajan at the winter solstice gathering. "[W]hen I got back I had immediate withdrawals from wearing white every day (because all my office wear wasn't white) and I had immediate withdrawals from Yogi Bhajan. And that's when I just knew. . . . In June I took the Sikh vows at solstice."

When interviewed, F. was a comparatively new member and definitely a convenience joiner, albeit one who had had a long-term connection with 3HO and an off-and-on interest in spiritual matters. She is cautious and has taken affiliation one step at a time; she is also quite droll:

> Well, I guess it was 1968 while I was in college. I guess
> I started to become interested in the New Age and
> expanding my consciousness. . . . And when I consid-
> ered myself really being a hippie in consciousness and
> everything was when I started to travel. My girlfriend
> and I, who later went into the ashram, she and I started
> going traveling. And we were still college students just,
> you know, looking for long-haired guys, smoking mar-
> ijuana every once in awhile, and just having fun. . . . She
> just called me one summer and said, "Let's go." So we
> did, and packed up all the stuff in our car, had all our
> money, all our possessions, our tent, and the whole bit.

In the course of her travels she met people with an interest in things
spiritual, and she felt more comfortable with such concerns than with
the political activities that had absorbed many of her friends: "I'm not a
really political person, and when we started moving into more spiritual
and esoteric and farmy type things I started getting into that more."

She met the friend of a friend who was involved with 3HO, and
periodically after this she took yoga lessons and made contact with 3HO
(and other yoga groups) as she traveled around the country for the next
nine years: "So it's been in and out, but I never had any idea in my mind
that I was ever going to commit myself to being a Sikh or being in 3HO.
I had no interest whatsoever. Even when I moved in four years ago it
was only, sheerly, because of my financial situation. . . . Then, because I
wanted to get my spiritual life in shape, I started doing *sadhana*. I had no
intention of being a Sikh."

She moved into the ashram because she needed an affordable place
to live. She continued to plan further travel and to consider a variety of
possible careers, but she received an unexpected response from people
in the ashram:

> "How long have you been doing this?" And it made me
> start thinking, you know, and looking at my life. . . . I
> wanted to be a dancer, and I wanted to be a chiroprac-
> tor, and I wanted to be a this and a that, and, you know,
> what am I really looking for? I found the spiritual part
> of me, and then I started feeling I was at home. So
> every time I'd say, "I'm going to leave" because of this
> or that, they'd just say to me, "Well the door is open,
> but where are you going to go? What are you going to
> do? How about your spiritual life?"

She kept delaying her departures, deciding to "stay for another two months," until finally, "after about two years I said to myself, 'All right, if you're going to be here why don't you start doing some work on yourself instead of complaining, "oh, I'd rather do this or I'd rather do that."'" And she continues to extend her stay.

When I talked to her, G. had been interested in spiritual matters for a number of years, but before her contact with 3HO she had followed a spiritual teacher who practiced raja (mental) yoga. It was because of this teacher's suggestion that she do some physical yoga that she first attended one of Yogi Bhajan's classes. She came as a businesswoman who had traded in commodities since she was eighteen. She is single, poised, and independent, and, as she put it, "I can trade commodities and fly planes and all this kind of stuff, but I'm afraid of the kitchen." She was bored with her job when she first encountered 3HO. Bhajan accused her then of a lack of occupational commitment, and she says that he was correct. Hers is clearly a case of recruitment by Yogi Bhajan. Here she describes her first impression of him (at a white Tantric yoga class):

> I'd never seen a yogi in action, and it was pretty amaz-
> ing with the fruit and the pillows and all the people
> were touching his feet and everything. It was just
> amazing to see that, and I'm sure my curiosity was
> blasting out. So he called me up on stage. . . . So I went
> up on stage and he asked me all these questions, and he
> was so charismatic, and his energy was just so neat and
> warm and wonderful to be around. . . . I got this really
> high feeling. . . . Being around him I felt like I was
> drunk or something—goofy. . . . We had the second
> part of the Tantra, and then at the end again I was just
> watching everything, . . . and he yelled over from really
> far away, "Invite her to the party."

She attended the gathering that was held after the class, and thus began her association with 3HO. Yogi Bhajan's interest in her continued and she was courted, and sometimes pressured. "He was really being firm with me," she remembers. "He wasn't being Joe Happy. So every-day I would talk to him, and he would say a lot of stuff to me about just being committed to something, and working, and having a career, and, 'what are you going to do with your life?' . . . He made me start to cry because he was really giving me a hard time about my job experiences. . . . He kept saying, 'Trust me and trust yourself.' And he asked me to work with him." Her affiliation with the 3HO businesses did not last long, however, and she moved on. I was not able to contact her and learn about the circumstances surrounding her departure.

While its original appeal appears to have been primarily to counterculture women, 3HO always appealed to people with a range of outlooks. The impetus to expand and legitimate the organization led to the incorporation of utilitarian points of view, and I have the impression that this was accompanied by an effort to attract women with a greater variety of talents and personality types. Increasingly, 3HO became an ideological umbrella that could shelter women with varying motivations and needs. There was little room for the political or feminist activist unless she reinterpreted her beliefs in a more spiritual or psychological form, but 3HO could serve a variety of needs. The ideologies developed by social movements are often ambiguous and thus flexible (Gerlach and Hine 1970). This leaves room for individual interpretations of various tenets and for their adaptation to changing economic and political realities. Such was the case with 3HO. It brought a cross-section of women into the organization, and these women have contributed to, and made sense of, the organization in their own distinctive ways.

The Washington Ashram: Beginnings

When she heard that another yoga student was going back to the East Coast to open an ashram in Washington, S. Kaur was interested, and she told Yogi Bhajan that she wanted to go too. Bhajan never really officially sanctioned her going, but neither did he discourage it. So when it was time for the other student to go, S. packed a bag and left with him. She and her companion arrived in Washington in October 1969. They had to make most of their arrangements ad hoc, and, fortunately, another 3HO member who had friends in the Washington area found S. a place to stay.

At the time, Bhajan was on his first teaching tour. He had gone to New York and, after speaking there, was planning to turn south and visit Washington. Publicity and preparations for his talk fell to S. She put up posters and was pleased when twenty people attended Bhajan's lecture. She had cleared her first hurdle but was still faced with the daunting task of establishing an ashram.

On November 15, the antiwar movement sponsored its mammoth Mobilization in Washington. S. attended the march, settling in near the Lincoln Memorial. At one point she began to repeat the 3HO mantra, *ek ong kar*. When she looked up, she found herself surrounded by a curious, but friendly, group of people. She began to talk with them, explaining her life-style and describing Yogi Bhajan. Later, some of these new acquaintances offered her a ride, and, as they drove through crowded streets, she told them about her desire to establish an ashram. She had spoken with the right people. They told her about a residence on Q Street, one of several communal facilities belonging to a group calling itself the Washington Free Community. Soon she was able to take over their lease, and after cleaning the building, painting the walls white, and sanding the floors, she renamed the house Ahimsa Ashram.

In spite of the changes S. made, some members of the resident hip community continued to live at the Ahimsa Ashram throughout the winter of 1969, but most elected to leave, and, slowly, beginning in the summer of 1970, the original residents were replaced by other, more spiritually inclined members of Washington's alternative community. An early resident believes that about twelve people moved in during the first year, and that by the fall of 1970, "the house had about fifteen solid members" (Khalsa 1984). Yoga classes were offered and publicized through contacts in Washington's counterculture community and via the distribution of flyers. Informal networks appear to have been an important source of students. The first classes were followed by a visit from Yogi Bhajan in December, when he taught some kundalini yoga classes, and shortly thereafter by the arrival of another yoga teacher sent from Los Angeles to become director of the ashram. He continued in that capacity until 1980.

Looking back, S. says, "I was just open." She feels that she was a channel, that God led her, that she was in tune with the times, and that all she needed to do was to let things happen.

CHAPTER 5

"Going through Changes": Interpreting and Adapting the Teachings

*I*n his introduction to a workshop that I attended, the leader asserted that "for most of us, 3HO is our first experience of real trust." And such trust, he noted, was a prerequisite to commitment. He went on to describe what he saw as a common phenomenon: Americans get caught up in a "self-esteem loop" in which self-worth becomes tied to tangible achievements, to doing things well. Life "becomes a scramble to always do it right." The end result, he warned, could be stasis, the self frozen in fear of failure. Here was where 3HO could be particularly helpful. Repeating, and believing, much-used 3HO affirmations, such as "God and me are one," could enable members to bypass the loop and the fears it generated. They could experience themselves as expressions of divinity and would no longer need to base self-esteem on others' judgments or on specific accomplishments. They could see the best in themselves and in others, and so begin to trust themselves and the world beyond.

The early members of 3HO were baby boomers, "the least trusting of all age groups toward social and political institutions," as Roof puts it (1993, 41). Without some degree of trust in the surrounding order it was difficult for them to settle into any established way of life. For many, there were no compelling social roles to give meaning to personal biography, and little in the way of social armature for the self or ego. Socially defined success was unappealing. Traditional roles and career paths did not beckon. Citizenship in the Vietnam era conferred little pride, and gender identities were increasingly subject to examination.

In such circumstances, 3HO seemed to offer particularly desirable resources: trust in self and leader and an acceptable place to strike roots and make commitments. For people who could not accept conventional identities, who saw little hope for constructing a meaningful life within mainstream settings, the organization represented a chance to move life forward on new terms. For those raised on constant demands for successful performance it offered new, and more acceptable, definitions of achievement. For those who could take no pride in their nationality, it offered an alternative citizenship in a Sikh "nation of steel." And for those who sought a limited rapprochement with the mainstream, 3HO provided the terms for this compromise and the boundaries that would establish its limits.

There was also the expectation that participation in organizational life and acceptance of Bhajan's leadership might profoundly change individuals. Members would enact rituals of quest, of trial by fire, and of self-renewal. They could make the prototypical American journey into the wilderness and return enriched. They could confront and overcome their weaknesses. Rather than seek conventional success, they could become real people, and "people," Bhajan declared, "are those who change environments to increase the beauty and comfort for each other" (1973a, 3). They might even experience enlightenment.

Offered such possibilities, members set about the business of becoming people in Bhajan's sense. They drew upon organizational metaphors, images, and rituals. They took on new identities and were exposed to a variety of identity processes (Robbins 1973). Soon the fabric of the self was shot through with the organizational thread. In some cases the thread was central to the overall design. In others, it was only worked into the background. But it was always interwoven. Many members matured with the organization, establishing adult identities as they defined their ties to 3HO. When they married, identities as spouses and parents were linked to 3HO and to Sikhism. Yogi Bhajan arranged or approved marriages and provided guidelines on marital life and appropriate gender roles. He and other leaders instructed young mothers in the art of parenthood. Being "strong Khalsa" came to mean being a responsible parent and householder. After the inauguration of the Khalsa Women's Training Camp in the mid-1970s, identities as Sikh, woman, mother, spouse, and employee were progressively elaborated and entwined.

The traditions on which 3HO builds provided powerful metaphors for personhood. These metaphors spoke to immediate concerns, allowing members to envision themselves as they would like to be: free of anxiety and doubt, never estranged from the best in themselves, and leaders in the construction of a new and moral order. The images also worked at more abstract levels. They provided members with visual means of conceptualizing the relationship between self and society. Members could incorporate those metaphors that seemed most helpful or promising, and in the process they could shape a self whose form was related to the organization of 3HO, to the surrounding culture, and to their images of an emergent order. This they could only do because they allowed themselves to trust Yogi Bhajan and his teachings. From this basic trust came trust in the future, trust in other 3HO members, and trust that a higher self existed.

Adopting the Life-style

In the course of this wide-ranging process of elaborating individual and collective identities, 3HO women have not necessarily left the past behind, nor have they simply been passive recipients of organizational socialization. Many have actively sought to accommodate 3HO perspectives and values to their own personal viewpoints and goals. In the process they have reinterpreted organizational teachings, thoughtfully altered their own identities and behaviors, and refigured their own biographies. In 3HO, this process has come to be called "going through changes."

As children of middle-class suburbia, members were raised on many of the values of a modern mobile society: individual striving, career advancement, and self-expression among them. Many found these values arid or oppressive and turned to countercultural ways of being which seemed more humane. But even though the hip subculture in which many found a temporary niche opposed many of the dominant values, it still retained the underlying emphasis on mobility, albeit in altered forms. Hip rhetoric depicted the dominant culture as repressive, lacking in energy, formalized, and "uptight." Social arrangements that might result in stasis or rigidity were rejected. To be tied to a single persona, to a system of formal roles and material rewards, or to a particular world view was considered undesirable. Self-esteem was to be detached from conventional statuses and achievements. Travel, a series of "relationships," active experimentation with identity and perception, and thoughtful sampling of philosophies and cultures were prized. The counterculture, as Musgrove (1974) noted, mounted a general "attack on fixed order in favor of openness, mutability and flux" (86).

Although many of the youth who encountered 3HO in the organization's formative years were questioning tenets of counterculture ideology, or felt that they were ready to move on to something new, they brought with them their expectations of, or at least the rhetoric of, continual change and personal evolution. In 3HO this was transmuted into a willingness to experiment with identity and with organizational beliefs and practices. This willingness to experiment has proved a valuable personal and organizational resource.

Each individual goes through her own "changes," although those who remain in the organization tend to accept the dominant customs and accounts. They tend to conclude that 3HO beliefs and practices "work," thus adapting the preference for pragmatic accounts. They learn to think in terms of central 3HO and Sikh principles, such as commitment and discipline, positivity and negativity, higher and lower selves, graceful behavior, neutrality, and service. They construct their individual spiritual paths in the light of such shared concepts. They adapt the symbols of collective identity, participating in *sadhana*, wearing *bana*, and incorporating new terminology. But their constructions are also shaped by personal biography, expectations, and circumstances. Members provide the accents and the nuances. They may choose those accounts that are in keeping with their usual concerns and modes of solving problems, or they may gain new and valuable insights by trying an unaccustomed approach.

The following examples illustrate these processes as individuals have interpreted, adapted, and sometimes struggled with some of the core ideals and gender prescriptions of 3HO/Sikh Dharma in the earlier years.

Bana

Originally, 3HO members wore a variety of clothing styles, which varied from ashram to ashram. Early on, Yogi Bhajan suggested that white was an ideal color choice because the "vibrations" were pure and the distinctive white dress would draw attention to members, and thus to the guidance and service that they could render. So more and more members began to dress in white, or at least in light colors. Soon, turbans and standard dress were introduced, and with Sikhism came the vow to keep the "five K's."

Members have found various ways of fitting such practices into their own frames of reference. Sometimes they do so easily and lightly, an attitude captured in the phrase "White is fun to wear." Sometimes a woman cheerfully admits her conformity to group norms: "I didn't feel like I had to wear a turban and I didn't feel like I had to wear all white, but because everybody else is doing it that's what you do. But you try to find out the underlying reasons why we cover our heads and why we do this and that, but still it's kind of vague sometimes." Others have to work harder at finding an acceptable interpretation:

> Everybody started wearing white. It was Yogiji's idea to wear white. It had to do, of course, with the vibrations. I didn't wear white because I had two little kids—two very active boys—and I said, "This is ridiculous." . . .

> Well, just about then was the first women's camp. . . .
> I was willing to try what they were saying. . . . [T]he
> thing that got me—you can always get me if you come
> at me from a scientific standpoint—was the vibration
> of the color. . . . I said, "Okay, I'll try wearing only
> white while I'm there." . . . I felt better in light colors.

Hers is a typical case of an individual who is not eager to adopt an emerging group norm but who *does* want the satisfactions of group belonging and of shared beliefs. She holds out for some time until she encounters a reason for conforming that is congruent with her self-image or her belief system. In this case, the woman speaking prided herself on being an intellectual, and when faced with a "scientific" explanation for the custom, she was willing to give it a try.

She also acted in accordance with two other 3HO norms: willingness to experiment and readiness to experience heightened sensitivity. Not all 3HO people say they can feel the physical effects of wearing white, but many do, and a belief in such effects and in the desirability of feeling them is widespread.

Another member who had wearied of dating and wanted to be spared men's advances, emphasized the modesty aspects of wearing *bana:* "I think the spiritual robe is something very nice, something very special. . . . [W]hen you put it on, it's like you dress for God. You don't dress to be sexy, those kinds of things." Hers is another example of a woman adapting a new practice to a preexisting frame.

At first, only men wore turbans. Yogi Bhajan said that the turban would channel and conserve a man's energy and protect him from stress and confusion. Later women began "tying a turban." 3HO tradition has it that Premka, then Yogi Bhajan's secretary, first tried one on for fun. He saw it, liked it, and praised it, and so other women began to imitate her.

As with the color white, there are beliefs about the effects of wearing a turban. Here is one version, from a Washington woman: "[O]nly the men were wearing turbans. . . . I told one of the men, I said, 'I'm going to teach a yoga class tonight and I want to wear a turban. Can you lend me some material?' So he lent some material and I tied the thing on my head, and it looked really weird. But I put it on and it felt really good. . . . I just couldn't believe how different I felt. I felt real centered and I felt this energy just like all in my top *chakra*s." Hers is a justification based on feelings and on the "sensitivity" that is expected to arise as members meditate and progress along the spiritual path.

While many people on the East Coast thought *bana* was "fun" or energizing, a number of people on the West Coast evidently rebelled at the prospect of wearing a turban. Even in the East it can still be a source of discomfort or contention. Members have experienced job discrimination because of the practice, and it can create social distance at work and in the community. Children have been teased for wearing their turbans to public schools, and 3HO people are subject to ridicule and stray comments when they wear *bana* on the streets: "Getting used to wearing the clothes, letting my hair grow—we don't shave—to me that was hard. . . . [L]ooking different was hard for me. . . . It still bothers me sometimes. I'll be walking down the street and someone will say, 'Hey, turban head,' or something less reverent than that; but it's not as bad as it used to be." Such stray comments from the public were particularly difficult during the Gulf War, when many people seem to have unaccountably associated the distinctive dress with Iraq.

When asked why she bothered with *bana*, given all the complications it added to her life, the woman cited above replied, "It's the relationship you have with your teacher. . . . [T]hese are the things that he's put down, and that's it. . . . I've gone out before, had my feelers out there, felt what it's like to dress in street clothes and shave and live like that. It does affect my consciousness. I found myself living on a lower rung, so to speak, spiritually, when I was out there."

Without the *bana*, she said, she felt like Samson without his hair. In 3HO clothing and consciousness are closely bound, and *bana* has been interwoven with her sense of identity and her feelings of independence from the larger culture. She is inclined to talk about the "muck and mire" in the larger world and her struggles to avoid it. *Bana* is a useful symbolic marker separating her from what she sees as the outside world's dangers and temptations.

The 3HO concern with clothing and its effects can be viewed as an extension of the countercultural emphasis on the symbolic properties of dress. Writing about a different group—the Amish—Kraybill (1989) notes the "symbolization of core values" which one often finds in such groups. This symbolization is evident in 3HO where *bana* encapsulates Sikh values and organizational boundaries. Whether her initial response to wearing *bana* is eagerness or reluctance, whether the practice is justified in intuitive or utilitarian terms, a 3HO women who regularly wears the turban and other items of clothing is reminded daily of her group membership in a concrete, constant, and kinesthetic way.

Sadhana and the Neutral Self

A central image in 3HO is that of union with God. "God is sort of like where everything is all right," said one woman. "I always have the image of a bright light and of all being in union with that bright light, which is a real common image, but it's sort of like where I feel like all of the anxieties, all of the tensions, all the cares, all the worries stop, and they stop just because you're united with your creator. I'm part of God and I just don't realize it fully, and that's where all the tensions and the anxieties and the anguish come from."

For the speaker, "union" represents serenity, trust in herself, and belief in the ultimate goodness of the universe. It implies a self that is free of internal conflict. It is a self in tune with its surroundings, a self that acts on the world but is not motivated by ego or will. Oneness with God, in 3HO accounts, sometimes seems to also be equated with an easing of the pangs of individuation and the difficulties of living with multiple perspectives and roles. It represents an alignment of external and internal presentations of self.

Its opposite is "separation" from God. One woman's description of alternating merger and separation from God captures both the desired and the feared states of mind:

> I might have a couple of weeks when I'm really feeling unplugged. I just can't feel God inside me, and I'm being short-tempered and over-eating, and I'm not loving myself, and then I'll kind of hit bottom, . . . fall at my altar and say, "OK, God, I give up." . . . Then, you know, I realize, "Oh, this is part of God's plan. I'm meant to give up. I'm meant to realize that by myself I can't affect change and just surrender to the part of me that already knows that everything's all right." So then I have maybe a couple of weeks of just cruising, doing what I need to do and feeling happy.

Members try to find a way of approaching everyday life that allows them to regularly experience this kind of "cruising." One woman describes her efforts:

> [T]he bottom line is always thinking about making God your focus twenty-four hours a day. . . . I have a long way to go but I try to. . . . It used to be me doing everything; now it's more me doing it through the presence of God. . . . I have to keep bringing myself

back to it, just really having those few moments of absolute connection with God that I have now to be constant, to be totally through me, so when I go to work it doesn't just disappear, or when I step in the car I don't think of other things. I mean, I step out of *gurdwara* and my mind goes right into movies.

One way to make the self a channel for God and to obtain this kind of unity with the divine is to attend *sadhana*. It is understood that this is a long-term project. The actual individual *sadhana* experience can vary from day to day. One day it may be viewed as an energizing set of exercises; on another day it is seen as a time of extraordinary peace and pleasure. Sometimes very little seems to happen; the yoga is a chore, the mind races during meditation, or perhaps the would-be meditator simply cannot stay awake. But participation is always considered valuable. It is said to ease the effects of stress, lift the consciousness, and balance the left and right hemispheres of the brain:

> The West has pressed the left brain to the limit. We have filled our lives with action-oriented, goal-oriented, linear, logical, verbal thinking. The right brain that rules intuition and is the doorway to the deeper self has not been valued. . . . Sadhana is a way of healing the left-right split and imbalance of our consciousness. It becomes a kind of therapy. Since it heals by stimulating the integrative mechanisms without the individual having to go into the origin of specific conflicts, it functions as a metatherapy. (Khalsa 1978, 23)

As we have seen, *sadhana* attendance is also said to foster "group consciousness" and to bestow benefits upon the entire group: "If in this whole group one person opens up to God just once, we all will be blessed in his openness" (Khalsa 1978, 2).

In the course of meditation, a 3HO member may visualize herself as she would like to be in everyday life, or as the evolved spiritual being she seeks to become. She may imagine herself as surrounded by light, at peace in all settings, or as gracefully submitting to God's will wherever she may be. Thus a woman describes her visualizations:

> One of the ones I use a lot is I imagine myself bowing before an altar, and the altar represents the highest, purest consciousness within myself and in all of us. . . . It's a sense of humility and surrender and love and

reverence. . . . Another is . . . I have an image of the eyes of this kind of ageless person, the most compassionate, loving eyes that I can imagine, looking at me in a totally accepting way, and then I literally look through those eyes and experience myself looking at the universe through them, absolutely accepting and loving.

The fruits of meditation should inform, and enhance, everyday thought and action. This is one woman's account of her feelings as she left the *sadhana* room (she wrote them down immediately afterward): "If I would *really* do this everyday I would be sooo *together!* My mind is clear, fast, calm and I *project* strength. I feel like I'm an inspiration to people I meet because I'm positive and happy and successful."

While the ideal is to feel energized, clear, and empowered, like the woman quoted above, the meditator should also accomplish some difficult tasks, such as breaking self-interested and circumscribed chains of thought; interrupting repetitive, emotional, defensive, or self-serving thoughts and actions; and "re-accessing" meditative states. Constancy at *sadhana* should pay off in small increments of God-consciousness during the day and in increased ability to reenter the altered state at will. As another woman recounted her thoughts upon leaving *sadhana* one morning, "I've just started my day positively. I can handle anything!! Instead of worrying or mindlessly thinking of a T.V. show or emotional response to something, the songs and mantras come into my mind. That's the best: it lifts the spirit."

The woman who regularly attends *sadhana* should find that she can extend the range of mental associations in most situations so that her mind reaches beyond the immediate and the practical. A job, for example, becomes an opportunity to channel grace to others. Events and situations become less discrete, more a part of a newly envisioned whole. In fact, *sadhana* should generally broaden the range of awareness. A spiritual person should be aware not only of her own feelings in a situation, but of others' reactions and interpretations, and of all the possible outcomes and implications of the situation. The long-term goal is a self that is always transforming everyday life by extending the horizons of sympathy, reference, awareness, and knowledge (Schutz and Luckmann 1973).

The individual who makes "a regular sadhana" should also begin to develop the "neutral self." The neutral self is detached from the passions, fears, and motives of the natural attitude (Schutz and Luckmann 1973). It should be capable of regarding experience without desire or expectation, and encountering different points of view with equanimity. It can serve an integrative function. It is also, most importantly, an aspect of the self that can be trusted, a point of stability in the midst of change.

As the neutral self develops, the meditator should slowly gain control over her own mind and circumstances. She should increasingly be able to focus her attention on feelings of love, clarity, bounty, and peace, and on images of unity and empowerment. Eventually, the meditator should "enter into *prabhupati* or mastery of God. This is the state of neutrality. Your motivation is neutral. No finite thing motivates you. No money, no fame, no sex, no personal advancement is enough to determine your actions. . . . The stage of *prabhupati* represents the opening and attunement to the superconsciousness" (Khalsa 1978, 15–16).

The image of the neutral mind may enable the individual to conceive of a new structure in the makeup of the self, one that is able to transcend trouble, conflict, and change. The image holds out the prospect of a future self that is not torn by internal conflicts, and one that does not reflect the lines of cleavage in the larger society. It should, according to a 3HO author, "stop the continual production and maintenance of the dualities of consciousness" (Khalsa 1978, 21).

While members typically attribute the development of the neutral self to the effects of "doing *sadhana*" and, perhaps, to living in an ashram, the demands of 3HO life may also encourage its formation. New members must learn to doubt many of their spontaneous responses. They must adapt to what is essentially a new culture and must learn a multitude of new responses and behavior patterns. This requires considerable self-awareness. So does the 3HO concern with graceful self-presentation and with achieving a balance between mysticism and practicality and intuitive and rational modes of cognition. The envisioned end result, in any case, is an observer self, rather like the modern emotion manager depicted by Hochschild (1983) or the rationalized self described some time ago by Brigitte Berger (1971), but it should have a depth, purpose, and serenity that are not necessarily aspects of the sociological model.

Grace

When it was first introduced, the term "graceful woman" appears to have been intended as an antidote to hip descriptions of women as "chicks" or as "old ladies." It was probably also intended as an alternative to feminist images of women. It implied a rejection of both the sexual freedoms of the counterculture and androgynous models of gender relations.

Women in 3HO reacted in a variety of ways to this conceptualization of womanhood. For some it was a relief or a revelation. The woman quoted in the last chapter who, before a divorce and her affiliation with

3HO, had been abused by her husband, responded with instant pleasure when she first encountered life in an ashram. "The thing that really got me," she recalled, "was the way the men respected me as a woman. I never had felt so much respect, and I just had a lot of problems with my father and with my first husband. To have these men treat me with so much respect, right away it affected my self-esteem."

This woman came to interpret the meaning of graceful womanhood in terms of her experience of abuse and her need for safety and respect: "It means [a woman] living with certain values and knowing who she really is inside, knowing her purity inside and holding that very high so that she never loses that grace. . . . [S]he always keeps that grace within herself so that she never gets abused or she never allows herself to be in a situation that would endanger her or make her embarrassed or something. For me, it's a whole way of feeling inside, and when you believe it inside it projects out, sort of like radiance from you."

Another woman complained of the impact of feminism (in terms often heard in 3HO): "Like women in today's society are very wrong. I mean, the women's movement and being sexually liberated, probably some of it was good, but I also feel they goofed up at some point. It's like now they are not very much respected. And what you see on all the media, it's too much sex-oriented. . . . Instead of women projecting their divinity they're projecting something else."

She defined grace in related terms: "Graceful, I think, is when a woman is aware of her divinity, aware of who she is, that she is not just a body or just a pretty person, but who is aware of her soul, of her strength, of her righteousness, a woman who loves God, who in her actions, in her words, is going to always be aware of her grace. Who is polite, sweet. . . . It's the opposite of being cheap, vulgar, rude or small-minded."

Grace implies significant differences between masculine and feminine natures. Each sex is said to have distinct talents and responsibilities. Several of the women I interviewed expressed relief at abandoning more androgynous ideals and accepting these differences. They felt that they came to trust and accept their womanhood. This is clearly one of the appeals that 3HO and graceful womanhood have had for a segment of the women members. The following quotation is typical of such attitudes:

> In college I was in a women's consciousness raising group, and I'm glad I was, and I still have a lot of feminist beliefs, [but] I grew up thinking of men and women as totally the same and they're really not. . . . I think there are a lot of the same things, but it makes life a lot

easier knowing that you don't have to try to be a man. Even though I think people realize that on a conscious level, if you look around you see that women totally do try to [be a man], and there are so many strengths that we have that men don't have and to deny those makes life a lot harder.

Or, as one woman put it, "It was a relief to learn we are different and don't have to make it. That felt right."

To some other 3HO women, grace originally suggested an unnatural, overly delicate, posing, or cloying kind of femininity, or it seemed too far from countercultural or feminist points of view. In their efforts to adapt to this new ideal these women worked their way toward what seemed like a more acceptable and authentic image. For them, the transition from hip chick to Sikh lady was not always easy:

> *Respondent A:* The first yoga class I went to my son wanted to nurse. I didn't think anything of it, but the next day one of the Sikhs said to me, "Sikhs don't take their shirts off." And I thought, "These kids are really uptight—they should smoke a joint."
>
> *Respondent B:* I went to Wisconsin and people there started talking to me about pinning my hair up, and wearing a bra, and being graceful, and that sort of thing—something I couldn't relate to at all. . . . Just be who you are, and if someone doesn't like it, too bad.

For such women it took some time and effort to process the approach and come to an acceptable understanding of it. The following is a typical (utilitarian) progression:

> I guess what I used to think a graceful woman was, before I wanted to be one, was someone who dressed pretty—I guess sort of vain or something—and that talked sweetly, and did all the things that I, for some reason, didn't want to do. And then, I guess, as I started feeling more like a graceful woman, my concept of it was basically thinking about your effect on other people. . . . And in order to have a positive effect you had to speak nicely, care about other people and what they're thinking, and even look a certain way in order to feel self-respect and earn the respect of others.

Others simply could not accept the concept and either left 3HO or simply ignored aspects of graceful womanhood.

As the concept evolved it typically implied poise, the capacity to nurture, a positive outlook, control over self and situation, and concern with one's impact on others. A graceful woman became one who "is positive, doesn't get down on people. Things don't bother her real easily, . . . real calm and collected and eager to help either other people's situations or her own situations. . . . It's someone who's confident about herself and feels good about herself." One woman said that she preferred the word "poise": "Poise to me comes from deep within, every word comes from deep within. . . . [I]t means being very reasonable, sensible, contained— not bottled-up, but contained." As one woman summed it up, grace could be construed as "serenity born of strength."

Graceful womanhood came to be valued not only for its own sake, but as a means to an end: cooperative, respectful, and loving relationships. Since 3HO women bear primary responsibility for relationships, grace is a tool as well as a state of being. One woman describes her struggle with this responsibility:

> In a marriage it seems like it's kind of sixty-forty: 60 percent from the women and 40 percent from the men, depending on the man, 'cause the woman seems to be much stronger, so more is her responsibility. . . . She's more nurturing, more intelligent. . . . Before I moved into 3HO I was always angry because, in the relationships I had had with guys, I was constantly striving for fifty-fifty, and I wanted them to be this and I wanted them to be that (what I thought they should be), and they were never measuring up, you know. I was always doing more than them and I resented it. . . . I was always the one who was cleaning up the mess of the argument, or keeping the relationship together, pushing for the honesty in the relationship. I found that I really had to fight in order to keep that relationship growing and keep my own rights in it, and not have it turn into a dry relationship, to keep it a really active relationship, and nurturing, and good. And so I was angry about it all those years. Now that I hear what the Siri Singh Sahib says. . . . [I]t just seems that it's true. I can really feel that inside when he says, "This is how women are. There's no sense in being angry about it, just accept how you are, accept that you can do these

things, accept that you can handle more pressures than he can—especially American men, because they've been pressured so much all their lives in America, to be this and that, macho and sexist, job and career."

This same woman describes her early distrust of 3HO attitudes toward gender differences:

> At first I didn't go for 3HO because I felt like, you know, "What's this 'be a woman' and all—it looks like their idea of being a woman is be a wife, take care of the kids and stay home. Forget it. No way." But then as time went on, I listened closely to what they were saying and started to realize that to them being a woman is just being a woman. It's being warm, being compassionate, and being very nurturing towards children, nurturing to all human beings. . . . At first I thought they were anti–women's movement, but then, as I said, when I looked more closely I found out it's not like that at all. . . . They're into being women, but they believe in equal rights. But they believe that women actually can do more than men—and I believe it; I agree with that philosophy totally.

Service (Seva)

Service to others is a Sikh value, and both men and women are supposed to generously give of their time and talents to their fellow Sikhs and to their communities. Service and surrender to others is also viewed as a means of reducing karma (Maple 1991, 67). For women, service also takes on additional meanings since a woman can become a saint by "serving a man of God," or by giving birth to such a man. In general, women are expected to be "serviceful."

For some 3HO women the idea of service was attractive from the beginning; others had some difficulty accepting it. As an ideal it had some affinity with the counterculture distrust of individualism, and with the hip preference for group living and sharing. It is my impression that, when new 3HO members, or their students, resist the idea of service, this resistance is typically explained in cultural terms. Americans are said to dislike the idea of serving because they have been raised to think that it violates ideals of equality and individualism. And it is understood that some American women are afraid that serving others will reinforce stereotypes of women as inferior or subordinate.

Longtime 3HO members insist that such interpretations miss the true meaning of service. To serve is not to be servile, and one can "serve without being a servant." Service should be performed with dignity and is intended, ultimately, as a gift to God. In the final analysis, they assume, people must do things for each other, and if ego is to be transcended this involves some subjugation of self to other. Moreover, they expect that life on a spiritual path will require submission to a teacher and will entail encounters with enlightened people who are due special respect.

As mentioned in the previous chapter, *seva* was part of the daily routine at the women's camp. Participants performed a variety of tasks such as serving meals, cooking, and cleaning. To introduce a personal note, when I was at the camp I tended to view this arrangement with some cynicism. I understood the training purpose, but still it did not seem quite "fair" to ask people who were paying to attend camp to work there as well. But I also had to admit that performing *seva* could prove particularly satisfying. One evening, for example, I joined several 3HO women, and the camp cook, to prepare hundreds of *chapatis* (a round Indian bread) for a special meal. The outdoor temperature was at least one hundred degrees, and in the kitchen, where large ovens radiated heat, it must have been twenty degrees hotter. We all kneaded and perspired and chanted together. In the midst of this labor I was surprised to find that I experienced great pleasure. I stopped caring that I was hot, ceased to think about how long it would take to complete the task, and simply enjoyed the sense of camaraderie and communal accomplishment. I was disengaged from my more accustomed mode of operation: time-pressured, individualistic, preferring to avoid "domestic drudgery." I was aware that this was happening and wondered if it was one of the intended effects of camp life, but I nonetheless found that I could not avoid questioning my usual stance toward life. I did not, however, abandon all skepticism, and immediately encountered another internal voice asking if it was possible to let down my guard without being forced into conventionally subservient women's roles. Can a woman today be graceful, gentle, and happy to serve without being exploited? I wondered.

Such questions arise when 3HO members seek to apply the ideals of service and selflessness to everyday life. Just how far should one go to serve a spouse, an ashram director, a spiritual teacher, or an employer? Where is the line between self-respect and submission, or between devoted service and naïve obedience? When is one diminishing karma, and when is one diminishing necessary aspects of the self?

There are no easy answers. At the level of personal relationships, individuals often decide these issues on a case-by-case basis. They may experiment with forms of service. Thus a woman quoted earlier describes her efforts to come to terms with the service ethic:

> To serve a man without feeling defrauded and without feeling lesser or not as equal, I guess that's all of it in that one sentence. . . . I keep stressing this service to men and stuff because I've found that when I'm combating with a man and trying to be his equal and rival that I'm not comfortable. When I'm serving him and seeing his appreciation—I don't mean I serve him and he beats me; I mean when I serve him and he's appreciative of it—it's like I've seen some men when they respect a woman and the woman serves them what the reward is. It's incredible. It's such a beautiful, flowing relationship that I've experienced at moments, like in the ashram, even with my boss, a few moments that I just drop my ego, try to be humble, and just really try to serve him and try to be supportive of him. He really responds and he turns around and turns it back to me.

At an organizational level, the norm of service can raise difficult issues. Members have served and obeyed ashram directors who were unnecessarily dictatorial or who violated their trust. By the mid-1980s some members were talking openly about this and saying that leadership styles had to change since members had matured and were successful in their business and family lives. One woman told me that she thought she had "learned victim scripts as a child," and that she had played them over and over in the ashram setting. She had heard too many people say, sweetly, "It's the dharma, ji," when rationalizing unkind acts. Others had no such experience, having had more thoughtful directors, or more assertive personalities. Today the directors have less power as leadership functions have been spread to governing councils.

Service to Bhajan is particularly valued. It is considered an honor to hold a position on his staff, and those not on the staff are often grateful for lesser opportunities to help the spiritual teacher: cleaning his home or offering medical advice, for example. The majority of women in 3HO encounter Bhajan only at special events, such as ladies camp and Tantric yoga classes, or on occasions when he visits their ashram. Women who are themselves in leadership positions or are married to such individuals encounter Bhajan more frequently, as do those with special skills or resources. He also has an entirely female private staff whose members are expected to devote themselves entirely to Bhajan and to the organization.

Marriage

3HO marriages may be arranged by Yogi Bhajan, and all should be approved by him or by an ashram director. As we have seen, the theory is that marriage is a "yoking of souls," and, as such, should not be based upon infatuation, physical attraction, or emotional needs but on the partners' potential for growth as a pair. A successful marriage is said to be a matching of "male and female polarities." Yogi Bhajan is said to be able to judge the rightness of a union by viewing the auras of the individuals involved.

Sometimes a marital arrangement simply involves Yogi Bhajan giving his stamp of approval to a couple who have already decided they would like to marry. Some couples were already partners when they joined; others have met at Dharma-sponsored activities or in their ashrams and have received permission to marry. In other cases, an ashram director, or Yogi Bhajan, has felt it "was time" for an individual to marry and has conferred with that person about a possible mate. And sometimes Yogi Bhajan has simply announced that two people are to marry. Today there are not many marriages to be arranged for the founding generation, and most of the young people who grew up in 3HO are choosing their own spouses and asking Bhajan's approval of the choice. There have, however, been some arranged marriages in this generation.

Arranged Marriages

The following histories should convey the 3HO sense of the institution of marriage and its place in a spiritual life. Each woman frames her experience in a combination of personal and organizational terms.

A Woman from the First Generation

This first account was provided by a woman who was clearly happy with her arranged marriage. She had a new baby at the time she was interviewed:

> We were in separate ashrams in the same city. So we would see each other every day, except that we never talked to each other, never really noticed each other. He was playing music every morning at the *sadhana*. . . . [A]nd after one year it came a time when everybody told me, "I think you should get married." Several people came to me and said I should get married, and several people also gave me suggestions. . . . [B]ut I was not

interested in anybody. Then the Siri Singh Sahib one day told me, "We're going to find somebody for you who's really handsome," . . . and then he said, "You're going to be married very soon and everything is going to be all taken care of." And then, as I was leaving, he asked me, "do you have anybody in mind?" And I said, "No."

And then I went home, and I thought, "My God, who could that be?" And then I started praying and meditating and reading from the Siri Guru Granth Sahib 'cause I was kind of nervous. And then his question kept coming back in my mind: "Do you have someone in mind?" And when I was reading or meditating my husband's name came into my mind, and I thought, "That's odd, because I even don't know him and we never talk to each other." I didn't really notice him, you know. But the name kept coming back again and again. And when I asked myself, "Well does it mean that you might want to marry him?" the voice inside of me said "Why not?" . . . Usually when I had asked myself this question it was always "No, for sure. . . ."

So I called the secretary of the Siri Singh Sahib. I told her, "whenever I meditate or read from the Guru this name comes in my mind and I even don't know him." So she said, "Okay, I'll get back to you." And then during the day I was thinking, and I actually saw my future husband because I had to go to his ashram and do something, and he opened the door. And when I saw him he was really nice to me, and I remember I kind of blushed and I didn't want to stay in his presence. Then I realized I was feeling a little bit shy around him. I thought, "that's funny." And then I kind of thought about it, and, subconsciously, I think I had noticed his kindness. I had seen him be very kind to others and I knew he was very devoted, and so I think I had been subconsciously attracted to his soul. You know, it was definitely his soul. So then the secretary calls me back and she says, "well the Siri Singh Sahib said that he would be perfect for you. He said that he is a great Sikh; he's very devoted, and it will be great match. . . ."

And the next day I saw him walking towards me, my future husband, and he talks to me and he says, "Sat

Nam, congratulations on your engagement." I said, "Oh, but I'm not engaged." He said, "Last night the Siri Singh Sahib talked to me and he said, "You know this lady? She's ready to be married. What are your plans?" And he said he was really happy about it, actually. And he said, "I think the best way for us to get to know each other would be that we get engaged. What do you think?" I said, "okay." And we started seeing each other once in awhile. We believe in being kind of chaperoned. You know, it's more graceful. So we just were getting along and it was really fun. We were totally different people. It was very amazing. It was nice. . . . Later he told me that he liked me, he had noticed me. What I appreciate is that he never showed it. . . . I've seen too many flirtatious men, you know. It's like as soon as they like you they're going to flirt. I got very, very tired of that. . . . [A]nd he, he just wanted to be one-pointed and just to relate to God, and he believed that when it will be time for him to be married God would give him a wife, and that's what happened. So that's what I really respected in him.

A Young Woman Who Grew Up in 3HO

This young woman was newly married when I interviewed her:

It was arranged—which I expected. . . . I felt good about it because in our society today, you know, the whole dating thing. . . . [Y]ou're always thinking about breaking the relationship—the thought is [in the back of your mind that] you're going to break the relationship with someone. . . . It used to be you'd go out and have fun with someone. . . . [B]ut now it's a lot more sensual; it's a lot more uncommitted, I think. I have a real confidence in the Siri Singh Sahib. He's been like a grandfather. . . . Because he's got the ability to see people different ways that people can't see, he can tell who needs what kind of person. I always felt confident and trusted him. As far as school goes, I never really dated anybody because wearing a turban kind of puts something in people's heads that you're different—I don't know, there's something about it. I had lots of boy friends—I always had more boy friends than girl friends—but they never ever tried anything or even asked me for a date.

I'm really happy with my husband now, so I feel grateful that there was a way I could meet my husband that wasn't an insecure kind of way that a lot of kids, I think, go through. I was actually graduating from high school, and I went to say "hello" to him [Bhajan], and he said he had found someone for me to marry and I should go meet him. And we did Tantric together. . . . I was definitely pretty scared. . . . I was kind of in shock. I always expected the Siri Singh Sahib to find someone for me, but I just didn't expect it then. . . . But then, afterwards, he [her husband] came to my house and he spent some time with us, and his mother came down. . . . We got married pretty quickly afterwards. I think if I had to do it over again I'd do it the same way. . . . [I]t worked out perfectly for us. It worked out very well.

Growing in the Marriage

Once they are married, women want to "keep up" and maintain a positive attitude in their marriages:

I think the biggest thing for me was learning to be really supportive, and when I would see my husband's faults or see things that really bothered me about him, never to bring them up to his face and never make him feel bad. . . . So I really learned how to just be real supportive and to raise his self-esteem by just concentrating on the positive aspects of him, and it took me a long time. You know, the Siri Singh Sahib always would say you should relate to your husband as a god and by doing that you won't feel the negative things; you see them but they don't really matter because you know how great he is. . . . Whenever I would think my husband was the worst creep and he was acting like a total jerk I always would try to remember that. At least if I didn't consciously think of it, I would at least not lay my trip on him, and I would try and come from a positive place.

This woman, and other 3HO women, remind themselves that marriage, in the final analysis, is not about individuals; it is about growth and commitment: "[M]y commitment to my marriage has definitely made me go through a lot of my changes, and I'm really glad for it. . . . The marriage means more than just being married to each other. For me it's like a commitment to myself, because I feel like if I left the marriage I would be denying all the stuff that I have to work out in this lifetime, 'cause, you know, I would just find it with somebody else and I'd have to work on it all over again. So it just means sticking in there and going through it."

The women are supposed to think of themselves as one half of a spiritual partnership in which they serve truth and guru by serving the husband. In Yogi Bhajan's words,

> As we all know, Truth is a very pure and simple matter and in contrast our minds and emotions are very complex. . . . No one can monopolize the truth; you hold a facet of it as does your husband and every other human being alive. Therefore when you are faced with a situation in which you and your husband disagree, and you are expected to give in (remember the three rules of a good wife when faced with a disagreement with her husband, she says only: "you're right; I'm sorry; it's the will of God." This was the lesson Guru Ram Das told his daughter before marriage), you must remember that you are not giving in to his ego. You are offering your portion of the truth to the higher part of your marriage. (From material distributed at Khalsa Women's Training Camp.) 1983(a)

This, clearly, is not the perspective that prevails in secular society, and many educated, hip, middle-class American women did not take readily to saying, "You're right; I'm sorry." In fact, at one point early in their history, women in the Washington ashram, no doubt influenced by the women's movement, got together and agreed that serving a man should mean serving his higher consciousness—not serving his every whim. They decided to perform only those domestic chores that could be done with love, and to not do those that would create resentment. They still, however, assumed heavy burdens within the home as they began the long-term process of modifying the tenets of *stridharma* while making accommodations to its demands.

Wives try to retain their opinions and distinctive views of the world but express these only in timely and graceful ways. Some speak of learning to hold back their criticisms and arguments: "Sometimes," said the young bride quoted previously, "when my husband talks to me about doing something I argue with him about it first, then I realize what he's telling me, and then I do it. I'm trying to get to the point where I can just realize what I should be doing in the first place." She was not assuming that her husband was always right, but that she ought to avoid routinized marital arguments and learn to gracefully appreciate his ideas. She wanted to cultivate the capacity to be sufficiently calm and centered that she could act upon an intuitive sense of right rather than on competitive impulses, superficial feelings, or conditioned reflexes.

In cases where their husbands are lapsing in their spiritual practice, are expressing doubts about the organization, or are withdrawing from active participation in ashram life, wives are encouraged to maintain their own steadfast devotion to the Dharma. In such cases the wife should set an example of piety and faith and find ways to encourage and inspire the faltering partner. If this fails, she should retain her own commitment and have the strength to resist a husband's arguments and doubts. Said one woman whose husband chose not to be Sikh: "I had to deepen my faith in order to maintain it, I had to find deeper resources and be more independent in my spirituality." She also had to learn to assert herself: "My husband is a very strong creative person and he really like his ideas also. So I've had to become a lot stronger. . . . I just sacrificed my weakness. And that wasn't that easy." Her husband's decision was interpreted as a test and as a goad to personal growth.

Given the 3HO concern with commitment, and the organizational preference for embracing rather than avoiding life's dilemmas, it is not surprising that divorce is discouraged for followers of Sikh Dharma. It is not proscribed, however, and it certainly happens with some regularity. In fact, in cases in which a spouse has turned on the organization and is seeking to remove wife and children, wives are supported and encouraged if they decide to remain in the Dharma in the face of the husband's disapproval. In such circumstances, divorce is considered understandable.

Motherhood

With arranged marriages came children, and, as families expanded during the late 1970s and early 1980s, so did the number of teachings surrounding pregnancy and child rearing. Many of these were enunciated by Yogi Bhajan. He taught that a mother's influence is greatest during pregnancy and in the first few years of life. This is the period when she leaves her imprint upon the child. She has the power to "raise a saint" and, indirectly, to alter society in the process. His teachings were often taken literally, and women began to look for examples of motherly influence, even for prenatal influences. "It's really interesting to see babies," said one woman. "If their mother did a certain thing, like chanted a lot, when they were pregnant, and they were real positive and all that kind of stuff, versus a mother who had a harder time, was going through a lot of stuff in her life, you definitely notice a relationship between the projections of the mother and the way the baby is when it's born."

People in Sikh Dharma believe that a baby's soul enters its body near the end of the fourth month of pregnancy (thus early abortions are acceptable in 3HO). Up until that time the mother should meditate and chant so as to attract a pure soul. She does not announce the pregnancy until the end of this period, but then, on the "one hundred and twentieth day," she is specially honored: "We usually do it on Sunday and in our *gurdwara* we sing all the *shabd*s, and all the songs are in honor of the mother, and everybody kind of thinks of the person. And then, later on in the day, we have kind of a party where everyone gives her gifts, and it's like the whole ashram is acknowledging her and saying, 'We support you, and we want you to have a great pregnancy.'"

Childbirth may be viewed as a spiritual event: "Having a baby was a really big experience for me. A lot of the things that Siri Singh Sahib talked about—Adi Shakti and creative energy—I really experienced. I found it a very spiritual, ecstatic experience."

In the Washington ashram, many of the babies were delivered by a medical group that specialized in home births. The mother-to-be could chant or play tapes of chants during labor, and for awhile an ashram resident would play music if that was requested. These home births were very much in keeping with countercultural preferences for "natural" and non-institutional ways of doing things.

After the birth a woman employs a *sevadar* for forty days, and members will sometimes speak of "doing someone's forty days." In the early years this task was performed as a free service, but later this changed, and another ashram woman, preferably someone close to the mother, was paid for her efforts. The *sevadar*'s job is to care for the mother, clean her house, and watch the new infant's older brothers and sisters so that the mother and baby can establish a bond and the mother can rest properly. "She did all the laundry and all the cooking, took care of my older son," recalled one woman. "She brought my food to me. She massaged my feet. And I just got to be with my child. I just never will forget it. I was in so much bliss just being with the baby alone."

I was told that this custom was intended to encourage bonding and to assure the mother's rest and recovery. Maple (1991) encountered another version of this explanation, one expressed in more symbolic terms: "The child's aura is intertwined with the mother's for forty days after birth. The mother will reduce her activities and contact with others to a minimum during this period to enable the vulnerable infant to "individuate" its aura and to ensure a close bonding. . . . The processes of individuation and of bonding can be ruptured by intrusion and handling, however well intentioned" (61). She goes on to note that "individuation fully charges the child as an agent of it's own destiny" (61). Then the infant is a separate being with a soul and karma.

Once the *sevadar* has left, the mother will face many of the same stresses other suburban mothers face. But she will be less isolated than many of these other mothers, and she will know that, in an emergency, there is always help available. She may have the option of working for one of the family businesses where she will find more flexibility than she is likely to encounter if she works for a large outside corporation. She is relatively well situated to attempt a holistic life-style that integrates motherhood, spirituality, work, and marriage.

Sikh customs and beliefs surrounding birth and child rearing elevate the place of motherhood and assure that women receive formal recognition when they become mothers. The role receives considerable attention. As we have seen, many of the special qualities attributed to women are said to issue from their roles as mothers. Women have, to quote one member, "a specially designed nervous system because they give birth and they have more intuition to go along with the child rearing." Not only are their roles appreciated, organizational life can ease the balancing acts and the role overload that modern mothers so often experience.

But some of the teachings and practices can also function as forms of social control. Women emphasize the positive aspects of the teachings and the opportunity they have to accomplish much in the role of Sikh mother, but the leadership's power to use that role to sanction women remains. The message sometimes seems to be that the children of an ungraceful or nonconforming woman will suffer. A woman can raise a saint, but she can also be held responsible for a child's failings, even for its physical problems. Yogi Bhajan has, for example, told his followers that a "bitchy," tense, or angry mother can inhibit her daughter's breast development.

The ideal 3HO mother should attempt to become the kind of person she would have her children become. She should also remember that a child is a temporary blessing, not a possession, and concentrate on pointing her children's minds in the direction of God and the Sikh gurus. As one woman put it, parents should work at "establishing it in their minds that God is the strong point in their life, having them turn that way instead of just to you, as parents. . . . I feel like children are God's children and not my children." Such sentiments are frequently voiced, and sound to me like a spiritual reframing of old countercultural and New Left themes.

As they grow, 3HO children generally progress from home, to a local Khalsa school, perhaps to a local public school, and then to boarding school in India. The first boarding school used by 3HO families was the same one that Yogi Bhajan's children attended. In the late 1980s there were close to 150 3HO children enrolled there, mostly in the lower grades. Today many of these children have graduated from high school. They have returned to the United States and Canada and are distributed around North America. Many have gone to New Mexico; others are in Florida and in Los Angeles. Some of these graduates are working in Sikh businesses, and some are attending college. There are also some graduates who have chosen to stay in India. Young people from 3HO/Sikh Dharma are now attending a different school in Amritsar. Some of the graduates are helping there as well. I am told that 3HO members feel that they have more control over events and curricula at this school.

Members can provide a number of explanations for the practice of sending children to India. When asked about their decision to send their children away to school, parents may mention "sex and drugs" encountered in American schools, the beginnings of a disrespectful attitude in their children, or their desire to provide an environment where the children are not troubled by social problems beyond their control and understanding. Parents say they want their children to maintain a higher consciousness than is possible in the "sensual," undisciplined, and materialistic American mass culture. There is a tendency to regard keeping children at home (when they might thrive in a supposedly more wholesome atmosphere) as a selfish act:

> It really is the best place for them. Drugs and sex are so heavy in school these days that I could just see them deteriorating after all the years that we put into raising them. . . . Maybe to other people it wouldn't seem that apparent, but to me—I could really see it—and when they came home from India this winter they were so

different. They were radiant. I mean they were so beautiful. I knew that I did the right thing. . . . They are independent beings that grow and have the right to grow in the best environment, and for us to want them to be here, just to be with us, ultimately is a very selfish reason when you think about it. But it takes a lot to really come to that place.

While parents feel strongly that they have done the right thing by sending their children overseas to school, this does not mean that they find the separation easy or that the sacrifice is not keenly felt. There are many days when the house feels empty and the children very far away, and parents know that these hours and days when their children are away can never be recaptured. They worry. They plan visits to India, and they anticipate vacations when the children will return.

Such separations do not begin with boarding school. When I attended the women's camp, many of the children were staying at a primitive campsite a few miles away, and they were not supposed to see their mothers throughout the camp session (girls aged seven to fourteen were an exception since they had their own *jatha* within the main camp). There were several explanations offered for this. Bhajan teaches that American children are overprotected and badly in need of opportunities to meet and overcome challenges on their own. He argues that they should be exposed to a variety of people and situations so that they will be socially skilled and flexible as adults. In addition, he advocates "distance therapy" during late childhood. By this he means separations that lead children to think of their parents with love and longing, rather than with rebellious feelings and resentment. He also says that mothers need the respite from childcare and time for personal rejuvenation.

Whatever the reasoning, mothers worried a great deal throughout the summer, and whenever someone had a reason to be at the children's site she would be asked by her friends to check on their children, and the report would be anxiously awaited. I would periodically hear women discussing their children's adjustment or homesickness.

The emotional impact of these separations came home to me when the woman living in the tent next to mine was told by Bhajan that it was time to send her child to India. The mother became deeply distressed. She was a single parent and strongly attached to her only child, a thoroughly charming daughter of about six years old. I thought back to the day that the young children had left for the camp site. This mother had asked me to walk her daughter to the bus while she finished packing a summer's supply of clean clothing for her. A bright and thoughtful child, wearing a little blue sweat suit, her hair on top of her head in a lace-covered knot, the daughter took my hand and chattered away. I asked about the children's camp, at which point she turned pensive, said that five weeks would pass quickly, then stopped, thought further, and finished, "but not at children's camp." Now I thought that an entire term in India would look interminable if this summer's separation seemed long and imposing. And I knew that even this shorter summer separation loomed long and difficult for the mother too, for she had told me that she never had enough time with her daughter during the school year and that she regretted the loss of their summer companionship.

More recently, talking with a young woman whose parents have now left Sikh Dharma, I was again impressed by the pain and difficulty of these separations. The woman had spent several years at the original school in India before her parents decided to leave the Dharma, and I asked her about the time she spent there. She was miserable at first, she said. She felt "abandoned," and she was lonely. Physical punishment was sometimes employed. She also said that it was understood that some of the boys were sexually abused. The facilities were not all that good. I asked why she and her friends didn't tell their parents about all of this. "We assumed they knew," she replied. She later came to love India and to value the deep friendships she formed at the school, but the scars remain, and the years apart have affected her relationship with her parents.

The first 3HO boarding school engendered controversy. There were accusations that funds allocated for the students were mismanaged. Parents expressed concerns about the quality of the children's diet there and about the severity of school discipline. An ex-member also described "unsanitary drinking water, unsanitary kitchen facilities, the lack of any medical supplies or facilities" ("Deep Turban 3," www.rickross.com/groups/3ho.html).

It is worth noting as well that impressionistic data suggest that the older students who have returned to this country upon graduation do not feel obliged to uphold all 3HO/Sikh Dharma norms and are inclined, as is so often the case with a second generation, to be less doctrinaire than their parents.

Varying Approaches to Membership

If we look at the ways that the women go about sifting, interpreting, and adapting the customs and beliefs they encounter in 3HO/Sikh Dharma, we find that the different categories of joiners employ distinctive approaches and narrative themes.

Intense Seekers

The intense seekers appear to turn readily to 3HO spiritual practices and to engage in these with particular devotion and pleasure. They are willing to take risks and leave the familiar behind. They wholeheartedly adopt and internalize many of the ideals presented to them. Here, for example, is one such woman discussing her vows: "I took Sikh vows almost immediately after I took my first yoga class. I took Sikh vows at summer solstice of 1972, and I took Amrit in India at the Golden Temple. . . . I remember things that I felt when I took Amrit. You know, I felt that I would never leave the path. Taking Amrit to me meant that you were a Sikh to the end, that you would live as a Sikh, die as a Sikh, and you would sacrifice your life if need be before you would cut your hair or anything like that."

The intensity of her commitment is reflected in her determination to live as a saint:

> My parents have accepted that people are a certain way, and that you have to deal a certain way. They've just accepted a lot of things which they chalk up to maturity and wisdom—and I chalk up to the fact that they don't have as strong a vision as I do of what the potential of a person's consciousness is and how it really is possible to change certain things. . . . I feel like, because I have the examples of the gurus and I believe in them, that it is possible for a human being to become a saint through practices and service, through the spiritual life, but it makes me a less compromising person.

As another woman describes her own spiritual development it is clear that there were leaps of faith as well as periods of steady evolution. She found that every step in her development required another. At times she had no idea where her spiritual feelings were leading her, and she was sometimes frightened and isolated in the process:

> I started becoming aware that what I wanted was a spiritual way of life, I became aware of my faith in God. That was the first step. But then, four months later, I went through incredible changes where I decided to become vegetarian, very naturally. . . . The same thing with stopping any kind of relationship I would have, becoming celibate. . . . [M]y changes became very obvious. . . . I went through the hardship of discovering

what loneliness is. There were no friends because nobody could understand me, and I couldn't relate to what they were doing. I was terrifying myself. . . . [B]ut it was very beautiful, it was like my heart opened and I felt that it was brimming. . . . And more and more I was in love with God. . . . [A]nd after I experienced yoga for awhile, one day I came back to my apartment, and I looked all around, and I knew I was making a big decision that I didn't want to be in that apartment anymore. I wanted a big change, and I wanted to live in an ashram. . . . Then, after two months, I had to make another big decision [not to return to college], and it became obvious to me that this style of life was my school and it was more important than anything else. And on and on. You realize your commitment is a commitment to God, where you want to live your life for God and you really want to work on yourself and give up other things. That's how it works.

Pragmatic and Intuitive Seekers

In constructing their narratives, these women are as likely to focus on their positions and activities within the organization as on their spirituality. Their lives are multifaceted, and they talk frequently about work, friendships, and personal growth. Some of these women (those with a more utilitarian approach) tend to compartmentalize their various roles while others work to integrate them into a pleasing whole. Those closest to the intense seeker end of the spectrum place considerable emphasis on uniting work and spiritual path.

An energetic woman, who is a fairly typical pragmatic seeker, listed some of the jobs she had held during 3HO's early years. She took on a variety of jobs in the Golden Temple restaurant: hostess, waitress, cashier. Then she was a bookkeeper for a 3HO business, and she later moved up to become the manager. She left that job when she became pregnant with her first child and then worked as a book keeper for another family business. When I interviewed her she had just had a second child and so was taking some time off, but even then her list of activities was impressive. "I'm one of those kinds of people that gets involved," she told me. "I do *sadhana* in the morning. And there's *gurdwara*: I've studied Gurmulkhi and *gurbani*. . . . [S]o I'm kind of personally in charge of the *gurdwara*, scheduling and protocol, teaching people how to play and read. . . . There's a lot of family kinds of things that go on—the Sunday meal, for instance, I'm always involved in that, either buying it or preparing it, and there's different holidays."

The next woman provides a variation on this theme. She has seen considerable change in her duties and expectations: "In my early days in the ashram . . . I was much more career-oriented and very involved in everything. . . . Being a central figure in our community was very important to me. I was feeling very fulfilled serving the director of our community and being so involved."

But an arranged marriage interrupted this way of life, a way of being that, in retrospect, she views as rather superficial. Soon she had a child, and her husband took on a responsible position. At this point, both her husband and Yogi Bhajan advised her to cut back on ashram activities and instead become a supportive wife: "My most useful function wasn't being a secretarial type or a doer of things. It was more just taking care of whatever needed to be taken care of so he could do what he had to do. . . . [W]hat he wants from me is that he knows that his family is taken care of, his home is taken care of. I always have to have a certain vibration about me, and be very flexible in whatever happens. . . . [I]t's a very interesting life. I enjoy it."

These two women tended to focus on different aspects of their lives at different stages. The following two exemplify a more broad-ranging and integrative approach.

The first woman is the lady who encountered 3HO people at a course in homeopathic medicine. As she became involved in Sikh Dharma she also developed a career in alternative medicine. Soon she met a man she liked who was also in 3HO, and they received permission to marry. When I first met her she was a mother, she was quite active in ashram activities, she was employed in a family business as a homeopathic nurse, she was teaching some classes in homeopathy, and she was the vice president of a newly formed homeopathic nurses association (separate from 3HO). She was also very interested in Waldorf education and looking into it as a possibility for her daughter, although this was not much approved by most of the ashram residents at that time.

She describes her life as a unity: "It's about eleven years now that I've been a Sikh. . . . I feel real into it. As a life-style I feel like my career goes right along with it." Her training and commitment have tended to go hand in hand. She went to London to study homeopathy because there were Sikh homeopaths and an ashram there. In the process she grew close to Indian Sikhs, learned to read Gurmulkhi, and traveled around to different *gurdwara*s playing music. Even her early friendship with her husband was based upon a shared interest in health issues.

The final example is a woman who had been politically active, but at the time she joined 3HO she was beginning to doubt the utility of a political approach to social change. Large-scale change, she was beginning to believe, had to start by altering the consciousness of single individuals. She decided to combine commitment to a spiritual path with a career in counseling, and so she began to study transpersonal psychology, neurolinguistic programming, and psychosynthesis. She combined these modalities with the yoga and meditations she learned in 3HO and used this eclectic approach in both private counseling sessions and in public workshops. Her basic premise was spiritual, her techniques both psychological and spiritual:

> All change really is remembering or reconnecting with that highest aspect of yourself. Everybody's got a sequence, steps, that they end up going through, uncovering who they are and experiencing it fully, and there's usually layers of different fears and complexes that have to be gone through. So each person is very individual. But the thing that runs through all people, the common thread, is that all beings, in the long run, want to experience an unconditional love and experience a unity or a sense of connectedness with the universe.

Throughout her affiliation with the organization this was her focus, and she served both Sikhs and non-Sikhs as a counselor. She also found time to do public relations work for the *sangat* and to be active in everyday ashram life.

Convenience Joiners

These women tend to take a particularly careful approach as they test the waters, experiment with techniques, question the motives of the leadership, and look for meaningful points of contact between their values and central organizational concerns. They embrace practices and beliefs that they find appealing, or acceptable, and experiment with some others, either because these are generally embraced or because they appear to have particular potential.

One of the women, who has already been introduced, told me frankly that she had joined simply for her husband's sake. He seemed to need the yoga, the meditation, and the structure of beliefs and routines that 3HO provided. Her reaction to his early contact with and enthusiasm for 3HO was simply to view it as a hobby: "he went to his yoga class and I went to my pottery class." When he convinced her to attend a yoga class, she went and thought it was "no big deal." In time, he convinced her to attend more 3HO events, and she found that she was impressed by the physical and mental challenges of white Tantric yoga. She continued, however, to question many practices, such as vegetarianism, and to fear that the organization would breed intolerance. It was only when she heard Bhajan condemn some attitudes as "fanatic" and heard him preach tolerance and an approach to life and social change which did not deny the importance of this-worldly commitments that she began to relax her vigilance. But still, she said, "I did it totally because of my husband. One of the things I've always felt extremely strongly about was the fact that a family should worship the same way. To me, *how* one worshiped was never all that important."

It was on this principle that she took her vows and set about establishing her stance vis-à-vis the organization. She tried to understand the thinking behind various practices. She embraced those practices and beliefs that were most in keeping with her logical, liberal, work-oriented approach to life. She retained her professional identity while most of the other ashram residents worked in the restaurant. Years later, when she was reminiscing for me, she said she was glad that she had resisted the group norm of working within 3HO. It seemed to her that, in general, she had been all too ready to be a follower, "wanting to belong, wanting to be like everybody else," and she was pleased that she had at least retained her profession. My own impression was that she had also, in many ways, been her own woman, even when she was firmly nudged in the direction of commitment. In the early days, Bhajan urged her and her husband to make their house into an ashram, and, when they agreed to do so, he promptly appointed them as ministers. She was willing to adapt, and, I would imagine, brought intelligence, energy, and fair-mindedness to bear on her commitments, but she was also selective in her appropriation of beliefs throughout her 3HO career and came to pride herself on being more "eclectic" and tolerant than the typical 3HO member. She consistently interpreted Bhajan's teachings so as to align them with her own strong preference for tolerance and an open mind, and she always retained her commitment to her profession.

Another convenience joiner (who has already been quoted on her interpretations of service and graceful womanhood) moved into the *sangat* primarily for financial reasons, as she required affordable housing. Always ambivalent about any commitment, she found that as soon as she was established in the ashram she began planning to leave. "I think I spent the first two years looking for somebody to do something wrong so I could leave," she said. "I'm a very cautious person, extremely cautious." At first she distrusted Bhajan because of the many tales she had heard of spiritual leaders who exploit their followers. "I didn't trust him much," but then, "as time went on, I started listening to him more and hearing his advice to other people and watching what he was saying to me, and analyzing this the whole time, feeling it in my heart and trying to balance out between my heart and my head."

She began to frame her ambivalence, and her pattern of moving from place to place and from job to job, in 3HO terms. In the past it had occurred to her "that what I was really looking for was God," and now she began to consider this possibility more seriously. She also began to look at the expectations which made it so difficult to settle for any one career or life-style: "I always felt like I should be doing much more. I should be better than what I am. I think it came from my mother's phrase, 'that's not how things should be.' The Siri Singh Sahib told me to relax and stop worrying about everything, things are what they are. . . . He even told me at one point, 'You're doing okay. You're doing great.' It blew me away—'I am? What about the list of things I should be doing?'"

She began to reexamine her life. Ashram residents suggested that she might experiment with breaking her past patterns of constant change and travel. It was probably this possibility of trying on the 3HO approach to life, of experimenting and taking things step by step without making a final commitment, that made it possible for her to begin to embrace a number of 3HO concepts and practices. She also asked to be given a spiritual name. She began to wear a turban. And "after about two years I said to myself, 'All right, if you're going to be here why don't you start doing some work on yourself?' . . . [S]o I decided, 'Well, one thing that I could do to enhance myself would be to go to *sadhana*,' so I decided just to go to *sadhana* every day. . . . I really started growing then, and really feeling my commitment starting to come out, and really seeing God is the foundation of this whole universe and for everything we do."

She was still ambivalent when I spoke with her, longing sometimes for a freer, lighter-hearted life and wanting to keep her options open, but she was working hard to appropriate and internalize 3HO concepts. Later, she took Sikh vows.

Interviews: Journal and Memories

I drive to one of the Sikh communities, and, as usual, I experience a range of expectations and feelings. If I am about to interview someone I have interviewed previously, or someone I know quite well, I look forward to the interview, but I also experience some strain. If I don't know the individual, or if she is someone with whom I am not particularly comfortable, I may be nervous and worried about how I will be received. These are pretty ordinary reactions, but there are others that do not seem to have much to do with the individuals involved. They seem to have more to do with my sense that I am about to cross a boundary. That boundary must be partly of my own making, a mental line that I draw. These are people much like myself, actually, but I create the Other. And I prepare for the business of understanding lives different from my own. Sometimes I feel subdued, my usual thought processes in suspension, as if making mental room for 3HO language and categories. Sometimes there is a tendency to judge myself by what I imagine to be 3HO standards. I might feel defensive about my restless energy, as if I should slow and calm myself. Or I might feel like a representative from the shallow, mechanical, everyday world and half-believe that my thoughts are too mundane, too conventional. And there is at times the feeling that I am lacking sufficient spiritual grounding and I am too academic. Sometimes my mind and body rebel at the 3HO rhythms, at members' efforts to think and feel in particular ways, and sometimes I weary of my own efforts to be completely free of judgments, completely open to what I hear. And then I wish that they and I could just be more spontaneous, and at the same time feel that I am being unprofessional to feel this way.

Then I arrive and am welcomed graciously, often with yogi tea, or with an offer of some other refreshment. Usually the interviewee reminds me that she has a limited time period available, or warns me of potential interruptions like a waking baby or a child who may need to be driven somewhere. Everyone is busy. I'm always worried about imposing, but I also want as much of each woman's time as I can get.

Soon the sense of strangeness dissipates. We find a place to sit where a tape recorder can be placed. I review my project and purpose, and soon the rhythm of the interview takes over. The woman is concentrating, remembering, and recreating scenes and memories—usually with considerable verbal skill. I am absorbed by her story and her personality. There is fascination, empathy, and sometimes affection and admiration. I look for points of contact—similar life circumstances, biographical details, values, or perspectives—and generally I find them. Most of these women are very easy to interview because they are so verbal, thoughtful, and interesting, and by the

(Cont'd. from page 201)

end of a session I have a wealth of information. Now it seems that there is something almost magical about this business of two people from different worlds, two women, meeting and sharing like this. And there is this sense of wonder: I have been gifted with a piece of someone's life.

Of course there are days when things do not go as smoothly, or as productively, as I would like. Occasionally the magic is just not there. I have difficulty finding the right question to ask, or I miss opportunities to follow up on a comment or idea. Sometimes my informant is preoccupied or just not forthcoming. Sometimes it seems that the woman I am interviewing is working very hard to say just the right things, and I hear the collective story more loudly than the individual tale.

There are also times when my reactions get in the way for awhile. I may feel slighted, as if my way of life has been devalued. I know that many 3HO people think that non-Sikhs live "unconscious," automaton-like lives, and sometimes I'll get the feeling that that judgment is being applied to me, and, in spite of myself, I'll take it personally. Or I'll feel that the woman is suggesting that only Sikhs have access to the Truth, or that her life-style is much more rewarding and demanding than any other, as if only Sikhs work hard at living well, as if the rest of us didn't struggle to attain maturity, insight, self-discipline, generosity, and the like. But these are the exceptions—usually there is a sense of mutuality, of experience shared, and of insights garnered.

I may leave happy, eager to jot down some notes in order to capture the insights, the new facts, and the scene that I have just left. Or there may come a point when my mind simply stops processing. Overload has set in. Sometimes I even wonder if I am actually losing my own voice and perspective with all this listening and empathizing. I experience a tamping down of identity. Then, after I leave, there's a slow revival.

As I drive home different internal voices may begin to speak up, or at least to whisper. Often they jostle each other. As the Efficient Ethnographer I feel I should engage my memory and retrieve salient details. Maybe I should stop somewhere along the way for a cup of coffee (but then I can't help but think that 3HO folks don't drink coffee, and I drink too much of it) and jot down notes. But then another voice, Everyday Me, says it wants to move on, drive, run errands, go back to ordinary life, to my life. From somewhere else comes the voice of the Mass Mediated Person who wants to turn the radio to a rock station and sing along while driving fast along the Dulles Access Road—speed up to the culturally approved pace after listening to measured voices in quiet peaceful homes. Another voice, the Defensive Social Scientist, may begin a conversation with a generalized version of the 3HO Other, arguing points, asserting the values of a secular, academic, feminist kind of life. It

may be answered by an Internalized Sikh Dharma voice which tells me that I am returning to addictions—to coffee, car, radio, noise, busy-ness, academic categories—and that I may be using these to numb my consciousness. And what 3HO folks might call the Neutral Mind notes all of these voices, and my eagerness to return to my usual routines, to my reality. It notes the constructed nature of my reality and of the 3HO reality, and notes itself noting, and notes itself noting it's noting.

Women gathering for Yogi Bhajan's daily lecture at Khalsa Women's Training Camp, 1983.

Decorating for a wedding at Khalsa Women's Training Camp, 1983.

Partial view of Khalsa Women's Training Camp site, 1983.

Entrance to Khalsa Women's Training Camp, 1994.

Summer solstice site outside of Española, New Mexico, used as a children's camp during the Khalsa Women's Training Camp in 1983.

Entrance to Guru Ram Das Ashram, Española, New Mexico, 1994.

PART FOUR

Collective Identity and Identity Struggles

CHAPTER 6

Identity and Charisma: A "Shadow Side"

*I*n the mid-1970s many of the new religious movements, which had been growing rapidly, found that their membership was now growing slowly, if at all. The heyday of the counterculture was past, the tumult associated with the war in Vietnam had subsided, and recession limited social experimentation. Wuthnow finds that for the new religions "the general picture appears to be one of growth until 1975 or 1976, followed by stability or decline" (1986, 16). Similarly, Wallis (1984) noted "the disappearance of the constituency for many of the youthful world-rejecting movements" and an associated need for these movements to adapt to changed circumstances, with the result that the groups "have either largely disappeared, or transformed themselves in still more conventional directions" (89). While this may be an overly pessimistic reading of the pressures facing the new religions (see Melton 1991), it is true that these organizations had to make some mid-course adjustments.

As Kirpal Singh Khalsa, himself a 3HO member, described the situation in his doctoral thesis:

> The loss in enrollment combined with a recessive national economy placed the new religions in a position that required the development of creative and practical techniques for group survival. Consequently, funding methods were needed that did not depend on ever-increasing numbers. Ideological changes were also needed that gave meaning to their statuses as small fringe religions. The move by 3HO and Vajradhatu during the mid-seventies to placing a greater emphasis on material wealth was not difficult nor contrary to any

of their religious principles. It was a practical and effective response for survival through a changing social and economic structure. (1986, 244)

Prosperity Consciousness

In the mid-1970s and in the 1980s, 3HO offered courses in "prosperity consciousness"—a New Age concept adapted to 3HO needs. The leadership actively encouraged entrepreneurship, further education, and professional attainments. Many 3HO people started small businesses, which were favored because they provided flexibility, sociability, shared values, and a way to avoid the discrimination or disapproval that were often the consequence of wearing *bana* in mainstream organizations. As early as 1973, *Beads of Truth* reported the establishment of several businesses in the Los Angeles area: a company that manufactured candles; another called Sunshine Scents that bottled perfume oils; Sunshine Services, a contracting and lawn care company; and Sunshine Brass Beds. The push in the mid-1970s and 1980s extended the number and variety of businesses.

Kirpal Singh Khalsa's list of small Sikh-initiated businesses functioning in 1986 further conveys the flavor of 3HO entrepreneurship:

> 3HO Foundation members are found nationwide in many professional and technical fields. Some have started manufacturing businesses such as health food products, furniture, and massage tools; others have become very successful in sales and distribution of products such as insurance, health food, shoes, and school supplies; and 3HO Foundation restaurants can be found in many cities in the country. Small businesses have been started in areas such as construction, janitorial service, landscaping, painting, auto mechanics, T.V. repair, security, and small business computers. (Khalsa 1986, 236)

Worldly success was considered desirable, as long as it was the result of honest work and was shared with the community. In 1978 the practice of tithing, or *dasvandh*, was established. People in Sikh Dharma were encouraged to tithe 10 percent of their income to the international headquarters, which then dispersed these funds. In addition there were, and are, local fees, and individuals may make additional donations for special projects such as establishing a local yoga center.

Members emphasized the return on giving. Khalsa found that "ten-fold return was talked about as a universal law, and a number of 3HO members could give examples of receiving ten times the amount of what they had recently given" (Khalsa 1986, 239).

Establishing businesses and succeeding in them are, of course, two different things. In the competitive environment of the 1980s, 3HO businesses were severely tested. It is difficult to get information on business outcomes, particularly because 3HO members feel obliged to speak positively about their endeavors, but the experience of one ashram suggests that the "family businesses" have an uneven record. The late 1970s and the 1980s saw the bankruptcy of a health food restaurant and the dissolution of a telephone business and of an alternative medical center. A shoe sales company was in trouble. A national cosmetic line, Oriental Beauty Secrets, which was taken on by many ashram residents, was short-lived. On the other hand, a jewelry business and individual massage and accountancy businesses were more successful. In 2002, independent businesses and professional practices, rather than "family businesses," seem to be more common, and many of these are doing well. At the national level, prosperity consciousness is once again a focus, and Bhajan and others are now writing and talking about "prosperity technology" (see, for example, www.sikhnet.com).

Like any new religion that adopts an achievement ethic and values material success, 3HO runs some risks. If members actively pursue business opportunities or academic and professional credentials, they may increase their commitments outside of the group. This may mean that they give less time to activities sponsored by the organization or that 3HO must find means of countering new external "pull" factors. Individuals who find themselves achieving in their field of endeavor may also demand more respect, authority, or autonomy within the religious organization.

This appears to have been the case in Española, New Mexico. In the mid-1980s much of the Española leadership, including the ashram director, left. Issues of autonomy and independence were the crux of their dispute with the 3HO leadership—or, at least, that is how it looked from the perspective of the individuals who left. Several people at the Española ashram, individuals who were gaining professional knowledge of group and organizational dynamics, became excited about reorganizing ashram life based on their new knowledge. In an interview after his exit from 3HO/Sikh Dharma, a central figure in this group said that he had come to feel that he and other leaders, by experimenting with new forms of leadership within the ashram and by encouraging the formation of various kinds of internal groupings, were creating an innovative and successful community. But, he said, in the end they also became convinced that the openness and creativity that they believed they were fostering was perceived as a threat by people at the top of the Sikh Dharma bureaucracy. He thought that, in fact, the national leadership actively discouraged their efforts. Lewis (1998), referring to this event, also reports that "[i]n 1984 a number of high-ranking leaders in the Sikh Dharma left the organization, complaining of the intense discipline and being cut off from the Sikh community as a whole and from American culture" (113).

Similarly, when a segment of the Washington population withdrew, the arrest of the ashram director was the precipitating event which led to their exit, but frustration with the way that the local community was run figured equally in the final decision to cut their ties with Sikh Dharma. The individuals (all couples) who left wanted a more open and democratic approach to ashram affairs. In both settings the innovators seem to have been a bit naïve about the likely reactions to their demands for change in an established organization, and their enthusiasm and openness to new ideas may have led them to act without giving much thought to timing and tactics and to likely outcomes. But their desire to enrich and improve community life was sincere, and their rebellions were a message that the leadership would have to accept some devolution of authority, and, if the organization was to thrive, that it would be necessary to think more creatively about how to best harness the growing maturity and expertise of the membership at large.

As 3HO members adjusted to changing circumstances, residents of several ashrams began to live more independent lives, and a variety of life-styles emerged. Some lived separately from other members, some even went to work in ordinary business clothing. Such accommodation eroded some of the barriers between the organization and the outside world. While many were happy with such changes, some members clearly felt the loss of the early community, the group-in-fusion. Some saw this loss as the inevitable byproduct of individual and organizational maturation. Others saw it as a failing in the organization. In the early 1990s an alternative 3HO newsletter called *Visions* flourished briefly in the Bay area. In one article the author writes about "then" and "now." Then, "a magical, mystical, and miraculous reality was our standard frame of reference." Then, "a feeling of mutual admiration and kinship developed between us. . . . This atmosphere made us feel comfortable enough to try new roles, in which our performance, in general, was not subject to criticism." Then, members were happy to abide by Bhajan's teachings and advice and believed that they were part of a mass movement. Later, "we began to echo the trends of our national culture in the '80's; we were less interested in flights of fancy, and became more materialistic. . . . Many of us no longer get to know each other well. . . . We are not sure how far we can trust one another. Inter-group politics and manipulation are common. . . . Now we no longer agree on issues. . . . Perhaps we find ourselves with more internal strength as individuals, but with less unity and direction as a group" (G. Khalsa 1991, 10–11).

Another risk associated with greater worldliness is that individual members may be tempted to indulge in questionable business practices and may justify these in the name of loyalty to the group. Like other groups, 3HO has its examples of this phenomenon. The best documented is the case of a telemarketing business centered in Monterey, California. Claiming to represent a nonexistent business called C. A. Services Corporation, the director evidently called senior citizens and told them that they had won a "double Canadian lottery." They were to send a percentage of their "winnings" as a "tax" in order to receive the prize, which was never forthcoming. Complaints to the Better Business Bureau eventually led to investigations by the Monterey County district attorney's office and to the arrest of three men, two of them Sikhs (Monterey County Office of the District Attorney, June 17, 1992). One was cleared, but the operator of the scam, Kirpal Singh Khalsa, pleaded guilty to "grand theft, money laundering and illegal telemarketing," and in October 1992 was sentenced to three years in federal prison (*Monterey County (Calif.) Herald* 1992a; 1992b; 1992c; *State of California v. Kirpal Singh Khalsa*, No. MCR 8425 [1992], Superior Court of California; *World Sikh News* 1992).

As previously mentioned, the head of the Washington ashram and an associate were indicted on charges arising out of a sting operation. Albert Ellis and Gurujot Singh Khalsa were accused of "engaging in a continuing criminal enterprise involving the importation of multi-ton quantities of marijuana during the 1983–1987 time period" (*United States of America v. Gurujot Singh Khalsa*, No. 88-210-M [1988], Order of Detention, U.S. District Court, Alexandria, Va.).

The two were accused of arranging, and making payments on, a series of marijuana shipments. One of these shipments was found on a fishing vessel, the *Oregon Beaver*, in San Francisco Bay in April 1985. The boat carried twenty-two tons of marijuana. In 1987, yet another load was intercepted, this time off the coast of British Columbia. By this time, a DEA special agent was working under cover on the case, and he claimed to have met with Khalsa and Ellis (*United States of America v. Albert Ellis and Gurujot Singh Khalsa,* No. 3880144 FW [1988], Criminal Complaint, Northern District of California, City and County of San Francisco). According to this agent, Gurujot Singh Khalsa suggested that the informants should invest in one of the 3HO businesses, Khalsa Financial Services. But he "did not want drug transaction proceeds going directly into it. Instead, he told Special Agent Ogilvie to invest his money first in shell corporations and then transfer the money into Khalsa Financial Services" (*United States of America v. Gurujot Singh Khalsa,* 3). Gurujot Singh was convicted on charges of drug trafficking and money laundering but gave state's evidence and received a sentence of unsupervised parole. He claimed that events were not as they appeared on the surface. Ellis is still a fugitive.

Naturally, such events cast a shadow over organizational life. In the wake of such incidents, members may face probing questions from family, friends, and people they interact with in the community. Within the group they may feel that they must take a stand in favor of, or in opposition to, an individual, or that they must "keep up" no matter how difficult life becomes. Some have searched for scapegoats. Some have chosen unquestioning loyalty, and others a measured kind of loyalty. Some have questioned and some have abandoned their commitment to 3HO/Sikh Dharma. These events were further complicated by the fact that, in the 1980s, 3HO had to cope with external problems as well. These grew up in the wake of Sikh separatism and Indira Gandhi's murder. After these events the nature of the Indian Sikh leadership changed. Political maneuvering in ethnic Sikh communities intensified, and local 3HO ashrams were occasionally exposed to the forces that had been unleashed.

Personal Encounters

Almost from my first contacts with 3HO/Sikh Dharma, I had a recurring feeling that some of the women I talked with were considering their words quite carefully. That made sense, given that (1) they were actively involved in assimilating a new culture and a complex belief system, and verbalization was a major means of doing this, and (2) I was an outsider, and they were thinking carefully about what they said to me. Many had been interviewed by journalists and other commentators and felt that their words, and the organization as a whole, were distorted in the descriptions that emerged. But still I had a sense of spontaneity denied, of pain and struggle that were glossed-over. I often had a vague sense of discomfort when I was in 3HO surroundings and could not determine if that was projection of my own unease, a minor case of culture shock, or something more.

Over time, I encountered quite a few stories of Bhajan telling women whether or not to pursue careers, when to have children, and how to conduct their marriages. These troubled me in the simplest, most commonsensical, and feminist ways: I felt that he was intruding on what should be personal decisions. I told myself that some of my reactions were stereotypically American, individualistic, and predictable, and that I should try and put them aside—not away necessarily, but to the side. When an interviewee told me that Bhajan had told her not to study to become a chiropractor, as she had planned to do, but to sing *kirtan* and tend to her spiritual development instead, I struggled to view this as sound spiritual advice. But I was too secular an individual to truly understand such a decision, and too practical and skeptical, and perhaps materialistic, to think that a woman should jeopardize her earning capacity on the advice of a man who might have an interest in her obedience and submission.

My concerns crystallized when the woman who had been my first informant told me that she had chosen to leave the organization. "I thought it was a much cleaner operation than it is," she said. She also told me about Simran's separation from 3HO, and so I interviewed Simran as well.

I know now that this was one of the most painful periods of Simran's life. The organization had been the whole of her world, and now she found herself ostracized and judged. She had suddenly lost her friends, her roles, her routines, and central aspects of her self-concept. The pain was both emotional and cognitive, for she was questioning the reality that she had been so instrumental in constructing. She surprised me when she told me that she had been "mostly unhappy" in her seventeen years of participation, for I had assumed that a longtime leader with high status in the organization would have been reasonably happy in her position. But no, she said that she was often "miserable," although, at the time, she could not find a way to explain her discomfort. Now she could. For one thing, she had been constantly battling her own doubts and perceptions. There had been 3HO teachings and behaviors that troubled her, but she turned away from these. The good student did not give in to doubts or negative thinking. Her discomfort, she said, was intensified by isolation. Contacts outside of staff circles were discouraged. The women in the inner circle were told that no one could really understand their unique situation or the demands of their daily lives. Adding to her pain was the fact that she longed for children but was told that marriage was not for people in her position. Bhajan said that her destiny was to serve God and to seek liberation, and that there was no place for a family in her future. She struggled to accept this version of her destiny, and it sometimes seemed reasonable that she should sacrifice what was most important to her in order to serve God. Not only did she give up her dreams of family life, but she also felt that, in her official role, "any creativity on my part was stifled." It seemed to her that the Khalsa Council, of which she was a member, had little power, and that individuals who truly wanted to contribute to and shape the organization were constantly frustrated as they encountered firm control from above.

Looking back upon all of this now, it is the alienation from her own perceptions that she sees as particularly injurious. She describes it as a "shutting down to one's own intuitions," an expectation that one will "override" intuition and "break the connection to one's own truth." She says this while acknowledging the context in which it occurred. People who participated in the social movements of the 1960s learned to examine their own consciousness and to question many of their responses and their perceptions on the assumption that these had been shaped by a culture and by a social order that they could no longer embrace or trust. Thus, it was not an alien mental exercise that she encountered when she was encouraged to doubt many of her intuitions. How could she know for sure that they were not just held-over feelings resulting from her early socialization, or recurrent symptoms of lower consciousness?

But too much of this self-questioning violated another strain in counterculture thinking, a strain that assumed that somewhere under the layers of false consciousness laid down by society was the truth. As Tipton puts it, "[T]he counterculture assumes that all persons can know with certainty what is good by means of direct experience and intuition. . . . The good of the individual is to be aware—to experience and to know herself fully" (1982, 17). While 3HO also teaches that the individual, via prayer and meditation and the raising of kundalini, can know the true and the good, it also suggests that this is a long-term project and that there may be considerable self-deception along the way. Thus 3HO can undermine or limit faith in this intuitive morality, and did so in Simran's case. The very basis of her self-concept and much of the ground on which she had previously stood was shaken.

The turning point for Simran had come when she had an opportunity to marry a Sikh man she cared for. At this point she had no intention of leaving the organization; she simply hoped to change her position within it and to become an ordinary householder. This choice, she believes, was interpreted as a betrayal, and in the end she found herself ostracized and condemned. She left 3HO/Sikh Dharma, and she and her new husband moved away. Now she began to see the organization in a new light. People who had claimed to love and respect her would no longer speak to her. No one in 3HO inquired into her side of the story. She uncomfortably recalled her previous assumption that anyone who left was probably misguided and motivated by ego and negativity. She had been troubled by the organizational hierarchy and the extent of control from the top well before she left, but now she roundly condemned it, at the time telling me that Bhajan was surrounded by "yes men" who "don't question, and reinforce the illusion that he is perfect and has only your best interests at heart, knows your destiny and knows what is best for you." And within that setting, she said, Bhajan had a knack for pinpointing people's weaknesses and using these to manipulate individuals and win their loyalty. In short, it seemed to her that much of what the organization stood for was rapidly being lost, that "it all got corrupted."

As a member of the staff, Simran had access to luxuries—to travel both in the United States and India, to the use of the Mercedes, to a nice place to live, and to gifts and admiration—but these were attached to her position, and when she left and married she discovered that she had to "start from zero in every way," as she had no home, money, conventional job experience, or major possessions.

After my conversations with Simran I spoke with other ex-members. As everybody who has interviewed former members of the new religions knows, it can be difficult to sift through their information. There are distortions due to anger and resentment and loss. I had to allow for interpretations that might be associated with particularly difficult or confusing separations and with efforts to protect the self-concept (Mauss 1998). I also listened for language that might be a sign that former members had been influenced by the anticult movement. There were, for example, pieces of Simran's story, and sections of the legal suit that she filed with another ex-member, that were similar to the "captivity narratives" that Bromley (1998) associates with apostates whose exits are influenced by the anticult movement. These accounts typically suggest that the individual was tricked into joining, manipulated by various psychological techniques once she became a member, and then was isolated and essentially held hostage while exposed to techniques that further undermined her "capacity for rational, autonomous decision making" (42). An interview with another woman who filed suit against Bhajan most closely follows the captivity narrative and may be the most troubling account I have encountered. The interview was conducted by an ex-member and has been widely circulated among people who were once attached to the organization. The larger part of Simran's personal account, especially as she tells it today, does not fit this outline. Most of it suggests that she assumes personal responsibility for her choices and takes a measured view of the organization, but the other elements are there, as they were in the accounts of other former members. A number of ex-members also express outrage at what they construe as illegal or dishonest acts by people affiliated with Sikh Dharma, or they express disillusionment with the nature of the leadership. Some, who feel that they were set up to take the blame for others' illegal behavior, are particularly angry. But overall, most take a thoughtful and reasoned approach in their analyses and criticisms.

Several male ex-members told me that Bhajan's publicly expressed, respectful attitudes toward women were quite different from those he expressed privately. Several ex-members recounted stories of Bhajan encouraging men to employ "silence" as a way of "controlling" a difficult wife. Indeed, one ex-member, Stephen Josephs, recounts such an incident in his doctor of education dissertation (written when he was still associated with 3HO/Sikh Dharma): "I was silent that day and silent for four more until I was sure her ego was broken. . . . My first words to her were important after such a long silence. 'You are my wife,' I said. 'Your place is by my side and you must help me. You must be there all the time with all your strength. . . . If you won't act as my wife, then you cannot be my wife.' She said, 'Thank you'" (1974, 82–83).

Former members also talked about what seemed to them to have been very poorly matched spouses, the pain that these marital arrangements caused, and the extramarital affairs that grew out of this unhappiness. Emotions and feelings were often not discussed in these marriages; instead, spouses tried to feel the appropriate feelings or play the appropriate parts. One such ex-member described years in an unsuccessful arranged marriage. He had a series of affairs with secretaries (he was an ashram head) until one woman told him that she loved him. He had been repressing his feelings, working to the point of exhaustion day after day, and suddenly he found himself face-to-face with raw emotion. Rather than being pleased, or flattered, or even feeling guilty about her declaration of love, he felt nothing but terror, and he simply broke. He turned to therapy and acknowledged a "closet" self, a self that was needy and caring and frightened, a self long denied.

His fear was a compound of many parts. It was composed of exhaustion and stress, and of repressed needs and feelings, but also of fears about 3HO activities. He believed that some 3HO members were in contact with Sikh separatists or terrorists. He had heard rumors of drug dealing.

Other ex-members expressed similar concerns to me. I was not in a position to judge the truth of their claims, but it was clear that they walked in shadows and that they were deeply disillusioned with the organization.

What I heard was sufficient to make me look more closely at the role of charisma in the organization, and at the beliefs and practices that fostered solidarity, loyalty, dedication, and even dependency.

Personal and Collective Identities

Lindholm (1990) depicts one strand of thinking about modernity that is associated with writers such as Bellah, Lifton, Riesman, and Goffman, all of whom portray modern actors as rudderless, pragmatic, and likely to shift from identity to identity; they are set "afloat in an uncertain and perilous world where meaning is hard to discern and secure commitment unlikely" (81). They suffer the anomie that accompanies normative ambiguity and extensive choice, and, additionally, they find that "this fluid, highly competitive society can lead to a tremendous anxiety about making 'correct' decisions" (81).

Lindholm goes on to say that these conditions can "push individuals toward immersion in a charismatic group," as solipsism and conflicting messages set up a yearning for their opposites: merger, clarity, communion, and wholeness (82). I think, in the case of 3HO, such arguments explain the organization's appeal to a portion of its members. Lindholm makes another relevant point. He notes an opposite route into charismatic commitment which "begins not with an individualistic ethic but with a communal ideology of identification with the masses and an absolute rejection of mainstream self-centeredness" (121). A segment of the 3HO membership certainly came to the organization carrying this deep distrust of individual striving and a conviction that the society as a whole was fatally corrupt. Once they sampled the Eastern spiritual wares, found pleasure in meditation and other practices and in the support of a caring group, they could finally allow themselves the luxury of commitment. Here, within the group was a chance, perhaps the only chance, to maintain a communal way of life, to eschew many forms of individualism, and to construct an alternative way of living. Here, perhaps, ideals could be realized, and sisterhood and brotherhood might become a lived reality.

Of course, it is easier to dream of such things than to actually construct an organization in which one can experience the just merger, the happy conjunction of self and group, particularly if one has been raised in a culture that embraces individualism and personal achievement. The would-be member is likely to turn to a leader who can symbolize the desired form of union—one whose performances and pronouncements can evoke shared enthusiasm, one who can promote shared rituals and can delineate the desired relationship between self and group.

But even in the presence of such a leader, members themselves must work to construct a collective identity and to align it with their individual goals and personalities. As I looked at the organization I became more and more interested in the ways in which individual biographies and an emergent collective identity were configured (Melucci 1995). In an effort to look at these, in a fair-minded way, I attempted to apply Robbins's concept of identity processes to 3HO life.

Identity Processes

Robbins suggests that "[i]f any society is to survive, it must have some institutional means of inculcating in its members knowledge of behaviors and symbols appropriate to given identities, and must periodically ensure that those identities are confirmed or reinforced. It must have means to ensure that individuals believe that they are what they are supposed to be, and means to facilitate identity transformations. These means are what we have called identity processes" (1973, 1208). He goes on to identify particular types of identity processes, some of which will be briefly surveyed here as they apply to 3HO. While most of these processes are not explicitly named elsewhere, some have figured in previous chapters and others will appear in more detail in chapters to follow. Most have been instituted by the 3HO leadership, some by rank and file members.

It is important first to note, however, that in 3HO, while identity and organization are closely intertwined, women members often have sources of identity available to them outside of 3HO. These include their familial roles as daughters and sisters to nonmembers and, for many, external occupational roles from which they garner social identities and self-esteem. All possess distinctive talents, skills, and perspectives which shape their self-concepts and their enacted identities. Moreover, the women are not necessarily passive recipients of 3HO culture; they work at socializing themselves and choosing those aspects of 3HO life that meet their goals or best affirm their self-concepts (e.g., Dawson 1990; Richardson and Kilbourne 1985).

Identity Diffusion and Dissolution

These are processes that dissolve old identities, or obscure the boundaries of the self. Robbins mentions fasts, trance, shame, and mortification under this heading, and, clearly, all of these are employed in 3HO. These are typically the techniques that worry anticult writers, and they do have the potential for abuse, but as Robbins and many others have noted, they also are used worldwide and in many settings; they are certainly not unique to the new religions.

In 3HO, members are sometimes encouraged to go on special diets, including "mono-diets" which involve eating only one food for a specified period of time to cure an ailment or some general form of malaise. Public shaming has sometimes been employed by Yogi Bhajan and by other leaders. For example, Josephs, in the doctoral dissertation he wrote while he was a 3HO ashram head, addresses his own use of this technique. (It should be noted that he is describing the formative years.) He does so in a context in which he explores the use of Kanter's commitment mechanisms in ashram life. He is explicit about the need to dissolve old identities:

> Public embarrassment is used as a form of what Ms. Kanter terms "a mortification process," or the breakdown of the individual's sense of separateness to give way to a sense of identity with the group. Often offensive behavior stems from a preoccupation with personal goals rather than goals seen in the light of group consciousness. . . . As the head of the house I sometimes feel it is necessary to criticize someone publicly. I do this only when circumstances or peers have not provided the proper teachings. (1974, 20)

He also describes other means of intentionally dissolving old identities: "When the new student moves in, I consider it important for him to make a clean break with the past. It is part of my office to give permission for trips to visit friends or home. I often exercise that right of refusal. . . . Other links with the past, such as listening to music associated with former conscious [sic] days, wearing hair down rather than in a turban, visiting old girlfriends or boyfriends, or simply escaping into a reclusive consciousness are openly discouraged" (1974, 5).

Other modes of mortification were extensively employed, particularly in the 1970s and 1980s. Depending upon the member's personal history and tastes, there was a degree of mortification involved in relinquishing colorful clothing or in accepting a vegetarian diet. For some, attempts to give up drugs, alcohol, and caffeine involved a real struggle. There was considerable mortification involved in rising daily before dawn and beginning the day with a cold shower and vigorous yoga, in accepting an arranged marriage that was not desired, in seeing one's child leave for boarding school in India, or in abandoning fond hopes for a chosen career.

The boundaries of the self are redefined when an individual becomes deeply involved with 3HO/Sikh Dharma. Karma, conditioning, child-hood conflicts, and the contents of the subconscious are said to be pow-erful determinants of behavior. Members believe that karma and conflict will be burned off by yoga and meditation and by the instructions of the spiritual teacher, but they assume that much of this occurs outside of conscious awareness. Members must accept the existence of such invis-ible processes, and of a dynamic that is understood and initiated by the spiritual teacher but is not necessarily accessible to the conscious self. Women also are told they are changeable by nature, and much of this variability is attributed to physiology. One woman said that she tells herself, "This is the way I feel about this now, but I'm a woman and my emotions change every two and a half days. How I feel about something now will be different in two and a half days."

The extent to which identity is diffused varies, of course, from one individual to the next, as does the interpretation of this process. Iden-tity diffusion in the new religions can have a particularly reflexive and intentional element. Many of the members of these groups understand identity processes clearly and choose to be exposed to them. They will-ingly experiment with identity, or at least choose to keep selfhood open and unfinished. Many are adventurers in this realm and willing to take the risks and to pay the price involved. Some, however, are less knowl-edgeable about, or are unaware of, the effects of such processes. They accept them because they are devoted followers, or because the prac-tices are normative. The costs may be more difficult for them to calcu-late because the risks are unrecognized.

Identity Formation and Transformation

Robbins refers to those practices that enable the individual to learn the nature of available identities and relevant behaviors and symbols as "processes of identity formation and transformation." These encourage the belief that one is "what he is supposed to be or wants to be, or what others want him to be" (1973, 1208). These processes represent a crucial link between personal and collective identities. Marital, Amrit, ministe-rial, and 3HO vows contribute to such identity formation. They specify statuses, duties, responsibilities, and attitudes associated with new iden-tities and wrap them in a tissue of symbols and values. Yogi Bhajan's lec-tures and classes also define his expectations of members, as do a variety of manuals, workshops, tapes, courses, and training sessions offered by Yogi Bhajan and by other leaders and significant figures in 3HO life. Major ceremonial occasions, such as the solstice celebrations and Baisakhi Day, become opportunities to experience and experiment with changing identities.

Identities may be further transformed and elaborated by Yogi Bhajan when he discusses aspects of the self in private interviews or in response to specific questions. He will claim to see a person's history and character in her aura. He may tell a woman that she is an "old soul," that she possesses special talents, that she has difficulty making commitments, or that she has been wasting too much of her energy on unworthy men. He may tell her that she has narrowly escaped death or faces trauma if she does not change her ways. (All of these revelations have been reported to me by members or ex-members.) Many 3HO men and women expect Yogi Bhajan to know them better than they know themselves and to define the nature of their unplumbed depths and of their nascent spiritual qualities.

Identity Confirmation

Robbins defines identity confirmations as "those cultural processes that function to permit or aid the individual in attaining consistency between his self and his social and public identities" (1973, 1215). Probably the most far-reaching form of identity confirmation in 3HO is the acceptance of the idea that one is on a unique spiritual path. This path links public and private selves, and provides a wealth of potentially integrative imagery. Yet, even given this context, 3HO members will find that their public and spiritual, or subjective and organizational, identities are at times in opposition, or are poorly aligned. In such circumstances there are a variety of approved interpretations of the situation. There are also diverse prescriptions for remedying it.

Thus 3HO beliefs about healing and disease can explain a disjunction between public and private identities. Remedies center on the idea of balance, the intent of 3HO healing systems being to reestablish a balance between mind and body or between inner and outer selves. An unhappy woman may be encouraged to alter her public identity. She may be told to pursue a "more graceful" or less stressful occupation because 3HO theories of healing hold that an unhealthy environment— for example, stressful or ungraceful—can cause illness. Alternatively, an individual may be encouraged to enhance or alter a public identity. She may be encouraged to seek a new occupation or to develop a talent. If she feels that she is not skilled enough to pursue the new career, or outgoing enough to develop the talent, she may be told to meditate on the self as empowered, able, and knowledgeable. She may visualize herself acting successfully. Thus, meditation and visualization are among the available remedies. Members are also reminded that they can become what they "project."

The emphasis on developing the neutral mind in the course of meditation further enables the individual to manage, or at least explain, any tension she may experience between organizational expectations and personal desires, or between her public identities and her private sense of self. She expects to observe a contest between positive and negative aspects of the mind, but she also expects to strengthen her own capacity to transcend these. She is taught that neither public nor private identity is final because both are subsumed under a higher reality. Thus, dissonance between inner and organizational selves is allowed for, and even expected, in the 3HO belief system, and members are encouraged to have some patience with it or to regard it as a form of negativity or "tantrum" that can, in the long run, be transcended. Members expect to encounter situations in which "ego" is interfering with "growth," and they use language with their children and with one another that assumes a level of internal conflict and a capacity to watch and contain one's own ego displays. The following excerpt from my journal describes a scene at women's camp that dramatizes this:

> It is 4:30 A.M. Lines of women in white terry cloth bathrobes around the shower stalls and at the bathroom. In the bathroom a young girl has been sick and her mother is making her presentable. She is telling her that her upset stomach is due to eating the wrong foods, but that she has learned a lesson and she should thank God for teaching it to her and just go on from there. When the child continues to cry and to say that she just wants it "to go away," her mother tells her that we must accept things and deal with them, and if she is afraid she should sing the song that begins, "We are the Khalsa."

Equally, their mothers are taught that even their strongest maternal feelings must be disciplined, and that it may be necessary for a child to live with another couple or attend boarding school in India in order to have the best environment in which to mature.

It is understood that, at times, the conflict between positive and negative may become an all-out battle. As we have seen, Yogi Bhajan has taught devotees that at some point on the spiritual path the individual's personal weaknesses may threaten to overwhelm her and her spiritual life. Some need—to feel important, to be successful, or to dominate others, for example—will lead her to doubt the teachings or to abandon the discipline. This is *shaktipod*. If she can triumph over her weakness she will have taken a giant stride on the spiritual path. If she succumbs, she may go astray and not regain the path; rather than experiencing joy and evolution, she will repeat the karmic cycle.

Identity Management and Identity Struggles

Identity management refers to an individual's efforts to maintain and perform identities and to get others to validate and confirm them. Struggles refer to "those interactions in which there is a discrepancy between an individual's claimed identity and the identity attributed to him by others" (Robbins 1973, 1214).

One of the major early 3HO efforts in the direction of identity management was the push to legitimate the organization by encouraging members to become professional, successful in businesses, better educated, tidy and well dressed, and to live in nice, well-kept houses. All of this made it possible for members to present themselves as ordinary middle-class people who happened to practice a minority religion and to rise early in the morning. This was furthered by the emphasis on careful speech, poise, and graceful self-presentation.

Meditation has also been used as a means of managing identities. The individual who, during a morning meditation session, imagines herself performing her job well later in the day is attempting to manage an identity. In fact, many women have assured me that they perform all of their roles better on days when they attend *sadhana*. Various small rituals also facilitate identity management. Acts which express respect and courtesy in 3HO, such as serving "yogi tea" (a spiced tea, similar to chai) to guests, offering a massage to the ashram director's wife, greeting other 3HO members as "ji" (a term of respect) all validate identities and leadership positions and affirm the special relationship between people on a spiritual path.

When they are communicating with non-3HO audiences, members gear yoga, cooking, and healing classes to their secular audiences and often do not mention Sikhism or Yogi Bhajan unless they are questioned about this side of their lives. When it occurs, they aim to appear poised, calm, and neutral in the face of harassment. They have learned to turn potential criticism to their advantage and to define and control situations that might otherwise prove damaging. Negativity in the form of skeptics and enemies is met with aggressive positivity.

It appeared to me that many classes and workshops were structured so as to minimize possible criticism. Questions and discussion were usually welcomed, but the stage was set so that certain assumptions were simply not questioned. Because sessions were often opened by chanting *ong namo guru dev namo* (a Sikh Dharma translation of this is "I bow to the wisdom of the Universe; I bow to the wisdom within"), thus establishing a religious, and even esoteric, framework, those who attended had to accept this framework and, perhaps, suspend disbelief out of tact and respect. Beliefs are stated as fact: this exercise *will* improve digestion, there *is* a transpersonal realm, healing *is* a matter of balance. Few people in any audience are likely to be rude enough to respond with the equivalent of "How do you know?" When questions did take that turn, workshop leaders were quick to say that this was their particular belief system or what their spiritual teacher had told them, and that of course they did not necessarily expect everyone else to agree.

Identity struggles can come in many forms, and they will be further examined in the next chapter. Instructions to marry, to change careers, to return or not to return to school, to have or not to have children can become occasions of struggle. Individuals may resist instructions and may chafe or rebel at the requirement for obedience. They may experience intense anxiety, be reduced to tears, or argue. In the case of a member's active resistance, the spiritual leader may insist that his instructions be followed, perhaps buttressing his position by claiming to be able to read the individual's aura and to perceive the individual's needs. Bhajan, or another leader, may argue that the individual's desires reflect an unhealthy preoccupation with a limited and repetitive identity, or that they are shallow, misguided, or egotistical. Rejection of organizationally assigned identities can lead to intense pressure from others, not to mention a pervading fear that resistance was indeed inspired by ego and by the lower aspects of the self.

Norms, Rewards, and Accounts

3HO identity processes are supported by a number of organizational norms, rewards, and sanctions, by institutionally endorsed means of accounting for experience, and, as we have seen, by members' own distinctive ways of interpreting 3HO beliefs and practices and integrating these into their lives.

Norms

Members subscribe to the norm that one should at least give a new idea or practice a hearing and a try. A member may wear a turban, attend *sadhana* regularly, submit to the instructions of the spiritual teacher, or take Sikh vows in order to test the effects of these practices. Even if the individual experiments and notices no immediate results, this need not indicate that a practice is ineffectual. The student is told that change will eventually occur and she need only persist. Here is Josephs again, explaining the desired attitude: "After a time the student gains the confidence that the eradication of his ego is in God's hands. Our only job is to do a good sadhana and 'keep up.' There is only so much one can do, and, realizing that, one becomes more relaxed about progress" (1974, 51). The experimental approach can extend to an effort to believe a teaching, or to behave as if one believes it. Eventually, the student should be rewarded by solid results. Thus there is a predisposition to verify teachings and to find within the self the approved emotions, sensations, attitudes, and motivations; or, failing this, at least to act for awhile as though one were indeed in possession of them.

Commitment is further enhanced by a belief system that often plays down the significance of specific individuals, roles, and circumstances. Thus, a marriage is a yoking of male and female principles more than it is a union of two distinctive personalities. Divorce is not likely to solve problems because whatever is going wrong in one's current marriage will just be repeated in the next, new spouse notwithstanding. Resistance to roles that are a systemic part of the organization, or a decision to leave the organization to take up another life-style, are denied validity. Whatever justifications an individual might offer for leaving 3HO/Sikh Dharma will be viewed as typical of the excuses that the individual always uses to avoid difficulties. Better to simply stay where one is, maintain commitment, and stop looking for nonexistent greener pastures.

In fact, one should color one's own pasture green by generally seeing the positive side of 3HO life and ensuring that one's self-presentation and speech are "uplifting." This means that members are on the lookout for personal and organizational strengths and successes, focusing not on organizational flaws but on the reasons for remaining a member. If a member does spot a problem, she should attempt to resolve it rather than dwell on 3HO's failings. Eager to belong and to be—and appear to be— generous, spiritual, and kind, members may swallow doubts and worries, or subject these to rationalization rather than to exploration.

Rewards

Snow (1987) found that Nichiren Shoshu Buddhism maintained group mobilization by offering several "ideological inducements for becoming and remaining active" (163). These inducements included a belief that the organization's mission was divinely given, that members were contributing "to a kind of cosmic plan that was divinely prophesied years ago" (164), and that individuals who participate in the movement will become public leaders when the movement comes to fruition (167). There are similar inducements in the strand of prophetic, and sometimes millenarian, thinking that periodically surfaces in 3HO. A 3HO member can believe that she is part of an elite ushering in the new order. As Bromley puts it, "[A]dherents gain biographical continuity and salvation by assuming charter membership in the tradition that is about to be born" (1997, 39).

Belief in the significance of the organization, the value of its practices, and in one's mission as a member gives meaning to everyday life and to continued and active participation, and is a major reward. But this belief does require confirmatory experience and additional rewards if the individual is to maintain faith and commitment on a day-to-day basis. Such rewards include the support of the community and the pleasure, calm, and empowerment that the individual experiences during *sadhana* and meditation. Over the years, 3HO members have also acquired rewarding skills, knowledge, and employment opportunities by virtue of membership. Women record and sell tapes of mantras, teach in Khalsa schools, and serve their community as therapists and medical workers. They have attained knowledge of another culture and language, of massage and alternative medicine, and of nutrition and gourmet vegetarian cookery. Many have improved their verbal, social, and organizational skills. Things have changed since Bailey visited the ashrams, and there are an increasing number of leadership opportunities open to women. While none serve as ashram directors, women have long been active as ministers, and in ashram administration, teaching, and outreach activities. Several ashrams have created administrative councils or steering committees. Appointees are responsible for financial planning, fund raising, school administration, devising plans for future construction, and the like. Women make up the majority of members in those councils that now exist.

There are also rewards related to gender roles. Many women see freedom from conventional "goal orientation" as an organizational benefit. They are free to actively pursue careers if they wish to, but they are equally free to choose a multifaceted life-style that combines community activities, family life, and time for spiritual enrichment. As one informant described it, "There was one woman who had tried a number of different jobs and nothing really worked out for her, and the Siri Singh Sahib said, 'Ok, your job is to be a spiritual wife,' and she was so relieved. The society would say she had to work or she's just a parasite or lazy or whatever. . . . Women here, they can work or not work. . . . I really feel I've had more flexibility here in 3HO." Similarly, a young woman who grew up in 3HO said, "There are some ladies in our community that are more into developing a career than others, but for me I see myself as 'doing things.' There are so many things to do in our community. . . . I do computer work. . . . I've done a lot of traveling. I've gone a couple of times to India, . . . and for my twenty years I feel like I've gotten a lot in."

Interpretations and Accounts

There are many standard explanations for difficulties in daily living when they occur. The most far-reaching of these is karma. Another inclusive explanation is separation from God. The individual may have an inflated notion of her own uniqueness, or she may forget that she is really an extension of God. If this is the case, she must cease to act as an isolated, willful individual and "let God do." Cultural programming may also be a cause of negativity and often contributes to separation. It can be the source of fear, neurosis, and low self-esteem. Similarly, physical causes may be cited. Poor diet, insufficient exercise, and feminine physiology are all possible sources of pain and negativity. Astrology can provide further possible explanations for trouble. A problem may be a typical issue for someone born under a particular sign.

Other troubles spring from encountering the behavior of people who are spiritually "unevolved." The spiritual person must protect herself from too much of their "unconscious" behavior or she will be dragged down by it. She should choose her occupation and her associates with this in mind, and she should leave a situation if she finds herself incapable of altering it for the better. She has every right to protect her own consciousness.

Of course, there may be more immediate and more individual sources of a problem. The individual may simply lack skills, tact, or the ability to communicate. She may be acting out of her own "lower consciousness." It may be that she is insecure and at the mercy of her emotions. She may be trying to manipulate, threaten, or control another person, or she may be trying to compete with a spouse. She may be failing in her spiritual discipline, not attending *sadhana*, perhaps, and therefore becoming irritable and erratic as negative aspects of the subconscious come to dominate her behavior.

Applying Pressure

One way that Bhajan and other leaders have encouraged compliance has been to use everyday living arrangements and major ceremonial events to confirm and intensify a collective identity. We have already encountered the image of the 3HO/Sikh Dharma life-style as a "pressure cooker" or a crucible in which the processes of spiritual evolution are accelerated. As one informant put it, "I felt as soon as I joined that, in a sense, I was in a pressure cooker because I lacked all my old routines and ways of thinking that kept me in a certain limited sense of self. They were being kind of gradually eroded, and I had this whole new way of experiencing things." Bhajan himself has used the image of a pressure cooker, applying it to ashram life, to the women's camp, and to solstice gatherings.

Solstice Gatherings

Solstice celebrations were an early innovation. The first was held in the summer of 1969. It was followed by summer and winter gatherings in 1971, with attendance reaching two to three hundred individuals. In 1972, one thousand people attended a summer solstice celebration (Bailey 1974, 104). The gatherings were soon institutionalized, and 3HO members and their yoga students began to regularly converge on Florida in the winter and New Mexico in the summer for these events. In the organization's formative years, solstices were an important setting for the definition and enactment of a corporate identity (Bailey 1974). Today the gatherings continue to cement that identity. Since ashrams are widely dispersed, solstice gatherings are a reaffirmation of community and an opportunity to be with Sikhs from around the country. They also link personal efforts to grow and discipline the self to organizational goals and expectations. They have both public and personal significance.

At the public, organizational level, solstice rapidly became a time to enact important rituals and to make public vows, including initiations into Sikh Dharma, marriage ceremonies, and opportunities for Yogi Bhajan to publicly assign people their spiritual names. Solstice was also the setting for mass ordination of ministers. Thus, Sikhism was spread and institutionalized at these gatherings. Dusenbery (1975) sees 1972 as a transitional year in the shift toward Sikhism. Heads of all existing 3HO ashrams, as well as other individuals, were ordained in 1972–73. Bailey found that by December 1972, sixty-two ministers had been ordained (1974, 111). In 1973, another observer, Alan Tobey, attended a solstice gathering and later wrote a description of the ten days that he dedicated to participant observation. He saw approximately eighty ministers ordained then (1976, 19). At that time there were many very small ashrams, each of which had a director. Each director, and his wife if he was married, had to become a minister. Evidently these early ordinations were sometimes performed with little advance preparation. In the course of answering my questions about the minister's role, one woman described her own ordination: "He was making our house an ashram, and then that summer when we went to solstice they were getting ready to have a ministers' ceremony and . . . the head of the East Coast came up to me and said, 'Where's your husband?' And I said, 'He's getting the boys ready.' And he said, 'Go get him and get in line.' And I said, 'What line?' And he said, 'This line, you all are going to be made ministers in five minutes'" (1985). She later had to study for a series of minister's examinations, but the procedure seems to indicate that some aspects of the organization's religious framework were introduced hastily.

The first solstices were clearly demanding and difficult events. The sites were primitive and the days were full. All activities were conducted without the accompaniment of conversation. The only speech at solstice was in the form of mantras, chants, and inflected uses of the phrase *Sat Nam*. Short written notes were allowed only if another form of communication was necessary. These rigors were meant to bolster members' confidence in their powers of endurance. Finding that they could break the patterns of daily life and overcome obstacles here, they would more readily believe that they could reshape themselves and construct a new way of life when they returned to civilization. Bhajan made this goal explicit in an address at the 1973 summer solstice: "Can we prove to ourselves that deep, deep in us we have the strength and are capable to do anything we want to do? . . . If we never learn in our lives to break our patterns of life for ten days we will never learn to live happy. . . . Can you remain silent. . . . Can you overcome your needs. . . . Here we want to build a nation which we have lost. . . . To prove to ourselves that we have the spirit to survive through every obstacle" (Bhajan 1973a, 6–7).

Disciplines such as silence were also intended to compel the individual to look inward. The talk and energy usually directed toward maintenance of personas, attitudes, and egos could be redirected. Free of their usual roles, and of the talk which supports them, solstice participants should learn to "drink the nectar within," as Bhajan said, since much human pain issues from a failure to recognize this spiritual core of the self. People accept socially constructed goals and identities rather than looking inward where the true self lies: "[Y]ou are influenced by A, B, C . . . all the time. Why? Because you are not *you* at all! . . . We care for society. We care for the image. We care to create an image, not to create what we are. And that is all which is bringing us pain. It brings fluctuation: 'Oh, I may not be right, I might be wrong. I have to be great'" (Bhajan 1972a, 11).

At solstice, accustomed identities are held in abeyance, or diffused, and the individual seeks to contact the higher dimensions of the self. But this always occurs within a structure. There are planned events and routines, and sessions of white Tantric yoga. The exercises, particularly in the early years, were, as an early observer noted, "usually of quite long duration. . . . [T]hey are difficult, either physically or emotionally; they may involve strong physical effort to the point of great pain" (Tobey 1976, 15).

Tobey described a composite Tantric session as he experienced it in 1973. One section of this description catches the intended effect:

> [Couples] rise up on their knees (so that their faces almost touch) and then kneel back down again, maintaining eye contact, in time with a complicated eight-part mantra chanted alternately by the men and the women. Although this lasts for sixty-one minutes without pause, in the concentration required to perform it properly all sense of time disappears. With every rising, great pain builds in the thighs and challenges one's will to continue. Locked in the tantric lines, though, the continuing effort of all the others is an encouragement to "keep up," to participate in the "group consciousness" of the exercise and not drop out because of individual discomfort. The concentration and the pain . . . and the hypnotic force of the mantra create a specific altered state of consciousness, in which individual ego is dissolved into this shared activity and disappears for the duration (1976, 16).

Tobey viewed the solstice as a modern-day errand into the wilderness. Like the Pilgrims, he said, 3HO members were trying to establish a model community. They were émigrés in their own country, going "to a new space within America" (1976, 29). It seems to me that they might equally be likened to Plains Indians embarking upon a vision quest. They venture into the wilderness where they undergo physical and mental trials, and induce altered states of consciousness, in order to establish a new identity and experience a form of spiritual empowerment. It is worth noting that this movement away from society and tradition to a wilderness where the "true" self can emerge is a frequent theme in American literature (e.g., Lewis 1955, Slotkin 1973, Smith 1950). The organization's spiritual orientation may be Eastern, but, in this case, it has adopted rhetoric, myths, and rhythms of selfhood that are prototypically American.

Charisma and the Role of the Spiritual Teacher

Identity in 3HO also has to be understood in terms of the charismatic leader. Charisma, as Wallis (1982, 1984) argues, is socially constructed. A leader's qualities and authority must be recognized and substantiated by members. Followers support the leader's claims and offer affection and admiration in exchange for the goods that he or she has to offer. Although charisma makes many things possible it is, by its very nature, precarious. Supporters can withdraw their approval and their willingness to legitimate a leader's claims. They may tire of emotional and physical demands. Group members also have, as Wallis (1984) notes, good reason to limit a charismatic leader's authority or to redirect it into conventional bureaucratic forms. As members assume positions of respect and responsibility within the organization they may wish to institutionalize these. They may seek to limit the leader's authority in order to increase or assure their own.

Wallis suggests that a charismatic leader can respond to such institutionalizing and rationalizing forces, and the potential threat that these may pose, in various ways. One response is to encourage them. The leader recognizes the advantages of institutionalization and "actively directs that process in such a way as to control it and utilize institutionalized structures and procedures to buttress his authority rather than allowing it to constrain him" (1984, 110).

Bhajan has periodically pursued this route since he first nudged 3HO in the direction of organized religion. He instituted formal Sikh vows, sought recognition from Amritsar, and encouraged his followers to pursue further education, enter businesses, become ministers, and reach out into their communities. But he has resolutely held onto the reins and has maintained a dramatic persona. He has always balanced institutionalization with beliefs and practices that undermine routines and everyday realities. He does not allow his students to become too comfortable in their secular lives. He interrupts the smooth flow of an individual's life with instructions to move to a different ashram, to pursue a particular spiritual discipline, to get married, or to send a child to school in India. The 3HO ritual cycle also breaks ordinary life with solstice celebrations, the women's training camp, and even daily *sadhana*.

Conger and Rabindra (1998) have examined the behavior of charismatic business leaders, and, although they have studied business settings, their observations are equally relevant to charisma in new religions. These authors identify three stages of leader behavior. In the first, the leader successfully evaluates the status quo, his followers' needs, and the resources available within the surrounding environment. Based on this reading, the leader then moves on to the second stage and articulates an "inspirational vision that is highly discrepant from the status quo yet within latitude of acceptance." In the third stage, the leader further elaborates on this vision and demonstrates the ways in which it is to be achieved. This involves personal example and "unconventional or counternormative" practices. Followers feel that the leader is passionate about the goals and is "incurring great personal risk and cost" to achieve them. This intensifies their trust and respect, and, finally, these steps lead to internal cohesion, consensus, and "values congruence" (50–51).

If we look at Bhajan's case, it is clear that he has followed these stages. He assessed the needs and values of his counterculture students and designed a distinctive spiritual path that he, and they, believed to be specifically tailored to their circumstances and to the North American environment. He recognized their need for structure, security, and meaning. He personified followers' hopes and embodied what they found best and most precious in themselves and in their past. Bhajan then elaborated his vision and tied it to Sikhism and to a future in which the Khalsa would lead. He inspired his students by example, by extensive teaching, and by including such "counternormative" practices as kundalini and Tantric yoga. He became a protector of their special qualities and potential and assured them that, in time, they would have the skills and the attitudes they needed in order to realize his vision.

Bhajan has proved particularly adept at portraying himself as someone who incurred "great personal risk and cost." He has consistently portrayed himself as an innovator and as a man willing to risk all for the sake of his mission, one who has suffered and sacrificed for his 3HO family. For example, he is said to have paid a price for introducing kundalini yoga to the public. According to 3HO tradition, before Bhajan taught it, kundalini was practiced only by an elite. He says that he formally introduced it because it was an appropriate spiritual discipline for the time and a good technique for Americans who expect rapid progress in all endeavors, but he says that he had to do it in the face of criticism and condemnation. In fact, when he was studying 3HO, Gardner was told that it was dangerous for Bhajan to teach kundalini publicly. "The legend within 3HO today," he wrote in 1978, "is that Yogi Bhajan himself became gravely ill in 1969 for daring to be an iconoclast . . . and was saved only by the great outpouring of prayers from his students" (130).

Bhajan speaks of how he must endure his students' "dramas," egoism, and doubts. Whenever one of them abandons the path, Bhajan's pain is said to be great. Like a parent he will do anything for his students, but, he says, they should realize that leadership exacts a toll, and they should treat him with appropriate respect and consideration. He suggests that there are few benefits, and many costs, to leadership.

Conger and Rabindra, like other writers on the subject, address the "shadow side" of charisma, contrasting what they call positive and negative forms:

> Negative charismatic leaders use the power of their position or office, rewards and sanctions under their control, and various impression management techniques to get followers to perform required behaviors and to demonstrate follower compliance. . . . Positive charismatic leaders, on the other hand, use empowerment instead of control strategies to bring about changes in the followers' core beliefs and values as they move the organization toward its goals. . . . At the heart of the negative form or the shadow side of charismatic leadership are two fundamental processes—follower dependence in the form of transference dynamics and the leader's own potential for narcissism. (1998, 216)

Presumably, most leaders fall into a gray area between positive and negative leadership. This is true of Bhajan. There is much about Bhajan's leadership that has proven positive and empowering. But there is also much in his approach that can foster dependency, and much that is aimed at obtaining members' compliance. Often he appears to use his image as a leader who has risked and sacrificed for others in order to elicit obedience and respect. His changeable persona can keep students worrying about Bhajan's reactions and make them anxious to please him. An entire mythology has grown up around him. He claims special powers, including the ability to see into the future. I was told that he can control water—he can bring rain or cause flooding—but he has eschewed use of this capability because it is magical, rather than spiritual, in nature. Bhajan is also said to travel on an "astral plane": while talking to an individual in Los Angeles he can respond to the needs of someone in Española or correct the mistakes made by a yoga teacher in Boston.

In contrast, students, particularly during the 1970s and 1980s, were reminded of their own fallibility and were already painfully aware of the mistakes they had made in the past. They accepted the premise that American culture was impoverished. They knew that they were in their spiritual infancy and had yet to learn about the proper etiquette and respect due to a teacher. They required guidance in order to construct new identities and new patterns of thought. Students of 3HO must have often felt like the proverbial ugly Americans bungling about in the wonders of the Eastern spiritual landscape.

But Bhajan also offered visions of future empowerment. Great powers are attributed to the awakened mind in 3HO. The individual mind is seen as an extension of the Infinite Mind, and so "anything and everything is influenced by the mind" (Bhajan 1973e, 27). The world, members were taught, can be imprinted by an active, focused mind. Equally, the mind's power could be directed inward and used to program, or reprogram, the self. As one 3HO counselor put it, "[C]hange the thoughts, to change the emotions, to change the desires, to change the actions" (personal notes, 1981). Bhajan taught his students that change is partially a matter of language and attitude. "Never say, 'I am bad.' Never say, 'I am miserable.' They are mantras!" he asserts (Bhajan 1972a, 12).

Attached to this call for positive thinking, however, was criticism of "negativity." This term has a range of connotations. It can refer to unpleasant "lower consciousness" attitudes and behavior such as greed and jealousy or can be applied to the fears, anxieties, angers, and compulsions that may haunt the subconscious. It can refer to a tendency to see the worst in others, in situations, and in the self.

Negativity casts a shadow on the 3HO psyche. However hard a member works at thinking positively and cleansing the subconscious, there is always the possibility of being overcome by negativity and of falling by the wayside. Bhajan teaches that negativity can be difficult to recognize. In the form of egotism it can even be mistaken for virtue—for devotion, strength, determination, or generosity. At its worst, the ego is said to be hydra-headed, constantly manufacturing desires and illusions that can lead the individual astray. As a spiritual teacher, Bhajan claims he can see what is hidden from the individual and can guide the ordinary person through the mind's toils. He can spot negativity and discern its sources. Lacking "the guidance of the man of God, one can never hope to find the way through the maze of the human mind" (W. Khalsa 1979, 335).

Ideally, the adherent should surrender entirely to the teacher and thus to the universal Guru. Bhajan describes the process:

> Why is it necessary to surrender? Is there any way other than surrender to get over your habitual consciousness? There is no other way—because when you surrender without, you find the within. . . . Outside you have given up, you do not exist—you are blocked. . . . Now all this energy, which forms you, has been blocked by surrender, by belonging to someone. So what happens? This energy is blocked, it cannot go outside, so it goes within. Everything will go inside and you will see your own potential. To take this potential out, you have to offer this gift. (Bhajan 1972c, 3)

Yogi Bhajan also teaches that a student should never argue with the teacher. "When you start arguing with him you are blocking his intuition," Bhajan warns. The teacher must be the guide, and his intuitive powers must be intact in order for him to give valid direction. There must be acceptance of his words without discussion or disagreement. Doubt and disagreement are a waste of time in any case, for, even if the teacher is not all he claims to be: "If you ask for help, and he is a guru, whether he's phoney or real, his prayer shall be answered" (1972c, 4). As long as the student goes in faith, help is inevitably forthcoming.

The teacher becomes the channel to the infinite, the source of pressure, and the protector when the ego is stripped away. He becomes the means through which the self can be reorganized because attachment to the teacher represents "the surrender of the lower self to the Higher Self" (Bhajan 1972c, 4). When such a reorganization of the self occurs it is often depicted as a kind of purging, and some 3HO women tell of how Bhajan has helped them to clean out the "debris" in the subconscious and to jettison aspects of the personality that were retarding spiritual growth. His followers say that he functions as a kind of spiritual mirror, reflecting back the individual's nature. This facet of 3HO belief goes back almost to the founding of the organization. As Premka, then secretary general, wrote, "Yogiji is like a two-way, reflecting mirror, he reflects to you your own ego, and he will always point up the areas of weakness, the hidden places where you never want to look because there are buried all of your fears and insecurities. Then, on the other side he is a mirror of the Cosmos, he reflects the light of purity and Truth and his very being is present as a manifestation of that Supreme Consciousness. Thus he is a symbol for the Infinite Truth within each of us" (P. Khalsa 1973b, 26). In this belief system students and teacher are aspects of a whole. The teacher reflects the student's identity, both negative and positive. The teacher's presence is internalized and represents access to truth.

Even though the teacher plays such a central role, and in spite of the necessity to submit to him, students often resist his authority and his claims. In 1979, on the occasion of Bhajan's fiftieth birthday, the organization published a commemorative volume (P. and S. Khalsa 1979). It includes a narrative which captures the 3HO view of doubt and redemption, at least as these themes were understood in the early years. In it, the individual questions Bhajan and the spiritual path, perhaps decides to leave the organization and is relieved by this decision, but then, upon leaving, succumbs to the many forms of lower consciousness behavior and thought that pervade American life. Finally there is the realization that he or she misjudged Bhajan.

> There was slander, there was gossip, and in my mind the question arose: can I really believe in this vision which I have glimpsed. . . . Experience had convinced me that I couldn't really trust the perceptions of my own mind; I had trusted before, I had loved before, and I had honestly had a vision and believed before. But, all of those dreams had been shattered. . . . So I chose to leave the discipline. . . . [A]nd I found that in order to do it, I had to involve myself in every type of escapist activity available in the American society. . . . Physical pain finally brought me crawling back for relief. . . . This very drama is enacted by nearly every individual who comes into any kind of contact with Yogi Bhajan—only each individual has it packaged in a unique wrapper. (P. and S. Khalsa 1979, 68)

Such cautionary tales served as a warning to other members, telling them that doubts are generated by their own weaknesses and, if pursued, will only lead them into pain and maya.

In the Eastern tradition the relationship with the spiritual teacher has often involved a close one-to-one relationship. The teacher is supposed to assess the student's character and adjust the exposure to new realities and practices accordingly. One individual may require gentle encouragement and persuasion; another may require shock tactics. The large-scale new religions put a strain on this method of spiritual training. There are hundreds of devotees, so it is not always practical to carefully tailor methods to individuals. Bhajan uses courses and workshops and, increasingly, videotapes, to spread his message. He also delegates authority to ashram directors. Inevitably, the spiritual path has been tied to bureaucratic procedures and to disciplines that are performed en masse. It has been standardized and in the process has lost some of its subtlety and flexibility.

Bhajan does balance mass activities to a degree by responding to individual questions and encouraging people to consult their own ashram directors. Residents can consult him about personal concerns when he visits the ashram. They can ask him about their marital problems, about disciplining their children, about career decisions, or about diet, for example. When he is not present they can raise problems in letters addressed to him, although it is not clear how many of these actually get to him and how many are handled by his staff. Because of this mix of personal and impersonal means of communication, some members have close ties with Bhajan while others have very little contact with him.

Replies to requests for advice can be encouraging and reassuring, but sometimes they are unexpected and unsettling. The woman (previously mentioned) who decided to go to chiropractic school wrote to Yogi Bhajan to get his approval for this step. When he did not reply, she took this to indicate agreement, only to find out later that he saw no need for her to pursue the training: "He said, 'You don't need to. You already know all that stuff. . . . You need to sing and you need to teach people about the Guru. . . .' That really freaked me out for awhile. But I did exactly what he said, and from there my current occupation started and it just blossomed." "My ego was jumping up and down," another woman said, referring to a time when she had difficulty obeying the teacher's instructions. She obeyed, and just observed her own reactions and endured considerable anxiety. By adopting this stance, she and other members may increase their self-control and extend their understanding of their own multifaceted personalities. But there may be costs as well. Some spontaneity is sacrificed. And too much denial of intuitions, feelings, and emotions may leave the individual less attuned to the warning functions that these serve (Hochschild 1983).

How, then, is one to evaluate Bhajan and his teachings? He, and his persona, are complex, changing, and contradictory. So are the effects of his teachings. He is the patient father whose children refuse to grow up and take advantage of all he has to offer them. He is the self-sacrificing teacher who suffers so his students may grow. He is the sensitive seer surrounded by people who doubt and attack him. Sometimes he is self-pitying. Sometimes he is the stern teacher—a powerful, even frightening figure, who shouts down the ego and publicly humiliates students. Then he is ready to exert authority, to demand obedience, humility, and sacrifice, and to minimize members' culture and background. He grows in stature as he denigrates his followers' culture and their secular roles and realities.

But he can also adopt a tongue-in-cheek tone, and many of his students share this style of humor. He tells them that a spiritual path need not be all work and earnestness and that life is to be enjoyed. His students can see the humor in their striving, and Bhajan's humor speaks to the lighter and more ironic vein that runs through 3HO life and even embraces it. This makes him, temporarily, a peer. It makes him a model for everyday conduct.

Several instances of humor at a Tantric course I attended in 1986 capture this tone:

> A member of the ashram gets up on the stage and starts warm-up yoga in preparation for Yogi Bhajan's coming. We do several sets of stretching exercises; one of them is in camel pose—the individual kneels and leans back over the feet with head tilted back. This pose is held for a long, uncomfortable time, and the leader's comment that "this exercise is very good for asthma," is received with laughter since it very hard to do with normal breathing capacity. . . . Finally Yogi Bhajan arrives and begins, "Are you ready for some fun?" Nods and laughter follow and the class commences.

> "Face your partner. Put your right index finger between his brows, and your left hand on your heart. Not his forehead! Don't you know what are the eyebrows? Those hairy outgrowths. . . ."

> There is some trouble starting the tape that is to accompany the next exercise, and Yogi Bhajan turns to the man who is struggling with the tape recorder and says, "So you go through life pushing the wrong buttons? Do you do it with Siri ——— [his wife], go to push one button and push the other?" (Journal)

Bhajan attracts, in part, because he is a puzzle. In the course of one class he can shift from humor to threats, to reverence, to anger. He tells his students that he wants them to be independent, but he expects obedience. He promises power and praises humility. He tells women that the creative force of the universe is feminine and that women can accomplish anything, but he balances this by telling them that they have been seriously damaged by their culture and that they cannot necessarily trust their own perceptions. He is both tolerant and authoritarian, humorous and imposing. He encourages independence of thought and then demands service and devotion. He allows for ad hoc interpretations of teachings and policies and then suddenly closes the door on these. He sounds an apocalyptic note and then offers salvation. He keeps his audience off balance and absorbed in efforts to dissolve contradictions or accept paradoxes. He hovers between explanations, adopts varying perspectives, changes tone, and upsets expectations. (See Lindholm 1990 for a discussion of the charismatic figure's tendency to adapt this fluid, shifting character.)

Although they may never decipher his motives and his character, his students can hope to share in his powers and to reap the benefits attached to his special abilities. They assume that Bhajan can warn them of coming hard times. He can purge their auras and their psyches and make them strong enough to face the most challenging future. He can instruct them in practices that are both esoteric and empowering, and, as Bird noted when such practices were first flowering in North America, the rituals "are not only authorized by a charismatic authority, but are felt to bestow a kind of secret, hidden charisma on practitioners themselves" (1978, 187). Charisma flows through the group and provides the energy for newly created and mutually constructed identities.

Prabhupati wrote:

> We didn't understand, of course, that as we listened to
> our teacher humiliate one of our brothers or sisters in
> our presence that he was actually controlling us as well.
> Naturally, as we watched, all of us were grateful that he
> was shaming someone else and we worked hard to
> avoid any behavior that would bring Yogi's wrath down
> on our own heads. However, this reverence we were to
> maintain for our teacher had deeper ramifications than
> merely keeping us in line. It was the philosophical construct . . . under which Yogi was able to create a very
> glamorous role for himself. (K. Khalsa 1994b, 6)

But in the same piece of writing, in a kind of backhanded tribute to 3HO, she goes on to describe the paradoxes of membership, the growth and empowerment that did occur, almost in spite of the tactics employed by the leadership:

> In the end there were three things that gave me the needed support and power to get out of that cult. The first was the experiential confidence I had developed in my own capacity to heal. Through all those hours of introversion, broken by the raging interpersonal conflicts inherent in group living, I slowly developed understanding of myself, others, and some self esteem. The second was the ironic and bittersweet awareness that although Yogi had not been able to withstand the temptations . . . many of his . . . students actually had succeeded in developing tested and true integrity, not to mention courage. That proved to be quite inspiring to me; very inspiring. And finally, sometime during those twenty years of meditating my brains out I actually came to trust in the Divine. . . . [I]t was a faith that had discovered that . . . it is within the human capacity, within my own capacity, to walk through life's fire with an open, brave and vulnerable heart and a compassionate and joyful spirit. (K. Khalsa 1994b, 13)

Many other ex-members could make similar statements. The magical setting, the exposure to alternative forms of perception and cognition, fresh imagery, even the "pressure cooker" atmosphere of organizational life, can and do open new pathways to growth. In the construction of a new reality, Yogi Bhajan is cast in the role of wizard. He forges new metal out of old traditions. He encourages his followers to transcend everyday realities, but he, and they, still must use these realities to accomplish this delicate task. He must both affirm the reality that he and his followers construct and simultaneously cast doubt on most accepted versions of reality. He reminds his followers that their cognitive processes are not entirely dependable, and, often, are in need of repair and refinement, and yet he offers faith that they can know the truth. He expects his followers to be both true believers and Pirandellos. They must have faith that there is a path, but may also be aware that it is being constructed. They can know that there is a wizard, but must not think that this is Oz.

On Light and Dark

Prabhupati once described herself as never quite fitting into the 3HO mold. Grace was not her strong suit. "I have red hair and a temperament to match. My turban was always a bit askew." When she said that I had an instant image from a book that I loved as a child. It was called *The Littlest Angel* and was about a very young angel with red hair and freckles whose halo was always crooked.

In spite of the fact that she never quite fit in, and, in fact, occasionally misbehaved or rebelled when faced by rules and expectations, Prabhupati now thinks that as a 3HO member she tended to repress her feelings. This tendency to repress aspects of the self, she would argue, takes some of the spark out of 3HO life: "You know, it takes a lot of energy to deny or ignore parts of the self." She now employs some Jungian concepts (among other psychological frameworks) in her efforts to make sense of her experience. Looking back on the years just after she left 3HO, she finds that she had to face the shadow aspects of her personality. She had to encounter some of the repressed aspects of her past before she could be whole.

In retrospect, it seems that she spent years trying to accept the discipline of those who sought to shape her behavior. Here is her account of one dramatic instance:

Guru R. Singh [head of her Ashram at the time] put me on silence after I moved into the ashram because I had a loose mouth and it wasn't very graceful. I just (sort of) said whatever came out of my mouth. My husband was forever kicking me under the table—which really pissed me off so I would start to act snotty. . . . For the first months I lived in an Ashram I was silent in the mornings through breakfast. I could talk while I worked at Wawa, of course, and when I got home I could talk until dinner. Then I was supposed to be silent until bedtime, but my husband and I cheated and talked some anyway. I could talk all day Saturday and I was silent all day Sunday. . . .

That little silence *sadhana* worked wonderfully. I didn't say much of anything after that (except what was the accepted rap, of course) for quite a few years. During this time I also read this very pink little book called *Fascinating Womanhood*. . . . It proposed that one should avoid conflict with one's husband at all costs by agreeing with him about everything or by staying mute. This would make your husband your eternal slave and he would worship you and shower you with endless romance and sentimental anniversary cards. Since arguing with everything my husband said hadn't worked to make our marriage happy, I gave up feminism, or my version of it, which had been my main thing before I moved into the Ashram. . . . [T]he joys of serving one's husband and being thought of as a Graceful Goddess had eluded me until I read *Fascinating Womanhood*. Always one for extremes, I underwent a stunning conversion similar to the one that hit Saul on the road to Damascus and I

(Cont'd. from page 241)

decided that I would be sweet and kind or die trying. . . . I would agree with every word that came out of my husband's mouth or at least pretend to. I pretended a lot of things back then and sometimes faking it almost did help me make it. . . .

I was "very good" for those first years. I got up for *sadhana,* and I tried to read my prayers each day. I wore white clothes and I tried to not get spaghetti sauce all over them. I didn't drink coffee and I didn't notice how cute the single or married guys were. (K. Khalsa 1994a, 21–21)

Prabhupati did not continue to be quite so good about observing 3HO forms, although she remained devoted to most of the spiritual principles. She moved to another ashram, and over time she gradually moved to the fringes of the organization. In the early 1990s she began to write articles for the new 3HO publication called *Visions*. She drew on the literature about dysfunctional families in order to analyze 3HO. She was surprised when she became "an overnight celebrity," receiving calls from ex-members and members who agreed with her depiction of the organization.

When she wrote the articles she had no intention of leaving 3HO, but after they read her work ex-members began to tell her disturbing stories that led her to question her affiliation. She was under pressure from within 3HO as well. But, as she told me in a letter, the greatest pressure was internal, as she faced her own shadow:

> By the time I had written the second dysfunctional 3HO family article I had been contacted by enough discouraged Sikhs and ex-3HOers to know that my articles were more right-on than I had ever suspected. . . . I was completely obsessed with learning everything about the dark side of 3HO. . . . I just couldn't help myself and I watched myself in horrified fascination as I challenged YB [Yogi Bhajan] nose to nose in private and public with both overt and covert actions. . . . (Letter, 1994)

She started a new meditation, "the 'Why did I joint a cult?' meditation":

> I practiced it with all the discipline that twenty years of rigorous spiritual practice had managed to instill in me. I also went into formal therapy to finally deal with the severe child abuse of my past. In time I concluded that I had joined a cult because it had provided that nice homey and familiar feeling of abuse that is happening secretly behind the cloak of purity. It was inevitable, given my background, that I would be drawn towards abusive men and organizations. What now seems a miracle to me is that I was ever attracted to a good and ethical man like my husband and that I was ever able to develop trust

and faith in the Divine. All in all, my Ashram years were tremendously healing. . . .

I now know that God is within all my feelings, pain and joy alike, and that God flows through my thoughts in the form of infinite paradoxes that tantalize, mystify and amaze me. One such paradox is the awareness that although Yogiji was the worst spiritual teacher imaginable, he was the best one for me. After all, it was in the process of grappling with him that I finally learned to look inwards and access my own symbol systems and guidance. And it was in the face of his corruption that I found the courage to trust in my instincts. . . .

If I was to judge Yogiji the way I judge a math professor, I would have to say that he was a wonderful teacher. He inspired in me, and in my brothers and sisters, a great amount of self discipline and he taught us hundreds of very useful meditations and really wonderful yoga sets. These practices were potent enough to make drug use seem primitive and unnecessary, and they made us less dependent on therapists, doctors and other magicians like himself. He also taught his students the mythological magic of Indian Tantrism which I personally love, particularly because I am a woman and models for female spirituality are scarce in our world. It certainly could be argued that Yogiji, unlike many less sophisticated cult leaders, was a bit of an artist and should be judged like one. No one ever claimed that Miles Davis or Pablo Picasso were saints who lived balanced, ethical and exemplary lives, rather they were fantastic channels of creativity and vision who gave us much more that we can ever repay.

The catch here, of course, is that spiritual teachers, at least, are supposed to live balanced and ethical lives. That is the whole point. When we compare Yogiji with the classical great religious leaders, the difference between Yogiji and the Buddha or Christ is very fundamental and apparent. Great saints, sages, and masters practice what they preach and thereby prove to us that love, honor, courage, and grace are rare but possible attainments for us all. (K. Khalsa 1994b, 5–14)

Today, Prabhupati draws on a variety of sources, including psychology and Tantrism. She studies dreams—her own and others.' She writes science fiction stories. She has worked as a performance poet and sings in a band. She has divorced and remarried. Symbolic realities for her still hold the highest truths. She realizes that there are risks and paradoxes involved in looking steadily inward and toward the symbolic realm, and that "paradox develops where the distinction between our inner realities and outer realities comes into question." But this is a risk she chooses to take, a form of paradox that she chooses to confront.

CHAPTER 7

"Keeping Up" and Letting Go: Identity Struggles and Disaffiliation

*I*n spite of the numerous identity processes and rewards that link them to 3HO/Sikh Dharma, members are vulnerable to centrifugal forces that can draw them away from the center of their religious and organizational life. People in 3HO frequently say that theirs is a difficult and demanding path. When they speak of their fears that it may prove too demanding, they are likely to say that they are afraid that they "won't be able to keep up." In fact, "keep up," is an often-repeated phrase in 3HO circles, a kind of organizational mantra. It is used in numerous situations: when a yoga set becomes difficult and painful, when individuals feel the need to "break through" psychological obstacles, or when members are facing a challenging task. It refers to members' efforts to maintain a positive attitude, to overcome ingrained habits, and to maintain their commitments.

Doubts and Identity Struggles

In groups like 3HO/Sikh Dharma, commitment "is *always* subject to interruption" (Wright 1987, 13). In the 3HO case, the potential "interruptions" are numerous. Because 3HO incorporates so many cultural tensions, and because it is a syncretic mix of traditions, it generates some internal contradictions, and, as in any religion, there are disjunctions between what is taught and what is actually done. These contradictions can give rise to doubts, and are even potential sources of disillusionment. Moreover, although 3HO could be described as a self-validating system (Snow and Machalek 1982), it is not as well insulated from external realities as are some of the more world-rejecting, communal, and high-demand groups. The more adventuresome and independent members are likely to be in regular contact with external systems of meaning. The organization is not the only potential supplier of identities and viewpoints for its members, and this may increase the pulls in the direction of defection (Bromley 1991, 178).

Given the demands of multiple commitments, and exposure to external points of view, the motivation to validate organizational assumptions is likely to wax and wane. The motivation may also vary as situations change. Bromley reminds us that individual positions in organizations imply a negotiated balance between an individual's rights in the organization and that person's responsibilities to the group. Any shift in this balance can prove disturbing. Thus, "the initial conditions for disaffiliation may occur whenever the organizational or individual requisites are either increased or decreased" (1991, 177).

All of these factors mean that many members are likely to experience periods of discomfort or of outright internal conflict. They may become embroiled in identity struggles, and these may be intense and poignant. By defining their path as difficult, their doubts as "negativity," and their task as "keeping up," members equip themselves to resist the factors that might undermine their loyalty and commitment, but they also recognize the force and presence of these potential disruptions. These are likely to be resisted as long as members find that, overall, life in 3HO is essentially rewarding. As long as members believe that they are realizing their goals, dreams, and preferred identities, and that they have a place in the community, they can manage doubt and ignore organizational failings. It is probably a tribute to the organization that so many members have done this for long periods of time and that the dropout rate is not higher than it is.

The leadership has also been quite creative in its elaboration and application of the belief system. Beliefs and values are deployed pragmatically. Tensions and temptations are acknowledged and then neutralized. Members come to expect to exert continuous mental effort, and they expect to actively work at maintaining their faith and commitment, and, to this end, they are supplied with numerous explanations for, and ways of dismissing, disconfirming experiences that they encounter.

It is worth noting that this work is not done solely with 3HO-supplied tools. There is probably insufficient reference, in discussions of new religions, to the predispositions that members bring with them into these organizations. Members must bring their own distinctive cognitive structures and narrative frameworks to bear on the symbols, beliefs, and practices that they encounter in the organizations they choose to join. Many enter with a store of personal values and goals which they expect the organization to further. Their persistence in the religion is at least in part dependent upon its continuing congruity with such preexisting inclinations. It also depends upon the organization's readiness to offer rewards that are attached to the goals, narratives, and dreams that members bring with them when they enter.

Thus, some organizational rewards must apply to members' original goals, and these rewards must appear to balance those that could be found in other settings where similar goals are realized and similar perspectives are valued. If members come to feel that cherished visions of self and society are not sufficiently rewarded, they may no longer attempt to contain their doubts and repair tears in the fabric of belief. They may curtail their efforts to keep up and confirm organizational truths. They may even conclude that the costs of membership are too onerous. It is at this point particularly that identity struggles lead to disaffiliation and 3HO appears to suffer its losses.

Women's identity struggles arise around several issues. They may arise around central concepts such as commitment, depth of personality, service, and obedience. They may develop around expectations of submission to teacher and husband or involve family life and such issues as accepting an arranged marriage, learning to be a good wife, planning a career, or deciding whether to send a child to school in India. They may concern decisions about careers. They may erupt along with desires to find new avenues of self-expression or opportunities to innovate within the organizational structure, desires that may threaten to alter accepted hierarchies and ways of doing things.

A struggle begins when a member claims an identity, a right, or a spiritual motivation that is troubling to other people in 3HO. These others will then deny the claim or offer alternative identities. Thus the woman who says that she is acting as a responsible mother by keeping a shy, retiring child at home may be told that she is actually being selfish in her decision not to send the child to India. The woman who is happy pursuing a career and living alone may be told that it is time to marry and to concentrate on the domestic sphere. One woman I interviewed had been told by Yogi Bhajan that her plans to go into a massage business were "ungraceful," and that she should instead develop her talents as a fine artist. She was a single mother and very concerned about the financial costs of trying to live on the income she was likely to produce as an artist. Rather than question the task assigned to her by her spiritual teacher, however, she was attempting to give up the identity she had attempted to claim. She was struggling to accept her instructions.

A decision to abandon *bana* or to leave the organization is almost certain to initiate a struggle. When a long-term member who had decided to leave 3HO/Sikh Dharma stopped wearing her turban and began to define herself as a "graduate" of 3HO, several members made a point of telephoning her in order to challenge her new identity and to tell her that now she had "lost her radiance."

These incidents suggest the tone of 3HO identity struggles; the following stories more fully depict and dramatize these contests. The first two simply capture the internal debates and ambivalence that have the potential to give rise to full-blown struggles. The others depict overt struggles concerning self-definition.

The first woman was introduced in a previous chapter as she attempted to combine her feminist sentiments with 3HO conceptions of service. At the time of the interview she was concerned about issues of "depth" and "commitment" and was beginning to give her life story a new plot line. She was beginning to see her self through a 3HO-ground lens which revealed a restless seeker who was finally finding a spiritual home. Since her move into the ashram she had come to view her early life as a restless shifting from one goal to another. It seemed that she had planned one career after another and pursued none. She had traveled from place to place but never settled. Previously, she had viewed herself as a traveling hippie and a free spirit, but she had now begun to see herself in a new light, as someone who was "uncommitted," too quick to abandon projects and to leave one place for another.

She also talked about renouncing "superficiality" and about her tendency toward fantasy. Members are expected to view the world with a neutral eye, recognizing and dealing with reality rather than escaping into fantasy. She spoke wistfully of the days when she was free simply to be and to dream and was not expected to observe and "work on" herself: "I want to deal with reality and how it is, and I want to keep going towards God. . . . [B]ut lots of times I say to myself, 'Why do we have to go so fast?' I would like to go back to a certain point in time and stay there because back then the earth was everything to me—my family, my relations, everything was perfect at that time—and why couldn't I have stayed at that point . . . extremely carefree, not a worry in the world, living really light."

She was clearly divided. A part of her was happy to maintain the attitudes of youth and to avoid adult roles, and that part distrusted commitment and earnestness and discipline. It held on to the identities she had claimed at earlier stages of her life. That part was very cautious as it tried out the 3HO life-style and was proceeding at a careful pace, even occasionally rebelling. The other part internalized 3HO language and now described the old life as a search for spiritual meaning. It now interpreted her previous restlessness as an emptiness "I've been wanting to fill up." Speaking from the perspective of 3HO, she concluded, "I feel more fulfilled within myself now than looking for fulfillment in a marriage, or in a relationship, or in a career. I just really want to be closer to God than ever."

One can imagine her in the future, occasionally torn between personas: the playful experimenter and the committed member, the feminist and the serviceful woman. The teachings of 3HO will encourage her to view this as a contest between superficial and committed selves, a choice between pursuit of a fulfilling spiritual path and aimless wandering. The organizational concepts may well channel and contain the conflict, but it may threaten to rise to the surface and overflow the well-maintained banks if 3HO cannot continue to speak to the value she places on laughter, lightness, ordinary life, and variety.

Ambivalence such as hers is often handled through identity processes. Sometimes it eased by the assumption of a new identity or managed by elimination of an identity. Thus, an ex-member who is now quite critical of the organization described her life in 3HO/Sikh Dharma as a procession of provisional and assigned identities. She remembers having constant doubts about remaining a member. She seemed to attend her first yoga classes and don a turban in spite of herself. When Bhajan suggested that she enter an ashram she believed she was only going to stay for six months; the identity was only temporary. But at each step along the way, Bhajan either eliminated old roles or assigned her a new role or identity. She released the old when she was told to and, with some mental crossing of her fingers, accepted the proffered identities. She originally joined in the company of a close friend, but was soon told that she was seeing too much of the friend, so that association was limited. She felt "miserable" and "kind of homeless" in the ashram but was convinced to stay until a major Tantric course. There, at the course, Yogi Bhajan arranged her marriage. Once married, she had doubts about her subordination to her husband, but she accepted the organizational teaching that women are responsible for a marriage and for any unhappiness within it. She soon had a baby, and when that child was still quite young Bhajan sent him to another family, claiming that the woman's aura indicated a need for this separation. At this point the woman's parents took legal action and finally had the child returned to the mother. From her current (anticult) vantage point she says that all of these events led her to believe that she was inadequate as an individual and as a parent and of value only as a follower and spiritual seeker.

A former member, but speaking then as a member in good standing, remembered the time when her marriage was arranged. She was contented with her single life—it was full and busy—when she learned that Yogi Bhajan had betrothed her to a man she did not know. She felt unready for marriage, certainly unready for marriage to a stranger, and she initially gravitated between tears and anger. Making her betrothed's acquaintance did not improve her outlook. She called Yogi Bhajan and said she simply could not do it. She cried, she pleaded. He and others attempted to convince her that it was the right step for her, that Bhajan had considered the prospective partners' characters and auras and knew that they would be a good match. It finally came down to a decision to leave or to obey.

In the end she obeyed and adjusted to the marriage. At the time when she told me her story she described her marriage as "very happy." She had adjusted and had found ways to rationalize Bhajan's choice of a partner. It was good for her because, left to her own devices, "I would've married a Jewish intellectual just like me. I would be always competing and looking for attention in the same ways that I did from my father. There's much more growth this way."

Later she was involved in another decisive identity struggle. She suffered a miscarriage at the Khalsa Women's Training Camp and was informed by her doctor that some of the more vigorous yoga exercises might have been responsible for her loss. In good faith, she conveyed the doctor's concern to members of Yogi Bhajan's staff, suggesting an announcement to warn other expectant mothers to avoid some of the exercises. Instead, she was stunned when she was singled out in front of the assembled camp and told by Bhajan that she herself had occasioned the miscarriage. He suggested that she had been wrapped up in herself and her ambitions and had not really wanted the baby, an accusation that she duly considered and then dismissed. She rejected the stereotype of hard career woman and began to seriously reassess her commitment.

She did not stand to lose a family or career if she left, but the woman in the following example did. When this woman reached a point of crisis it was clear that a decision to leave would cost her both family and position. Her identity struggle was cast as an episode of *shaktipod*.

As she described herself, she had always enjoyed being busy, involved, and central in a group. She said she has a talent—and a weakness, as she now sees it—for enjoying the surfaces of life. She was once very active in ashram affairs but then was asked by her husband and by Yogi Bhajan to cut back on these activities and put her family first. This was a turning point:

> [M]y whole role was changing. I was no longer needed to function in the capacity that I had. I didn't quite know what I was supposed to do. I sort of had lost my foundation. I got tested in a way that went to my Achilles heel, which had to do with love, with wanting to be loved in a certain way, and being unfulfilled with my marriage. . . . I was very depressed. I was very angry. . . . It was something I was pursuing, a lack of fulfillment that I was experiencing. . . . [I]t was a fantasy that I had. . . . It had to do with everything being perfect, harmonious. You know: your husband adoring you and willing to do anything for you—and me being the perfect person who would be worthy of all that. . . . I was developing a life that was having nothing to do with him [her husband] because I was so angry. . . . What Yogi Bhajan did was he saw it in me immediately and he took me to be with him. He had me live in New Mexico and Los Angeles for about six months. . . . He yelled at me a lot. And what it did was it really crashed through my whole facade, my ego. . . . I always thought that being just nice was the best thing you could be, but sometimes, if a person is really stuck in their negativity, you have to smash it really, to get through to them. . . . I was in tears for months, literally. . . . I didn't have my protective layer of my ego on me and at any moment I would burst into tears. What I realized was that I had made a step that was ultimately going to destroy my life. I mean I was ruining my marriage, I was ruining my children, I was ruining my relationships because I had just gotten into this framework which was no longer placing any importance on my spiritual values. . . . I was totally withdrawing. I was trying to create my own life and my own relationships. . . .
>
> He [Bhajan] gave me *sadhana*s to do, meditations to do, projects all in the spiritual realm. . . . I started working my way up and growing. . . . You know, the main thing was I wasn't the person in my fantasy so nothing else around me would be that way. . . . Somehow

he showed me that the work had to first be on myself and then everything would change and I would have exactly what I wanted. And that is what happened, and I couldn't believe it. You know, when I saw it starting to fall into place I was completely amazed, and I continue to be amazed to this day. . . .

I feel like I had lived a very shallow life. . . . I can ride the surface real easily. I can be very happy and just exist in that place. This required more depth from me and I had to learn it. That experience gave me an awareness of what to strive for. . . . [I]t took about a year or so, but when I realized that I had actually gone through this experience, had changed and had come out on top of it, I was tremendously happy and had a lot more faith.

Devoted members typically describe such struggles as an instance of *shaktipod*, or as a necessary breaking down of the ego. They speak, as she did, of increasing the depth of the personality, of overcoming ego and negativity, of outgrowing fantasies, or of Bhajan's wisdom. And, like the woman above, when they accept the proffered identity they find ways to work these themes into their biographies and into their cognitive and emotional schemas.

As long as they believe that membership is a means to valued ends, they can continue to weather such storms and assimilate such lessons. They will draw meaningful lessons from interruptions to the life course in part because "it would be devastating to learn that one had acquiesced to a demand for a major life change that had been based on a miscalculation or poor judgement by the Siri Singh Sahib" (Maple 1991, 123), in part because they have faith in his superior insight. They will persist as long as they believe that the guidance is wise and that they are realizing their goals, as long as internal social networks are satisfying, as long as the good in the organization seems to outweigh the bad, or as long as they feel that being a devotee is their only choice. If they come to believe that the essence of the self or the dream have been violated, however, or if new perspectives and opportunities seem to outweigh the old, such struggles may issue in a new and oppositional identity.

Disaffiliation

Of the eighteen women with whom I conducted intensive interviews in the Washington, D.C., area during the early 1980s, I know of seven who are no longer associated with 3HO. One ex-member, whose position afforded him sufficient knowledge to speak on the subject, suggests that this is representative, and a typical rate would be close to one-third per year, with new members being the more likely to leave. This is substantial, but well below the defection rates found in some new religions. Bromley (1991, 173) reports that some have rates as high as 50 percent a year. I have been unable to learn whether there have been long-term patterns in membership fluctuations, but there have been the relatively large-scale defections in the Española and Washington ashrams while I have been studying the organization.

The following discussion of disaffiliation incorporates the experience of three groups of former members with whom I have had contact. It is based on (1) interviews with those who left the two ashrams during periods of major organizational upheaval (these interviews included both women and men); (2) interviews and correspondence with, and content analysis of exchanges among, the members of a loose network of approximately thirty ex-members; and (3) interviews with women who have left the Washington *sangat*, as well as people from other ashrams, both male and female, who, since separating from the organization, have taken public or legal stands in opposition to 3HO/Sikh Dharma. This is not a representative sample, but it is an accessible group of ex-members. A segment of the sample is also longitudinal. Individuals I interviewed between 1983 and 1987 have since left the organization and I have been able to follow their progress. This adds considerably to the depth of the analysis.

The major reasons these women cite for leaving are (1) their doubts about the ethics of the leadership and of some 3HO-sponsored businesses; (2) their belief that the organization as a whole has become rigid, dogmatic, overly hierarchical, and unresponsive to the membership; (3) their disillusionment with ashram politics and policies; and (4) in a minority of cases, their experience of psychological or sexual abuse (see Jacobs 1989, 92).

Both Wright (1987) and Jacobs (1989) found that disillusionment with leadership that has been presumed to be exemplary is a major factor in disaffiliation from new religions, and this is true in the 3HO case. Feelings of betrayal are common in the literature on disaffiliation from high-demand groups, and this is a common thread in the accounts of ex-3HO members.

It seems to take a distinctive turn in the 3HO case, however. While ex-members are well aware of, and angry about, failings of the leadership, they seem even more resentful of the ways in which the organization finally rejected or misused those aspects of themselves that were most creative and giving. In her interviews with men and women who had left new religious movements, Jacobs found widespread "disappointment with the emotional dimension of the leader-follower relationship." Her respondents, in fact, experienced the "pain of unrealized love" (1989, 99). While this certainly is true of some former members of 3HO/Sikh Dharma, the leavers I spoke with seemed to suffer more from other members' failure to affirm valued identities and self-concepts (see Mauss 1998). It is not so much that they were not loved, but that they felt that the best of the self was not acknowledged, utilized, or valued. Many of these leavers had, as members, wanted to explore new institutional possibilities. Rather than simply accepting the 3HO-approved forms, they wanted to experiment with alternative forms of meditation, different types of schooling for their children, or various types of therapy and discussion group. They felt that they were discouraged, by both the leadership and their peers, when they sought to do these things. They say that they wanted to contribute to organizational growth and evolution and were seen instead as negative trouble makers. The women tried to be the kinds of positive, environment-altering women that the organization said they should become, and when they attempted to manifest their spiritual values in practical ways they felt that they were sanctioned for their efforts.

In Washington, this feeling of betrayal was acute. The arrest of the ashram director in 1985 and his indictment on drug-smuggling charges precipitated the process of withdrawal. Many ashram residents were present when police arrived, with guns drawn, and searched his house. Remembering this, those who later left said that they had been subjected to a form of humiliation that they should not have had to experience while living in a spiritual community. The director, they argued, even if innocent, should not have done anything that could so readily involve and shame the community. Although they did not use such language, they clearly felt that their spiritual and secular identities had been damaged.

The director later gave state's evidence and was released on suspended parole. Throughout the director's ordeal, residents, including those who were later to leave, gave him the benefit of the doubt and stood by him. But the leavers anticipated acknowledgment and reciprocity in return. They also expected to see more democratic procedures within the ashram, but instead they felt things became, if anything, more autocratic: "I actually experienced being held at gunpoint, with a shotgun, here in this spiritual community. . . . It wasn't so bad that he was arrested—and maybe he did this, and maybe he didn't—but the way it was portrayed in the ashram. He never apologized. We never really got the whole story." Their identity claims, as loyal friends and as people whose standing in the community had been jeopardized, were not recognized.

The Stages of Leave-taking

Bromley (1991) describes several stages in the disaffiliation process. The first is a gradual disaffection. The individual experiences a series of doubts and conflicts, and these intensify to the point that they are no longer manageable within the organizational structure. The disaffected member begins to pull back from organizational involvement, and devotees and outsiders respond to the "cues" that this member now emits. Devotees may be able to pacify and reintegrate the individual. If not, the process is likely to intensify, and a precipitating event can now lead to "a line of action toward separation from the group." The exiting process may be drawn out and followed by "a period of considerable personal turbulence" (181).

In general, these stages appear to fit the 3HO experience. It is worth noting, however, that before, or in lieu of, withdrawing, many 3HO members attempt to reform the organization. One can remain a member even with a critical eye and a heavy load of ambivalence. It is also possible to remain on the fringes of 3HO, not quite in and not quite out, and quite a few individuals select this option (see Barker 1998). The organization is a wide umbrella.

Disaffection and Separation

Interviews indicate that doubts typically tend to reach a point where they cannot be managed or ignored under four circumstances. The first is when members create a satisfying group or network within 3HO/Sikh Dharma which is then disrupted or marginalized. Typically, such a group has become a means of actualizing ideals, and it offers a number of social rewards. The prospect of membership without this group becomes unattractive, or the group itself becomes a vehicle of exit. In the second circumstance external perspectives become more convincing, typically because the individual is marginal within the 3HO community or because the person becomes deeply involved in activities outside of 3HO/Sikh Dharma. These activities are now seen as supporting the individual's basic values or essential self, and the member dons valued identities outside of the 3HO community. The third circumstance is when major events, such the arrest of the ashram director, intervene. And in the fourth, the individual hears troubling information about the leadership via other 3HO members or former members. If these sources are people whom she trusts and knows to have access to the inner circles, and if she is already questioning her affiliation, she is likely to reexamine her commitment to the organization.

Exits via a Group or Network

In the two ashrams where relatively large numbers of people exited within a short period of time, group affiliation was a significant factor. In 1983 the Española ashram was large (110–120 members), and, as we have seen, the director thought he had been innovative in the way that he divided it into administrative subgroups. The people in charge of these subgroups spent a great deal of time together and felt that they were having considerable success in creating, as one former resident put it, "a real and open community." When the ashram director and one of these subgroup leaders became disillusioned and left, their going appears to have led to an exodus over a period of months. These people did not necessarily talk with one another about their plans; rather, the loss of close group ties and of shared, meaningful work appears to have been an important factor in their leaving.

During the period of tension in the Washington ashram, several members asked a facilitator to direct a series of open ashram meetings. According to the rules established for these meetings, each individual was entitled to speak until he or she was finished, so this became a setting in which members could speak their minds without being corrected or admonished. The usual pressures to conform to group opinion were eased, and what had been an ashram custom of speaking up freely and interrupting another speaker was dropped. The topics were broad: "It was how can we live together, how can we work together, how can we work this out." Over time a core group emerged. Others ceased to attend, and the core came to be viewed as "negative" by other residents of the ashram. As an ex-member reflects, "[T]his group acquired a name, a stigma to it. These were the negative people who were sitting around talking about the ashram and talking about the leadership and generally being negative. Which, in fact, we weren't doing at all. . . . They thought we sat around talking about them, but we sat around trying to figure out our own minds and how can we come to peace with ourselves. . . . It helped me drop a lot of resentment and a lot of anger." Those who regularly attended these meetings finally left.

Exits via External Identities and Contacts

The more world-accepting strands of 3HO thought are readily interwoven with liberal causes and New Age psychologies, which can provide an alternative foothold for the sliding member. Some members
have pursued goddess-based and American Indian spirituality. Others
have participated in various support groups. In San Francisco, some of
the American Sikh men became involved with the men's movement.
Such activities can supply critiques of life in 3HO/Sikh Dharma, and
they have been important stops on the route out of the organization.
They need not inevitably be used in this way—many belief systems can
be reinterpreted in 3HO terms—but they may be, particularly if the
suspicions of other members marginalize the individual who actively
looks outside of the usual circles. Some degree of marginalization may
well happen because other 3HO members are quite likely to question
the worth or relevance of other belief systems or of therapeutic groups.
When, for example, I have asked 3HO women whether they have an
interest in goddess religions or have participated in various groups,
some have expressed interest, but others have questioned the need for
such activities. The following is a fairly typical response of this sort:

> We do believe the Adi Shakti is God manifest as a
> woman. I don't feel God is he or she. And all this stuff
> about the goddess and this and that, I don't know, I
> don't feel a need for it. I feel it's true that I am divine
> and that every woman is divine, and the Divine Mother
> is in all of us. But there's so much to do in Sikh Dharma
> I don't feel any need to go anywhere else and look for
> anything else. People, honestly, who have gotten into
> that, it's because their egos don't get enough gratifica-
> tion in Sikh Dharma; they're looking for some approval
> somewhere else.

For this woman, the alternative identity is mere ego satisfaction.

A return to school or pursuit of professional training can be important in the disaffection process, as is career success. In the literature on
disaffiliation these activities are often cited as a means of reintegration
into the larger society after disaffiliation, but, in a group like 3HO
which encourages professional and economic success, they may prove
to be important "pull" factors. The juxtaposition of career and organizational norms, or of academic and Sikh values, may lead to high levels
of discomfort or cognitive dissonance:

[M]y career has become more important to me, and in the process I have the desire to be accepted. So here I am wearing full *bana* to work every day with people who've never seen it before and don't know anything about it, except they think about cults and stuff like that, and me not wanting to be related to that, and just wanting to be treated as a peer and respected for who I am and for what my skills are. So I downplay it, even to the point where I'm ignoring it. . . . I have shunted off my spiritual beliefs.

For one couple who left together, the juxtaposition of occupational and 3HO norms provided the precipitating event. The husband worked as a trainer at the Massachusetts Institute of Neurolinguistic Programming. He has told this story publicly and the following account appeared in *Common Boundary* magazine (where he is referred to as "Singh"). I have previously referred to the incident, and to "Singh"'s dissertation:

One day, a devotee who had suffered a miscarriage was severely berated. . . . Yogi Bhajan stood her up in front of several hundred people and accused her of killing her own baby, sacrificing the child to her "professional ego." The language he used was crude and humiliating. A few days later, one of Singh's dearest colleagues, who wasn't a devotee, refused to appear on a public podium with Singh. The friend had heard about the incident and couldn't believe that Singh would not protest such inhuman treatment. "Something shifted in my chest," says the man who used to be Singh, "as if a key were turning. I began to make plans for leaving." (Callahan 1992, 33)

His colleagues' repudiation of Bhajan's actions and of Singh's affiliation and complicity set up an identity struggle. His colleagues denied Singh his identity as a respected therapist in their world. The only way to reclaim that identity was to repudiate Bhajan's actions, and perhaps even end his association with 3HO. Singh clearly valued his colleagues' good will and his professional standing and finally made his choice. External realities may function in this way—by setting up an identity struggle—or by helping a member confirm a valued identity, and, in general, an opportunity to critique the 3HO reality is an important aspect of disaffiliation. In this context, contact with ex-members may hasten the process. Productive and happy ex-members are proof that there is life beyond Sikh Dharma. Former members are also aware of litigation involving 3HO/Sikh Dharma and can provide well-thought-out critiques of the organization. A potential leaver who takes her concerns to ex-members or to other doubters within the organization is much more likely to leave than is one who primarily confides in the leadership. A spouse who is willing to listen is very helpful, and one who will not hear anything against the organization represents a major obstacle to leave-taking.

Efforts at Reform

Before leaving, members may elect to try to work from within. Those who think that the organization has lost its creative spark or that it has become too autocratic often feel that they ought to try to remedy this situation. Those who imagine a different kind of organization may try to enact their dreams, hoping to prod the organization to move in the desired direction.

Occasionally these efforts are formalized, as in the case of *Visions*, the newsletter published in San Francisco. It clearly began as an effort at reform rather than rebellion. In an introduction the editor described his goals and took care to disavow any destructive intent: "Over eight years ago, the Siri Singh Sahib, in a fit of rage, accused me of being 'shallow.' . . . *Visions* is a direct product of a desire and, for me, effort to look deeper at any given situation. . . . *Visions* does *not* come from any agenda of gossip, slander or 3HO/Siri Singh Sahib bashing. Any suggestions to the contrary could not possibly take into account my strong desire and commitment to live and serve as Khalsa" (J. Khalsa 1991, 2).

Included in the newsletter were a number of articles that either analyzed 3HO from external viewpoints or attempted to integrate Sikhism with other perspectives. Implicit in most of them was the assumption that boundaries must fall and that 3HO/Sikh Dharma must become much more open to external ideas and to the free flow of information.

One previously discussed newsletter series, written by Prabhupati, compared 3HO to a dysfunctional family. In one article, she identifies roles such as "Addict," "Co-dependent," "Hero," and "Scapegrace" in 3HO. Thus, "[m]any of the early male heads of Ashrams were these Scapegraces turned Addicts or we could say, rebels turned tyrants. As in any dysfunctional family, these . . . were forever ranting and raving, praising and blaming and, at times, participating in typical addictive behavior usually around power, money or sex" (K. Khalsa 1991, 13–14).

Prabhupati goes on to say that addicts are power brokers, often changeable and difficult to please, but also charismatic, and "stabilizing, nurturing, containing, controlling, pleasing and living up to the high standards of the Addict is the life work of the dysfunctional family. . . . I assert that we force the Siri Singh Sahib into an Addict role. This is ultimately our problem, not his" (ibid., 12).

It is easy to imagine that many members were offended by being called "dysfunctional" and by the identification of Yogi Bhajan as an addict type. The article was intended as a call to organizational self-examination, and it undoubtedly gave some readers a reason to think, but it also alienated others.

Several other *Visions* articles, drawing on the men's movement and New Age thinking, treat both Eastern religions in general and the Khalsa in particular as products of a patriarchal historical period. These religions are said to place too strong an emphasis on transcending the emotions and the senses. Sikh Dharma is urged to abandon such patriarchal attitudes and, instead, to respect embodied experience and creatively unite the feminine and masculine principles.

Thus, in one article, Vikram Singh Khalsa asks, "In the Punjab, we see a vicious and brutal struggle for Khalistan [the name given to the independent Sikh state which many Sikh activists aspire to create]. . . . Is the Khalsa way always to be about physical death? In this age of so much enlightenment, why so much violence?" He continues, "[T]he attitudes, prejudices, emotions and ideas of eighteenth century India still define the Khalsa today. If the Khalsa is to survive it must change and adapt" (1991, 8).

Then, in an interesting twist, he argues that the Khalsa is actually in a position to lead in the New Age. Khalsa ideals and imagery could readily speak to the concerns of the men's movement. If only Sikh Dharma would be sufficiently flexible, its members could "take everything we have learned and transmute it into an entity which will transform this planet." Another male author suggests that members rechannel the old militaristic ideals of the Khalsa and become "warrior/lovers of an interspecies protectorate" (1991, 7).

The articles indicate a shared vision of a revitalized and reformed 3HO. The stated goal of the newsletter was to "rekindle the spirit and the soul of this community," but there is a strong tendency to reinterpret the teachings and to reconsider organizational forms.

In his study of a UFO cult (an early form of what later became the ill-fated Heaven's Gate), Balch (1985) found that members who were beginning to disengage often reconceptualized cultic beliefs and activities. In so doing, they refashioned their identities and used the group's vocabulary "to justify defection" (42). They were engaged in what Balch calls a "bridge-building process" in which they attempted to bridge the gap between the cultic and the general seeker milieus. There is a similar process at work in 3HO members' attempts at reform as they attempt to tie 3HO beliefs to the premises of other belief systems in which they have lodged identities, but the effort often begins with a reforming impulse.

San Francisco is known as one of the more liberal *sangat*s. Members there have historically been active outside of the 3HO community and inclined to freely interpret dogma and rules. It is in such settings that one might expect successful efforts at either frame-bridging or internal reform. So far, it appears that efforts have tended to lead not to reform but to disaffection. Several contributing writers for *Visions* have left the *sangat*. This newsletter, and similar expressions, have not met with general acceptance. When the would-be reformers realize that they are perceived as wreckers, they often become disillusioned and increasingly find themselves isolated from the 3HO mainstream.

Bromley found that "the response to signs of disaffection by insiders and outsiders is pivotal to the disaffiliation process" (1991, 181). As we have seen, there are a variety of responses when an individual challenges, or is perceived to challenge, the approved identities and actions. The first line of response is likely to be persuasion and encouragement to "keep up." If this is not sufficient, the individual can be given special spiritual exercises or can be transferred to a new location, or given a new responsibility or a new identity. She most likely will be told that "the thoughts you're having of defecting are just the negative aspects of your ego." If none of these work, there may be confrontations and threats. (One ex-member, for example, reports that when her husband began to do a form of yoga not taught in 3HO, Yogi Bhajan took her aside and told her that her husband would become impotent and the marriage would collapse if her husband continued in this vein.) There is always the threat that if one leaves the organization one will return to where one was before entering and become mired in maya. One's marriage will crumble, as will one's confidence, willpower, and clarity of thought. The person who persists in the face of these sanctions is likely to find that she is being routinely labeled as "negative," and that she is shunned or accorded only minimal social courtesies. The friends of many years' standing simply redraw the boundaries of the community, leaving the dissenter and her doubts outside of the magic circle.

Rejection acts as a spur to disaffiliation and contributes to the feeling that the organization has spurned the individual's loving gifts. The increasingly disillusioned member may turn to family, to other "fringy" members, to ex-members, and to outside interests for support. If the individual is already part of a supportive group of reformers or activists, this group may provide the impetus to leave.

Reintegration

Jacobs (1989) found that leavers first sever their social ties to a new religious movement as they become disillusioned with the authority structure. Next they break their emotional bonds with its charismatic leader, who is seen to have behaved in ways that "are inconsistent with his role as spiritual figurehead and loving parent" (1989, 128). Then, finally, after a time of isolation and mourning, they completely separate from the movement. I do not have sufficient information to judge whether this sequence holds true in the 3HO case, but I have the impression that 3HO leavers do follow it, with the proviso that the stages are not so clear-cut in this group.

Social withdrawal in 3HO may be hampered by several factors. Members may own or rent houses in the community. They may own property in partnership with, or work in a business with, other 3HO members. It can be difficult to sell a house in the middle of a religious community or to negotiate with co-owners who remain in the movement. Children may be in school in India, and parents may have to wait for an appropriate time to withdraw a child. Children may rebel, or one partner in a marriage may be ready to withdraw before the other. Given these circumstances, it is not uncommon for social and physical detachment to take two to three years. A great deal of emotional work can be accomplished during this period, so social leave-taking, detachment from the leader, final withdrawal, and the early stages of reintegration may occur simultaneously.

The picture is further complicated by the fact that there is considerable variation in the degree of attachment that individual women feel to Yogi Bhajan. Women who are in leadership position themselves, or who are married to men in such positions, and women who have special resources to offer the organization are most likely to be strongly bound. Others appear to be more deeply attached to the spiritual practices, to the local community, to special friends scattered throughout 3HO, and to a communal vision than to their spiritual teacher.

Balch describes a period of "floating" when defectors find themselves lodged "between two symbolic worlds" (1985, 45). It is a period of ambivalence and confusion. Leavers regularly find themselves in this condition, but it is worth noting that the network of ex-members can provide support and guidance to the individual as she experiences this difficult stage.

Because there is the growing network of former and peripheral members it is no longer necessary for the disaffected individual to entirely break ties with the movement. In fact, it may not be practical. Ex-members' children may continue to associate with the children of devoted members, and ex-members may join with members in some activities. Marginal members may associate with both ex-members and the active membership. A former member may be married to a devotee. The individual who no longer associates with Sikh Dharma has the option of affiliation with another Sikh *sangat*. Boundaries are not absolutely clear.

Some of the leavers now say that they would prefer to belong to a network of spiritual seekers rather than to an intentional community, and for them the image of a network has replaced the spiritual path metaphor. In fact, for a period of about two years (1994–96), the network image was transformed into a reality. Participants wrote to a facilitator who then combined their letters with her own thoughts and distributed these. Individuals mailed in essays, thoughts on 3HO/Sikh Dharma, or information about what they were now thinking and doing. They also corresponded with other individuals in the network via letter or e-mail and provided hospitality to traveling "graduates."

The network was a freewheeling and spontaneous form of sharing which participants sometimes referred to by whimsical terms such as "our aquarian group grope" or the "Inner Net." Some of the participants employed central 3HO/Sikh concepts in their sense-making, and some continued to claim a version of Sikh identity. A few continued to draw on 3HO teachings about, as well as their own readings of, Tantric and kundalini yoga traditions. Like the contributors to *Visions*, quite a few were environmentally conscious. They were aware of ideas from both the men's and women's movements, and they were concerned with balancing "male and female principles." They were also quite creative—devising new rituals, writing poetry, drawing, and imagining new lives.

They were struggling to find images for their future ways of being, and some clearly felt that they needed to guard against repetition of old patterns. One woman told me that both she and her husband agreed that any new community must be a spontaneous, grass-roots affair, not willed and formal: "We might get together with some people and meditate and chant if we want to, but we'll feel free to say we don't want to do it next week."

Her husband suggested that I read a book titled *Reimagination of the World*. The subtitle, *A Critique of the New Age, Science, and Popular Culture*, suggests the content. The authors start with the assumption that the concept of a New Age has been trivialized, but one of the authors, David Spangler, suggests that the concept is nonetheless important:

> As the Dutch futurist Fred Polak wrote in his seminal book *The Image of the Future*, Western culture does not have an image of the future. Instead it has an image of progress, which is really an extrapolation of the present, a continuity of the familiar.
>
> This is where the idea of the New Age comes in. It restores our imagination of the future by confronting us with images of transformation, not just of change. . . . The New Age idea calls us to replace projection with vision . . . to live with a transformative vision that opens us to the metamorphic and regenerative qualities of life. (Spangler and Thompson 1991, 22–23)

The network sought to further that sort of transformative vision. Participants attempted to manage the delicate task of sharing and imagining together without institutionalizing their interactions and thus provided a valuable way station en route to new identities.

Most of the leavers I have interviewed left after ten or more years of active participation in 3HO life. In the case of those who left in the midst of a crisis, circumstances dislodged members who had expected to spend their lives within the community. After so many years, the tasks of separation and readjustment are formidable. Biographies and identities have long been entwined with organizational hopes and history, and the task of disentangling from these, and of substituting new identities, frames, and narratives, can prove distressing, exhausting, and consuming, even if one takes on some identities and memberships that come ready-made. One woman I interviewed said that she cried daily for three years after dissolving her ties with 3HO/Sikh Dharma; another told me that she felt that she had been through the equivalent of a divorce and death at once. For such leavers, the support of a network, or the opportunity to jointly create images of new social forms, has been a crucial step in the construction of a new life.

Jacobs found that "the new affiliations selected by former devotees tend to be characterized by loosely structured organizations, with few hierarchical arrangements and a style of leadership that is less authoritarian in character" (1989, 105). She found a preference for a "more maternal ideal of spirituality," and this, in fact, is the case for many of these 3HO "graduates."

Modes of Reintegration

There are questions and difficulties that most of these women highlighted in their accounts of leave-taking. They reported anger and grief and rejection. Those who could not physically leave had to manage daily interactions with the community. Most had to decide what to do with the communal dream. Were they to relinquish it, to replace it, to displace it, or to reformulate it? And they had to reinterpret their biographies. Were they to view the years invested in 3HO as wasted years, or view 3HO as a necessary experience? And how much responsibility should they assume for their own loyalty and persistence?

Most of the women I have talked to have not chosen to reject the whole of the dream. Most are still involved in some spiritual discipline or New Age activity. They will go through further stages, but their initial modes of readjustment can be arranged along a continuum.

At one end of the continuum are those who might be called the "spiritual leavers." They retain whole segments of the 3HO belief system. Typically these beliefs are drawn from Tantra and are tied to an interest in feminine spirituality and empowerment. These individuals may believe that 3HO distorts their favored belief system, and several are actively involved in reclaiming and reworking it. The majority of the women I interviewed, including the women in this group, would no longer call themselves Sikhs, although Prabhupati has retained a strong feeling for the Sikh community and occasionally writes for an on-line Sikh news service, and Simran is still drawn to Sikh ritual and prayer (but is presently active in a Buddhist group).

Since Prabhupati is a prolific writer and fits into this category, I cite some of her letters and articles in order to capture her perspective. For some time after she left 3HO she was preoccupied with the practice of Tantric yoga as a means to experience God directly without the intermediaries of group and spiritual teacher: "I committed myself to never giving my power away to another religious flim flam man. . . . [A]nd I decided to just skip the intermediaries and take God on directly" (K. Khalsa 1993).

In an unpublished article titled "The Guru Paradox," she wrestles with the paradoxes imposed by her hunger for the advice of a truly wise and encouraging teacher, the likelihood that any "guru" she follows will exploit this need, and the pitfalls of "declaring myself my own Guru." She reinterprets "guru" to mean a proper balance between male and female principles. She views women as the source of *shakti* and argues that Yogi Bhajan and other men in the organization have misused 3HO women's *shakti* powers. Women should learn not to give their power away, she says, but should use it for themselves.

In keeping with the Tantric tradition and 3HO teachings, she views women as the creators of environments. "We weave the web, create the mood, set the stage or tell the story," she declares. "It is our power to dream." Indeed, she calls the network members "new dreamers" and describes their purpose: "to perk enough Shakati to dramatically cleanse our subconscious minds and make all our dreams come true" (K. Khalsa 1993).

Closer to the middle are those who practice some form of spiritual discipline—perhaps meditation, but not a form employed in 3HO—and who draw on psychology (particularly transpersonal psychology), New Age thinkers, and sociology for their understanding of selfhood and human motivation. Individuals who fall at this point on the continuum have drawn particularly from various psychologies in order to make sense of their experience within 3HO and to explain the behavior of the leadership. They may have also read sociological literature on sects and new religions, perused anticult literature, studied dysfunctional family theory, or browsed through organizational theory. People in this category may also continue to believe in a transpersonal realm, to meditate, to probe the nature of consciousness, and to explore New Age philosophies. They may draw on the women's movement. They are likely to overlap with the first group in their interest in esoteric Eastern modalities.

Three years after leaving, a woman in this category reported, "My beliefs now are closest to Taoism and the I Ching, but I'm very unthematic. I dropped *sadhana* and the chanting with ease. It was just a bunch of busywork. I spend more time in my body now, sleeping late, enjoying life."

She was (and still is) inclined to take a very critical view of 3HO and of Yogi Bhajan and implied that she was subjected to mind-control techniques. When I first interviewed her she described Bhajan's verbal techniques as a form of hypnotism. She was also convinced that he intentionally breaks bonds between parents and children and inserts himself. "He made me hate my parents," she recalled. She had sad, and sometimes bitter, memories of the way Bhajan sent her son to live with another couple (as previously recounted) and taught 3HO parents to keep children on a strict schedule and not "love them too much." When she left it was with the fear that she had neglected her child. "How could any of that be good?" she asked.

Contacted another five years later she appeared to be moving toward an even more secular approach to life. She reported that she had become interested in therapy and psychodrama and had participated in an improvisational theater company. She had returned to college with plans to complete a degree so that she could work as a therapist. While in school, however, she became fascinated with expressive art therapy and discovered that she had "some artistic talent." She had just completed her degree and had decided to explore that newly discovered talent.

At the far end of the continuum are "secular leavers." These women look primarily to family, school, or occupation for identity, although they have not necessarily abandoned all spiritual interests. They have jettisoned most 3HO beliefs and practices and are eager to get on with new lives. They have largely exchanged community for society. As one leaver put it, "A big part of me doesn't want to replace that community. I would like to sort of look at the community at large. You know, just look at the universe as a community rather than such a small, insulated community. . . . It's just a certain feeling of freedom."

Narratives

The following are the stories of four women, all among the women I originally interviewed, who have since left 3HO/Sikh Dharma. They represent a cross-section of women interviewed in that they joined for different reasons and have followed different strategies in their leaving. They first recounted their biographies for me when they were devotees. After exiting, they revised their histories and, in some ways, reconceptualized the selves that had originally embraced the organization.

Their stories, however, do not reveal extraordinary shifts in narrative and self-concept. There is consistency in their motivations and in their sense-making. An intense seeker has remained just that. She still values mystical experiences and seeks to attain them through meditation and yoga. She is as emotionally expressive and impassioned as she was as a 3HO member. A woman who viewed the study of psychology and consciousness as a vehicle for liberating people has not changed her goal. She performed outreach activities and taught workshops in 3HO and continues to do those things now, but in another setting. Her dedication to living her beliefs has only increased and matured. A woman who joined 3HO less out of a spiritual hunger than for a life-style consistent with her values left the organization when she felt 3HO no longer stood for those values. She entered as a woman who kept her own counsel and left as one. She entered because she valued autonomy and respect for others, and thought that these goods were more read-ily available in 3HO than in the outside society, and when she decided that those values were being undermined by the organization she sev-ered her ties to it. A woman who joined primarily because of her hus-band's enthusiasm for 3HO was strongly motivated by family considerations when she decided to leave. For each, there was clearly a point where the line was drawn. Certain things were not negotiable. When overriding beliefs, values, and conceptions of self and reality were threatened, the 3HO identities lost their luster. The costs of con-tinued membership began to outweigh the benefits.

Spiritual Leaver/Intense Seeker

A. was originally introduced as an intense seeker. Throughout the period of this study her approach to life has consistently been spiritual, intuitive, and emotional.

Both as a devotee and as an "ex" she has portrayed herself as differ-ent from her family of origin, which she describes as outer-directed and achievement-oriented. The contrast between intellect and feeling has been central to her interpretation of her biography. When she was in 3HO that organization represented an opportunity to express the mys-tical, intuitive, and caring sides of her personality which, she felt, were not valued by her parents. Membership also precipitated a struggle with what she viewed as the controlling, critical, and overly intellectual aspects of her self, some of which she had come to equate with inter-nalized aspects of her mother's personality. Within 3HO these unde-sired aspects of the self could readily be described as expressions of the negative mind or as symptomatic of the intellect ruling where the soul should hold sway.

When she was still a 3HO member, she told me that her family had exhibited little concern with such virtues as compassion or with such goals as spiritual growth. They cared, she thought, primarily for exter-nal achievements. She tried to live as they expected her to live, but she was unhappy: "I was always doing. I never stopped doing. I had a black book with a list of things that had to be done and that was all it was. I was very compulsive. Everything was suppressed. . . . I was just totally success-oriented and the result was I was being a total failure in terms of developing myself."

Parts of her story have already been recounted. She rebelled when she reached college. There she encountered the hip scene and experimented with psychedelic drugs. Turning her gaze inward, she found a highly visual and, increasingly, spiritual world. She married, lived overseas, and gave birth to a son. After some years, she and her husband returned to the United States, where they traveled in a van and looked for an alternative community or a promising parcel of land. But their marriage was fraying. It was at this point that she encountered a 3HO yoga class. This led to attendance at a solstice ceremony, and there the spiritual identity that she had been slowly forming finally became concrete. At the same time she decided that the gulf that had been growing between herself and her husband was too wide to be bridged. She essentially relinquished the role of wife and took on a new spiritual role. She also moved to repair the daughter role as she had been estranged from her parents: "I wrote my parents telling them I wasn't doing drugs anymore, and they were very happy and wanted me to come visit. So I packed up . . . and I went to Washington, thinking it would just be for a weekend for a Tantric course. . . . And I never went back to the piece of land where I was living."

She settled into an ashram, and in time she remarried. The 3HO emphasis on mothering and on the divinity of children became very important to her. It enabled her to give her children the attention and easy affection that she felt was lacking in her own childhood: "I wanted to take care of my kids. Even if I could have afforded help I didn't want it. I'd been raised by servants. . . . I wanted to do everything, including breast feeding them, massaging them daily, being there for them day in and day out."

The organization provided her with a blueprint for the spiritual self she had set out to explore, and it also provided discipline and justification for her inward-turning gaze. It provided her with explanations for powerful emotional highs and lows, and it was rich in the visual and symbolic material that she clearly craves. The belief system assured her that the mystical, caring, and intuitive aspects of her being were valuable, and she was able to assign priority to the inner life while finding a spiritual purpose in more instrumental activities. The crevices of self-doubt, and even self-dislike, that she attributed to her upbringing could now be formulated in terms of a negative self. I asked her to describe herself, at a time when she was still a wholehearted 3HO member, and this is what she said:

I'm a mixture of a whole lot of different elements. The best of me is the part that is totally one with God, and I do have a big part that longs for that, and can experience that, and can come back with the knowledge that it's there for everybody. . . . [A]nd the worst is the self-pitying, anxious, irritable, doubting thinker who is trying to change things somehow by worrying about them—which doesn't do any good at all.

There's a very simple, happy me that loves to be out in the garden and cook and clean and hug children and read them stories, and I'm glad I've had the opportunity to give a lot of my life to that.

There's a business part of me that's coming out more now that my kids are gone. That I'm comfortable with now, and I see that it gives me a way to do things for other people. . . .

I'm not normal in anything that I do—not that I know what normal is. . . . [T]he way I see things and speak about them makes me stand out, and when I'm feeling strong and God-filled I don't mind that. I'm also very strong in negativity, which is one reason I think that I needed such a rigorous path, because my mental negative mind was just devastating. . . .

I think I'm mostly a good mother. . . . People say my children look like me, and it's wonderful because I never thought I was beautiful. . . . [A]nd when people say I look like them it makes me feel there must be some beauty.

Many of the thematic elements in her interpretation of her biography are in that self-description: mothering, feeling versus thinking, intensity, and being different and self-critical.

At approximately the same time that she provided this self-description she also told me that she found Bhajan's image of a horse-drawn carriage helpful, and it is easy to see how that image offered release from internal conflict: "The body is the vehicle, the horses are the mind, the driver is the soul. Often we (in our ignorance) let the horses determine where we go, how fast, etc. . . . Yogiji recommends that the driver pick up the reigns and direct the life. . . . [T]he mind does well as the servant of the soul. . . . I feel more relaxed when my soul is in charge. I feel nuts if I allow my mind or emotions to lead the way. I become more relaxed and peaceful when my soul is in charge."

Aspects of the belief system were clearly liberating for her. But the intuitive, expressive self that found justification in the teachings also posed a potential threat to organizational discipline—although, throughout most of the time that she was a member, this was a fact of which she was cheerfully unaware. She chafed at anything that would curtail her creativity. Thus as a Montessori teacher for Khalsa children, "the really fun time was creative time, just letting things flow." But "I didn't like the restrictions placed on me by the next level Montessori teachers who were saying, 'By this stage the children need to have mastered this, this, and this.'" Her approach to teaching yoga and meditation or to participating in *sadhana* was to "tune in and let the God energy come through." She would say whatever came to her and do as she was prompted.

For a very long time she simply did not notice any of the more restrictive, materialistic, or opportunistic sides to 3HO life. But then she was present when the ashram director was arrested. The event left her frightened and disturbed. Its aftermath was even more trying as ashram residents experienced severe anxiety attacks and depression. This, she thought, was most certainly not healthy, happy, or holy.

She struggled through the following weeks and found herself closeted in her room every night once the children were fed. There she cried and cried. She learned of video tapes of drug deals involving the ashram head, and she simply could not reconcile this with her picture of the organization. She was in pain and did not fully understand why; all she knew was that "things did not compute." The ashram director told her to "have faith," but her faith in him was shattered, and that loss of faith, although to a lesser degree, extended to Yogi Bhajan and to the organization as a whole.

The pain and the sense of loss were acute, but she began to take action. She participated in the meetings of the "dissident" ashram group. She began to call ex-members of 3HO, saying, "I don't understand." They provided her with a new picture of the organization.

She began to assert a new identity and found herself embroiled in identity struggles. She called her family and told them about the arrest. They were caring and supportive. She taught independent yoga classes. She tried to withdraw money from a Khalsa financial investment company, only to be accused of "undermining the economic security of the community." She removed her turban, and for this was told she could no longer play music for *sadhana*. She was labeled "negative."

She had little choice but to construct a new identity and a new interpretation of 3HO life. She studied attitudinal healing. She took up

Vipassana meditation (a Buddhist form), which encouraged a belief she had held for some time but not always acted upon: "the divine and the answers are within." She wondered if 3HO, in spite of many of the organization's teachings, had encouraged devotees "to find God outside ourselves" and decided to take the time to listen to the internal voice. Now it seemed that the forms of meditation practiced in 3HO had required "doing rather than being." 3HO mantras demanded effort and "pushing through" resistance and feelings; much of the meditation was "like eating and not noticing the taste." Now she would sit, she would feel, she would taste. Never one for half-measures, she gave herself over to the process of grieving and reconstruction.

She began to read literature on cults and on dysfunctional families and organizations, and she incorporated these in her sense-making. She reinterpreted her biography as a movement from one dysfunctional family (her family of origin) to another (3HO). Aspects of the organization began to appear "repressive," and, in fact, it seemed that 3HO youth were "under pressure to be successful and professional" just as she had been in her youth.

She decided that, for her, ashram life had supplied a set of "blinders," so that she could seek God and not be distracted. "The world was too dangerous, too tempting," and she had needed a way to "break from the mental." Indeed, she had developed "an absolute disdain" for the mind, believing that it had "gotten her into trouble." Now she began to wonder if she had carried this too far. The 3HO practice of meditating on mantras began to look like a way of avoiding reflection and self-knowledge. Now she chose to enter "the noisy, dirty, basement of my mind, to witness and detach from thoughts and feelings." She used "the inspiration of moments of immersion in the Divine" in order to "keep on sludging through."

She ceased to wear *bana*. Nevertheless, there was continuity in her life: she was able to retain her business, she remained in her house, and her children and husband were loyal to her and understanding of her withdrawal. In fact, one son, himself disillusioned with 3HO, asked, "What took you so long?" She remained very much the mystic that she had long been.

She continued to view her life as a search for truth or *Sat Nam*. She talked to ethnic Sikhs and was reassured that she could still follow the faith; she decided it was a matter of retaining content but not form. But she also began to try to meld other belief systems with Sikhism. She choreographed and began to teach a form of yogic dance, and she developed her interest in goddess religions. She could even see herself—and her mother—as reflections of the Goddess. She found a Sufi group to worship with.

In spite of the pain she suffered, she continued to look for signs that 3HO/Sikh Dharma had been a good experience and that it might be evolving toward a more open, "true" religion. She was determined to forgive and even "to love Yogi Bhajan unconditionally." She spent some time floating between worlds. She remained as emotional, as intuitive, as desirous of faith and "immersion" in divinity as she ever was. Years into the separation process she was still hurting and still looking for a place to lodge her faith, her strong feelings, and her creativity. She still needs some structure, but she wants to avoid hierarchies and prescriptions. "All isms should be wasms," she quoted to me recently.

Psychological Leaver/Intense Seeker

The next woman, B., was also an intense seeker. Unlike the previous woman, however, she has more respect for the mind, and her decision to affiliate with 3HO was tied more closely to intellectual constructs. She has been more willing to incorporate ideological and academic ideas into her self-concept. She seeks a life of praxis and is more inclined than A. to take on long-term instrumental roles. When she first encountered the organization, 3HO appeared to offer an ideal setting for the enactment of her ideals. She was not aware of it then, but the structure of 3HO was probably also compatible with the demands of her strong superego and her desire to excel and to strive for perfection.

B. was politically active before she encountered 3HO. She did not find her activities entirely fulfilling, however, and when she first found yoga and meditation she knew that these filled a gap in her life. She increasingly came to feel that social change could only be accomplished at the level of individual consciousness:

> I started revolting when I was in college and got involved politically—radical groups and so on . . . against the whole capitalist class system, and feeling a need for people to mobilize and get what they needed on the planet, and wanting to support that process. It had values of equity and opportunity for all, that kind of thing, in it. Over the years, though, it kept getting deeper and deeper, so it became me rebelling against a value system that prevented people from realizing their highest potential. . . . [B]ottom line it always comes down to each being and their own relationship to consciousness, their own consciousness, their own awareness.

As she explored meditation and yoga, she also trained as a counselor and began to integrate Eastern techniques with her studies and her work; 3HO was part of her effort to further change and enhance consciousness. She encountered therapies, such as neurolinguistic programming (Cameron-Bandler 1978), that harmonized with her spiritual insights, and she worked at blending these with yoga and meditation.

While she was still a member, she told me that the practices she learned in 3HO fed a sense of her own "inner beauty." Her sense of her potential had increased, she said, as had the range of her skills and her ability to further others' growth. For a while she felt that she was successfully formulating a path that integrated all of the major elements in her life. But over time, aspects of 3HO life appeared less and less attractive as she began to view them from the perspective of growth therapies. For some time she respected Yogi Bhajan as a teacher of yoga and meditation, but she was bothered because some people were dependent on him for advice about the smallest details in their lives. She began to feel that he encouraged dependency and even guilt in some of his adherents.

She had not joined 3HO in order to find a spiritual teacher. It was the community, the dedication, the practices that were foremost, a chance to live a life that was "devotional, with meaning and purpose." But Bhajan soon became an important figure in her life. She had "a real emotional investment in being a good student of his . . . and in feeling that there was a relationship with him." She accepted his spiritual authority and respected his knowledge.

This is not to say that she did not find herself in conflict with him or in doubt about his judgments, but for some time she retained her faith in his leadership. Because there are, as she notes, "a lot of messages that if you make any other choice than staying it's ego," it was difficult to credit her occasional desires to leave the organization. "It easily becomes your truth versus Yogi Bhajan's truth."

Periodic clashes with the leadership created some doubts about the organization, but none sufficient to lead to an exit until Bhajan berated her before the assembled women's training camp. This incident was pivotal because it altered her view of Bhajan. She saw him "doing something abusive. . . . I understood that he was just a man being abusive." She "no longer trusted his legitimacy or spiritual authority," and for her this was "a pivotal and radical departure."

She was no longer convinced that his life-style and his advice qualified him as a guru. She also looked more closely at the organization and came to the conclusion that it was not a healthy environment: "[T]he . . . following and the structures that develop—a lot of the materialism . . . I think is excessive. There's just a lot of guilt-based messages that come across. . . . And to me that was the biggest paradox that I couldn't live within: that someone was telling me, 'You're divine and experience it.' On the other hand, 'If you don't do these things, if you think like that, or act like that or talk like this'—all the do's and don't's—'then the devil will take you.'"

Regretfully, she came to the conclusion that she should leave the organization, that this was not her path. She continued her *sadhana* and some of her personal friendships, but she ceased formal affiliation. At that time she described the process:

> I meditated myself beyond believing I was going through *shaktipod*, and I used meditation and prayer the whole time in my withdrawal, as a way to keep anchored in my higher self, to not get angry in my pulling out. . . . I definitely had to deal with parts of me that thought that maybe I wasn't good enough [to manage outside of 3HO], or I couldn't work things out on my own well enough, or might make bad decisions, or might fall to my lower nature, . . . but that's been the beauty of it, that rather than copping to it and bowing to the pressure of my superego I just kept using meditation and prayer to reassure myself that I was fine. So I feel like I've grown a whole lot by just doing it.
>
> Beyond the personalities and the politics, the vision and the beauty of a group of people dedicated to consciousness, getting up early for *sadhana*, living vigorous, healthy, natural lives; community—I love it, I still love it. That makes me saddest. . . . I love the practices and processes, but when enough static is created by the organization . . . then the only thing I know to do is to try to keep the same idealism and bring it to my personal relationships and my life-style outside of the organization.

Looking back, she feels her leaving was eased because she had an established professional life and was a new mother. "I was focused on my child and what I already had going. . . . I didn't have to create a new life." But even so, "I was dealing actively with 3HO for five years. . . . [M]y dreams were chock full of it [,] . . . with wanting, sadness, and fear."

Almost immediately upon leaving she embraced Vipassana Buddhism, and her practice provided a further critique of 3HO. From that perspective, it seemed to her that 3HO did not further mature self-acceptance or acceptance of life in all of its varied forms. It was too hierarchical and unsympathetic to feminine principles. Thus she now sees the leaving and starting over process as "coming to trust myself in a deeper way." 3HO made it "difficult to trust one's own inner wisdom." One doubted one's ideas and was always in "fear of making a mistake." She and other members were always told not to "be so emotional." She now equates this with "a denial of the feminine," a tendency which she now finds in many religious traditions with their "hierarchies, higher and lower selves, their need to sublimate the lower self." In retrospect, she thinks that 3HO members constantly felt there was "something wrong with the self." This was, at least, true in her case. "I felt the sense of guilt and shame that comes when you are in a hierarchical and judgmental system. . . . I felt I had to cover up things," she says.

Today she is teaching Buddhist insight meditation and continuing her therapeutic practice. Buddhism has convinced her that "awakening is through our nature, not denial of it. . . . [H]onoring our emotions . . . honoring ourselves is how we awaken." She feels that she has had to discover her emotions and acknowledge her embodied self: "I had to wait until I was in my late thirties to know when I was attracted to a man and to realize when a man was attracted to me. I had to learn that whole dance." She believes that in 3HO she was busy trying to change herself and others. Insight meditation has taught her to cease that constant effort and simply allow herself, and her clients, to be.

Now she feels she has acquired "spontaneity . . . capacity for intimacy . . . ease and appreciation for the life around me. . . . I'm less judgmental . . . more creative, more alive, more receptive and not trying to judge and control." Her practice is "about openness and receptivity to life as it is," and it teaches that efforts to control lead to "contracting and pain." As for the future, "I don't think so much in terms of external goals and plans . . . although the externals are happening." Her concern is "to live fully and be present . . . keep open to living, to my son and friends . . . have fun. . . . It's all so sparkly out there."

In spite of the upheaval she has experienced and the ways in which her thinking has changed, there is considerable consistency in her motivations and concerns. She has retained her spiritual focus and her desire to teach and to facilitate others' growth. She has continued in her profession and in her efforts to unite psychological, political, and spiritual insights. She still seeks a role in which she can wholeheartedly enact her beliefs. In fact, she has enthusiastically embraced another system of beliefs, although this time she is avoiding a hierarchical organization. Her critique of 3HO is ideological, much as her defense of the organization once was. Her self-description is still institutionally informed and now incorporates the ideals of Insight Meditation.

When she was in 3HO she described herself as "always playing hard, working hard, trying hard. . . . Always wanting to get the most out of things, always concerned that I'd be missing out on something—that kind of a personality." This is clearly not the description of a calm, accepting Buddhist, and in seeking to live by Buddhist ideals she has learned to moderate the striving and demanding aspects of her personality. But she still excels in her world. If this is not an oxymoron, she might be described as a high-achieving Buddhist teacher.

Secular Leaver/Pragmatic Seeker

C. is thoughtful, petite, humorous, and lively. Like so many of the women who have had ties to 3HO, she is verbally skilled and readily conveys the flavor of her experience and the nature of her convictions. She is positive in outlook, independent, seems to gravitate toward leadership positions, and keeps her own counsel. She is clear about her values, and 3HO originally appealed to her because it appeared to offer a life-style in tune with her convictions. She also describes herself as "solution-oriented" and eager to "have things resolved." She is a musician and was attracted by the extensive use of music in 3HO.

She describes her parents as "old traditional types" who managed to raise a family "with real good values." Those values gave her a stable point from which to measure what she saw around her, and much of what she saw in high school and college seemed unkind, self-serving, or dishonest. When she found a 3HO ashram in her college town, "it was something I could relate to more." She began to attend *sadhana* regularly but did not reside in the ashram. Then she moved, and after a period of time she became an ashram resident in her new city. From there she moved to the larger Washington ashram.

For awhile, "all I did was yoga and meditation, and I played music and taught yoga classes." But soon she was doing more. When Sikhism was introduced she welcomed the opportunity to sing the *shabd*s and learn Gurmulkhi. She worked in 3HO businesses, and her managerial skills matured along with the businesses. She became a bookkeeper and a store manager. She was increasingly active in ashram life and instrumental in planning Sunday worship and meals.

She readily embraced the 3HO admonition to keep up since it was congruent with her desire for a positive, energetic approach to life. Interviewed when she was still an enthusiastic resident of the ashram, she said, "Things I really think a lot about are: one is to have a positive outlook, and the other is to be solution-oriented. I'm real solution-oriented. Where some people just look at everything as there may be a problem in it. . . . I try to figure out how it can be a good thing, how to make it nice."

This approach was enhanced by marriage and motherhood. She savored the early years of motherhood and the 3HO approach to childbirth and child care. Detailing the different life stages she had passed through, she spoke at length about the ways in which motherhood had changed her. "The births of my children are the highest points in my life, ever," she said. With motherhood, past and future faded for awhile into the timeless world of childhood and an eternal, practical, now: "It's hard to think of the past for me. I hardly even remember it, . . . and with children it's hard to live in the future that much. . . . [I]t's like I'm so much in the present I can hardly think about what I'm going to do tomorrow."

Her contentment was periodically interrupted, however, by difficulties in the ashram. She encountered occasional strains in relationships with other residents, and, more troubling, she observed what she thought were unhealthy patterns of leadership and submission: "It was hard seeing other people totally relating to the head of the ashram as God, rather than following the teachings, because I'm more into living the way of life than relating to the person. . . . [I]t was watching other people kind of not grow within themselves but just following, which is not what we're all about."

In addition, she became embroiled in a dispute about schooling for her children. She wanted to try a type of schooling that was not favored in the 3HO community, but she was pressured by the ashram director and fellow residents to send her child to the school that the other ashram children attended. She succumbed to group pressure for awhile, but was finally dissatisfied with the group school and pursued her own course. Later, she remembered, "there was a real sore feeling there. . . . We were given this message: 'you can if you want to, but if you don't agree you're certainly wrong.'"

Such events began to register in her mind. Although there was a new ashram director, she again saw people following too willingly. She was bothered by "things like a hierarchy where there were the higher and the lower . . . within the ashram and then within the bigger ashram community, nationally and internationally." She noticed that "there were businesses, like telephone sales, that would come and go and disappear. . . . [A]nd I just never felt they were so righteous."

She began to feel increasingly distanced from many of the people in the ashram. After awhile she allowed herself to wonder if the group was, little by little, deserting it's ideals. True to her preference for positive action, she tried to "be part of the solution." She joined committees and worked with a group that attempted to revitalize what had, in their eyes, become a repetitive daily *sadhana* routine. But she constantly encountered resistance and opposition, and "every time I put my two cents in, I'd be sort of put down. 'Negative' was a word I heard a lot." She began to think of some members as the "thought police."

The arrest of the ashram director confirmed many of her misgivings, although she appears to have been equally bothered by its aftermath, when little changed and there was no apology or explanation forthcoming. She became part of the discussion group and found it very helpful to finally voice some of her doubts and discontents. But participation meant more disapproval from ashram leadership, and that "symbolized things that I had felt for a long time: that it's not accepted to seek outside of the system in 3HO. . . . I always used to like to go to other groups and do different things. What I always felt, which was uncomfortable, was that when we went to these places we only went to offer them *our* great teachings. We didn't go to meet with them on common ground. I just felt a certain arrogance that I didn't want to be part of."

She decided that "maybe I can live here and not be part of the politics, but be part of the group. I took off my turban and tried to just live there." But "slowly people just didn't talk to me." She felt that they slighted and judged her children as well. Alienated from the community, frustrated in her efforts at reform, no longer believing that the organization reflected the values that she cherished, she had little choice but to withdraw.

She struggled with fears that she was making a mistake in leaving and that she was ill-equipped to cope with the outside world. She found it both amusing and helpful when a friend and ex-member reassured her that "'none of the curses are true.' I just really appreciated it because it wasn't like anyone really even realized they were curses, but there were all these little subtle fears."

She and her family have now moved to a new home. She was already a teacher, but she went back to school to solidify her credentials. She has ceased to practice Sikhism and has no desire to find another organization like 3HO: "There's a lot of dogma in every organization and every group. I just want to keep my distance from it." She retains the 3HO practices, such as vegetarianism, that are consonant with her own value system, but she has adopted no other religion or set of practices. Always one to want closure and to look at the positive side of things, she has readily left a share of the past behind, although she is in regular contact with other ex-members. "I love being out, I really do," she says.

Secular Leaver/Convenience Joiner

As a member, D. viewed her path as a trajectory toward empathy and autonomy. She described herself as more career-oriented, intellectual, and analytical than many of the other women in 3HO, and she did not share their hip background. These areas of difference posed some problems for her as she accommodated to the 3HO life-style, and they were important to her interpretation of her biography. Also important was a long-held allegiance to principles of tolerance and open-mindedness. She tended to depict the organization as moving in directions that paralleled her own growth, a not uncommon perception.

As a member, she adopted a critical tone to describe the person she had been when she first encountered 3HO: "I was insecure. I was striving. I was selfish. But I did have . . . some commitment to a community, a group of people, and I had some awareness of social change that I wanted to take place, and I was doing something about it in a small way."

She was speaking then as a member of many years' standing and felt that she had made progress and that some of those traits had been transmuted: "I think that I'm still striving, but in a very different kind of way. I think that I see possessions and money and all that kind of thing in a different way than I did then. . . . I also think I'm a much more universal person than I was then. . . . I think I've become much more eclectic."

She told me that she remembered with distaste her grandmother's religious intolerance. As a child she began to read about different cultures and religions, and when she asked about people who didn't believe in Jesus, her grandmother replied, "'They're going to hell.' Well to me that was the break. That's when I stopped being a Christian, in my head."

When she encountered 3HO people whose attitudes were similar to her grandmother's she was disturbed, but she was relieved and impressed by the tolerance she originally perceived in Yogi Bhajan's approach to religious practice. She was so troubled by one individual's attitudes that she spoke to Yogi Bhajan about these, fearing that he might share that individual's rigidity. She was relieved when he responded that "some people in 3HO are fanatics." And she has never forgotten an incident in the early years: "[Yogi Bhajan] went through all of these ideals—now this is what should happen, you should do this, you should do that—and for a lot of us, we had already blown it. . . . This one woman sitting not far from me started to cry. . . . [A]nd she said, 'I've blown it; it's hopeless,' and just about then the Siri Singh Sahib walked by. . . . [A]nd he said, 'all things are redeemable.'" It was his assumption that change and redemption are always possible that impressed her.

She looked for tolerance and a willingness to forgive both in the organization and in herself. She criticized herself for having been an "intellectual snob" in the early years. She was delighted when her son told her that she was one of the most open-minded and easy-to-talk-to parents in the ashram. For a long while she assumed that the thrust of Yogi Bhajan's teachings and disciplines was toward disseminating such openness and empathy.

Always fairly pragmatic and worldly herself, she valued those strains in Sikhism. She was pleased that Yogi Bhajan taught that you could not serve people by withdrawing from the world: "You had to know where they were coming from. You had to be part of the world they related to. This was another thing I think that for me personally was really important and appealing, the fact that you were trying to change the system from within it, as it were. You were trying to change the world by being in the world."

She continued her professional role, even in the face of some peer pressure, and in her struggle to pursue her own goals, to find honest points of contact with the organization, and to learn from its tenets, she felt that over the years she developed depth, flexibility, and independence.

She tended to see parallel trends in the organization: a loosening of some of the rules, greater tolerance for other perspectives, and a desire on Yogi Bhajan's part for a more self-reliant following as he grew older. She focused on aspects of 3HO life that supported her long-held values and modes of processing experience, but she also incorporated less familiar aspects when they seemed to offer opportunities for growth and accommodation.

Slowly, however, she began to perceive more of the intolerance and rigidity that she so dislikes. She concluded that she had grown more open-minded than the organization. As longtime members, she and her husband

> created a spiritual community that was very eclectic. . . .
> There were Sufis, Buddhists, and Catholics. That was
> the mixture we usually had, besides ourselves. I got to
> feeling really much more comfortable with that. Much

more a feeling of what I thought was the Sikh philosophy, which was for each person to choose the expression that they felt was most meaningful to them at that particular time and place. And I felt 3HO had evolved, in practice, and to some extent in theory even, to something very narrow. While I was getting wider and broader, it was getting narrower and more restrictive.

She perceived strains in her family life, which she attributed to 3HO, and family had always been central to her identity. She also felt a need for greater privacy and individuation:

I think the main thing was just being tired of the group-living situation. . . . Another part of it was always doing what someone else was telling me to do, whether I wanted to do it or not. And coming to the realization—as I was talking to an old friend it just sort of hit me. . . . [I]t had been so long since I stopped and said, "what do *I* want to do?"

I think the thing that really cinched it for me was my mother-in-law's death. . . . [T]here were just some really emotional things that happened with the extended family . . . and our own personal nuclear family that made me realize that one of the things that was happening with 3HO was a move away from family. . . . I saw it as a pulling-away from my biological family. And I just felt a really strong tie to my husband's biological family and to my own, to my husband and my sons, and that I think was the real turning point.

She also began to wonder about the costs of being a minority member in 3HO: "I think that in some ways there was part of me that always felt kind of on the edge of it. And I would . . . try to explain it away to myself: I was older, you know, I was the oldest woman in the ashram, in this area anyway. . . . And even though people tried to say that race wasn't an issue, I thought that it was."

The arrest of the ashram director brought these issues to a head, particularly because the publicity seemed likely to affect her position at work. Because of this publicity the name "Khalsa" was associated with the legal case, and she and her husband finally decided to change their names. Soon after that they moved away from the ashram. They hoped to retain 3HO friends, and to that end they carefully composed a letter to all the local 3HO members saying how they valued the ties they had made and the years they had shared in 3HO. They received almost no replies. It seemed a sad way to end years of shared living.

For now, D. is content to live without either an organized community or a distinct spiritual path. She will occasionally attend a church, but has come to the conclusion that she is unlikely to find one that will meet most of her requirements. In any case, her life is full with her work, her friendships, and her hobby. The exit did not leave a very large gap in her life since she already had a demanding and absorbing job and many non-Sikh friends.

There is, however, a price she paid, and one that still angers and troubles her. It is the cost of having submerged her ethnic identity while she was in 3HO and the associated fear that her children have been left without the understanding that might have better equipped them to live in a world that seems to her to be growing less tolerant. "You know what really makes me angry?" she asked. "It's what I lost with my family, my nuclear family. . . . I'm angry at the organization and I'm angry with myself. . . . I didn't give my boys an awareness of their community. I didn't tell them the stories they needed to hear . . . or not enough. And now it's too late. They needed to hear that when they were younger. To give them that inner firmness they need."

Although she qualifies as a secular leaver, she has certainly not abandoned all of her spiritual interests. When she and her husband were struggling with the decision to leave 3HO, she felt that their decisions were in tune with some spiritual force or direction. When asked about the most satisfying aspects of 3HO she unhesitatingly replied, "[D]iscovering the Divine was within me, that there was a direct connection that I could make." She feels that that connection remains, but she does not have a need to formalize it with a religious affiliation or even with regular yoga and meditation.

She values lessons that she learned in 3HO, and sees no sense in jettisoning all she gained from the experience. You can't deny it, she says, "it's your identity." But Sikhism and 3HO are clearly behind her, and the pleasures of everyday life and her newfound autonomy loom large.

I am struck by the continuities in these women's lives. Central themes, preoccupations, motivations, and values keep reappearing in their biographies. What each of these women appears to have gained, via membership in 3HO and the hardships of exiting, however, is a capacity to employ alternative ways of viewing and encountering the world in addition to those that they began with. Thus A. has learned to balance her thoroughly open, accepting approach to life with a mild dose of skepticism. B., a striving achiever, has learned to moderate her intensity and to enjoy life. C., a positive problem solver, has realized that some situations are intractable and sometimes it is best just to leave them behind and move on. And, finally, D, originally an externally oriented woman, now cares less for possessions and positions and more for her own personal and spiritual needs. Ironically, each of these women has, in her struggles and her leaving, moved closer to the Sikh ideal of equipoise.

Making Meaning

As I was browsing Borders' new books display, I noticed a paperback called *There Are No Accidents*. That is the sort of thing that my New Agey and ex-Sikh friends are always saying—and the sort of belief that makes me very uncomfortable. But the subtitle was *Synchronicity and the Stories of Our Lives*. The stories aspect appealed to me, as did the possible synchronicity of being drawn to a book about synchronicity. So I bought it.

The author, Robert H. Hopcke, defines synchronistic events as "meaningful sequences of unusual, accidental events" (19). These events could be dismissed as coincidences, except that they are too meaningful to us. We can't seem to dismiss them. They just seem to be too closely connected to what we have been thinking, seeking, and needing to have "just happened," but we know that we did not cause them and can find no ordinary explanation for their occurrence. They tend to occur, he finds, at times of transition in our lives, and they have "a rather distinctly dramatic or novelistic quality to them, because of the way in which an internal, emotional state . . . is reflected in a chance occurrence in the external world" (1997, 5).

They can lead us to question the assumption that internal and external realities are separate and distinct. Often, they also challenge our ideas about what our lives should be: "What occurred in many, if not most, of the synchronistic events as told to me was that what people in fact wanted to believe about themselves and their lives—emotionally, professionally, psychologically, and spiritually—was revealed to them, against their will by sheer coincidence, as not at all what it seemed" (ibid., 186).

The individuals who experience synchronistic events seem to learn to see their lives from a less egocentric perspective, and their lives, in turn, take on a new coherency. Moreover, "synchronistic events confront us with the fact that sometimes the stories we make up about ourselves, the stories we would like to live, are not necessarily the stories we are actually living or, to go a step further, are meant to live" (ibid., 9). In fact, Hopcke notes, "we receive in a synchronistic event a reminder of an important truth: that our lives are organized, consciously and unconsciously, the way a story is, that our lives have a coherence, a direction, a reason for being, and a beauty as well. Synchronicity reminds us how much a work of art the stories of our lives can be" (ibid., 47).

Hopcke does not insist that these events are necessarily signs that the God of traditional religions is sending us the help and the lessons that we need. Obviously, many people will explain a synchronistic event in these terms, but he is content with a broader approach. It is the meaning we create out of these events and out of our deep need for wholeness that renders synchronicities significant, for "the plot of our life stories, is not written simply by what we know about ourselves but comes from a much deeper place, from our innately human capacity to experience wholeness through living a symbolic life." It is the ability to see/assign the symbolic content to these events that gives shape and depth to our stories when this is combined with a heightened sense of possibility.

Many of the new religions create just such a sense of possibility. They teach that there are layers of truth behind appearances. There are signs behind events. Devotees often are encouraged to believe that there are no accidents, that all the events in their lives are significant, that meaning is to be found in every nook and cranny of their lives. There is, for example, a reason that a devotee happened upon a spiritual leader or was introduced to the group at a particular time. But, more interestingly, 3HO introduces elements of chance and new possibilities for synchronicity. When Bhajan arranges a marriage, encourages someone to pursue a particular career or to stay at home and be a spiritual wife, tells a couple that he thinks they ought to have another child, or asks people to take up a new responsibility in the *sangat*, he introduces the unexpected, the turn of events that is not in the individual's plot for her life, but he insists that it has purpose. If the individual accepts his instructions or his information, she has no choice but to release some of her expectations and plans and to alter her self-concept. She has to search for and create meaning so that she can weave this occurrence into her personal story and her view of the world. And my impression is that this often leads to an effort to achieve wholeness and balance within the self. I think this is one of the reasons that members persevere: there is this necessity/opportunity/challenge to create a deeper, and more interesting, personal story.

PART fiVE

Maturity

CHAPTER 8

Re-visioning

This chapter considers the viewpoints of several women who are currently refining their understandings of womanhood, taking on new identities, and venturing in new directions. I include three women who are longtime 3HO/Sikh Dharma members, two women who have left 3HO, and Simran, who temporarily returned to the fold. The chapter is something of a collage of stories and voices. It is an attempt to capture hesitant steps in new directions, experimentation, confusion, and growth, and an effort to place these portrayals in a broader context, tying the women's thinking to some developments in women's spirituality and to recent conceptualizations of the feminine principle.

Feminism and the Feminine Principle: East and West

These women are making sense of their lives at an interesting moment in history when understandings of gender and issues of concern to women are tossed about in a cross-cultural current of ideas. Women residing outside of Europe are examining Western forms of feminism and deciding which elements to absorb and which to discard. Western women are appropriating goddesses and rituals from every Eastern and native tradition that offers a candidate. Women worldwide are actively redefining the "feminine principle."

Because 3HO/Sikh Dharma is a small part of this extensive undertaking, an understanding of women's lives in 3HO, and a fair assessment of the organization, cannot be based simply upon Western perspectives. Sikh and Hindu traditions offer distinctive resources to women, and women raised in these religions and within the Indian cultural matrix encounter unique opportunities, pleasures, challenges, and hardships.

So do women who voluntarily embrace these religions. They mature in distinctive cognitive worlds. Crucial terms such as self, identity, religion, family, motherhood, individualism, service, and feminism take on special implications within these worlds.

Indian women's critiques of Western-style feminism are illustrative, and obviously relevant, to a comprehensive understanding of women's lives in the Eastern-oriented new religions. I would like to look briefly at some of these and apply them to the 3HO/Sikh Dharma experience.

Respect for the feminine principle has a long history in Hinduism. There patriarchy presents different features than in the West and is not so likely to be perceived as a final explanation for women's troubles: "It must be remembered that in India patriarchy is only one from among the several hierarchies that oppress women. Some of the most oppressive of these are the hierarchies of age, of ordinal status, of relationship by marriage. . . . [I]n most families, the principal oppressor is the husband's mother, or his unmarried or widowed sisters, not the husband" (Chitnis 1988, 92).

Moreover, "the firm tone of western feminism . . . can strike a discordant note in the ethos of Indian life," because this ethos favors compromise over conflict and values "the capacity to live with contradictions and to balance conflicting alternatives" (1998 93). Indian women are likely to believe that it is desirable to subordinate one's ego for the good of family and community and therefore are likely to question the Western insistence upon autonomy and the priority of personal growth.

Viewed from this perspective, Bhajan's rejection of American feminism is not only a male strategy but may also be a point of view grounded in the Indian context, as is his assumption that patriarchy is not the crux of the problem that women confront. It is interesting that most 3HO women have accepted the premise that Bhajan is an ally in their struggles and so do not employ the type of criticism that would issue from an assumption that, as a man, his interests are different from, or opposed to, their own.

Young (1994b) provides thought-provoking sketches of some contemporary activists. One of these activists is Madhu Kishwar, who has been involved since its inception with *Manushi: A Journal About Women and Society*. Here, Young quotes Kishwar discussing a view of feminism that is shared by many Indian women: "While I stand committed to prowomen politics, I resist the label of feminism because of its over close association with the western women's movement. . . . The definitions, the terminology, the assumptions, even the issues, the forms of struggle and institutions are exported from west to east, and too often we are expected to be the echo of what are assumed to be more advanced women's movements in the west" (93). Kishwar goes on to say that an Indian women's movement, while it should not be slavishly indebted to the past, ought to build upon Indian traditions: "In order to move our society in the direction of greater justice and freedom we need to develop a creative relationship with the more humane and potentially liberating aspects of our cultural traditions" (ibid., 95).

This is a controversial position, and Kishwar has been accused of clinging to oppressive and outdated mores, but hers is a perspective shared by many women of Indian descent, and it is clearly one that has considerable potential. A women's movement built upon the foundations of tradition can have a broad appeal in India, it can mesh with the personality forms and styles of interaction that are favored there, and it can be adapted to local needs.

It can also be radical, as any reader of Vandana Shiva's critiques of Western-sponsored development knows. Shiva uses tradition as both shield and weapon, striding into ecological battles with the courage of Durga. "Ecological destruction and the marginalisation of women, we know now, have been the inevitable results of most development programmes," she asserts. She advocates a response based upon spiritual principles: "Indian women have been in the forefront of ecological struggles to conserve forests, land and water. They have challenged the western concept of nature as an object of exploitation and have protected her as Prakriti, the living force that supports life" (1988, xvii). Prakriti, the "primordial energy which is the substance of everything, pervading everything," is also, she notes, worshiped in other female forms as Aditi and as Adi Shakti, "the primordial power." Adi Shakti is, of course, a central concept in 3HO/Sikh Dharma, and one that some former members also draw upon for inspiration in their dedication to protecting the web of life. It is one name for what has come to be called the feminine principle.

A more academic interpretation of the feminine principle comes from Nikky-Guninder Kaur Singh, who has written a thoughtful interpretation of Sikhism titled *The Feminine Principle in the Sikh Vision of the Transcendent* (1993). The purpose of the work is to present—to both Sikh and non-Sikh audiences—a wealth of female-centered ideals, symbols, and imagery to be found in Sikh religious and literary traditions. "The Sikh tradition," she writes, "provides a striking instance in the history of religion of a faith that acknowledges the significance of the feminine component within human existence. . . . The feminine principle in Sikh literature is a great resource for uplifting women's psyche, but needs to be rediscovered" (14).

Underlying her analysis is her conviction that Nanak and the other Sikh gurus intended, as they each made their individual contributions to Sikhism, to include and reverence the feminine principle. Nanak, she believes, wished to "shatter" old icons and ways of thinking, including those that treated the masculine as the norm or ideal. She also argues that the poetic form of the Granth Sahib, and particularly of Nanak's syntax, creates "a theaological vision" in which "the dialectic between the finite and the Infinite is constantly maintained, giving equal ontological status to both men and women" (ibid., 40).

Her presentation focuses on several aspects of the Sikh heritage. First, she discusses the image of mother as the divine source and ground of being as presented in the Guru Granth Sahib. Next she considers the bride imagery which is so prevalent in Sikh religious literature. She also analyzes the compositions attributed to Guru Gobind Singh in which Durga ("the autonomous Hindu goddess") is the central character. She concludes with a look at the works of contemporary Sikh writer Bhai Vir Singh, who makes women the central characters of his novels and poetry.

Singh begins with the image of mother (*mata*) as "Infinite Matrix." She notes that in Nanak's writings the One, the Transcendent, is not treated as either masculine or feminine and quotes from the Granth Sahib: "It itself is man; It itself is woman" (1993, 52). She finds that the Sikh gurus describe the One in a multitude of feminine images or feminine nouns and that "the Sikh Scripture is not reticent in regard to birth imagery: female body, flesh, the natural female processes are fully affirmed" (56). She contends that, in the Sikh scriptures, nature and intellect, as well as mind and body, are not opposed, making it possible for the mother figure to represent both wisdom and nature.

When Singh looks closely at the bride imagery which Nanak used so freely, she, like other commentators, finds that the bride embodies the principle of love which is central to Nanak's message. But, in Singh's reading, the bride also represents Nanak's refusal to separate the spiritual sphere from the practical everyday world. The bride is depicted as a woman grounded in family and relationships, as one who "opens the way to the Transcendent by living fully and authentically in *this* world, maintaining her connections with her own self, her family and friends, and nature around" (ibid., 117).

Turning to Guru Gobind Singh and his efforts to regenerate Sikh society, the author looks at the stories of the goddess Durga that are attributed to Gobind Singh. Gobind Singh, she argues, employed the figure of Durga to show that religious persons "should be prepared to act in behalf of the moral choices they make. They should be ready to act not only for themselves but also for others where injustice and oppression are involved. They should be fearless" (ibid., 148). For Gobind Singh, she says, Durga is represented by the sword—that which destroys injustice, illusion, enemies and "opaqueness." Thus women are strongly associated with courage, action, praxis, and clarity. Singh admits that there is considerable controversy surrounding this element of Gobind Singh's writings, and, as we have seen, a number of commentators argue that he is not the author of these stories. Some Sikhs argue that Gobind Singh would not have made Durga a central figure in his work because this would not be in keeping with the Sikh rejection of polytheism, but Singh argues that this is too literal an approach to the stories, which represent not worship of Durga but a powerful and dramatic use of myth to make a point.

Singh concludes by discussing four works by Bhai Vir Singh, a Sikh renaissance writer. In all of his writings Bhai Vir Singh employed women characters to epitomize Sikh ideals. Singh uses his writings to make several points. One is that Sikhism has a strong existential component. The focus of one poem, for example, is upon individual experience, "the journey inward—a probing of the layers of the self—the main action, and reaching into the innermost core of the self its finale" (1993, 172). This form of quest, narrated in the poem and embedded in Sikhism, Singh notes, is similar to the feminine quest forms suggested by authors such as Carol Christ.

Another point Singh makes is that Sikhism has models of courageous women. Thus, Bhai Vir Singh was also the author of a very popular novel featuring a heroine named Sundari, "the paradigm of Sikh ethics." Sundari is something of a modern-day personification of Durga, and somewhat similar to the Western figure, Joan of Arc. She joins her brother in his military exploits, asking, "[W]hy should I not be the first woman to fight courageously like my brother?" (ibid., 191). She proves herself a heroine, but one who is always committed to selfless service and to righting injustices. On her deathbed (she dies courageously in battle) she urges the men around her to respect women as the gurus did.

Bhai Vir Singh also created a character who exemplifies Sikh mysticism in Rani Raj Kaur, the protagonist in *Rana Surat Singh*. The story begins with her widowhood and intense longing for the lost beloved, who, as it happens, was the king of a realm. Her longing is so intense that she has no time or interest for the duties she should assume as the surviving queen. As the story unfolds, it becomes clear that she longs not just for her dead husband but for the ultimate Divine. In her grief, she slips from longing into a swoon, and in an altered state of consciousness, experiences worlds of great beauty. She travels through the five stages depicted in the Sikh morning prayer. These are the states of approach to mystic union with the divine: duty, knowledge, beauty, grace, and truth. After she experiences the ultimate state of union, she returns to her duties, thus enacting the central Sikh axiom that one must live one's religion. Praxis is every bit as important as enlightenment. Singh notes that in Sikhism, everyday relationships "are the raison d'être of the human condition," and "Rani Raj Kaur finds her authentic self not in isolation but in relations" (1993, 24).

Nikky-Guninder Kaur Singh argues that in this literary tradition one can find all of the components that feminists might seek in a religion: meaningful feminine imagery, appreciation for the senses, rejection of hierarchies and dualist modes of thinking, a practical this-worldly ethics which asserts the primacy of human relationships and the necessity for justice based not just on abstract principles but upon active caring, and models of women who are strong, autonomous, and courageous, figures who can experience the divine directly and act upon their illumination.

But she laments that Sikh scholars ignore or downplay the feminine principle so deeply embedded in the Granth, and that "the role of women is narrowly circumscribed. It is tragic to observe how the literature of this culture includes them so fully and the society excludes them so despairingly" (1993, 254). Her work reaffirms a finding by Catherine Wessinger that "the various world religions demonstrate that religions in patriarchal contexts remain patriarchal, even when they conceptualize the sacred in terms of goddesses and impersonal principles" (1993a, 11).

Nonetheless, Singh looks to the future and claims that "the voice of western feminists is in perfect harmony with the literature of Sikhism, and it only remains to turn our mutually validating experiences into an envigorating dialogue. This dialogue calls for a vigorous interaction amongst Sikh women and other Asian women and feminists in the West" (1993, 257). Working as she is in a Western academic setting, Singh attempts to bridge American and Indian cultures and proposes her interpretation of Sikhism as a vehicle for a rapprochement between women of East and West.

I have covered Singh's work in such detail for a number of reasons. First, she provides a summary, and thorough discussion, of many of the elements in Sikhism that can make it particularly appealing to women. Second, her interpretations throw some light on teachings I have encountered in 3HO/Sikh Dharma, and I would like to briefly review these. Third, I would like to look at some of the themes she enunciates as they are rendered by women who are currently, or were at one time, associated with 3HO. I would also like to branch out further and simply look at how these women envision and enact the feminine principle.

For example, Singh's discussion of bridal imagery slightly altered my view of women's garb in 3HO. While I always understood the symbolic meaning that the white clothing holds for 3HO members, and recognized the importance of *bana* as a tool for establishing a collective identity, I had been bothered by scenes at the camp when women sat dressed like brides listening to Bhajan. While this still makes me uncomfortable, I can now also more readily see it as an extension of this central Sikh metaphor.

In a similar vein, I was originally surprised by 3HO members' acceptance of the sword as a symbol. It seemed thoroughly opposed to the antiwar sentiments of the counterculture and to traditional women's values. When I asked 3HO women about this, they talked about the sword as a symbol of their dedication to justice and to defending the oppressed, but while that seemed very abstract, the sword seemed quite real, aggressive, and warlike. The associations Singh makes with Durga, and with women as heroines, renders the symbol more palatable. My understanding of grace has been expanded as well. Singh reminded me that it is not only a 3HO ideal for women but also a stage encountered by the soul as it journeys toward enlightenment.

In the course of my research I have often been struck by Bhajan's insistence that his students persevere in human relationships, no matter how difficult these might prove. Informants have told me of times when a personal relationship left them angry, resentful, or hurt and Bhajan warned them not to give into the emotion, not to sever human ties. Many of these individuals are grateful that they took this advice, however unappealing it seemed at the time. Singh places this teaching in a broader context and makes the primacy of relationships in Sikhism clear. It is in relationship that one enacts the religion. Again, this is a theme with which I was familiar, but her rendering of it, her explicitly feminist understanding, impressed upon me the significance that this ethic holds for the women of 3HO.

Singh also reconfirmed my conviction that Sikh wholism has been a central factor in the religion's appeal to 3HO members. She was quoted earlier on this topic, but I would add now that she sees much of the wholistic imagery as feminine. For example, she finds that in Bhai Vir Singh's works, Sundari, the warrior, "transcends contemporary sociopolitical reality. Her society was divided into different religious and racial factions," but Sundari refused to use this to her advantage and would not whip up strife (1993, 198).

Beyond these general assertions, what stood out most for me in Singh's work was that the ethical principles she finds present in Sikhism are not only steeped in the feminine principle, but appear to be particularly well suited to a group of people holding convictions nurtured in the counterculture. As we have said, she finds that, in Sikh thought, everyday relationships "are the raison d'être of the human condition, and they only exist because we are ultimately related to the Ultimate One" (ibid., 240). For people seeking a communal, group-oriented way of life this was an appropriate underlying theology—just as it is a central principle in the thinking of many contemporary women theologians. Singh's sense of Sikhism as an existential religion that requires a "journey inward" to the core of the self, a religion that encourages a probing of the layers of consciousness, is in tune with the motivations and concerns that 3HO members brought from the counterculture. The exploration of consciousness—through drugs and other modalities—was a central theme of the counterculture.

In her survey of women theologians working within several different religious traditions, Bednarowksi (1993) finds some consistent themes:

> There is apparent a growing preference for Goddess(es) rather than God; an emphasis on divine immanence rather than transcendence; affirmation of the body in addition to spirit as the source of both spiritual and earthly wisdom; descent as the prototypical spiritual journey rather than ascent; community and interconnectedness over—or at least in addition to—individualism; relationship as an organizational principle rather than hierarchy; self-knowledge or transformation as the worthy goal rather than perfection; sin as self-denigration rather than pride. (229)

Most of these themes are clearly present in Singh's reading of Sikhism. The presence, or potential presence, of these themes in Sikhism is important, both as incentive for women to affiliate and remain with 3HO/Sikh Dharma, and as ideals to pursue if women separate from the organization.

Former Members and the Feminine Principle

We can see these themes in the lives of several women who are no longer affiliated with Sikh Dharma. I should state at the outset that these women are not representative of all former members. They are particularly concerned with finding a spiritual approach to life which can replace the identity and the meanings that they found in 3HO/Sikh Dharma. Further, they are dedicated to understanding and living by the feminine principle, as they understand it.

Mother/Goddess

Not too long ago, I visited a Sikh woman who had been kind enough to loan me copies of women's camp transcripts. She lives in a quiet wooded area and is a close neighbor of a former member whom I know quite well. This particular day, as I was leaving the Sikh woman's house and walking toward my car, I happened to look up and see two ex-Sikh women walking through the woods. They waved me in their direction and announced that they were in the process of "dedicating the property to the goddess," and they asked if I would like to participate. I already felt rather like I was playing hooky since I had squeezed in time on a work day to drive out here, and their invitation added to my sense of freedom from routine. I gladly joined them, walking around the perimeter of the lot and marking it, with "song, incense and intention," in the name of the Goddess. It turned out that Rahima had recently "felt guided" to dedicate the property to the Goddess and had plans to make it into a place of refuge, therapy, celebration, and renewal where there would be a variety of events such as yoga classes, healing lodges, solstice celebrations, and rites of passage.

Some time later I sat down with Rahima and asked her to elaborate on the genesis of her plans and on her understanding of the Goddess or feminine principle. By then she had produced a flyer about the property which describes it as "a private home which selectively opens its doors to the public through the introduction of what we call 'devotional circling.' . . . [It] is lovingly dedicated to the service of the Divine Mother and supports the 'feminine' principles of inclusiveness and heartfelt nurturing."

I realized in the course of our conversation that Rahima had been reinterpreting her biography, creatively mining it for inspiration and new directions. She had also found in the Goddess a spiritual teacher to replace Bhajan, and she had found a way to give the feminine principle the central place in her story.

Rahima has studied, borrowed from, and experimented with many religious traditions—her approach is definitely eclectic. Some time after she exited 3HO she began to study the works of Lex Hixon, a scholar and a spiritual teacher she had known when she was young. Hixon's knowledge extended to Sufism, Zen Buddhism, Eastern Orthodox Christianity, and Hasidism. She first met Hixon when she was in college. Now she sees that meeting as her first solid contact with the spiritual life: "[T]he smell of incense, the candles, the holy books, the whole environment was just like, 'ah, this I feel at home in.' And he shared with me that there was such a thing as a spiritual path, that there was such a thing as enlightenment, that I wasn't crazy, that I just had a spiritual yearning. I felt affirmed, understood, acknowledged, and appreciated."

Much later, when she and her husband and friends found themselves "on the outs with the 3HO family" and she seriously studied Hixon's work, she found that "Lex's work was about bringing forth the feminine aspect of all religions. . . . [M]y understanding of the Goddess really stems from his work." His work assured her that "God can be approached as mother," and "because I'm a mother, and I have very strong feelings of wanting to both be mothered and be a mother it made sense to me." Hixon's work also affirmed all forms of experience, and "that included sacralizing pain, tears, confusion." He did not deny the value of physicality or sexuality.

She began to develop a form of yoga that (with intentional whimsy) she calls MaPa yoga. It has roots in Bhajan's version of Tantric yoga in that "the MaPa yoga is partly the balancing of the male and female facets of self." But she points out that it is more expressive than many of the 3HO forms of worship as it includes such activities as spontaneous dancing. It also allows for the expression of frustration and pain as well as joy, and it celebrates connection with nature, a theme not central in 3HO/Sikh Dharma. Her yoga is also based on the concept of oneness that can be found in Sikhism, but with a greater emphasis on the immanence of the feminine divine than she found in 3HO. Also, like Sikhism, her approach honors the *sangat*.

Rahima is also involved with a group that sponsors "Dances of Universal Peace." She tells me that the "work with the Dances of Universal Peace is to be able to take a sense of the sacred and to look at another person and say, 'yes, we are one.'" Again, the theme is oneness in divinity, which is metaphorically and physically expressed when the dancers form a circle and say to one another, in different ways, "I see the Beloved in you" and "We're all part of the great mystery." By the end, "we're all standing in a circle, shoulder to shoulder, arms over arms, swaying, feeling loved and loving, knowing that we're the Beloved."

This circle metaphor has been imported to rituals that she designs: "Part of what is really important is the power of circling, that there's no teacher, that there's no hierarchy . . . in all traditions they talk about when people come together in the spirit of love or truth that the Holy Spirit is there." Rahima contrasts the circle with its eye-to-eye contact, equality, and interweaving movements to the layout of the *gurdwara* where all participants face the Guru Granth Sahib, men on one side, women on the other, "either with their eyes closed or looking toward the guru."

Rahima, like Vandana Shiva, ties her feelings about the earth to her understanding of the feminine principle. She has long been interested in peace and environmental issues, and she adds these to Hixon's teachings. To the extent that her teaching diverges from his, it is in her tendency to synthesize. He suggested "drinking from one stream at a time," but she finds that, in her personal practice, she cannot keep different paths separate. She is always defining and redefining her direction and intent, but in general she aims to

> connect with the Divine and say, "Thank you for this opportunity, and may I serve in the liberation of all human beings. May I exemplify peace, love, and harmony within, and share it with all who wish it, and may I die having done all that I could do . . . or all that I'm supposed to do, in service of the evolution of humankind." . . . We're all involved in something that's hard to talk about. . . . [I]t's something that's saying, "Stop doing in the normal way of doing; be and let that be your doing." It's like a song that a Sufi sister sings, "Let the beauty we love be what we do." And where it goes, only Goddess knows.

She shares Vandana Shiva's horror at "the desecration of the earth." Her activism, however, lies more in discovering a new way of being and in setting aside a place for others who can share her vision.

Some time before I joined the two women in our goddess-inspired circuit, I had been talking to Rahima about her spiritual concerns. She had mentioned one of Hixon's books then, although she told me nothing about his expanding role in her life. The book was *Mother of the Universe: Visions of the Goddess and Tantric Hymns of Enlightenment* (Hixon 1994). It is an expressive, almost mystical, look at the goddess tradition as encountered through the poetry of the Hindu devotee Ramprasad. Hixon writes that, through Ramprasad's works, he learned to "enter Mother's presence, commune with the entire spectrum of her manifestation, and gradually merge with her." He finds in Ramprasad's poetry a goddess of many faces. She is "the uncompromising Warrior of Truth . . . gradually removing all limits. Her teaching is that of indivisible oneness" (2). Her sword is an important symbol of "release from the mundane categories of egocentric experience." She is "the limitless one who wears limitation as a garland of heads, freshly severed by her sword of nondual wisdom" (22). Realization of her love comes through "enlightened play" and free acceptance of life's forms and dramas. It means giving up resistance to life's unexpected or unwelcome events and instead learning to be "free and happy under every condition" (Hixon quoting Ramprasad, 15). The author concludes that Ramprasad's vision of the Goddess, an image of both power and nurture, offers twentieth-century women an alternative to conventional images of womanhood: "It is comforting and important to remember that this beautiful, uncontainable, sword-wielding goddess, who destroys what needs to be destroyed, simultaneously nurtures what is real in us" (216). Hixon finds that she fosters acceptance, but not in a passive or fatalistic form; it is an active, playful, joyous movement in concert with the rhythms of life (see also McLean 1998). This image of Mother/Kali is the one to which Rahima and her friend dedicated the property. Rahima said that she made a decision (guided, she felt, by Hixon's spirit) to let the Goddess determine the ultimate use of the land.

In spite of its whimsy and idiosyncratic qualities, some of Rahima's work and thinking remind me of the ideas of Vicki Noble, a woman who is active in the world of feminist spirituality. Noble writes:

> The work of seizing back what has been taken from within us by centuries of female repression and early, often brutal childhood conditioning is a long, laborious process, requiring faith and vigilance and the willingness to learn by trial and error. . . . It is not a question of returning to the past but one of reawakening the instinctual senses and the empowerment needed to act on what our bodies know to be true. . . . For a woman actually to repossess herself and to center there is a monumental task, taking years of difficult, painstaking work. This is the work I am calling female shamanism, a gradual mastery of oneself, and a healing or recovery from the chronic dis-ease of our time. Once a woman has done the work of re-membering herself, she is much more able to change the world effectively. (1991, 5)

In Noble's sense, Rahima is a shaman, turning more and more to intuition, to the body and its cycles, and to nature for her sources of inspiration. She would probably agree with Noble, who sees the individual body as an extension of nature: "Since our bodies are literally cells in the larger body of the earth, we feel and respond to the experiences she registers in her body" (1991, 51). Rahima feels every insult to the earth personally. She is ready to do whatever is required to express her sense of the life-force, to "heal the planet," and to live honestly and from her center.

If Rahima has explored a variety of traditions and teachers in her search for meaning since her parting with 3HO, Prabhupati has explored several identities. It has been a painful, as well as creative and imaginative, search. Not too many years ago, she regularly spoke on a radio program on the West Coast and sometimes taught college in the field of religious studies. She was very busy and she felt successful. Looking back, she calls it "show-boating," but she was happy and engaged in what she was doing at the time. Then she began to experience anxiety attacks and confusing flashbacks—symptoms, she now believes, of post-traumatic stress syndrome attached to early abuse. And, as if this weren't enough, she confronted the leadership in 3HO and withdrew from the organization, encountering all the stresses and loss of identity associated with this process. Next, her family moved to the Southwest, where her husband had taken a new job, and she found herself separated from friends and routines. She became the coordinating figure in the network of ex-3HO members. At that time she was fascinated by the possibility of minding reality into being and posited that "if you get enough people aligned in their intentions (prayers) then "reality" shifts. I don't know if this is true or not, but I know that my life has become an experiment in this laboratory."

At this time she and her husband decided to divorce. Prabhupati had to find a new house and job and adapt to life without her husband and older children. She went through a very difficult period, and, chastened, she settled down for awhile to what she called "my humble period," as an "anonymous urban dweller." That continued until she decided to join Rahima and to help plan and organize events, teach yoga, and act as a counselor. She was happy for some time, but she moved on from there into another unsettled, but productive, period. In response to my question, here is part of her description of who she is today: "I am a dreamer, a pray-er and a novelist. I am a feminist writer who is just now, at age forty-four, beginning to make her living at it. I am lead singer in a band. . . . I am a mystical poet. I am a novelist and I know it. So I focus on making fiction really dramatic and I keep praying that the facts of my life get a whole lot more peaceful."

A backward glance tells her "[i]t is simply that I didn't fit, being me, into my own life for twenty-five years. I was trying to please my brilliant and wealthy husband, . . . trying to please my distant spiritual teacher and all the Sikhs around me, and my students too, and my friends too. . . . But I had a great time, for all that, and I would do it all again and I would probably choose to make all the same mistakes, because I can see now . . . that the suppressed novelist in me was always headed for the most amazing story." She recently remarried, "playing the bride in a couple of wonderful and powerful High Ritual performances" of her own designing.

She has dropped and taken on identities at a dizzying pace. Each of the upheavals in her life has led to self-examination and to encounters with what she would probably call the shadow aspects of her personality. Such encounters have alternated with periods dedicated to creating realities and, as she would put it, to "shifting" them.

Vicki Noble, to quote her one more time, describes a struggle that is remarkably similar to Prabhupati's:

> Our willingness to face the dark is the key to our own development. What we're afraid of is actually the treasure at the center of our being, the female source energy from which we have so long been severed. The dragon that always gets killed by the hero, the monster that lives under the ocean, the ogress that hides in the deepest recesses of the female psyche is the liberator and savior for the Shakti woman. . . . There is, naturally, suffering in these descents, which take us down into the unconscious psyche. (1991, 31)

Prabhupati's journey has taken her closer to that source and its energy.

A.'s new spiritual perspective was described in the last chapter. She is now studying and teaching Vipassana meditation while continuing her work as therapist and mother. I would like to look at the way she now views the feminine principle.

A number of contemporary commentators fault Buddhism for its historical distrust of women, its paucity of women teachers, for its emphasis upon archetypically masculine virtues (such as wisdom, intellect, and control) over the traditionally feminine attributes (such as open-heartedness, feeling, and sensuality), and its otherworldly preoccupations. Western women in all of the Buddhist traditions are now redefining their roles and altering rituals and rules (Friedman 1987, Paul 1979).

A. is one of the women who is shaping American Buddhism to better fit current Western understandings of gender. She finds that Vipassana is an appropriate vehicle. Vipassana, with its Theravada roots, is a relatively recent arrival on the American scene. The first teachers to transplant this tradition, Jack Kornfield and Joseph Goldstein, established the Insight Meditation Center in Barre, Massachusetts, in 1976. Both had studied Theravada in Southeast Asia (Ellwood 1987, 40).

A. has been much influenced by Kornfield. Kornfield's approach is evident in the title of one of his books, *A Path with Heart* (1993). His emphasis is on compassion and loving-kindness—directed toward both self and others. He encourages his students to sit quietly and face whatever pain or rage is locked inside and to recognize that healing occurs as these feelings are released. Lives, he maintains, change with the slow but inevitable processes of catharsis and self-acceptance. The goal is a full life, lived from the heart: "We can actually converse with our heart as if it were a good friend. In modern life we have become so busy with our daily affairs and thoughts that we have forgotten this essential art of taking time to converse with our heart. . . . Whatever we choose, the creations of our life must be grounded in our hearts" (12, 17).

These are age-old teachings of Buddhism, but they often become secondary in the teachings of masters who urge students to transcend the self and the world. A. speaks of an "imbalance" in the way that Buddhism has been presented over the years, and in this she echoes other female teachers. For example, Friedman (1987) cites another Vipassana teacher, Christina Feldman, who is similarly critical of a "lack of balance in the way Buddhism is usually presented" (28). Summarizing many of the objections that Western women have raised, Feldman notes, "In traditional teachings the world is generally seen as something which you get out of as quickly as possible. There is a whole value system in which things like relationship, connection with nature, and social activism are presented as being inferior to a fully dedicated spiritual life. And inwardly, things such as your body, your feelings, your emotions are things to get over, to be transcended. Basically one is to aspire towards seeing them as empty" (1987, 28).

Friedman quotes from a teacher-training workshop that Kornfield gave in 1986: "Some of the important changes in Buddhism in our time will be the positive result of reintroducing the feminine. Specifically I mean a return to the heart, the validation of feelings and emotion, receptivity, and connection to the earth. Til [*sic*] now, Buddhism has been preserved in a fundamentally masculine context, with stress on knowing rather than on heart and feeling. And it's gotten out of balance" (Friedman 1987, 32).

It is Kornfield's consistent emphasis upon the feelings, the heart, and the embodied nature of our experience that was particularly appealing to A. She weds these attributes of Vipassana to her interest in the concept of a feminine principle. She put some of her thoughts together in a talk she gave to her students, and I summarize this and quote from it in order to portray the nature of her thinking.

She begins with the assertion that the feminine archetype, representing "compassion, holding, and nurturing," has been historically neglected in favor of the more intellectual qualities of wisdom and understanding. The latter, she agrees, are essential, but they must be grounded in everyday life and in a caring attitude. The feminine is "the lover archetype, that which deeply appreciates beauty and life and feels connection, feels aliveness." Because the feminine has been neglected we carry an unhealthy distrust of emotionality, a fear of chaos and of losing control. We are faced with the necessity of awakening to the feminine side, but this is not an easy thing to do because there is a shadow side to the feminine. There are several aspects to this shadow. There is shame attached to the feminine self because it has so long been undervalued. There are our inappropriate (from a Buddhist point of view) responses to feelings of pleasure and to our awareness of the beauty of life: we seek to grasp and hold these things, and in the process we just grow small and fearful. And there are our fears of rejection and pain, and the many repressed feelings that keep us "contracted" and fearful.

"How," she asks," do we develop a wise relationship with the feminine?" The first step may be to admit our shame, to own our imperfections and mistakes, for liberation occurs, says A., quoting a Zen master, "when we are without anxiety about our imperfections." Then there are "skillful means" that one may employ in order to attain the goal, and many of these fall within the framework of the five spiritual faculties enumerated by the Buddha: faith, effort, mindfulness, concentration, and wisdom. Students of Buddhism will certainly recognize these qualities. What is distinctive in A.'s approach is that she views them as skillful means of opening to the feminine, and her interpretation of each always stresses acceptance, connection, and love of life in all its forms. Her belief is that, as the end result of developing the five qualities, "we can let go and live in the mystery. We can let go and live fully in our lives." She is convinced that with the transplantation of Buddhism into the West there is "a very beautiful awakening of the feminine side, a recognition of the importance of relatedness, of our connection with each other and this earth and the universe, and it's in that sense of relatedness and a sense of open-heartedness that we really wake up fully."

Growing in the Dharma

Women who have remained "in the Dharma" do not tend to talk about the Goddess, but they too talk about empowerment and touch on many of the themes that engross the women who have left. A number are experiencing sufficient prosperity to be able to pursue careers of choice rather than necessity. Several of the women whom I have interviewed are now embarking upon new careers, are taking college courses in order to obtain credentials and skills, or are taking on new responsibilities. One of the women I interviewed in 1984 has just completed training and is working as a chaplain in medical settings. Another has completed a counseling degree and has established a private practice. A young woman who grew up in 3HO is a marketing director for Sikh Dharma businesses. Another, who has always painted, has been able to pursue a bachelor of fine arts degree and is beginning to find the imagery and the style that allow her to express her spiritual and personal view of the world. Another woman in the ashram, not someone I interviewed, has just published a book. These women appear to be finding ways to combine community commitments, faith, and self-expression. They seem to be arriving at a reasonably successful balance between the personal life and the life of the *sangat*, and between service and self-fulfillment. Often they use Bhajan's teachings on women when faced with decisions, difficulties, and dilemmas, choosing those ideas that best fit their circumstances. Choosing different symbolic material at different stages of their lives, they have selectively employed 3HO and Sikh metaphors or concepts. I would like to look now at some of their interpretations and reinterpretations of their years in 3HO/Sikh Dharma, and at their current understandings of what it means to be a woman. To do so I will briefly profile several women.

"Coming into My Grace"

A. and her husband (then a friend) were consciously seeking a spiritual community when they encountered 3HO in the early 1970s. They were hippies who had abandoned drugs and were seeking a spiritual path. When they attended their first *sadhana* they had already visited several communities, none of which seemed right for one reason or another. A.'s brother-in-law was briefly in 3HO, and she and her husband visited him in Santa Fe. This led to contact with the organization. They found the people friendly and welcoming and soon became affiliated with 3HO, although they lived at a distance from other members for quite some time on their ashram farm in West Virginia. Now, twenty years later, she and her husband are still with the group and, at my request, she is looking back. I ask why she has stayed all of this time:

> We laugh about how we can't believe some of us are
> still around after our early days and some of the fanatics
> we had to put up with, or crazy rules at some ashrams.

. . . There is a part of me that knows that this is my destiny. I experimented a lot when I was younger. I got to see a lot of different ways to live, and what it came down to was, "What's the most important thing to me in life?" And the most important thing to me in life is spirituality. The soul is the only thing that lasts through everything. The body can change: you can still chant and meditate. You can be in all kinds of difficult situations, but you can still think about God and feel that connection and build that connection. My ultimate goal would be that I don't ever forget God, ever. . . . I want to have that awareness. I know this [Sikh Dharma] can give it to me. I also don't feel like shopping around. I've been doing this for twenty three years, and I've been very blessed, and this is my path. . . . And I think it's just God's grace and the guidance of Yogi Bhajan that I'm still here.

The organization's understandings of gender have been of considerable importance in her life. In the early years, she was struck by the 3HO approach to marriage. "It was just so interesting to be in an environment where people talked about marriage in a positive way," she says. Here were people of her age and background praising an institution that people she knew held in low esteem. She came to Washington for a course taught by Bibji (Bhajan's wife) on women as the grace of God: "It gave me confidence again that it's good to be a woman." She began to experience a sense of security and a new level of self-esteem.

A. has raised two children since that time. She spent some time working with her husband and has taught Gurmukhi and Sikh Dharma studies. When she could do so she "finally decided I'm just going to go for the fine arts because that's really what I'm interested in. So I've been fortunate enough that I can pursue that and teach yoga."

She maintains a regular *sadhana*, sometimes attending the group devotions, sometimes holding a family *sadhana* at home. Lately she, and others in the ashram, have been practicing a new form of meditation, a healing technique which has led to a new kind of awareness: "I used to think the lower centers [*chakras*] were not as good as the higher centers. And then I started to realize that it's the yoga of awareness. . . . All the *chakras* need to be activated and balanced. You become more and more aware of everything. . . . God is everything. . . . [B]ecoming more aware of everything you're becoming more aware of God."

Like so many spiritual women today, A. is discovering a spirituality that is more accepting of the whole person, both intellect and senses. It is a spirituality that supports her self-esteem: "Something that has developed over the years for me is to come into my own grace, which is something that I sort of denied myself for a long time. That's a personal thing, but I've found it's more universal than I thought. Myself and other women I've talked to don't feel a lot of self-esteem. But through meditation, and through women's camp, and also through my own experience, through life, I've realized my own grace and dignity and manifest that more and more."

This grace is expressed in a number of ways. One manifestation has to do with aesthetics and style:

> I think it's a self-elegance, doing things the way you really want to, rather than just accepting something less. ... I notice I wear nicer clothes than I used to. ... That's an outward manifestation of something inside. . . . I think it's bringing more of what you really want to see in life, and the beauty you'd like to live in, into your life, rather than just accepting less because you don't think you deserve it. I think it's living up to what you know you deserve. And there's a certain elegance that everyone can have in their life.

As an artist she may be particularly concerned with bringing beauty into daily life, but, as we have seen, this is a significant aspect of Sikh Dharma and perhaps a more important part of contemporary women's spirituality than is generally recognized.

What she calls elegance may also contribute to the capacity for "projection" that Bhajan talks about: "Yogi Bhajan often speaks about when you come into a room your presence should work, just the fact you're there should help people. You shouldn't have to say a word, eventually." She says that she has experienced this increasingly, and that other 3HO members have as well.

Asked about the nature of womanhood, A. has a great deal to say, some of which I have heard from many other women in 3HO/Sikh Dharma: men and women "are like two different species," women are more intelligent and sensitive, and we should accept the differences rather than imitating men or competing with them. But she goes further:

> The way women have gotten into trouble through history is by being too compassionate. They let their compassion take over their sense of self-preservation and

protection. That's why women so many times do get exploited. . . . They give beyond what they should in order to keep their own dignity and grace. . . . [A] woman has to put her foot down . . . and not expect a man to do it for her, to say, "Oh honey, I noticed you're really tired, maybe you should meditate. . . . It's really up to the woman to say, "This has to be. I need to go to women's camp for at least a week this summer, or "I need to take a walk. I need to have some time to meditate." . . . It can be dangerous to think, "Well, I should just keep helping here or keep working there," and just keep giving, giving, giving. Too much giving leads to exploitation and even illness.

I asked her, as I asked several of the women I interviewed, if she has participated in any kind of political action for women. She said that, beyond some marches, she has not, but "I always felt very strongly about women's rights. . . . When I was growing up I was a tomboy because boys always seemed to have more power, so I wanted to be like them. They got all the goodies." But she does not expect much progress from external sources. "The only way I can see to really change things is for women to become more aware of who they are so that they will change," she says. That, for her, implies a kind of spiritual evolution: "The way for everything to get better is for people to become more spiritually aware and spiritually active. When you become more aware through meditation and yoga you start to see what's going on in your life and how to change it. It has to start from that base rather than from outside somewhere."

Asked about her own future, and that of other women in the *sangat*, she replied,

I see more outreach . . . just trying to get the teachings out so more people can be happier. . . . It's more gradual than I ever thought it would be, but it's probably much more organic that way. . . . More and more women have been getting involved in business because as children have grown older they don't need their mother so much. . . . And women are very good in business. It's because of the motherly attitude. They know how to take care of things, and how to look after the details, and they're not afraid to work. . . . There are a lot more women all through 3HO who are working in businesses or professions. And among the younger generation that's been an emphasis because we've seen through our lives you just don't have very many families where the husband's the only one who needs to work. . . . [A]nd also, because of divorces and things like that, it's a very good thing for a woman to have something in which she can earn a living, a good profession or something.

I asked her at one point, "If you were going to write about women in 3HO/Sikh Dharma, where would you focus?" She answered, "I think I'd focus on the whole thing of women realizing who we are, recognizing the God within, and manifesting that more and more. And the infinite potential, the power, the ability to uplift others and yourself, the infinite possibilities for women, and the healing power that women have naturally, and can develop. The bond of sisterhood is growing stronger and expanding to include all women as we realize more in actuality that all people are part of one world family."

Valuing the Self

When I interviewed her, B. was working toward a degree in counseling. Like A., she points out that it is very important for women to take time for themselves: "I always see a big conflict between women doing for themselves and doing for others. . . . [T]o encourage women to take time for themselves, that's really important too, as much as the doing for others." And she assumes that a woman who takes that time is likely to have spiritual feelings. "I do feel that there's an innate spirituality in women," she says, although a woman may need to uncover and recognize her spiritual yearnings. "Women need to take the time to work on it."

She also agrees with the old principles of the Grace of God movement: "women being important, women being equal to men, women being the inspiration . . . women being the center of the household." But she prefers not to overstress the differences between men and women when the similarities are so great. Thus she assumes that women may have a particularly well-developed or innate capacity for intuition, "but I think if any guy cared to he could probably develop his intuition." And some of a woman's skills in this area are probably not so much inherent in the female character as attributable to the experience of child rearing: "I mean having a baby you give up your whole life to caring for someone's needs. It's transforming, uncomfortably transforming I thought at the time. . . . [N]ow my husband never had that transformation."

When she is counseling women she encourages them to place a value on their opinions and their time:

> The teaching is that women are the creators of the universe. Women's role is very important. . . . [S]o I teach that to my family, and in counseling I use that too, because I do find that women suffer from lower self-esteem. I know that, probably—because they are women—they've suffered a lesser identity. And when I hear it, I work on that. It could be like a situation when a woman and her husband are talking and he has one idea and she has another, and she defers to his idea even if she doesn't like it. She doesn't feel even entitled to stay with her ideas, even if they're perfectly fine.

She will encourage the woman to "take herself more seriously." The end result, she hopes, will be enhanced self-esteem and a lessening of the "subtle anger" that may accompany continual deference and self-doubt.

For many 3HO women, issues of self-assertion appear throughout the course of a marriage as the wife attempts to both foster a spiritual union and nurture her own personal growth. These women may work particularly hard to create a peaceful atmosphere, to serve and encourage a husband, and to appear graceful and serene. They also take motherhood and homemaking very seriously and invest a considerable amount of time in these activities. If they are also attending *sadhana* and meditations regularly and working for pay, or doing a great deal of volunteer work for the ashram, finding time for themselves, and just getting sufficient rest, may require thought and planning. B. has no doubt that a woman owes herself sufficient time and consideration.

"All Paths Lead to God"

When I first met C. she was very active in ashram affairs. She was hardworking and devout, a manager. The initial interview took place in her office, where she was constantly interrupted by the telephone. In between calls, she recounted her pleasure in learning about Sikhism when it was first introduced in 3HO. She spoke about Sikh ideals: sainthood, striving for perfection, and the concept of the soldier-saint. She also talked about the trials and tests encountered on a spiritual path.

That first interview was rather awkward. I was intruding on a busy day, and I think she was impatient with my presence and my predictable, outsider kinds of questions. When I began another interview fourteen years later, I was pleased to find that we were both enjoying it. C. had more time to talk and was far more relaxed than she had been at the first interview, and I was probably much more understanding of her way of life.

She has recently turned from accounting toward the helping professions. She has commenced training in medical pastoral education. "I'm not sure exactly where it's taking me," she says, ". . . but I like it because it combines people skills with a spiritual kind of bent. "

Entering the program meant exposure to another world. Born to Jewish parents, a Sikh by choice, and of generally liberal political outlook, she has found herself working with Christians, many of them conservative: "I was very sheltered living in this community all these years. And now I've started coming out and meeting just regular mainstream kind of people who have completely opposite political views than me, and . . . religious views, . . . and I had to bridge that gap. I think I did a really good job of it."

She reminded herself that "all paths go to God," and that enabled her "to look at any other person and see the beauty of their spirituality and see God in them." In the course of her training she devised ecumenical services when it was her turn to lead Sunday devotions, and she found that she "was able to appreciate Jesus, and actually to pray to Jesus with patients."

She is still a very devoted Sikh. She is convinced that "my effectiveness in my work totally depends on my *sadhana*." *Gurdwara* is still a central part of her life. And, she declares, "Guru Ram Das is a really big thing in my life. The Golden Temple is very important to me. I feel like I'm constantly kind of dipping there for spiritual strength and nourishment."

She speaks much less about facing trials and tests and being a soldier-saint than she did in her previous interview. I mention this, and she says it is no wonder she talked about tests at that time: she was going through a very difficult period in her life. Since then she has settled into a different and happier life, but she still values the activism inherent in the warrior-saint image: "I still believe in it. . . . I actually wish I was more of a warrior-saint. But there have been times when I've needed to be, and I have been. . . . When I look at the Siri Singh Sahib I see that one way that the Khalsa contributes to this world is that we have guts. . . . It's hard to describe the quality, the feeling, that you get from a Sikh, but it's a much more active, kind of dynamic, way of being spiritual than a lot of other paths." She still values that dynamism, assertiveness, and creativity, but there is less of sense of struggle.

I ask her if specific teachings on women are currently important to her. At first, she speaks only generally: "You're always confronted with how you were raised and really understanding the power you have as a woman, and just learning how to use that power. Or else, learning how to not use it." I ask what using the power means for her:

> For me, it's realizing the fact that I'm different from my husband, like the fact that I might be emotional, or whatever, it can be a contribution instead of just something to be ashamed of. And my marriage has been very challenging. I feel like I've discovered a lot about my strength as a woman through it. . . . The way my husband thinks. . . . [I]t comes in handy, but we [women] have a much deeper way of seeing the world. I don't know. I'm really glad I'm a woman. Because I feel men really have a hard time being complete. . . . When my husband is focused he just doesn't see anything else. . . . I have an ability to see situations in a more overall sense. . . . Because he's very focused he's extremely powerful, but there's just something missing. And I suppose what's missing in me, because I'm the other way, is that focus, that ability to get things accomplished. He's better at that.

The assumption that women can think about and do many things at once while men must focus on a single task is incorporated in the 3HO gender system. She has used this particular teaching in her efforts to be more accepting of her own nature and not to be overwhelmed by his "focus." She has learned to value her own broader insights, her feelings, and ways of perceiving the world and to believe that these are as valid as any masculine approach to living.

In general, she has applied 3HO frames to new situations as she has encountered them. When she needed it, she used the image of the soldier-saint. Later, she selectively applied gender beliefs so as to maintain self-esteem and balance in her marriage. As she moves into the work world outside of 3HO she looks to the technology and the belief system for ideas and support. *Sadhana* provides the necessary centering, her belief that "all paths lead to God" allows her to appreciate another religion, and her assumption that women are by nature different from men has helped her to pace her movement into her chosen profession. And 3HO/Sikh Dharma has supplied the concepts and images she has needed in order to establish a satisfying life-style and a meaningful narrative over the course of her affiliation.

Returning to the Dharma

While I was in the process of writing this book, Simran reconnected with 3HO. Here I attempt to describe some of the ways in which she was composing, editing, and revising her story as she reencountered the organization and her past.

The feminine principle is central to Simran's current understanding of her biography. The feminism that was spreading at the time she first joined 3HO had little meaning for her then:

> I never got the feminine aspect until five or six years ago. . . . I didn't get into the women's movement. I couldn't understand it. . . . I was perfectly okay with a male teacher, a male authority figure—all of that was fine with me. . . . I followed my mother's tradition, which was just to give self away, just to be in nurturing, just to be in support, just to be in service to the masculine principle—to the husband, to the father, to the whatever.
>
> In the course of my separation from the Dharma— in the pain that I experienced, and the sense of betrayal and abandonment and abuse—I really became alienated from my former concept of God. I had had profound experiences in the Dharma, spiritual experiences, and had real kinesthetic experiences with that. And when I felt so utterly betrayed, [it led to] a real examination of 'what is God.' . . . Now that the source of my concept of God had chosen to cut me off I had to reexamine that concept. I saw that what I had done was I had given power outside myself to an external concept of God and Guru. . . . How did I connect with it? I had no clue, and that was true for about five years. It was like, "There's only self, there's only me."

She saw a counselor and took the time to look into interior spaces:

> I just really got in touch with the emotional, intuitive, feminine part of me. And saw how I had bought into a model that didn't value it. You know, bought into a system and culture, and my parental upbringing, that didn't ever value the feminine, didn't value a daughter, didn't value a female, didn't value the heart and compassion and the giving nature that is the feminine. And

> I was getting more of an understanding of what that
> was. . . . I saw the feminine. I saw the ways that I had
> been a "good daughter" of the fathers.

These insights led to a rethinking of her experience as a Sikh woman and appear to have guided Simran in an effort to design a way of living, and a form of spirituality, that honors the feminine and is in keeping with her emerging sense of the Goddess. She notes, as does Nikky-Guninder Kaur Singh, that "[t]he Sikh tradition puts the Adi Shakti, the primal feminine power, as what you bow to, what you acknowledge, first. And then you go on to all these other things, which are much more masculine. But it's the feminine first: 'I bow to that.' Now, in practice, it continues to look like the masculine stuff gets all the perks, gets all the acknowledgment, gets to the forefront."

Before she returned to 3HO she returned to some of the Sikh practices such as reading Japji or occasionally wearing a turban. She kept remembering the beauty of the observances, even felt Nanak's presence, and came to the conclusion that Sikhism was still a part of her, that "twenty-nine years of connection to this dharmic practice was not a mistake." Her life still felt incomplete, unresolved. There was this identity aching for expression and continuity. She had "a profound sense of connection to this particular community," and "dreams and visions guiding me to come." There seemed only one possible response: "If I could not get over this experience I would get in it." She would come back as her own person, on her own terms. She would work at "keeping centered, on my ability to keep my own counsel, my own strength, my own knowing," and she would come "with the intention to stay focused on what I'm grateful for, what I love." She would delight in the sound current, in *sadhana*, in the beauty of the music, in the concern with healthful living and good wholesome food. "It's rich, a rich fabric of feeling, with so many levels of sensual gratification—the smell and the taste of morning *prasad* dripping with ghee and honey . . . beautiful and brilliant when people are dressed up."

It would be even better if, in addition to reestablishing her own spiritual path, she could also influence the organization. She thought that she might be able to do this if she could act as a "gateway" and encourage greater openness to the outside world, and "if the community can receive me back and get out of judgment with me, they can do it with anybody." Perhaps her presence could truly matter. "I used to think I was a lightweight, kind of pink and sweet," she said. But now, "I think I'm heavy medicine."

There were some more practical reason for coming as well. Most of her efforts to generate personal income at this time were not particularly successful. She put this down to a lack of motivation; her heart was entangled in issues from the past. She began to contact people in 3HO who might support her return.

When we discussed some of this I reminded her that her original encounter with Yogi Bhajan many years previously occurred in similar circumstances. Then she had just gotten divorced; now her second marriage was over. Then she had been feeling alone, vulnerable, unprotected. Now she was again vulnerable and in need of stability. But this time, she said, she had years of experience behind her and was determined to change patterns of dependency.

She did return, and talking to Simran later in the year, I found she was again engaged in the organization. She was intent upon changing her angle of vision and, by extension, her world. "There is a point in consciousness," she said, "when you get that everything in your world is a reflection of you . . . . If things are reflecting to you judgmentally and harshly the highest medicine is found through transforming that, shifting it. . . . That in a nutshell is what I'm doing here. We all have our patterns we come into this life with. . . . [I]f we want a different outcome, the key to getting it is to do something different." And so, slowly, step by step, she was "moving across the old conditioned patterns, from parents, previous incarnations, and forcing those to submit to a new intention." She would make her world change its aspect and "look the way I want it . . . in a state of gratitude and blessing." She would "not be affected by words of praise and blame, not be determined by the outside world."

As for her first parting with 3HO, that now seemed "injurious." There were too many accusations, too much anger. "I wish all of us could have done it in a more graceful fashion," she said. The way it happened hurt all who were involved, and she now thought that it reinforced the organization's tendency to turn inward. She spoke about the 3HO approach to language. Since all speech "has a vibration," and an effect, "if my time and my energy is spent putting forth anything negative about anyone then I'm just reinforcing that reality." It is generally better to say only the "uplifting things," to not "speak disparagingly, to focus in on strengths not weaknesses." That was not how language was used when she left, and looking back on all the upheaval associated with her leaving, and at its effects, she concluded that she should have acted and spoken more thoughtfully. She tried to do so this time. Now Simran has returned to her son and her home on Maui and has recently adopted a Buddhist practice. We will encounter her again in the conclusion.

While their paths are different, these women have much in common. For each, spirituality lies at the center of identity. All are coming to value their womanhood and the feminine principle in new ways. They believe that their self-esteem and self-acceptance have been enhanced by their spiritual practices. They look back and see a self that was too ready to meet others' needs and expectations, to doubt its value, even to accept abuse. Often, others' identities loomed larger than their own. Now they are entering new worlds, learning to trust the self and to value intuitions. They are more accepting of their own emotions and rhythms. Although they wouldn't necessarily use her words, most of these women could echo Simran's sentiment—"now I think I'm strong medicine"—in some form. Bhajan says that women should alter and transform their environments, that their presence should be a "projection" of strength, serenity, and hope. These women, in their own ways, are fulfilling this image of womanhood, whether they are in 3HO or not. And they are all serious about making the world a better place, about finding ways to give of their gifts. They could all agree that growth requires us to turn inward and explore the self.

There are differences, of course. Rahima and Prabhupati are more eclectic and experimental in their approaches. They have sought out, and created, identities, structures, sacred spaces, and networks in their efforts to recreate the special sense of purpose and meaning that was lost when they left 3HO. The tone of these efforts has ranged from exuberance to desperation, from whimsy to earnestness, from joy to intense pain. They are more expressive and uninhibited than women still in 3HO, and they tend to be impatient with the idea of graceful womanhood. They are determined to avoid hierarchical organizations in the future and to follow no gurus. They, and Simran, are perhaps more ready to act on the premise that the world reflects our thoughts, that it is, in some respects, as Prabhupati would have it, a dream. They will stake all on making the dream a reality. They will treat "the Goddess" both as concept and reality, trying to live her into being, finding courage in the effort. The Buddhist woman is less dramatic and eclectic in her style but equally committed to realizing her visions and to honoring the feminine.

Those who have remained in the organization are also determined to live their dreams and act upon their beliefs. These dreams and beliefs are firmly embedded in Sikh Dharma and in 3HO beliefs and narratives. They accept more givens, more structure, but they too venture into new fields, find courage from the divine within, and are willing to base a life on the belief that there is indeed such an internal spark, and that, in honoring it, they, in concert with their fellow Sikhs, can alter the world. After years of *sadhana*, of life in a spiritual community, and of devotion to Sikh Dharma, they believe that they are reaping rewards and planting new seeds.

Scenes from a Workshop

After some talk and sharing of yogi tea, six women, myself included, settle ourselves in a circle on the floor. We attend regular workshops with a Sikh counselor. Tonight's topic is "polarities." Our leader begins by telling us that her clients often experience life in dualities and that this is a theme that she has been encountering frequently in her practice. She asks for examples from us—examples of oppositions that structure and strain our thinking—and they are readily forthcoming. One woman says that she tends to oppose duty/practicality to joy/spontaneity. I come up with a similar theme, opposing the exercise of will and self-discipline to relaxing, letting life happen, and generally "going with the flow." Another participant builds on this and says that she constantly fails to exert her will and capacity for decision making because she fears that she would then be responsible for the results of her decisions. The next speaker opposes periods of calm and tranquility to times spent smoldering with anger, and the last to offer an example speaks of an opposition between spirituality and practicality.

The workshop leader then asks us to come up with examples of situations in which each of the poles might be desirable. She reminds us that life is not really a matter of either/or, that any trait can prove valuable in the right circumstances, and that individuals can blend traits rather than choosing one or the other. After we do this and talk for awhile she leads us in an exercise in guided imagery, which is intended to help us synthesize seemingly opposed characteristics. We are to imagine three cities: one in which everybody has the trait that we are inclined to view as negative; one run solely on the polar alternative; and, finally, one that blends the best of both. We are to imagine what each city would look like, what the residents would be doing, what the architectural style would be, and so on.

At first I have trouble doing this, but then I see my place of rationality and self-discipline: a town of buff-colored low-lying adobe houses, carefully spaced, surrounded by brick walks and revealing an occasional touch of green. It is very orderly and attractive, and people are purposeful, energetic, and well dressed as they go about their business. Conversation is lively and enjoyable. But nobody understands what you mean if you talk about a feeling or an intuition, and there are no spontaneous acts. The other town is set on a river. Small houses blend with green hills and are barely visible as they merge into the landscape. Children are everywhere, running, shouting and playing. Adults wander about and talk. They also make paintings together, although they don't bother to frame or hang them. Things often go unfinished and get messy, but people don't seem to care, and they are happy and friendly. My third place is composed of scenes from each of the two previous towns and is divided into sectors with many bridges and passageways going from one section to the other; each sector is distinct from all others.

When we describe our imaginary cities someone points out that I haven't really unified any opposites in my third city; the polarities remain separate, although there is access from one to the other. This inspires the workshop leader to add an exercise. She tells us that it will help us to "release anchors." She chooses work and play as polarities. We are all to imagine our right hands filled with work associations, both positive and negative, and our left hands filled with similar play associations. Then she tells us to shake out each hand and raise both arms above our heads, palms to the ceiling. We are to keep shifting our attention from right hand to left, from a work trait to a play trait and back again. The idea is for the traits to begin to merge in our minds. After a few minutes we are told to bring our arms down and our palms together and think about the self being greater than any internal divisions.

Then we do a yoga set and follow that with a period of relaxation. As we lie prone and close our eyes, the leader taps a gong, at first softly, then louder, until I fancy that I can see waves of sound moving across the room, their amplitude rising and falling, the waves occasionally converging. Then she taps quietly again, softer and softer until the air ceases to vibrate. We sit up and recite a chant that is intended to reconcile and unite any cognitive polarities. Then we extend our arms outward, raising them and imagining an aura spreading from the palms and encircling the self. Next we are told to bring our arms down and sit quietly, breathing slowly and visualizing light encircling us. We are to become aware of the self as a source of wisdom and to experience it as greater than any of its parts. We are to think of this self as one piece of a beautiful universe.

I work at visualizing endless space and my place in it. Soon, I see a door opening into space, stars scattered in the dark and light pouring in, and myself as a glowing shape touched by the light as it enters. This is one of the nicest moments I have experienced in five years of workshops. I am convinced that the light pouring into this room carries a kind of benign power and that whatever is out there is good. I feel an enormous longing for it, but also peace because it is there. I am finally experiencing the unity and surrender that is the desired outcome of meditation. I have seldom felt complete trust and safety, but I do so now.

CHAPTER 9

Final Thoughts

> There is the odd and persistent fact that it is only after a faithful journey to a distant region, a foreign country, a strange land, that the meaning of the inner voice that is to guide our quest can be revealed to us. And together with this odd and persistent fact there goes another, namely, that the one who reveals to us the meaning of our cryptic inner message must be a stranger, of another creed and a foreign race.
>
> —Heinrich Robert Zimmer, 1946

In the epigraph above, Zimmer refers to an old and recurrent mythic convention: the adventure in search of wisdom, the quest for a guru who issues from an unfamiliar and "exotic" place. Over time, this myth may vary in its details as it is passed from one generation to the next and is carried to new settings, but the underlying structure remains much the same. Even in the United States, where there is a preference for things practical and contemporaneous, this myth retains its appeal. Its attraction has been particularly strong for participants in countercultural and religious movements. For those who were active in the counterculture of the 1960s and 1970s, the availability of low-cost travel made the quest a realistic possibility; heretofore inaccessible sites of pilgrimage could now appear on the itineraries of young middle-class seekers. A mythic convention soon became a youthful trend. Religious teachers and would-be gurus in the East soon perceived the opening of a new market, and many welcomed the influx of youth from the West while others brought their wares to the home countries of the seekers. Soon the young could choose to travel or to satisfy their mythic yearnings in their own back yards.

At the same time these migrations were occurring, the visual media were increasing their reach and influence; the information age was dawning. Increasingly, the public swam in a sea of mass-produced stories and images. Commercial symbols took over more physical and mental spaces. And the very meaning of space and distance was changing. People were not yet spending hours at personal computers or meeting on the Internet, but they were electronically, symbolically, and digitally linked. Life was increasingly about chemical transformations, flashes of energy, bits of information, and constant change. People found themselves in a world in which image and substance, subjective and objective experience, and possibility and probability were thrown into new and unexpected alignments.

Over the three decades in which 3HO/Sikh Dharma evolved and matured the globe grew smaller. The media spread their nets wider; new digital technologies became necessities. Corporations spanned nations; virtual organizations proliferated. Migrations and tourism blurred old boundaries. The exotic became ever more elusive. In the midst of so much change big dreams and big fears spread. If, in the 1950s and 1960s, many commentators feared technocracy and mass society, new, but similar, misgivings now emerged in the 1980s and 1990s. Denzin's picture of the world we have created is a good example of an academic version: "We confront the cultural logics and corporate machinery of late capitalism. . . . This faceless, irrational, bureaucratic conglomerate, which traverses local, state, and national boundaries with electronic ease, will destroy anything that threatens to impede its progress" (1997, 194).

He doubts that, under current circumstances, the old narratives and quest myths ring true. "It is," he remarks "a truism, as the post-Oedipal feminist theorists remind us . . . that there are only two basic plots in fiction . . . (and here he quotes Smith): 'one, somebody takes a trip; two, a stranger comes to town'" (ibid., 192). Now "you do not have to leave town. The world and its troubles come to you, so there is only one story: the story about constant displacements—how do I make sense of myself in this world that will not go away?" (ibid., 195).

Certainly the world and its troubles have come closer, but the quest, the trip out of town, and the special stranger arriving, continue to be compelling narratives. Even though he draws a grim picture, Denzin has a hopeful, even romantic, vision of the role of ethnography in this late capitalist world: "Ethnography is a moral, allegorical, and therapeutic project. . . . [T]he ethnographer's story is written as a prop, a pillar, that . . . will help men and women endure. . . . The ethnographer's tale is always allegorical, a symbolic tale. . . . It is a vehicle for readers to discover moral truths about themselves[,] . . . a utopian tale of self and social redemption" (1997, xiv, 284).

There are echoes here of Jeffcutt's (1993) description of the quest genre in organization studies (see the introduction to this book), and of an earlier work I read when I was contemplating my fieldwork: Maurice Stein's *Eclipse of Community* (1960). Stein analyzes a number of the major community studies that have been conducted in the United States. Following the historical trajectory of these studies he finds that they reveal a slow "eclipse" of community identity and feeling, and he views this as symptomatic of a burgeoning mass society. He finds a paucity of communal symbols, dramas, and rituals. Life appears shallow and mass-produced, a soul-starving individualistic search for career success. But he assumes that somewhere under the surface reality that is documented in these studies, new forms are emerging. It is, he assumes, more likely that community has been "eclipsed" than that it has been completely obliterated. This means that an important task faces social scientists: they should be the ones to reveal the new, emergent forms of community. He suggests that there are both scientific and personal reasons for doing so. The social scientist can identify important new modes of expression and growth within the culture, and, in doing so, he or she can also grow as a human being. He advocates research based in the suburbs, where American society is now being shaped. The social scientist can look behind the facades of conformity, probe the prevailing anxiety, look for new symbols, and follow peoples' attempts to "find their way through the banalities of mass society."

I found that approach appealing and clearly relevant. An emergent form of community situated in the suburbs, 3HO was a case in point. Now, so many years later, what can I report? Did I find emergent forms of selfhood, maturity, or community? Did I encounter symbolic riches? Moral tales?

Self-Symbolizations and Maturity
American and Eastern Narratives

Puzzling over American approaches to the self, Hewitt (1989) finds that the United States "has produced incessant discourse about the self and its fate, its relationship to society, and its problems and prospects" (11). In fact, he suggests that "American culture lives in discourse about the person and the person's relationship to society" (24). This discourse has found its way into, and has been shaped by, authoritative renderings of American history and culture. Americanists, for example, have described contexts in which the American self has supposedly been forged: the early Puritan "errand into the wilderness," the settling and subduing of the western frontier, the later encounter between the "virgin land" (Smith 1950) and the industrial machine (Marx 1964), to cite a few examples. Academic, and more popular, commentators have claimed to discern a variety of personality types that have emerged as waves of people have settled, claimed, and reshaped the land. Many of these types have been masculine: the American Adam (Lewis 1955), the practical Yankee, the cowboy, the self-made man, and the other-directed personality (Riesman [1950] 1973) among them. Indeed, the formation of the "American personality" or character has often been depicted by male observers and in terms of men's experience. We do hear about the cowgirl, the pioneer woman, the nurse at the front, the spiritualist, and the suffragette, but until quite recently much of the literature on the American self leaned heavily toward the masculine experience, and it has often been the male experience that has found its way into the national lore. In the 1960s and 1970s, women who wanted to participate in the dialogue about the self or to live out great mythic stories and adventures, or, on a less romantic note, who simply wanted to explore the nature of consciousness or find new models of womanhood and social interaction, had a limited field from which to choose—if they wished to select female exemplars. The Eastern traditions, with their goddesses, their tales, and their sense of a spiritual order penetrating the everyday world, seemed a promising place to begin.

Just as they have attempted to define what is unique in the American identity, numerous commentators have identified various settings as loci for the creation of an "American character." The East has been identified as one these settings. As Ellwood puts it, "[T]he spiritual East is a presence that has long haunted America" (1987, 5). Here, too, much of the literature centers on male figures: literary figures such as Emerson and Thoreau, interpreters and teachers of Zen and Hinduism such as Alan Watts and Swami Vivekananda, and followers such as the male Beats. But America also has a history of women leaders in nontraditional religions (e.g., Haywood 1983; Wessinger 1993a, 1993b), so a group like 3HO is not a surprising choice for women setting out on a spiritual path.

Women, both 3HO members and ex-members, have been deeply engaged in the prototypical American activity of discussing, defining, and redefining the self. One of the benefits of affiliation (long or short term) with an organization like 3HO is that it affords the individual time to reflect upon and alter the self, and, at the same time, enables those seekers who are so inclined to undertake a mythical journey and to link the individual story to one, or more, of the great communal tales. Many

3HO women seem to have been able to do this, to at least some degree, and this has been possible because Sikhism, however uneven the actual practices, does have a rich repertoire of inspiring stories for women, and 3HO provides access to the tales of goddesses—and to the intellectually challenging explanations for the nature of being and consciousness—that come via the Hindu tales and the Hindu pantheon. Tapping into these, a woman can temporarily become Rani Raj Kaur, the Adi Shakti, or Kali in one of her various forms. There are also the organizational images such as the image of the graceful woman, or of the spiritual path, that can give structure and direction to a life. When the individual successfully links self with myth and image, her yearnings and joys, her anxieties and disappointments are more readily tied together in a logical narrative. They can be linked to those of other people across time and territory. Her life takes on added meaning and she assumes her place in the flow of history.

Women in 3HO also gain opportunities to alter their relation to the stories that are normative in their time and place, or to adjust the old plots and themes. Rather than seeking the perfect suburban home and family, for example, the 3HO woman can turn to the Golden Temple as home and to the *sangat* for support. Rather than looking for Prince Charming and hoping to live happily ever after with him, she can accept an arranged marriage (with, supposedly, the perfect spouse, but "perfect" only in the sense that he will spur her spiritual growth) and view her marriage and her life within the nuclear family as part of a larger mission. One member told me that she found the concept of *maya* particularly helpful. "Maya," she said, "is in the mind. If it's what you're attached to, then it's maya." This interpretation allowed her to change the way in which she looked at the roles and possessions of a middle-class life. They were desirable, if one was not overly attached to them, but "my main priority in life is not so much to have the things I have or accomplish the things I've accomplished, but to be who I want to be." No doubt many non-Sikhs could say the same thing, but it is not easy for people from hardworking, achievement-oriented families to frame their lives in this way and detach themselves from accomplishments, possessions, and appearances. Illustrative stories and biographies that give life to concepts such as *maya* make this easier and more likely.

The organization even endows its members with an assortment of images and narrative forms, however traditional they may be, that can be fruitfully applied in efforts to align the self with the new world of global forces, virtual realities, high-speed transfers, and energy transformations. There are, for example, images of the individual as a channel for and container of energy. The devotee seeks to raise kundalini energy up through the *chakras*. Women strengthen their auras by performing appropriate yoga sets. They speak of "tuning in" to others and of using energy for healing. Their world is going through a transition period in which "the vibrations" are changing.

Identification with another culture also provides access to alternative images of the self and exposure to people whose thinking, biographies, and personality structures differ from those encountered at home. There are, for example, aspects of Indian family life and child rearing that may foster forms of selfhood less strongly based on ego functions than are the doing, accomplishing, planning selves of the West. Kakar (1981) finds that, for the Indian, "[r]eality is not primarily mediated through . . . the ego; it emanates from the deeper and phylogenetically much older structural layer of personality—the id. . . . [T]hrough those archaic, unconscious, preverbal processes of sensing and feeling (like intuition, or what is known as extra-sensory perception) which are thought to be in touch with the fundamental rhythms and harmonies of the universe" (20). The world of the ego with its boundaries between inner self and outer world "is the stuff of reality in western thought and yet maya to the Hindus" (20).

Kakar also asserts that Indians may have a superego that is less fully developed than the Western version. "Much of the individual behavior and adaptation to the environment that in westerners is regulated or coerced by the demands of the superego, is taken care of in Indians by a communal conscience," Kakar notes (1981, 135). This results in a "relative lack of tension between the superego and the ego in Indian personality," and "there is much less pressure and guilt on the ego to appease the superego by means of productive activity and achievement in the outside world" (ibid., 136).

Of course, most 3HO members have grown up in Western families, and they must earn a living in a society where individuation and the intense pursuit of individual goals are admired. They have reason to exhibit a Western personality structure. But this alternative way of being is visible to them and aspects of it are embedded in the structure and beliefs of their organization. This may help them to ease the considerable pressures exerted by the Western model of personality. It opens the possibility of respecting and trusting the intuitive, sensing, merging form of selfhood which some would describe as characteristically female (e.g., Chodorow 1974, 1989; Gilligan 1982). It can allow the women at times to hand over ego functions to Bhajan, the *sangat*, or the Dharma and to let spiritual yearnings and aesthetic feelings unfold, or to allow the personality to be reconfigured with the aids of meditation, group support, and new identities.

As 3HO members and as Sikhs they also have the opportunity to sample another culture's modes of organizing sense experience, of defining and refining the emotions, and of viewing the relationship between the individual and the group. They have opportunities to concretize emotion through taste or smell, or to consciously use music to elicit a specific spiritual state of mind. They may know, at least fleetingly, what it means to experience personhood in another system, to merge self with family, or to depend primarily upon a group, rather than individual conscience, to control personal behavior.

In an earlier chapter I cited Palmer speaking of young women who join new religions. She sees them as having "egos as wobbly as caterpillars" and using the religions as "protective cocoons" while they take time to "gain a temporary distance from their culture and its bewildering mixed messages" (1994, 259). This time away from the culture, she says, can "facilitate the difficult metamorphosis from girlhood to womanhood" at a point in history when female roles are anything but clear. Time out in a new religion can afford the young woman necessary time to experiment and to avoid, or reconstrue, some of the conflicting demands imposed outside of the religion. But for many 3HO women, "time out" has become the better part of a lifetime. They have had sufficient time to accomplish a significant restructuring of their patterns of acting and feeling. Something more than cocooning is going on here. The caterpillar becomes the kind of moth or butterfly that its parents were; the 3HO woman may adopt significant aspects of another culture.

Guilt, Anxiety, and Feminine Identity

Many 3HO women are idealists and spiritual strivers. They want to be good, even saintly. Many appear to have been idealistic and striving before they entered the 3HO community, and they may well have needed to muffle the superego's judgments and demands. A number have spoken to me of the relief they have experienced when Bhajan has reassured them that they are fine the way they are, or that guilt is a waste of time, even a sin. The issue of guilt is an important one for women. Some time ago, Jessie Bernard (1981) sought to describe the essence of "the female world." It had, she said, long been a "kin and locale-based world." It was characterized by its integrative functions, and by an emphasis upon trust, loyalty, association, and identity. It had a love-and/or-duty ethos" (29). This female world has many virtues, but one of the costs that it can impose upon women is the burden of guilt. As Bernard puts it, "Women have so many—sometimes cross-cutting—obligations, responsibilities, and loyalties that no matter what they do there is plenty of room for guilt. They should have done more. Guilt . . . is the inexorable flip side of the love-and/or-duty ethos" (ibid., 503). This suggests that, for women in an organization like 3HO which espouses some traditional female values and draws in women who demand much of themselves, a philosophy that minimizes or diffuses guilt may be both appealing and necessary. My conversations with 3HO women have convinced me that many have found relief from burdens of guilt and excessive self-consciousness in the organizational teachings.

They have also encountered justifications for regarding the female, rather than the male, experience as normative, and ways of defining that experience. Marion Woodman, writing from a Jungian perspective, argues that "[m]ost contemporary women are the daughters of patriarchy; their mothers and grandmothers were daughters of patriarchy. They know very well how to organize, how to set a goal in some transcendent perfection. They know, too, the shadow of that perfection that never ceases to judge, to blame, to find them guilty for the crime of being themselves" (1992, 352). This take on women's experience is found in the kinds of circles that many 3HO women frequented before they were affiliated with 3HO, and it is found in the kinds of groups that they may encounter now if they actively seek insights outside the borders of the organization. These include Human Potential, New Age, women's spirituality, feminist, and Jungian groups. Rather than turning to one of these groups, or to psychotherapy, however, once they are affiliated with 3HO/Sikh Dharma most women look to Sikhism and to 3HO teachings, and there they have found a philosophy that says to forget the past and to simply value yourself for being a (spiritual) woman. By embracing many of the virtues that have been traditionally associated with the ideal female they are in their own way refusing to devalue womanhood. They are also following a route that sometimes parallels the road taken by other spiritual women who have been more influenced by Jungian psychology. That path calls for rejection of internalized masculine standards, and a turning away from what are seen as archetypal masculine traits (traits such as incessant judging of people and ideas, continual efforts to prove oneself through action and production, and acceptance of hierarchies, stress, and competition). Women who adopt this approach tend to assume that many Western women have learned to imitate men in order to survive in the world as it is. This may be unavoidable, they say, but there comes a time when the price is too high and a woman must throw off the persona she has adopted and find the "true" nature within: "When a woman overidentifies with her mask, with a show of strength and achievement, or if the social role she plays is too heavily invested in a masculine status quo, then this role clouds the inner woman" (Toor 1987, 19).

Therapists working in this mode tend to urge women to become more accepting of the senses, to accept their own unique way of being, and to allow love and gentleness the place that these traits may have been denied in a world that sets too little value on them. Here Marion Woodman quotes from the diary of a woman involved in this quest for the inner woman—a woman seeking to live by the wisdom of the feminine archetype: "The possibility is love, the known fact that the essence of all matter is love. When my consciousness expands, . . . the beauty of the reality of love existing within all forms of life softens me into a gentleness that cannot force itself into action. Instead I discover a beautiful quality living within me that radiates strength and direction" (1992, 187). Women in 3HO take a similar pleasure in their capacity to nurture and love. They can list numerous ways in which feminine knowledge and spirituality have been devalued in the west, and they believe that their practices enable them to uncover their submerged spirituality and to live as women deserve to live.

In addition to the opportunity to proudly embrace culturally devalued qualities that have been traditionally attributed to women, and the chance to leave aside some burdens of past guilt, submission to the Dharma and to the spiritual teacher, and acceptance of the guidelines for graceful behavior, may offer some women surcease from the generation of new layers of guilt and anxiety. If a 3HO "lady" is, in general, behaving like 3HO's exemplary woman, then she is doing very little that *could* lead to feelings of guilt. Moreover, she has handed over some of the responsibility for her own evolution to her teacher and her environment so that it need not entirely depend upon her own actions. In short, she may have less reason to feel that she is failing, exceeding limits, or choosing the wrong direction. Certainly she should be less inclined to feel this way than she did in her youth when she may have been experimenting with drugs and sexual freedom in the counterculture.

She is also spared some of the confusion and pain associated with rapid social change. The new religions can ease dilemmas posed by role conflict and overchoice, but, equally important, they may also ease the emotional tangles and the ambivalence associated with multiple options and responsibilities. Rather early in the study of the new religions, Bird alluded to this function: "The personal sense of moral accountability" can be "aggravated" by contemporary conditions, he wrote. In a complex society we are exposed to varied, and sometimes conflicting, moral expectations. We are also increasingly held responsible for our "own health and personal well-being." Under these conditions, "persons experience moral unease" (1979, 345), and "it seems reasonable, in our utilitarian, somewhat anomic milieu, that persons subjected to its relative standards, who yet hold high career and personal expectations might develop aggravated feelings of inadequacy and guilt" (1978, 177). The new religions, he thought, addressed these feelings by clarifying expectations, but also by offering healing rituals, and, via chants and meditation, easing "wandering, anxious, distracted states of mind, occasioned perhaps by the anomic absence of compelling norms" (ibid., 180). Through the group rituals, devotees were also able to "reinforce a sense of selfhood connected not with particular roles . . . but with their intrinsic dignity as anonymous human beings" (ibid., 181).

While Bird's observations are not recent, they are as timely now as when his articles were originally published. By offering clear principles and practical remedies, 3HO eases anxiety and "moral unease." Further, 3HO women have available a "technology" for explaining and managing stress and troubles. There is a yoga set for almost any imaginable form of distress. There are specific diets, meditations, and chants. The spiritual leader can provide direction when a member is too confused or ambivalent to make her own interpretations and choices. Conflicting cultural norms and discordant pieces of information are filtered through a firmly established system of beliefs and through the boundaries of the group.

The organization is also rich in boundary imagery. While it is useful to any individual struggling with the circumstances Bird describes, such imagery may be particularly valuable to women. If the bounds of a woman's ego are more flexible than a man's, imagery that enables a woman to visualize and to metaphorically manage the joys and pains associated with this ego structure can be quite helpful. In 3HO, the boundaries of the body and the self are reimagined and women are taught that, although their auras may sometimes be "like Swiss cheese," they can learn to "center" the self, to give to others only within reason, and to resist others' opinions and expectations if these seem to endanger the spiritual self. Women who might not be able to act assertively on their own behalf find that they can do so when acting in defense of their spiritual qualities.

Of course, the new religions may both appease and create guilt and anxiety in women members. The woman with a strong need to please or to excel, when faced by the multitude of 3HO techniques to master, by powerful images of graceful womanhood, by the expectation of being tested on the path, and by a vast amount of information to absorb as she learns about Sikhism and Indian traditions, may make excessive demands on herself. Women have long been expected to be good students, to follow the rules, and to prove themselves loyal and virtuous, and such expectations for the self can simply be reinforced and intensified in 3HO past the point at which a woman feels she is successfully meeting them. Thus, although 3HO offers avenues of escape from guilt and anxiety, it may in fact generate these feelings.

Maturity

Under optimum conditions—if 3HO functions according to its ideals—3HO women have interesting opportunities for personal growth and should be able to move in new and interesting directions. Potentially freed from the constraints and demands of more conventional personas, they are not encompassed by any single familial or career role and they need not permit the broader society to provide ready-made identities or determine their priorities. As embodiments of *shakti*, they can envision themselves as individuals who are free to define their own priorities, to respond creatively to modern contingencies, and to depend upon no person or position for their self-esteem. They can recast their biographies, reimagine themselves, and ease some of the cognitive and moral burdens of contemporary life. Not all have been as free-spirited and creative as these opportunities would warrant. Indeed, they have often carried heavy burdens of responsibility—for household chores, for their own and for family members' spiritual status, and for maintaining the organization—and have used much of their energy in efforts to be obedient and graceful and behave appropriately. But if they have not always leapt forward in imaginative new directions, many have made steady progress.

When they first encountered Bhajan and the organization, many of the youth who took yoga lessons and participated in 3HO-sponsored events viewed American culture as superficial, hypocritical, and something of a Disneyland writ large. For them, the East represented wisdom and a culture with much greater depth than the culture they encountered at home. It represented a matrix in which they could grow, and that desire for growth has remained a constant. The stories recounted in this study indicate that members' growth proceeds along organizationally shaped channels, as well as flowing along more individually defined routes. The starting points differ depending on whether individuals enter as intense seekers, pragmatic seekers, or convenience joiners, but most of the stories I have gathered indicate that members have moved toward a higher kind of integration in which they add balance to their personalities. For example, those who enter as intense, emotional seekers certainly do not become phlegmatic, but they do mellow a bit. And those who enter for more worldly and practical reasons become more interested in spiritual practices and in increasing the "depth" of their personalities. Women who enter as very dependent individuals become more assertive, and those who come in as outspoken, feminist, or career-oriented grow more receptive to domestic concerns and to nurturing others. It is equally clear that 3HO membership does not obscure or overwhelm long-term themes and preoccupations that recur in individual lives. In fact, each of the women I interviewed after she had exited the organization indicated that she had left because she felt that she was no longer able to pursue the kinds of growth and the personal goals that had originally led her into 3HO.

It is undoubtedly possible to stagnate or slide backward in 3HO, just as it is in any setting, but the main impression one takes away from contact with current and ex-members is of intentional efforts to evolve, to grow both in the directions that mattered in youth and in new directions defined by spiritual beliefs and organizational directives. Sometimes the organization furthers this growth by defining, encouraging, and channeling it. At other times personal goals and values come into conflict with organizational expectations. Under these circumstances growth can still occur and may come in a number of forms. Women members grow by resisting group pressures and taking stands in defense of their personal values and desires, and they grow by taking the opposite tack, by sacrificing old ways of being in order to align themselves with the group. Growth may mean different things in each case. In the first it is a strengthening of convictions, an enhanced trust in the individual's own perceptions and judgments and heightened ability to stand alone and make decisions. In the second case, growth involves learning to sacrifice, to compromise, to put the joint enterprise ahead of the individual's immediate desires, to relinquish fantasies and repetitive behaviors.

Community

3HO has seen some dramatic leave-takings, but for a group of its type, turnover is not excessive. As Beckford suggests, the new religions are seen by prospective and actual members alike as *sources of various kinds of power.* The expectation and the experience of many recruits is that membership empowers them to cultivate and to achieve a number of things more easily than through other means. The chance to cultivate various spiritual qualities, personal goals, or social relationships is the attraction. . . . [S]ome members are prepared to tolerate high levels of discrepancy between their beliefs, experiences, and the movement's practices for the sake of exploring their potential for development in unforeseen and only dimly perceived directions. (1990, 55)

I have been, at various times, impressed, puzzled, and troubled by 3HO women's perseverance on their spiritual path. Women have remained through economic hardships, through husbands' apostasy and through arranged marriages that would seem unlikely to meet even minimal emotional needs, through upheavals in various ashrams, and through intense criticism from, and even betrayal by, their leaders. Inspired by their desires and by Bhajan's insistence that they cope with, rather than run from, difficult conditions, they persist.

The reasons for this persistence and the benefits that accrue to women by virtue of membership have been examined throughout this book, and they are wide ranging. But while it is a community that provides important rewards for its members, it is not, perhaps, what the romantic researcher might look for when seeking examples of innovative, democratic, and freely evolving forms of organization. It is ironic that alternative groups like the new religious movements have given rise to rather rigid modes of organization just when a growing body of organizational theory challenges old images of bureaucracy. Certainly for 3HO members who read organization theory and who would like to believe that they belong to a cutting-edge organization, this discrepancy presents a challenge. In fact, this is a matter that I have frequently heard raised by former members.

Looking at the future of leadership in alternative religions, Bird (1993) suggests that most of the leaders of new religions employ a "personal charismatic" style of leadership. The leader's imprint is upon all aspects of the organization: such leaders recruit their following, develop personal relationships with them, and "author the normative visions that function as the mandates for the groups or movements they lead" (77). Members of these groups can be intensely committed to the leader and his vision and feel energized by that attachment, but there are particular problems associated with this type of leadership. One is that leaders tend to become isolated from most followers and are well protected from criticism. Whistle blowing is almost impossible, so discontented members have little choice but to swallow complaints or leave, and, if and when they do leave, they may carry with them years of accumulated resentments. The organization is thus not responsive to criticism from within and is generally resistant to change.

As we have seen, Bhajan has modified the organization and moved it toward greater institutionalization, and he has modified the personal style of leadership, becoming not only the originator of the message but the interpreter of an existing tradition. One might expect such changes to moderate the role of the leader's charisma, but Bird finds that "it is not clear, however, whether these institutional arrangements greatly modify the personal charismatic character of the leadership of these groups" (1993, 87). My limited knowledge of the working of 3HO suggests that this is so, but that change is occurring.

People experience this leadership in different ways. There is a striking gulf between the enthusiastic views expressed by some current woman members and the tales of some who have exited the organization. This is not entirely surprising, given 3HO's many faces and the different interpretive schemas available within and outside of the organization, but it does raise questions about the effect of the organization on its members. For a less positive view of personal charismatic leadership, let us look at the organization through the less sympathetic eyes of leavers and with a dose of skepticism.

At its least creative, 3HO simply reproduces contemporary conflicts and dilemmas in its metaphorical and structural arrangements. It frequently requires conformity. The creation of a collective identity demands imagination and persistence in the face of an often indifferent or mocking world—it is important work, but there is often a price involved. A member may actively work to discount or submerge any doubts or anger and, in so doing, may blunt her capacity to evaluate her environment and her own emotions. If a woman is constantly convincing herself that the teachings are valuable, and that the latest organizational directive is enlightened, there may be little energy left for critical analysis. When members are deeply involved in creating and protecting a reality, it is tempting for them to avoid those groups and individuals who might call that reality into question, and thus to live in a circumscribed world. Members may turn on other devotees who question the group's shared symbols and icons and thus create a charged and tense social atmosphere. Moreover, if 3HO women feel that they should appear calm, pleasant, and graceful, and that their statements and actions ought to be indirect, they are not always in a good position to oppose practices that threaten their well-being.

In addition to the costs attached to maintaining personal and collective identities, there are other very significant stresses that some members have encountered. These arise from financial struggles, from overwork, from loyalty to leaders who prove disappointing, from difficult marriages, and from finding themselves associated with businesses that have been mismanaged or run in a dishonest fashion. I know of several women, members and former members, who have experienced significant emotional and physical symptoms which appear to have been attached to such hardships.

The difficulties that Simran has encountered are illustrative. Many years after exiting 3HO, the manner of her leaving still looms large in her mind. Her ties to Bhajan, to organizational practices, and to an ideal image of 3HO remain strong. In her returning, she struggled to keep her own counsel, to view things clearly, to grow and expand. In an August 1995 letter to some of "the graduates" she stated her purpose concisely: "I wished to stand in his [Bhajan's] presence, in my own truth and purity, and see who he is, see who I am, and complete and heal, if possible, the painful injuries we had inflicted upon each other and upon the people around us. . . . [T]o stand in the presence of this man and know my own self, to be able to stand there in love and gratitude for all of the gifts of experience and learning which he brought to my life, and to see him in his totality: light and shadow."

She feels that she was able to do this. But listening to her, one is aware of the power of the bond and of the imagery that she has carried with her for all these years, and one can hear her return occasionally to the rhetoric, attachment, and romanticism of the old Simran. It was not easy for her "to stand in the presence of this man and know my own self." She still struggles to attain the degree of autonomy she desires; she is still not free of the emotions evoked by her contacts with the organization.

How is one to assess the costs and benefits involved in membership or the directions that 3HO is likely to take in the future? One way of looking at the organization as a community and as a setting for women's lives is to compare it to current thinking about religions that benefit women. Sered (1994) made a study of "female-dominated religions," and while neither 3HO nor Sikhism is female dominated, it is interesting to compare them to the profile that emerges from Sered's work. She finds that these religions are likely to "sacralize profane experience" and tend toward "the elaboration of a rich ritual repertoire focused on concrete problems" (145). Both Sikhism and Tantra, as interpreted in 3HO, have a strong this-worldly orientation, and most of the rituals and yoga sets are said to have practical applications. Sered also finds that women create religions that posit the immanence of the divine, and while this is an inconsistent element in 3HO teaching, it is certainly a significant strand. In Sered's sample of women's religions, the body is treated as sacred, not as the site of weakness and temptation. Clearly, 3HO teachings in this realm are contradictory, but there are many ways in which the female body is strongly valued. Pregnancy is considered a cause for celebration and community support. There is continuing stress on health and physical activity and a tendency to ground all teachings in bodily practice and imagery.

None of the women's religions studied by Sered worshiped "a single, all-powerful, male deity" (285). Again, 3HO/Sikh Dharma shares this trait, although there is a strong focus on the male gurus. Interestingly, Sered also found that "these religions teach that men and women are essentially different, and that while both male and female are necessary in this world, the two are often in tension" (ibid.). She suggests that this feeling of tension may reflect economic realities: the fact that women are dependent on men for at least some economic help in child rearing, and often, in the societies she studied, this help is "erratic." 3HO also sees men and women as essentially different, and, in the economic history of the organization there is a parallel with Sered's sample since male support for mothers was quite undependable in the counterculture from which 3HO arose.

As we noted in the previous chapter, 3HO also encompasses many of the themes that Bednarowski (1993) finds in the work of woman theologians: the immanence of the divine, an inward-looking spiritual journey, and "community and interconnectedness over—or at least in addition to—individualism" (229). But there are also quite a few of the traits that Bednarowski finds in these women's writings which are clearly not present in 3HO. Among them are a preference for goddesses rather than gods; imagery of the spiritual search as descent; "relationship as an organizational principle rather than hierarchy;" and, to some degree, "self-knowledge or transformation as the worthy goal rather than perfection" (ibid.).

The traditions upon which 3HO has built its theology assume that the sacred has both male and female aspects, and 3HO women value this belief, but the Goddess has received relatively little attention in 3HO. The explicit image of the spiritual journey as descent is not often invoked in 3HO/Sikh Dharma. It is there as an undercurrent, and there is certainly the idea of turning inward in the course of meditation, but the primary imagery is of kundalini rising, of living from ever "higher" *chakras* and of transcending "lower" aspects of the self. Although women are encouraged to accept the feminine self and Bhajan urges them to dismiss guilt, 3HO members, in fact, are often trying to "keep up," and some are even seeking after perfection—while always encountering one more hurdle along the way. Several of the "graduates" featured in this account have found it necessary to set aside the constant physical and mental efforts that marked their lives in 3HO in order to become more self-accepting. As for hierarchy, it is omnipresent in 3HO but does not displace relationship as an important value. It is interesting to note, though, that Sered found that in actual women's religions (as opposed to ideal formulations) hierarchy is commonly found. What may make the women's religions distinctive, she finds, is the fact that position in the hierarchy is likely to be based upon spiritual development rather than upon education or social class (1994, 217).

Thus 3HO beliefs share a number of premises with woman-centered religions and with women's theologies, but they also manifest significant differences. There is much in 3HO theology and practice that women can employ in efforts to create community, to express their faith in a personally meaningful way, and to attain personal growth and liberation. There is also much that should prove useful to those seeking leadership positions and full equality in 3HO. But theology is only part of the story. Wessinger finds that, while theology and gender roles are important, so is tradition, and "the social expectation of the equality of women is crucial" (1993b, 10). The expectation of equality is certainly present in the organization, in part because it is the expectation in the larger society. Women have moved into more and more responsible positions, and there is every reason to expects this trend to continue. But progress may be limited by Bhajan's point of view. As Simran describes it, "[T]he way that he asks women to participate continues to feel like it . . . has to keep putting forth men and the masculine and catering to it, and therefore it [the masculine] still holds dominion. It still holds the primary place. . . . In what he teaches and in what he exemplifies, the position of women is a very responsible one. It's like women kind of have to carry the responsibility, carry the blame, carry the weight of a lot, really a lot. And it can feel out of balance."

Sered finds that women derive the most long-term benefit from religions with certain characteristics:

1. In these religions, women's association is long-term; they live together or share a lifetime association. Like many of the new religions, 3HO offers women this potential basis of support. Sered finds that a model of sisterhood is common, and this, as well, exists in 3HO.

2. These religions "occur in societies in which women not only work, but in which they produce items that receive social value" (1994, 270). Women work in 3HO, although it took time for Bhajan to accept American customs and recognize women's economic role. Many 3HO women joined the organization without completing college, and a number have since returned to school or are doing so now. Thus 3HO women's economic clout is likely to increase as their education levels rise, and as they increase their earning power this may yield more leadership positions and a stronger voice in the organization.

3. In these religions women are empowered to control their own fertility and sexuality. Sered finds that "no female-dominated religions ritually bestow on men institutionalized control over women's fertility or sexuality (ibid., 274). This is a complex issue in 3HO. The very fact that Bhajan has arranged marriages can be construed as a form of control over women's bodies, although that is not the cultural spin placed on the custom in 3HO. Similarly, control is manifested in the cases in which Bhajan has advised a woman to have a child at a certain time. There are accusations that Bhajan himself may have taken advantage of his position to gain sexual access to women in the organization. But it is important to point out that many 3HO women have chosen their own partners and most have determined the number of their children and the spacing and conditions of childbirth. They support the right to choose an abortion, and they can, and do, obtain divorces. Single women often feel that 3HO actually protects them from the excesses of the sexual marketplace.

4. Women do not join these religions because of illness, nor rise to leadership because of long-term illness

and suffering. Women are not equated with physical weakness and their bodies are not considered frail and prone to distress. In general, this is the case for women in 3HO. Women are expected to be healthy and physically strong. As anyone who has attended *sadhana* or a Tantric weekend can attest, a 3HO yoga workout is not for the unfit. In the area of physical fitness and diet, 3HO clearly encourages women to enjoy their own strength. But it is also worth noting that, while women are expected to be physically fit, they are seen as mentally and emotionally sensitive, and vulnerable in many ways.

Thus, 3HO/Sikh Dharma exhibits many traits that are likely to benefit women members, although some of the exceptions to the ideals presented by Sered and Bednarowski are significant. Some of these exceptions arise from traditional Indian and Sikh practices, others from 3HO leadership.

Imagining the Future

It is difficult to know what legacy these refugees from the counterculture will leave behind. Theirs has been quite an adventure, a global adventure, and the story is still unfolding. Beginning as a loosely organized alliance, rapidly becoming a tightly structured and relatively demanding organization, and now moving toward somewhat greater flexibility and openness, 3HO/Sikh Dharma has gone through a common series of stages. The organization, and groups affiliated with it, are not large, or even growing in numbers, but members are committed and increasingly professional in their outlook. They are preparing for the future, attempting to put businesses on a solid footing, to train more teachers and market their skills, to maintain a global presence, and to work closely with youth.

Hexham and Poewe (1997) distinguish between two types of contemporary religions. One type consists of recently expanded global religions that are extensions of old religious traditions. They participate in a broad "metaculture" and retain basic tenets of a religious tradition, but they also take on "a local, or situationally distinct, cultural dimension" (41). Then there are other religions, which the authors view as genuinely new (under this heading they would include, for example, the Church of Jesus Christ of Latter-day Saints and the Children of God).

These truly new religions go further. They take fragments of several traditions, recombine these in new ways, and then link them to a local folk tradition (42).

At the time of its founding, 3HO/Sikh Dharma seemed to be heading in the direction of a truly new religion. Not only did it combine several traditions, but one could argue that it was linked to an American folk religion: in this case, the New Age movement. Members could, perhaps, have continued dipping into New Age thought, creating new cultural combinations, singing *kirtan*, and taking readings from the Granth Sahib. Instead, they chose affiliation with Amritsar and the Khalsa. A firmly Sikh organization emerged, albeit one that was generally separate from the *gurdwara*s of Punjabi Sikhs living in North America. Nevertheless, 3HO remained as a sister organization, and the Americans retained their distinctive enthusiasm for yoga and meditation. Will their creations become firmly entrenched? Will they become well-established local expressions of a global religion?

Many questions revolve around Bhajan. His future health will be a major factor in determining the organization's direction. But other factors are also important. There is Sikh Dharma's position in the larger world of the Sikh diaspora and the organization's relationships with Sikh authorities in India. The global economic climate and the success of 3HO businesses will be important, as will the attitude taken by 3HO youth.

It is not difficult to imagine that 3HO will continue with its work. A number of kundalini yoga teachers have been recently trained under its auspices, and programs in Europe are growing. The future profile of Sikh Dharma is more difficult to envision. Only a portion of the next generation will choose to wear the *bana* and to follow their parents' life-style. They will have to create their own blend of East and West, and it will be based on their very distinctive experience. Members have to plan for leadership when Bhajan steps down. He has been the major tie to, and symbol of, the larger Sikh world, and he will not always be able to function in this capacity.

A survey of the fate of new religions after the death of their founders (and this can presumably apply to retirement as well) revealed that "[t]he death of the founder rarely proves fatal or leads to drastic alteration in the group's life. . . . [P]ower passes to new leadership with more or less smoothness depending upon the extent and thoroughness of the preparation that has been made ahead of time. . . . When a new religion dies . . . it is from lack of response of the public to the founder's ideas or the incompetence of the founder in organizing the followers into a strong group. Most new religions will die in the first decade, if they are going to die" (Melton 1991, 8–9). Based on this prediction we might expect to see Sikh Dharma/3HO remain on the scene. It may be that 3HO and its affiliated nonprofits will retain their distinctive identity, while in the future, the American-grown Sikh Dharma will be somewhat less distinct and separate from the communities established by Sikhs of Indian descent.

Relations between these two groups generally appear to have improved. In 1993, Gurudharm Singh Khalsa found that "after two decades the relationship between the two cultural groups has become increasingly close and cordial" (1993, 1). Punjabi Sikhs, he noted, were more accepting of the inclusion of yoga than they had been originally. Their fears that Sikh Dharma would become a separate sect had eased. There were still tensions over Bhajan's position, particularly if his title was interpreted to imply authority over both Punjabi and non-Punjabi Sikhs in the Western Hemisphere. On the American-born side, there was continuing discomfort with the role of caste in the Indian community. But Khalsa predicted closer ties as "the next generations will share an American outlook on culture which will increase the role of English in Gurdwara ceremonies, raise the status of women in the social fabric, and lessen the influence of caste consciousness for the selection of marriage partners" (ibid., 7).

One sees points of contact and arenas for cooperation. In Canada, Sikh Dharma sponsors camps for Sikh youth, and there is a camp for Sikh women as well. The attendees are ethnic Sikhs. I am told that the make up of the Washington community's *gurdwara* is now about 80 percent Indian Sikh. There is a Dharma school during *gurdwara* which is attended by both the Indian and American children. Members of the two communities recently spent a weekend away together in order to get to know each other better.

It would seem that such contacts might benefit the youth, in particular, and that youth from both the ethnic and Sikh Dharma families have much to offer one another. They share some common concerns. The children of the converts have gone to school in India and are comfortable with both cultures. The children of Sikh immigrants have also constructed their identities out of both cultural fabrics. They may well need one another's support and insights. Bhajan seems to have staked out a moderate position in his approach to the younger generation of ethnic Sikhs. Here, for example, is a quotation from an article posted on the 3HO web page in which the author describes Bhajan's discussions with Sikh youth in England: "When faced with questions such as: Is it permissible to watch TV? Is it OK to sing shabds in English? Is it OK to intermarry between castes? He answered clearly and definitively. 'Of course it is OK to watch TV. How else will you know what is happening in the world? Of course it is OK to sing shabds in English, or French, or German. The Guru's Bani is beautiful and powerful in all languages and we should serve the entire world. Intermarriages should not even be a question. There are no castes in the Khalsa!'" (Khalsa 1997).

When he speaks to ethnic Sikhs, either in North America or abroad, Bhajan generally encourages them to adapt to their cultural environments and to social change as long as they keep to their vows. Of course, 3HO/Sikh Dharma has also had to adapt. The 1990s saw many changes —generally ones that moved Sikh Dharma in the direction of institutionalization and renewed emphasis on financial success—and these have continued into the new millennium. One of the first changes was structural. Several ashrams instituted elected councils. Women became more active in administration at higher levels. Sikh Dharma now sponsors an interfaith Peace Prayer Day. At this event, individuals are awarded grants that are financed by one of the Sikh Dharma businesses, Peace Cereal. As previously mentioned, there has been a concerted effort to rationalize businesses. The larger businesses today include a security business, the Yogi Tea Company, Peace Cereal granola, a Lotus Notes consulting firm, and the Natural Foods Brokerage Company. All told these companies employ four to five thousand individuals (not all are Sikhs), the largest employer and most successful company being Akal Security. This security firm has had a contract with the U.S. Marshal Service. The fact that these businesses are on a solid footing seems to augur well for the future of 3HO/Sikh Dharma, although their very success could tempt individual businesses to separate from the organization and expand on their own.

I recently asked several people in leadership positions within 3HO/Sikh Dharma to list some of the changes that have occurred since the late 1980s. Said one, with a touch of humor, "We're less fanatical." She thought that people are more comfortable in their Sikh identity now and that they practice the faith out of personal need and conviction, with less concern for appearances and with less perfectionism. She also thought that people have learned to better balance their personal lives with their participation in the *sangat*. Attention to self and family was previously described as a failing, an excess of "ego," but that point of view has moderated. Another individual said that he thought people had become more tolerant. They were more likely to maintain ties with people who left the Dharma. He also saw increased professionalism and efficiency in the organizations that make up Sikh Dharma/3HO. Another mentioned new concerns surrounding health and aging.

It is possible, though not highly likely, that, around the organization's fringes, new groupings will develop. These groupings could consist of ethnic Sikhs, youth raised in 3HO but not willing to take on all the trappings associated with affiliation, sympathetic students, and even a few former members. There are precedents for this. Already, some of the 3HO youth appear to drift in and out of organizational life. Recently an ex-member requested a healing ceremony, and this turned into a significant event attended by former and present 3HO members alike.

Personally, I hope that the next generations of Sikhs—those born abroad, those of ethnic background but born here, and those whose parents found the religion via 3HO/Sikh Dharma—will find common ground. I also hope that 3HO will continue its outreach activities since I know that I, and others, have met spiritual needs and have gained insights at 3HO-sponsored workshops. I have delighted in the Sikh *kirtan*. I have found some time for a spiritual life where otherwise I might have made no time at all. I have also met people I respect, and these people have enriched my life.

As for lessons, or moral tales, contact with 3HO has encouraged me to be more accepting of some of the "womanly" traits that are all too frequently denigrated in our society. It has certainly not healed, but has left me more accepting and understanding of, the ambivalence and the internal conflicts that have shaped my life. They now look more like conflicts that shaped whole segments of our generation. And I remain impressed by the drive of people who set out to enact their beliefs and their dreams (as opposed to those of us who are more inclined to analyze and dissect them) and continue to do so over the course of a lifetime. I am well aware that this determination may be associated with a tendency to think that they have a monopoly on the truth, with an inclination to accept premises that many of us would categorize as magical or mythical, or with a high degree of suggestibility, but this may be a price tag that is attached to this calling and to this steadiness of purpose. I am also impressed by the difficulties associated with social innovation. One step in the direction of creativity and innovation is often followed by two steps in the direction of the old ways and of conservative thinking. Charisma and faith are often the only forces that can keep a vision alive, even if in an attenuated form. And they often flourish without the safeguards that are built into older and more conventional forms of organization.

I have also been recently impressed by the way that 3HO/Sikh Dharma can efficiently provide information services for Sikhs in the

United States and Canada. Thus, Sikh Dharma responded vigorously after the terrorist attacks of September 11, 2001. Like Muslims, Sikhs were attacked in the aftermath of the events. When Indian Sikhs were attacked, and one, a gentleman by the name of Balbir Singh Sodhi, was killed, the Sikh Dharma web page (Sikhnet) gathered information, provided news reports, published safety precautions, and provided flyers, posters, and press releases for Sikhs to use in their efforts to educate the public about Sikhism.

It is possible that some of the members who have shared their lives with me will see this book as a betrayal because I have expressed some criticisms of 3HO life and leadership. I hope this is not the case and that they realize that my essential feelings are of affection and respect. I am grateful to them for their generous sharing of their life experiences, for their graceful hospitality, and for their tutelage. I am equally grateful to the former members who shared so much—pain, confusion, hopes, ideas, and new joys. I feel a strong responsibility to convey all of these women's experience honestly and respectfully. A life, I think, is sacred, no matter what routes that life may take or how mistaken some choices made in that life may appear in retrospect. The distillations and transformations and magical twists and inspired stories that we make of our lives are important, certainly as important in the final analysis as the organizations and social trends, the junctures, and paths, and turning points we encounter in the course of living.

And here, perhaps, I should let Simran say some final words. I asked her once if 3HO had helped her to unify aspects of the self; when she first encountered 3HO, was she internally divided? She agreed strongly that she had been:

> It challenged me to really try to calm some of that. In some ways it brought it to a head. It's something I would say I'm still dealing with. . . . I think probably you could put it in the word of 'trust.' It's like there's the place that wants to control and direct and order things by the mind, by the left brain, by logic and reason. And then there's the heart—for me this is one of my big dichotomies and life challenges. I would say at this point that where I'm at is I will choose my heart, hopefully, over my head at all times. . . . I'm going to be true to my heart, to my feelings, to my guidance from Spirit. . . . I said the word 'trust' to begin with. It's about all the calculating and all the concerns, and

all the fears of anything, versus your place of being in trust and surrender and acceptance of your journey, however it may unfold. Ultimately, it's just a play and ultimately it's just a movie, in a way, and once we step outside of it and look at it from an overview, it's like, "You don't have to take it so seriously. You don't have to take it seriously at all." And you play it according to your highest passion, dream, desire. You can play it any way you want. And you play what you have chosen to play. You can play it any way you want—but you have also chosen. So here it is. Like Arjuna on the battlefield—the classic Gita example. He saw that he was going to have to be taking a side to wage war, and that on both sides were his relations. And the perspective on that is, "It's okay, it really *is* only a play. You're just playing a part."

Perhaps Simran and Prabhupati are right: life should be viewed as a kind of play, or dreaming, or storytelling. Perhaps it is only understood if one adds a touch of the improbable, a hint of magic to one's interpretations. Perhaps it is only tolerable for many who are morally sensitive if it is viewed as a play or a role. Perhaps in times of rapid change one must trust a bit in mysterious forces. In a complex and contradictory culture perhaps one must, like Arjuna, simply dive in and act. In a highly rationalized world, where efficiency and material concerns tend to dominate other realms, the new religions, at least in their early years, seemed to represent a setting in which such magic and some enabling myths could be injected into everyday lives. In 3HO, members can periodically enter the realm of myth and story; a woman can know that she is *shakti* incarnate. She can return enriched and refreshed, or she may find herself laboring under a magician's spell.

A Brief Biography of Yogi Bhajan

Yogi Bhajan was born Harbhajan Singh Puri in 1929 in the small village of Tehsil Wazirabad in what is now India but was then Pakistan (Lewis 1999). He was born into a landed, professional family, attended boarding school, and later earned a bachelor's degree in economics from Punjab University. People in 3HO depict him as a spiritual prodigy who began the study of yoga at a very early age. They also say that when he was a young boy an astrologist predicted that he would travel overseas and would teach and liberate people in the West.

I have heard him speak of the partition of India and of walking miles with his family when his home became a part of Pakistan. A man who knew Bhajan in his early years describes these events in the commemorative volume: "Mobs ruled. . . . The scale of transfer of a population was unknown in history. . . . Yogi Bhajan and I were undergraduates at that time. . . . Like a million others, both our families wandered to safety, security and hovels in Delhi. . . . In 1948, the University of Punjab opened an evening Camp College in New Delhi to cater to the Punjabi students. . . . The events of 1947 had radicalized the youth. . . . We were too ill at ease to settle in classrooms. . . . Suddenly, we took on the government of India making two simple demands: tents to live in and loans for college fees" (S. Singh 1979, 44). This experience undoubtedly made it easy for Bhajan to understand alienated American youth in 1967.

After his graduation he married Inderjit Kaur and is the father of three children. He began to work as an Indian customs and security officer. Bailey (1974) was told that Bhajan "taught yoga therapy while working as a Customs Officer at Palam International airport in Delhi" (74). Lewis describes him as "a customs official and Interpol officer" (1999, 33). People in 3HO say that during this time period, as an act of service and devotion, he also washed the steps of the Golden Temple daily for four years.

In 1968 he traveled to Toronto, evidently expecting to take up a teaching position which did not materialize. He went on to Los Angeles, where he taught yoga at a YMCA and at the East-West Cultural Center. It was as a yoga teacher that he encountered the young people who joined him to found 3HO.

In the early 1970s he led groups of students to Amritsar and met with Sikh authorities there. They recognized him and his followers, and Bhajan became a figure in the world of western Sikhism. He has adopted Guru Ram Das (the fourth Sikh guru) as his special master, and this guru is of particular significance to his students as well. He has been active in interreligious affairs and has served as co-president of the World Parliament of Religions and co-chair of the World Fellowship of Religions (Lewis 1999).

Glossary

Amrit. Literally "nectar." Sweetened water used in the initiation ceremony of the Khalsa.

Arjuna. The hero of the Bhagavad-Gita. The Gita is embedded in the epic Mahabharata, which tells the story of the Bharata dynasty and features five brothers (the Pandava brothers). Arjuna is one of the brothers and a warrior. He and his brothers are assisted and instructed by Krishna.

Baisakhi. A festival held at the time of the New Year in Punjab. It is celebrated as the anniversary of the Khalsa.

Bhakti. Religion which stresses devotion to a divinity.

chunni. A long scarf worn by Sikh women. It is traditionally worn around the neck, but women in Sikh Dharma wrap it over their turbans.

Dasam Granth. Sacred writings attributed to Guru Gobind Singh, the tenth Guru and founder of the Khalsa.

Devi. Goddess. The divine in its female aspect.

dharma. Law or duty. Also morality or, in Sikh Dharma, "righteousness."

five K's *(panj kakke)*. Worn by all members of the Khalsa, they are *kes* (unshorn hair), *kangha* (a comb), *kirpan* (a dagger), *kara* (a steel bracelet), and *kacch* (breeches that are worn as an undergarment).

Golden Temple. Called Harmandir Sahib in Punjabi. The most sacred Sikh temple, located in Amritsar. Guru Ram Das began work on it in 1577.

gurdwara. A Sikh place of worship. It can be in a public place or in a private house, but it should house a copy of the Guru Granth Sahib.

Gurmukhi. The language in which the Granth Sahib is written. It is a written form of Punjabi.

Guru Granth Sahib. Also called Adi Granth. The sacred text of the Sikhs. It includes the words of the Sikh gurus as well as hymns composed by *sant*-singers before the advent of Sikhism. After the death of Guru Gobind Singh the guruship was placed in the scriptures. The Guru Granth Sahib is treated with veneration, and Sikhs remove their shoes, cover their heads, and bow in its presence. It is kept on a richly decorated platform with a canopy above it.

Khalsa. Translated as "the pure ones." Refers to all initiated Sikhs and is traced back to Guru Gobind Singh.

kirtan (gurbani kirtan). The singing of the words of the gurus, the hymns in the Guru Granth Sahib. "The poetic excellence, the spiritual content, and the haunting, lilting melodies of the hymns of the Adi Granth are Sikhism's greatest attractions to this day" (Singh, Kushwant 1989).

kriya. Action, ritual. In yoga, a combination of posture, breathing, and mantra.

kundalini. A power or energy (sometimes called the "serpent power"), a manifestation of *shakti,* which lies dormant in the individual. Various yoga *kriyas* are intended to awaken this energy and move it upward through the "subtle body." It is said to be a powerful force capable of rising to the highest *chakra* in the body and creating bliss and union with the Ultimate.

langar. A communal meal shared by Sikhs at a *gurdwara.* It is shared by people of all castes. Instituted by Guru Nanak.

Mahadevi. The great goddess. The goddess is an incarnation of *shakti,* the female aspect of divinity, and is worshiped in India today. She may be referred to as Mata (mother) and by numerous other names. The Mahadevi can subsume the Hindu goddesses Durga, Parvati, and Kali. Durga is a warrior goddess. Parvati is beautiful, nurturing, loving, and an ideal wife and mother. Kali is the destroyer of *maya,* the one who destroys the old so that the new can emerge. She is pictured wearing a necklace of skulls.

mantra. A sacred sound. It may be one or several syllables and is used in meditation to focus the mind and free it from ordinary associations. In Sikh Dharma, members talk about using *mantras* to create a "mental vibration."

Manu, Laws of (or Code of). A code of behavior which lays down norms, rules, obligations, and responsibilities for the different segments of society. It includes numerous rules regarding the behavior of women and the nature of marriage. It was originally a Brahman document but was also imposed as a law code by a colonial governor in the eighteenth century (Mitter 1991, 88).

panth. A path or way. Sikhs may speak of the Sikh *Panth* when referring to the Sikh community.

Punjab. The home of the Sikhs located in northwestern India. Often described as the land of the five rivers (the Jhelum, Chenab, Ravi, Sutlej, and Beas, all of which flow into the Indus). It is a land of flat plains and productive agriculture. Most of India's invaders have entered through the north, so this area has been influenced by many peoples and has often been the scene of strife. The Punjab was divided in 1947, and the West Punjab became Pakistan.

prashad. The broader meaning is "gift, received during worship." In 3HO it is used to refer to *Karah prasad,* which is served near the end of worship at a *gurdwara.* It is made of flour, sugar and ghee (clarified butter).

sadhana. A spiritual discipline. In Sikh Dharma, "personal spiritual effort on a regular basis" (Khalsa, Shakti Parwha Kaur 1996). In Sikh Dharma the term is generally used to refer to the morning worship. Tantric traditions emphasize the importance of specific practices and rituals as a means to empowerment and liberation and use the term *sadhana* to describe them.

sant. The word *sant* (not to be confused with "saint") derives from *sat*— "truth"—implying a seeker after truth. The *sants* looked inward, meditating upon the divine word.

sati. Immolation of a widow on her husband's funeral pyre. A practice opposed by Sikhs.

shakti (sakti). The feminine, and active, aspect of divinity. Primal power or life-force that creates and gives form to the cosmos and pervades all matter. In 3HO/Sikh Dharma one may refer to a woman as a *shakti.*

Shiromani Gurdwara Parbandhak Committee (SGCP). Central Gurdwara Management Committee.

Tantras. Texts referred to as Tantras date back to the ninth century, although they draw on much earlier sources. They are Hindu scriptures that elevate goddesses and *shakti.* Tantric practices draw on these sources, as well as others, and aim to unify the relative and the absolute and to raise kundalini energy up through the *chakras* of the subtle body.

Bibliography

Aidala, Angela, A. 1985. "Social Change, Gender Roles, and New Religious Movements." *Sociological Analysis* 46:287–314.

Ammerman, Nancy T. 1987. *Bible Believers: Fundamentalists in the Modern World.* New Brunswick, N.J.: Rutgers Univ. Press.

Anthony, Dick, and Thomas Robbins. 1974. "The Meher Baba Movement: Its Effects on Post-Adolescent Social Alienation." In *Religious Movements in Contemporary America*, ed. Irving I. Zaretsky and Mark P. Leone, 479–511. Princeton, N.J.: Princeton Univ. Press.

———. 1982. "Spiritual Innovation and the Crisis of American Civil Religion." *Deadalus* 111 (1): 215–34.

Bailey, Raleigh Eugene, Jr. 1974. "An Ethnographic Approach toward the Study of a Spiritually Oriented Communal Group in the USA: The Healthy, Happy, Holy Organization." Ph.D. diss., Hartford Seminary Foundation, 1973. Ann Arbor: UMI, 7418679.

Barker, Eileen. 1998. "Standing at the Crossroads: The Politics of Marginality in 'Subversive Organizations.'" In *The Politics of Religious Apostasy: The Role of Apostates in the Transformation of Religious Organizations*, ed. David Bromley, 75–93. Westport, Conn.: Praeger.

———. 1999. "New Religious Movements: Their Incidence and Significance." In *New Religious Movements: Challenge and Response*, ed. Bryan Wilson and Jamie Creswell, 15–31. New York: Routledge.

Barrier, N. Gerald. 1993. "Sikh Studies and the Study of History." In Hawley and Mann, *Studying the Sikhs*, 24–45.

Beckford, James A. 1990. "Religion and Power." In *In Gods We Trust: New Patterns of Religious Pluralism in America*, ed. Thomas Robbins and Dick Anthony, 43–60. 2d ed. New Brunswick, N.J.: Transaction.

Bednarowski, Mary Farrell. 1993. "Widening the Banks of the Mainstream: Women Constructing Theologies." In *Women's Leadership in Marginal Religions*, ed. Catherine Wessinger, 211–31. Urbana: Univ. of Chicago Press.

Bellah, Robert N., Richard Madsen, William M. Sullivan, Ann Swidler, and Steven Tipton. 1985. *Habits of the Heart: Individualism and Commitment in American Life*. New York: Harper & Row.

Berger, Brigitte. 1971. *Societies in Change*. New York: Basic.

Berger, Peter L. 1970. "The Problem of Multiple Realities: Alfred Schutz and Robert Musil." In *Phenomenology and Social Reality: Essays in Memory of Alfred Schutz*, ed. Maurice Natanson, 213–33. Evanston, Ill.: Northwestern Univ. Press.

———. 1977. *Facing Up to Modernity: Excursions in Society, Politics, and Religion*. New York: Basic Books.

Bernard, Jessie. 1981. *The Female World*. New York: Free Press–Macmillan.

Bhajan, Yogi. (See also Harbhajan Singh Khalsa.) 1972a. "From UCLA Lecture." *Beads of Truth* 16 (Winter Solstice Edition): 11.

———. 1972b. "Yogi Bhajan Speaks." *Beads of Truth*, Summer Solstice Souvenir Issue, 33.

———. 1972c. "Living Surrender and Rebirth." *Beads of Truth*, Summer, 3–5.

———. 1973a. "Solstice Sadhana: A Lecture by Yogi Bhajan." Kundalini Research Institute, June 18. Reprinted in *Journal of Science and Consciousness for Living in the Aquarian Age* 1, no. 2 (May 1975): 1–7.

———. 1973b. "Scriptures of the World." Originally published in *Beads of Truth* 17 (Mar.): 9–11.

———. 1973c. Untitled article. Originally published in *Beads of Truth*. Reprinted in Khalsa and Khalsa, *Man Called the Siri Singh Sahib*, 331.

———. 1973d. "Remember the Martyrs of the Aquarian Age." Originally published in *Beads of Truth*. Reprinted in Khalsa and Khalsa, *Man Called the Siri Singh Sahib*, 331–34.

———. 1973e. "Mind Projection." *Beads of Truth* 17 (Mar. 1973): 27–30.

———. 1974a. *Beads of Truth*, vol. 22.

———. 1974b. *Beads of Truth*, vol. 23, 8.

———. 1978a. "The Challenge: Woman Be a Woman." In *Women in Training III*. Reprinted in Khalsa and Khalsa, *Man Called the Siri Singh Sahib*, 196–99.

———. 1978b. "What Is Yoga." In KRI, *Kundalini Yoga/Sadhana Guidelines*, 4–8.

———. 1979a. "Significant Events in the Establishment of the Sikh Dharma in the Western Hemisphere." In Khalsa and Khalsa, *Man Called the Siri Singh Sahib*, 132–35.

———. 1979b. "Early History" frontispiece. In Khalsa and Khalsa, *Man Called the Siri Singh Sahib*, 15.

———. 1979c. "The Blue Gap." In Khalsa and Khalsa, *Man Called the Siri Singh Sahib*, 348–50.

———. 1982. *Relax and Rejoice: A Marriage Manual*. 2 vols. Pomona, Calif.: KRI Publications, 1:1–36.

———. 1983a. "Aquarian Marriage." Duplicated material distributed at "Yoga and the Spiritual Woman" course, Khalsa Women's training Camp.

———. 1983b. Lecture to Khalsa Women's Training Camp, Española, N.M., July 1. Author's tape.

———. 1983c. Lecture to Khalsa Women's Training Camp, Española, N.M., July 5. Author's tape.

———. 1983d. Lecture to Khalsa Women's Training Camp, Española, N.M., July 6. Author's tape.

———. 1983e. Lecture to Khalsa Women's Training Camp, Española, N.M., July 7. Author's tape.

Bharati, Aghananda. 1965. *The Tantric Tradition.* London: Rider.

———. 1985. "The Self in Hindu Thought and Action." In *Culture and Self: Asian and Western Perspectives,* ed. Anthony J. Marsella, George De Vos, and Francis L. K. Hsu, 185–229. New York: Tavistock.

Bhasin, Kamla, ed. 1972. *The Position of Women in India.* Proceedings of a seminar held in Srinagar, Sept. 1972. Bombay: Arvind A. Deshpande.

Bird, Frederick. 1978. "Charisma and Ritual in New Religious Movements." In *Understanding the New Religions,* ed. Jacob Needleman and George Baker, 173–89. New York: Seabury Press.

———. 1979. "New Religious Movements and Moral Accountability." *Sociological Analysis* 79, 40:335–46.

———. 1993. "Charisma and Leadership in New Religious Movements." In *Religion and the Social Order: The Handbook on Cults and Sects in America,* ed. David G. Bromley and Jeffrey K. Hadden, vol. 3, pt. A, pp. 75–92. Greenwich, Conn.: JAI Press.

Bird, Frederick, and William Reimer. 1982. "Participation Rates in New Religious and Para-Religious Movements." *Journal for the Scientific Study of Religion* 21:1–14.

Bleier, Ruth, ed. 1986. *Feminist Approaches to Science.* New York: Pergamon Press.

Blofeld, John. 1992. *The Tantric Mysticism of Tibet.* New York: Penguin.

Bromley, David G. 1991. "Unraveling Religious Disaffiliation: The Meaning and Significance of Falling from the Faith in Contemporary Society." *Counseling and Values* 35 (Apr.): 165–85.

———. 1997. "Constructing Apocalypticism." In *Millennium, Messiahs and Mayhem: Contemporary Apocalyptic Movements,* ed. Thomas Robbins and Susan J. Palmer, 31–45. New York: Routledge.

———. 1998. "The Social Construction of Contested Exit Roles: Defectors, Whistleblowers, and Apostates." In *The Politics of Religious Apostasy: The Role of Apostates in the Transformation of Religious Movements,* ed. David Bromley, 19–48. Westport, Conn.: Praeger.

Brooks, Douglas Renfrew. 1990. *The Secret of the Three Cities: An Introduction to Hindu Sakta Tantrism.* Chicago: Univ. of Chicago Press.

Bruner, Jerome. 1990. *Acts of Meaning.* Cambridge: Harvard Univ. Press.

Burkheimer, Graham J., and Thomas P. Novak. 1981. *Capsule Description of Young Adults Seven and One-Half Years After High School.* U.S. Department of Education, National Center for Education Statistics. Available on line at http://nces.ed.gov.

Butler, D. R. 1979. "Instant Cosmic Consciousness?" In *Kundalini, Evolution and Enlightenment,* ed. John White, 184–88. New York: Anchor.

Callahan, Jean. 1992. "Leaving the Ashram." *Common Boundary* 10, no. 4 (July–Aug.): 32–39.

Cameron-Bandler, Leslie. 1978. *They Lived Happily Ever After.* Cupertino, Calif.: Meta Publications.

Carroll, Theodora Foster. 1983. *Women, Religion and Development in the Third World.* New York: Praeger.

Chitnis, Suma. 1988. "Feminism: Indian Ethos and Indian Convictions." In *Women in Indian Society,* ed. Rehana Ghadially, 81–95. Newbury Park, Calif.: Sage Publications.

Chodorow, Nancy. 1974. "Family Structure and Feminine Personality." In *Woman, Culture, and Society,* ed. Michelle Zimbalist Rosaldo and Louise Lamphere, 43–66. Stanford, Calif.: Stanford Univ. Press.

———. 1978. *The Reproduction of Mothering.* Berkeley and Los Angeles: Univ. of California Press.

———. 1989. *Feminism and Psychoanalysis.* New Haven, Conn.: Yale Univ. Press.

Christ, Carol P. 1980. *Diving Deep and Surfacing: Women Writers on Spiritual Quest.* Boston: Beacon Press.

Christ, Carol P., and Judith Plaskow, eds. 1979. *Womanspirit Rising.* New York: Harper & Row.

Clifford, James. 1988. *The Predicament of Culture.* Cambridge: Harvard Univ. Press.

Clifford, James, and George E. Marcus, eds. 1986. *Writing Culture: The Poetics and Politics of Ethnography.* Berkeley and Los Angeles: Univ. of California Press.

Cohen, Abner. 1977. "Symbolic Action and the Structure of the Self." In *Symbols and Sentiments: Cross-Cultural Studies in Symbolism,* ed. Ioan Lewis, 117–28. London: Academic Press.

Cole, W. Owen. 1990. "The Sikh Diaspora: Its Possible Effects on Sikhism." In *Sikh History and Religion in the Twentieth Century,* ed. Joseph T. O'Connell, Milton Israel, and Willard G. Oxtoby, with visiting editors W. H. McLeod and J. S. Grewal, 388–402. New Delhi: Manohar Publications.

Cole, W. Owen, and Piara Singh Sambhi. 1978. *The Sikhs: Their Religious Beliefs and Practices.* London: Routledge & Kegan Paul.

Comeau, Rama Kirn Singh, and Shama Kirn Singh. 1975. "3HO: Happy, Healthy, Holy Living in a Spiritual Community." *Communities* 14:35–41. (Mar.–Apr. 1975 in the Underground Newspaper Collection.)

Conger, Jay A., and N. Kanungo Rabindra. 1998. *Charismatic Leadership in Organizations.* Thousand Oaks, Calif.: Sage Publications.

Cott, Nancy. 1977. *The Bonds of Womanhood: "Woman's Sphere" in New England, 1780–1835.* New Haven, Conn.: Yale Univ. Press.

Cox, Harvey. 1968. "God and the Hippies." *Playboy* 15 (1): 94.

Davidman, Lynn. 1990. "Women's Search for Family and Roots: A Jewish Religious Solution to a Modern Dilemma." In *In Gods We Trust: New Patterns of Religious Pluralism in America*, ed. Thomas Robbins and Dick Anthony, 385–407. 2d ed. New Brunswick, N.J.: Transaction.

———. 1991. *Tradition in a Rootless World: Women Turn to Orthodox Judaism.* Berkeley and Los Angeles: Univ. of California Press.

Davies, Bronwyn. 1992. "Women's Subjectivity and Feminist Stories." In *Investigating Subjectivity: Research on Lived Experience*, ed. Carolyn Ellis and Michael G. Flaherty, 53–76. Newbury Park, Calif.: Sage Publications.

Dawson, Lorne. 1990. "Self-Affirmation, Freedom, and Rationality: Theoretically Elaborating 'Active Conversions.'" *Journal for the Scientific Study of Religion* 29 (2): 141–63.

Denzin, Norman K. 1997. *Interpretive Ethnography: Ethnographic Practices for the 21st Century.* Thousand Oaks, Calif.: Sage Publications.

Douglas, Ann. 1977. *The Feminization of American Culture.* New York: Knopf.

Downton, James V., Jr. 1979. *Sacred Journeys: The Conversion of Young Americans to Divine Light Mission.* New York: Columbia Univ. Press.

Dumont, Louis. 1970. *Homo Hierarchicus.* Chicago: Univ. of Chicago Press.

Dusenbery, Verne A. 1975. *Straight Freak Yogi Sikh.* Master's thesis, Univ. of Chicago.

———. 1989a. "Introduction: A Century of Sikhs Beyond Punjab." In *The Sikh Diaspora: Migration and the Experience Beyond Punjab*, ed. N. Gerald Barrier and Verne A. Dusenbery, 1–28. Delhi: Chanakya Publications.

———. 1989b. "Of Singh Sabhas, Siri Singh Sahibs, and Sikh Scholars: Sikh Discourse from North America in the 1970's." In *The Sikh Diaspora: Migration and Experience Beyond Punjab*, ed. N. Gerald Barrier and Verne A. Dusenbery, 90–119. Delhi: Chanakya Publications.

———. 1989c. "Sikh Persons and Practices: A Comparative Ethnosociology." Ph.D. diss., Univ. of Chicago. Ann Arbor: UMI.

———. 1990a. "On the Moral Sensitivities of Sikhs in North America." In *Divine Passions: The Social Construction of Emotion in India*, ed. Owen M. Lynch, 239–61. Berkeley and Los Angeles: Univ. of California Press.

———. 1990b. "Punjabi Sikhs and Gora Sikhs: Conflicting Assertions of Sikh Identity in North America." In *Sikh History and Religion in the Twentieth Century*, ed. Joseph T. O'Connell, Milton Israel, and Willard G. Oxtoby, with visiting editors W. H. McLeod and J. S. Grewal, 334–55. New Delhi: Manohar Publications. 1990 South Asia Edition.

Eckland, Bruce K., and Louise B. Henderson. 1981. *College Attainment Four Years After High School.* U.S. Department of Education National Center for Education Statistics (NCES 82216). Available only on-line at http://nces.ed.gov/pubsearch.

Eichler, Margrit. 1983. "Leadership in Social Movements." In *Leadership and Social Change*, ed. William R. Lassey and Marshall Sashkin, 286–305. 3d ed. San Diego: University Associates.

Eliade, Mircea. 1969. *Patanjali and Yoga*. New York: Funk and Wagnalls.

Eller, Cynthia. 1993. "Twentieth-Century Women's Religion as Seen in the Feminist Spirituality Movement." In *Women's Leadership in Marginal Religions*, ed. Catherine Wessinger, 172–95. Urbana: Univ. of Illinois Press.

———. 1995. *Living in the Lap of the Goddess*. Boston: Beacon Press.

Ellwood, Robert S., Jr. 1978. "Emergent Religion in America: An Historical Perspective." In *Understanding the New Religions*, ed. Jacob Needleman and George Baker, 267–84. New York: Seabury Press.

———. 1987. Introduction to *Eastern Spirituality in America: Selected Writings*, ed. Robert S. Ellwood, 1–48. New York: Paulist Press.

Erikson, Kai T. 1976. *Everything in Its Path: Destruction of Community in the Buffalo Creek Flood*. New York: Touchstone–Simon & Schuster.

Erndl, Kathleen M. 1993. *Victory to the Mother: The Hindu Goddess of Northwest India in Myth, Ritual, and Symbol*. New York: Oxford Univ. Press.

———. 1997. "The Goddess and Women's Power: A Hindu Case Study." In *Women and Goddess Traditions: In Antiquity and Today*, ed. Karen L. King, 17–38. Minneapolis: Fortress Press.

Feldstein, Donald. 1984. *The American Jewish Community in the 21st Century—A Projection*. New York: American Jewish Congress. http://www.Adherents.com.

Fenton, John Y. 1988. *Transplanting Religious Traditions: Asian Indians in America*. New York: Praeger.

———. 1995. *South Asian Religions in the Americas: An Annotated Bibliography of Immigrant Religious Traditions*. Westport, Conn.: Greenwood Press.

Ferrucci, Piero. 1982. *What We May Be*. Los Angeles: J. P. Tarcher.

Feuerstein, Georg. 1991. *Sacred Paths: Essays on Wisdom, Love, and Mystical Realization*. Burdett, N.Y.: Paul Brunton Philosophic Foundation.

———. 1998. *The Yoga Tradition: Its History, Literature, Philosophy and Practice*. Prescott, Ariz.: Hohm Press.

Fine, Gary Alan. 1995. "Public Narration and Group Culture: Discerning Discourse in Social Movements." In *Social Movements and Culture*, ed. Hank Johnston and Bert Klandermans, 127–43. Minneapolis: Univ. of Minnesota Press.

Foucault, Michel. 1979. *Discipline and Punish*. Hardmonsworth: Penguin.

———. 1980. *Power/Knowledge*. Ed. Colin Gordon. Brighton, Sussex, England: Harvester.

Fox-Keller, Evelyn. 1985. *Reflections on Gender and Science*. New Haven, Conn.: Yale Univ. Press.

———. 1989. "The Gender/Science System: or, Is Sex to Gender as Nature Is to Science?" In *Feminism and Science*, ed. Nancy Tuana, 33–57. Bloomington: Indiana Univ. Press.

Friedman, Debra, and Doug McAdam. 1992. "Collective Identity and Activism: Networks, Choices, and the Life of a Social Movement." In *Frontiers in Social*

Movement Theory, ed. Aldon D. Morris and Carol McClurg Mueller, 156–73. New Haven, Conn.: Yale Univ. Press.

Friedman, Lenore. 1987. *Meetings with Remarkable Women: Buddhist Teachers in America*. Boston: Shambhala.

Gamson, William A., 1992. "The Social Psychology of Collective Action." In *Frontiers in Social Movement Theory*, ed. Aldon D. Morris and Carol McClurg Mueller, 53–76. New Haven, Conn.: Yale Univ. Press.

Gardner, Hugh. 1978. *The Children of Prosperity: Thirteen Modern American Communes*. New York: St. Martin's Press.

Geller, Jean H. 1979. "Ashram (Sikh) Communities and Self-Actualization." Ph.D. diss., U.S. International Univ., 1976. Ann Arbor: UMI, 7909547.

Gerlach, Luther P., and Virginia H. Hine. 1970. *People, Power, Change: Movements of Social Transformation*. Indianapolis: Bobbs-Merrill.

Gill, Pritam Singh. 1975. *Heritage of Sikh Culture*. Jullunder: New Academic.

Gilligan, Carol. 1982. *In a Different Voice: Psychological Theory and Women's Development*. Cambridge: Harvard Univ. Press.

Gitlin, Todd. 1987. *The Sixties: Years of Hope, Days of Rage*. New York: Bantam.

Glazer, Nathan. 1972. *American Judaism*. 2d ed. Chicago: Univ. of Chicago Press.

Glennon, Lynda M. 1979. *Women and Dualism*. Philadelphia: Longmans, Green.

Goldman, Marion S. 1999. *Passionate Journeys: Why Successful Women Joined a Cult*. Ann Arbor: Univ. of Michigan Press.

Greeley, Andrew M. 1990. *The Catholic Myth: The Behavior and Beliefs of American Catholics*. New York: Charles Scribner's Sons.

Grewal, J. S. 1990. *The Sikhs of the Punjab*. New Cambridge History of India II.3. Cambridge: Cambridge Univ. Press.

———. 1997. *Historical Perspectives on Sikh Identity*. Patiala: Publication Bureau, Punjabi University.

Griffin, David Ray. 1988. Introduction to *The Reenchantment of Science: Postmodern Proposals*, ed. David Ray Griffin. Albany: State Univ. of New York Press.

Gross, Rita M. 1994. "Studying Women and Religion: Conclusions Twenty-five Years Later." In *Today's Woman in World Religions*, ed. Arvind Sharma. Albany: State Univ. of New York Press.

Guenther, Herbert V. 1975. *The Dawn of Tantra*. Berkeley, Calif.: Shambhala.

Gupte, Pranay. 1985. *Vengeance: India after the Assassination of Indira Gandhi*. New York: W. W. Norton.

Hall, John R. 1987. *Gone from the Promised Land: Jonestown in American Cultural History*. New Brunswick, N.J.: Transaction.

Hans, Surjit S. 1981. "The Gurbilas in the Early Nineteenth Century." *Journal of Regional History* 2:43–56. Department of History, Guru Nanak Dev Univ., Amritsar, Punjab.

———. 1984. "Social Transformation and the Creative Imagination in Sikh Literature." In *Social Transformation and Creative Imagination*, ed. Sudhir Chandra, 91–106. New Delhi: Allied Publishers.

———. 1988. *A Reconstruction of Sikh History from Sikh Literature*. Jalandhar: ABS Publications.

Harding, Sandra. 1986. *The Science Question in Feminism*. Ithaca, N.Y.: Cornell Univ. Press.

———. 1991. *Whose Science? Whose Knowledge? Thinking from Women's Lives*. Ithaca, N.Y.: Cornell Univ. Press.

Hart, Stephen. 1996. "The Cultural Dimension of Social Movements: A Theoretical Assessment and Literature Review." *Sociology of Religion* 57, no. 1 (Spring): 87–100.

Hawley, John Stratton, and Gurinder Singh Mann. 1993. *Studying the Sikhs: Issues for North America*. Albany: State Univ. of New York Press.

Hayim, Gila J. 1980. *The Existential Sociology of Jean-Paul Sartre*. Amherst: Univ. of Massachusetts.

Haywood, Carol Lois. 1983. "The Authority and Empowerment of Women Among Spiritualist Groups." *Journal for the Scientific Study of Religion* 22 (2): 157–66.

Helweg, Arthur W. 1989. "Sikh Politics in India: The Emigrant Factor." In *The Sikh Diaspora: Migration and the Experience Beyond Punjab*, ed. N. Gerald Barrier and Verne A. Dusenbery, 305–36. Delhi: Chanakya Publications.

Hershman, Paul. 1977. "Virgin and Mother." In *Symbols and Sentiments: Cross Cultural Studies in Symbolism*, ed. Ioan Lewis, 269–92. London: Academic Press.

Hewitt, John P. 1989. *Dilemmas of the American Self*. Philadelphia: Temple University Press.

Hexham, Irving, and Karla Poewe. 1997. *New Religions as Global Cultures: Making the Human Sacred*. Boulder, Colo.: Westview Press.

Hiltebeitel, Alf. 1989. "Hinduism." In *The Religious Traditions of Asia* (Religion, History and Culture). Ed. Joseph M. Kitagawa. Readings from *The Encyclopedia of Religion*, ed. Mircea Eliade. New York: Macmillan.

Hixon, Lex. 1994. *Mother of the Universe: Visions of the Goddess and Tantric Hymns of Enlightenment*. Wheaton, Ill.: Quest Books.

Hochschild, Arlie R. 1983. *The Managed Heart: Commercialization of Human Feeling*. Berkeley and Los Angeles: Univ. of California Press.

Hunt, Scott A., Robert D. Benford, and David A. Snow. 1994. "Identity Fields: Framing Processes and the Social Construction of Movement Identities." In *New Social Movements: From Ideology to Identity*, ed. Enrique Laraña, Hank Johnston, and Joseph R. Gusfield, 185–208. Philadelphia: Temple Univ. Press.

Jacobs, Janet L. 1984. "The Economy of Love in Religious Commitment: The Deconversion of Women from Nontraditional Religious Movements." *Journal for the Scientific Study of Religion* 23 (2): 155–71.

———. 1989. *Divine Disenchantment: Deconverting from the New Religions*. Bloomington: Indiana Univ. Press.

———. 1991. "Gender and Power in New Religious Movements: A Feminist Discourse on the Scientific Study of Religion." *Religion* 4 (Oct.): 345–56.

Jameson, Frederic. 1984a. "Postmodernism, or the Cultural Logic of Late Capitalism." *New Left Review* 146:53–93.

Jeffcutt, Paul. 1993. "From Interpretation to Representation." In *Postmodernism and Organizations*, ed. John Hassard and Martin Parker, 25–48. Newbury Park, Calif.: Sage Publications.

Johnson, George. 1995. *Fire in the Mind: Science, Faith and the Search for Order.* New York: Alfred A. Knopf.

Johnston, Hank, Enrique Laraña, and Joseph R. Gusfield. 1994. "Identities, Grievances, and New Social Movements." In *New Social Movements: From Ideology to Identity*, ed. Hank Johnston, Enrique Laraña, and Joseph R. Gusfield, 3–35. Philadelphia: Temple Univ. Press.

———. 1995. "A Methodology for Frame Analysis: From Discourse to Cognitive Schema." In *Social Movements and Culture*, ed. Hank Johnston and Bert Klandermans, 217–46. Minneapolis: Univ. of Minnesota Press.

Josephs, Gurushabd Singh. 1974. "Education of the Spirit: The Dynamics of Personal Growth in a Spiritual Commune." Ph.D. diss., Univ. of Massachusetts. Ann Arbor: UMI, 74-25, 847.

Judah, J. Stillson. 1974. *Hare Krishna and the Counter Culture.* New York: Wiley.

Juergensmeyer, Mark. 1979. "The Forgotten Tradition: Sikhism in the Study of World Religions." In *Sikh Studies: Comparative Perspectives on a Changing Tradition*, ed. Mark Juergensmeyer and N. Gerald Barrier, 13–23. Working papers from the Berkeley Conference on Sikh Studies. Berkeley, Calif.: Graduate Theological Union.

———. 1993. "Sikhism and Religious Studies." In Hawley and Mann, *Studying the Sikhs*, 9–23.

———. 2000. *Terror in the Mind of God: The Global Rise of Religious Violence.* Berkeley and Los Angeles: Univ. of California Press.

Kakar, Sudhir. 1981. *The Inner World: A Psycho-analytic Study of Childhood and Society in India.* 2d ed. Oxford: Oxford Univ. Press.

———. 1988. "Feminine Identity in India." In *Women in Indian Society*, ed. Rehana Ghadially, 44–68. Newbury Park, Calif.: Sage Publications.

Kanter, Rosabeth Moss. 1972. *Commitment and Community: Communes and Utopias in Sociological Perspective.* Cambridge: Harvard Univ. Press.

Kaufman, Debra Renee. 1991. *Rachel's Daughters: Newly Orthodox Jewish Women.* New Brunswick, N.J.: Rutgers Univ. Press.

Kelly, Aidan A. 1990. "Tantra." In *New Age Encyclopedia*, ed. J. Gordon Melton. Detroit: Gale Research.

Keniston, Kenneth. 1971. "A Second Look at the Uncommitted." *Social Policy* 2 (2): 6–19.

Kent, Stephen A. 1988. "Slogan Chanters to Mantra Chanters: A Mertonian Deviance Analysis of Conversion to Religiously Ideological Organizations in the Early 1970s." *Sociological Analysis* 49 (2): 104–18.

———. 2001. *From Slogans to Mantras: Social Protest and Religious Conversion in the Late Vietnam War Era.* Syracuse, NY: Syracuse Univ. Press.

Khalsa, Gurucharan Singh. 1978. "Morning Sadhana." In KRI, *Kundalini Yoga/Sadhana Guidelines*, 14–29.

Khalsa, Guru Darshan Kaur. 1991. "The Healthy, Happy, Holy Organization Through the Years." *Khalsa Family Visions* 3, no. 1 (Dec.): 10–11.

Khalsa, Gurudharm Singh. 1993. "Disappearing Differences: Sikhs Becoming Americans, and Americans Becoming Sikhs." Paper delivered at Conference on "The Sikh Diaspora," Columbia Univ., Apr. 3.

Khalsa, Gurushabd Singh. 1977. "Recovering the Lost Art of Marriage." *Beads of Truth* 33–34:2. Reprinted as "It is Possible!" in Khalsa and Khalsa, *Man Called the Siri Singh Sahib*, 235–36.

Khalsa, Harbhajan Singh. (See also Yogi Bhajan.) 1980. "Communication: Liberation or Condemnation." Ph.D. diss., Univ. for Humanistic Studies. Pomona, Calif.: KRI Publications.

Khalsa, Inderjit Kaur. 1983. "Family Counseling" course at Khalsa Women's Training Camp, Española, N.M., July 6. Author's personal tape.

Khalsa, Japji Singh. 1991. "Letters from the Editor." *Khalsa Family Visions* 3, no. 1 (Dec.): 2.

Khalsa, Kamlapati Kaur. 1991. "Healing the Dysfunctional 3HO Family #3." *Khalsa Family Visions* 3, no. 1 (Dec.): 12–15.

———. 1993. "The Guru Paradox." Unpublished essay.

———. 1994a. Unpublished and untitled autobiography.

———. 1994b. "In the Magical Soup: Meditations on Twenty Years of Cult Living." Unpublished manuscript.

Khalsa, Kirpal Singh. 1986. "New Religious Movements Turn to Worldly Success." *Journal for the Scientific Study of Religion* 25:233–47.

Khalsa, Livtar Singh. 1979. "In the Image of Guru Gobind Singh." In Khalsa and Khalsa, *Man Called the Siri Singh Sahib*, 344–45.

Khalsa, Manjit Kaur. 1982. "A Psychological Evaluation of Ladies' Camp." Ph.D. diss., Boston Univ., 1982. Ann Arbor: UMI, 8213459.

Khalsa, Premka Kaur. 1971. *Peace Lagoon*. San Rafael, Calif.: Spiritual Community Publications.

———. 1972. "Birth of a Spiritual Nation." In Khalsa and Khalsa, *Man Called the Siri Singh Sahib*, 343.

———. 1973a. "Manifesting the Grace of God." *Beads of Truth*, Winter Solstice Edition, 6–9.

———. 1973b. "Mission Possible." *Beads of Truth*, 25–26.

———. 1979. "Early History." In Khalsa and Khalsa, *Man Called the Siri Singh Sahib*, 18–33.

Khalsa, Premka Kaur, and Sat Kirpal Kaur Khalsa, eds. 1979. *The Man Called the Siri Singh Sahib*. Los Angeles: Sikh Dharma.

Khalsa, Sat Peter Kaur. 1985. Letter to the author. Sept. 25.

Khalsa, Shakti Parwha Kaur. 1973. "High Times." *Beads of Truth* 17 (Mar.): 32–36.

————. 1979. "High Times." *Beads of Truth* 2, nos. 1–2 (Apr.): 45–63.

————. 1996. *Kundalini Yoga: The Flow of Eternal Power.* Los Angeles: Time Capsule Books.

Khalsa, Shakti Parwha Kaur, and Gurubanda Singh Khalsa. 1979. "The Siri Singh Sahib." In Khalsa and Khalsa, *Man Called the Siri Singh Sahib*, 117–23.

————. 1983. Introductory course, Khalsa Women's Training Camp, Española, N.M., July. Author's personal tape.

Khalsa, Shanti Kaur. 1997. "Song of the Khalsa." Available on-line at http://www.yogibhajan.com/articles/sikhconf.html.

Khalsa, Shanti Shanti Kaur. 1979. "From Mantra, to Meditation, to Movement." *Beads of Truth* 2, nos. 1–2 (Apr.): 42–44.

Khalsa, Siri Daya Singh. 1991. "Transcendence and Transformation." *Khalsa Family Visions* 3, no. 1 (Dec.): 6–7.

Khalsa, Soorya Kaur. 1984. Letter to the author. Feb.

Khalsa, Vikram Singh. 1991. "The Khalsa in the New Age." *Khalsa Family Visions* 3, no. 1 (Dec.): 8–9.

Khalsa, Wha Guru Singh. 1979. "A Turning Point in History." In Khalsa and Khalsa, *Man Called the Siri Singh Sahib*, 334–37.

Kishwar, Madhu. 1988. "Nature of Women's Mobilization." *Economic and Political Weekly*, Dec., 24–31.

Kornfield, Jack. 1993. *A Path with Heart: A Guide Through the Perils and Promises of Spiritual Life.* New York: Bantam Books.

Kraybill, Donald B. 1989. *The Riddle of Amish Culture.* Baltimore: Johns Hopkins University Press.

Krishna, Gopi. 1971. *Kundalini: The Evolutionary Energy in Man.* Berkeley, Calif.: Shambhala.

Kundalini Research Institute (KRI). 1976. *Kundalini Yoga Manual.* Pomona, Calif.: KRI Publications.

————. 1978. *Kundalini Yoga/Sadhana Guidelines.* Pomona, Calif.: KRI Publications.

LaBrack, Bruce. 1974. "Neo-Sikhism and East Indian Religious Identification." Midwest Conference on Asian Affairs. Lawrence, Kans., Nov. 1–2.

Laird, Joan. 1989. "Women and Stories: Restorying Women's Self-constructions." In *Women in Families*, ed. Monica McGoldrick, Carol M. Anderson, and Froma Walsh, 427–50. New York: W. W. Norton.

Lasch, Christopher. 1978. *The Culture of Narcissism: American Life in an Age of Diminishing Expectations.* New York: W. W. Norton.

Lawless, Elaine. 1988. *Handmaidens of the Lord: Pentecostal Women Preachers and Traditional Religion.* Philadelphia: Univ. of Pennsylvania Press.

Lewis, James R. 1998. *Cults in America.* Santa Barbara, Calif.: ABC-CLIO.

————. 1999. "Bhajan, Yogi." In *Peculiar Prophets: A Biographical Dictionary of New Religions.* St. Paul, Minn.: Paragon House.

Lewis, R. W. B. 1955. *The American Adam*. Chicago: Univ. of Chicago Press.

Lilliston, Lawrence, and Gary Shepherd. 1999. "New Religious Movements and Mental Health." In *New Religious Movements: Challenge and Response*, ed. Bryan Wilson and Jamie Creswell, 123–39. New York: Routledge.

Lindholm, Charles. 1990. *Charisma*. Cambridge, Mass.: Basil Blackwell.

Lopez, Alan R. 1981. "Reality Construction and Transformation in an Eastern Mystical Cult: A Sociological Study." Ph.D. diss., Univ. of Connecticut, 1980. Ann Arbor: UMI, 8115319.

———. 1992. *Reality Construction in an Eastern Mystical Cult*. New York: Garland.

Lorenzon, David. 1995. "Introduction: The Historical Vicissitudes of Bhakti Religion." In *Bhakti Religion in North India*, ed. David Lorenzon, 1–32. Albany: State Univ. of New York Press.

Lynch, Owen M. 1990. "The Social Construction of Emotion in India." In *Divine Passions*, ed. Owen M. Lynch, 3–28. Berkeley and Los Angeles: Univ. of California Press.

Mailer, Norman. 1968. *Miami and the Siege of Chicago*. New York: World.

Mandelbaum, David G. 1988. *Women's Seclusion and Men's Honor: Sex Roles in North India, Bangladesh, and Pakistan*. Tucson: Univ. of Arizona Press.

Mann, Gurinder Singh. 1993. "Teaching the Sikh Tradition: A Course at Columbia." In Hawley and Mann, *Studying the Sikhs*, 129–59.

———. 2000. "Sikhism in the United States of America." In *The South Asian Religious Diaspora in Britain, Canada, and the United States*, ed. Harold Coward, John R. Hinnells, and Raymond Brady Williams, 259–76. Albany: State Univ. of New York Press.

———. 2001. *The Making of Sikh Scripture*. New Delhi: Oxford University Press.

Maple, Michele Schwartz. 1991. "Commitment and De-Idealization: A Study of Symbol and Process in a Community of American Converts to Sikhism." Univ. of California, Los Angeles. Ann Arbor: UMI, 9221874.

Marcus, George E., and Michael M. J. Fischer, eds. 1999. *Anthropology as Cultural Critique*. Chicago: Univ. of Chicago Press.

Marcuse, Herbert. 1964. *One Dimensional Man*. London: Sphere.

Margolis, Diane Rothbard. 1985. "Redefining the Situation: Negotiations on the Meaning of 'Woman.'" *Social Problems* 32, no. 4 (Apr.): 332–47.

Marriott, McKim. 1976. "Hindu Transactions: Diversity Without Dualism." In *Transaction and Meaning*, ed. Bruce Kapferer, 109–42. Philadelphia: Institute for the Study of Human Issues.

Marx, Leo. 1964. *The Machine in the Garden*. New York: Oxford Univ. Press, 1967.

Matthiessen, F. O. 1941. *American Renaissance*. New York: Oxford Univ. Press.

Mauss, Armand L. 1993. "Research in Social Movements and in New Religious Movements: The Prospects for Convergence." In *Religion and the Social Order: The Handbook of Cults and Sects in America*, ed. David G. Bromley, 3:127–51. Greenwich, Conn.: JAI Press.

———. 1998. "Apostasy and the Management of Spoiled Identity." In *The Politics of Religious Apostasy: The Role of Apostates in the Transformation of Religious Movements*, ed. David G. Bromley, 51–73. Westport, Conn.: Praeger.

McAdam, Doug. 1994. "Culture and Social Movements." In *New Social Movements: From Ideology to Identity*, ed. Enrique Laraña, Hank Johnston, and Joseph R. Gusfield, 36–57. Philadelphia: Temple Univ. Press.

———. 1996. "The Framing Function of Movement Tactics: Strategic Dramaturgy in the American Civil Rights Movement." In *Comparative Perspectives on Social Movements*, ed. Doug McAdam, John D. McCarthy, and Mayer N. Zald, 338–55. New York: Cambridge Univ. Press.

McLean, Malcolm. 1998. *Devoted to the Goddess: The Life and Work of Ramprasad*. Albany: State Univ. of New York Press.

McLeod, W. H. 1976. *The Evolution of the Sikh Community*. Delhi: Oxford Univ. Press.

———, ed. and trans. 1984. *Textual Sources for the Study of Sikhism*. Totowa, N.J.: Barnes and Noble Books.

———. 1987. *The Chaupa Singh Rahit-Nama*. Dunedin, New Zealand: Univ. of Otago Press.

———. 1989a. "The First Forty Years of Sikh Migration: Problems and Some Possible Solutions." In *The Sikh Diaspora: Migration and the Experience Beyond Punjab*, ed. N. Gerald Barrier and Verne A. Dusenbery, 29–48. Delhi: Chanakya Publications.

———. 1989b. *The Sikhs: History, Religion and Society*. New York: Columbia Univ. Press.

———. 1989c. *Who Is a Sikh: The Problem of Sikh Identity*. Oxford: Clarendon Press.

———. 1997. *Sikhism*. New York: Penguin Books.

———. 1999. "Discord in the Sikh Panth." *Journal of the American Oriental Society* 119 (3): 381–89.

McLuhan, Marshall. 1973. *Understanding Media: The Extensions of Man*. Mentor–New American Library.

Melton, J. Gordon. 1986. "Sikh Dharma (Healthy, Happy, Holy Organization)." In *Encyclopedic Handbook of Cults in America*, 182–86. New York: Garland.

———. 1990. "Yoga." In *New Age Encyclopedia*, ed. J. Gordon Melton, 500–510. 1st ed. Detroit: Gale Research.

———. 1991. "When Prophets Die: The Succession Crisis in New Religions." In *When Prophets Die: The Postcharismatic Fate of New Religious Movements*, ed. J. Gordon Melton, 1–12. Albany: State Univ. of New York Press.

———. 1992. "Sikh Dharma." *Encyclopedic Handbook of Cults in America: Revised and Updated Edition*, 280–86. New York: Garland Publishing.

Melucci, Alberto. 1989. *Nomads of the Present: Social Movements and Individual Needs in Contemporary Society*. Philadelphia: Temple Univ. Press.

————. 1994. "A Strange Kind of Newness: What's 'New' in New Social Movements?" In *New Social Movements: From Ideology to Identity,* ed. Hank Johnston, Enrique Laraña, and Joseph R. Gusfield, 101–30. Philadelphia: Temple Univ. Press.

————. 1995. "The Process of Collective Identity." In *Social Movements and Culture,* ed. Hank Johnston and Bert Klandermans, 41–63. Minneapolis: Univ. of Minnesota Press.

Merchant, Carolyn. 1980. *The Death of Nature: Women, Ecology and the Scientific Revolution.* New York: Harper & Row.

Miller, Timothy. 1991. *The Hippies and American Values.* Knoxville: Univ. of Tennessee Press.

Mitter, Sara S. 1991. *Dharma's Daughters: Contemporary Indian Women and Hindu Culture.* New Brunswick, N.J.: Rutgers Univ. Press.

Monterey County (Calif.) Herald. 1992a. "Seaside Man Cleared in Bilking Scheme." Oct. 15, 3c.

————. 1992b. "Man Pleads Guilty in Phone Fraud." Peninsula Edition, Aug. 25, pp. 1c, 2c.

————. 1992c. "Khalsa Gets 3-Year Jail Sentence." Oct. 28.

Monterey County Office of the District Attorney, Press Release: "Arrests in Elderly Canadian Lottery Scam," June 17, 1992.

Mookerjee, Ajitcoomar, and Madhu Khanna. 1977. *The Tantric Way: Art, Science, Ritual.* London: Thames and Hudson.

Musgrove, Frank. 1974. *Ecstasy and Holiness.* Bloomington: Indiana Univ. Press.

Noble, Vicki. 1991. *Shakti-Woman: Feeling Our Fire, Healing Our World.* San Francisco: Harper.

Notes. 3HO Foundation, Women in Training Series. 1976, 1977, 1979, 1981, 1986, 1987, 1990, 1992, 1995. Ed. S. S. Sat Kirpal Kaur Khalsa. Transcriptions of lectures delivered by Yogi Bhajan at the Kahlsa Women's Training Camp, Eugene, Oreg.

Oberoi, Harjot. 1994. *The Construction of Religious Boundaries: Culture, Identity, and Diversity in the Sikh Tradition.* Chicago: Univ. of Chicago Press.

————. 1995. "The Making of a Religious Paradox: Sikh Khalsa, Sahajdhari as Modes of Early Sikh Identity." In *Bhakti Religion in North India: Community Identity and Political Action,* ed. David Lorenzen, 35–66. Albany: State Univ. of New York Press.

Ortner, Sherry B. 1974. "Is Female to Male as Nature Is to Culture?" In *Woman, Culture, and Society,* ed. Michelle Zimbalist Rosaldo, and Louise Lamphere, 67–87. Stanford, Calif.: Stanford Univ. Press.

Palmer, Susan J. 1994. *Moon Sisters, Krishna Mothers, Rajneesh Lovers: Women's Roles in New Religions.* Syracuse, N.Y.: Syracuse Univ. Press.

————. 1997. "Woman as World Savior." In *Millennium, Messiahs and Mayhem: Contemporary Apocalyptic Movements,* ed. Thomas Robbins and Susan J. Palmer, 159–71. New York: Routledge.

Parsons, Arthur. 1974. "Yoga in a Western Setting: Youth in Search of Religious Prophecy." *Soundings LVII* 2:222–35.

Paul, Diana Y. 1979. *Women in Buddhism*. Berkeley, Calif.: Asian Humanities Press.

Pettigrew, Joyce. 1975. *Robber Noblemen: A Study of the Political System of the Sikh Jats*. London: Routledge and Kegan Paul.

Pintchman, Tracy. 1994. *The Rise of the Goddess in the Hindu Tradition*. Albany: State Univ. of New York Press.

Plaskow, Judith, and Carol P. Christ, eds. 1989. *Weaving the Visions: New Patterns in Feminist Spirituality*. San Francisco: Harper.

Pond, Toni Kaur. 1972. "Sikh Dharma." *Beads of Truth* (16): 7.

Puttick, Elizabeth. 1997. *Women in New Religions: In Search of Community, Sexuality and Spiritual Power*. New York: St. Martin's Press.

———. 1999. "Women in New Religious Movements." In *New Religious Movements: Challenge and Response*, ed. Bryan Wilson and Jamie Cresswell, 143–62. New York: Routledge.

Rama, Swami. 1979. "The Awakening of Kundalini." In *Kundalini, Evolution and Enlightenment*, ed. John White, 27–47. New York: Anchor.

Ray, Reginald A. 1989. "Accomplished Women in Tantric Buddhism of Medieval India and Tibet." In *Unspoken Worlds: Women's Religious Lives*, ed. Nancy Auer Falk and Rita M. Gross, 191–200. Belmont, Calif.: Wadsworth.

Richardson, E. Allen. 1985. *East Comes West: Asian Religions and Cultures in North America*. New York: Pilgrim Press.

Richardson, James T. 1986. "Structural, Group and Personality Factors in Proselytization of Jews to New Religions: We Have Met the Enemy and It Is Us." *Journal for the Scientific Study of Religion*, Annual Meeting.

Richardson, James T., and Brock K. Kilbourne. 1985. "Social Experimentation: Self-Process or Social Role." *International Journal of Social Psychiatry* 31 (1): 13–22.

Richardson, James T., Mary White Stewart, and Robert B. Simmonds. 1979. *Organized Miracles: A Study of a Contemporary, Youth Communal, Fundamentalist Organization*. New Brunswick, N.J.: Transaction.

Richardson, Laurel. 1993. "Narrative and Sociology." In *Representation in Ethnography*, ed. John Van Maanen, 198–221. Thousand Oaks, Calif.: Sage.

Riesman, David. [1950] 1973. *The Lonely Crowd*. New Haven, Conn.: Yale Univ. Press.

Robbins, Richard C. 1973. "Identity, Culture and Behavior." In *Handbook of Social and Cultural Anthropology*, ed. John Honigman, 1199–1222. Chicago: Rand McNally.

Robbins, Thomas, and Dick Anthony. 1981. "Getting Straight with Meher Baba." In *In Gods We Trust*, ed. Thomas Robbins and Dick Anthony, 191–213. New Brunswick, N.J.: Transaction.

Robbins, Thomas, Dick Anthony, and Thomas Curtis. 1975. "Youth Culture Religious Movements: Evaluating the Integrative Hypothesis." *Sociological Quarterly* 16 (1): 48–64.

Robbins, Thomas, Dick Anthony, and James Richardson. 1978. "Theory and Research on Today's 'New Religions'." *Sociological Analysis* 39 (2): 95–122.

Robertson, Roland, and Joann Chirico. 1985. "Humanity, Globalization, and Worldwide Religious Resurgence: A Theoretical Exploration." *Sociological Analysis* 46:219–42.

Rochford, E. Burke, Jr. 1982. "Recruitment Strategies, Ideology, and Organization in the Hare Krishna Movement." *Social Problems* 29 (4): 399–410.

———. 1985. *Hare Krishna in America.* New Brunswick, N.J.: Rutgers Univ. Press.

Roland, Alan. 1984. "The Self in India and America: Toward a Psychoanalysis of Social and Cultural Contexts." In *Designs of Selfhood,* ed. Vytautas Kavolis, 170–91. Cranbury, N.J.: Associated Univ. Press.

Roof, Wade Clark. 1993. *A Generation of Seekers: The Spiritual Journeys of the Baby Boom Generation.* San Francisco: Harper.

Roof, Wade Clark, and William McKinney. 1987. *American Mainline Religion: Its Changing Shape and Future.* New Brunswick, N.J.: Rutgers Univ. Press.

Rose, Susan D. 1987. "Women Warriors: The Negotiation of Gender in a Charismatic Community." *Sociological Analysis* 48 (3): 245–58.

Roszak, Theodore. 1969. *The Making of a Counter Culture.* Garden City, N.Y.: Anchor-Doubleday.

———. 1972. *Where the Wasteland Ends.* New York: Doubleday.

Said, Edward. 1978. *Orientalism.* New York: Pantheon.

Sartre, Jean-Paul. 1976. *Critique of Dialectical Reason.* Translated by Alan Sheridan-Smith. Atlantic Highlands, N.J.: Humanities Press.

———. [1956] 1994. *Being and Nothingness.* Translated by Hazel E. Barnes. New York: Gramercy Books/Random House.

Sashkin, Marshall, and William R. Lassey. 1983. "Theories of Leadership: A Review of Useful Research." In *Leadership and Social Change,* ed. William R. Lassey and Marshall Sashkin, 91–106. San Diego: Univ. Associates.

Schutz, Alfred, and Thomas Luckmann. 1973. *The Structures of the Life-World.* Translated by Richard M. Zaner and H. Tristram Engelhardt Jr. Evanston, Ill.: Northwestern Univ. Press.

Sered, Susan Starr. 1994. *Priestess, Mother, Sacred Sister: Religions Dominated by Women.* New York: Oxford Univ. Press.

Shanker, Rajkumari. 1994. "Women in Sikhism." In *Religion and Women,* ed. Arvind Sharma, 183–210. Albany: State Univ. of New York Press.

Shapiro, Judith. 1995. "Gender Equity and Gender Folklore." *Barnard Magazine,* Fall 1995. New York.

Shiva, Vandana. 1988. *Staying Alive: Women, Ecology and Survival in India.* New Delhi: Kali for Women.

Shupe, Anson. 1998. "The Dynamics of Clergy Malfeasance." In *Wolves Within the Fold: Religious Leadership and Abuses of Power,* ed. Anson Shupe, 1–12. New Brunswick, N.J.: Rutgers Univ. Press.

Sikh Missionary Center. 1990. *Sikh Religion.* Detroit: Sikh Missionary Center.

Singh, Fauja. 1979. "The Weaver." In Khalsa and Khalsa, *Man Called the Siri Singh Sahib,* 408–9.

Singh, Harbans. 1994. *The Heritage of the Sikhs*. New Delhi: Manohar Publishers.

Singh, Kushwant. 1963. *A History of the Sikhs*, vol. 1. Princeton, N.J.: Princeton Univ. Press.

———. 1989. "The Sikhs." In *The Religious Traditions of Asia*, ed. Joseph M. Kitagawa, 111–18. New York: Macmillan.

———. 1999. "The Sikhs of the Panjab." In *The Arts of the Sikh Kingdoms*, ed. Susan Stronge, 13–31. London: Victoria and Albert Museum Publications.

Singh, Nikky-Guninder Kaur. 1993. *The Feminine Principle in the Sikh Vision of the Transcendent*. Cambridge: Cambridge Univ. Press.

Singh, Shamser. 1979. "The Fruits of Inner Searching." In Khalsa and Khalsa, *Man Called the Siri Singh Sahib*, 44–46.

Singh, Sulakan. 1981. "The Udasis in the Early Nineteenth Century." *Journal of Regional History* 2:35–42. Guru Nanak Dev Univ., Amritsar.

———. 1983. "Udasi Beliefs and Practices." *Journal of Regional History* 4:73–98. Guru Nanak Dev Univ., Amritsar.

Singh, Trilochan. 1977. *Sikhism and Tantric Yoga*. Model Town, Ludhiana, India: privately printed.

Slotkin, Philip. 1973. *Regeneration Through Violence*. Middletown, Conn.: Wesleyan Press.

Smith, Henry Nash. 1950. *Virgin Land: The American West as Symbol and Myth*. New York: Vintage–Random House.

Smith, M. Brewster. 1985. "The Metaphorical Basis of Selfhood." In *Culture and Self: Asian and Western Perspectives*, ed. Anthony J. Marsella, George De Vos, and Francis L. K. Hsu, 57–88. New York: Tavistock.

Smith-Rosenberg, Caroll. 1975. "The Female World of Love and Ritual." *Signs: Journal of Women in Culture and Society*, Autumn, 1–29.

———. 1985. *Disorderly Conduct: Visions of Gender in Victorian America*. New York: A. A. Knopf.

Snow, David. 1987. "Organization, Ideology, and Mobilization: The Case of Nichiren Shoshu of America." In *The Future of New Religions*, ed. David G. Bromley and Phillip E. Hammond, 153–72.

Snow, David A., and Robert D. Benford. 1992. "Master Frames and Cycles of Protest." In *Frontiers in Social Movement Theory*, ed. Aldon D. Morris and Carol McClurg Mueller, 133–55. New Haven, Conn.: Yale Univ. Press.

Snow, David, and Richard Machelek. 1982. "On the Presumed Fragility of Unconventional Beliefs." *Journal for the Scientific Study of Religion* 21: 15–25.

Snow, David, E. Burke Rochford Jr., Steven K. Worden, and Robert D. Benford. 1986. "Frame Alignment Processes, Micromobilization and Movement Participation." *American Sociological Review* 51:456–81.

Spangler, David, and William Irwin Thompson. 1991. *Reimagination of the World: A Critique of the New Age, Science, and Popular Culture*. Santa Fe, N.M.: Bear & Company.

Stacey, Judith. 1991. *Brave New Families*. New York: Basic Books.

Stein, Maurice. 1960. *The Eclipse of Community.* New York: Harper Torchbooks, 1964.

Swidler, Ann. 1995. "Cultural Power and Social Movements." In *Social Movements and Culture,* ed. Hank Johnston and Bert Klandermans, 25–40. Minneapolis: Univ. of Minnesota Press.

Tatla, Darshan Singh. 1991. *Sikhs in North America: An Annotated Bibliography.* Westport, Conn.: Greenwood Press. Bibliographies and Indexes in Sociology 19.

Tipton, Steven M. 1982. *Getting Saved from the Sixties: Moral Meaning in Conversion and Cultural Change.* Berkeley and Los Angeles: Univ. of California, 1984.

Tobey, Alan. 1976. "The Summer Solstice of the Healthy-Happy-Holy Organization." In *The New Religious Consciousness,* ed. Charles Y. Glock and Robert N. Bellah, 5–30. Berkeley and Los Angeles: Univ. of California Press. Reprinted in abbreviated form as "3HO's Summer Solstice" in *Beads of Truth* 2 (1, 2): 10–23, 1979.

Toor, Djohariah. 1987. *The Road by the River: A Healing Journey for Women.* San Francisco: Harper & Row.

Toulmin, Stephen. 1982. *The Return to Cosmology: Post Modern Science and the Theology of Nature.* Berkeley and Los Angeles: Univ. of California Press.

Tuana, Nancy, ed. 1989. *Feminism and Science.* Bloomington: Indiana Univ. Press.

Turner, Victor W. 1967. *The Forest of Symbols.* Ithaca, N.Y.: Cornell Univ. Press.

———. 1974. *Dramas, Fields and Metaphors: Symbolic Action in Human Society.* Ithaca, N.Y.: Cornell Univ. Press.

Van Maanen, John. 1995. "An End to Innocence: The Ethnography." In *Representation and Ethnography,* ed. John Van Maanen, 1–35. Thousand Oaks, Calif.: Sage Publications.

Varenne, Jean. 1976. *Yoga and the Hindu Tradition.* Chicago: Univ. of Chicago Press.

Wagner, John, ed. 1982. *Sex Roles in Contemporary American Communes.* Bloomington: Indiana Univ. Press.

Wallis, Roy. 1982. "The Social Construction of Charisma." *Social Compass* 29 (1): 25–39.

———. 1984. *The Elementary Forms of the New Religious Life.* London: Routledge & Kegan Paul.

Weigert, Andrew J. 1991. *Mixed Emotions: Certain Steps Toward Understanding Ambivalence.* Albany: State Univ. of New York Press.

Welter, Barbara. 1966. "The Cult of True Womanhood." *American Quarterly* 18 (Summer): 151–74.

Wessinger, Catherine. 1993a. "Going Beyond and Retaining Charisma: Women's Leadership in Marginal Religions." In *Women's Leadership in Marginal Religions: Explorations Outside the Mainstream,* ed. Catherine Wessinger, 1–19. Urbana: Univ. of Illinois Press.

———. 1993b. "Woman Guru, Woman Roshi: The Legitimation of Female Religious Leadership in Hindu and Buddhist Groups in America." In *Women's Leadership in Marginal Religions,* edited Catherine Wessinger, 125–46. Urbana: Univ. of Illinois Press.

———. 1997. "Millennialism With and Without the Mayhem." In *Millennium, Messiahs, and Mayhem: Contemporary Apocalyptic Movements*, ed. Thomas Robbins and Susan J. Palmer, 47–59. New York: Routledge.

West, Candace, and Don H. Zimmerman. 1987. "Doing Gender." *Gender and Society* 1, no. 2 (June): 125–51.

Westby, David L. 1976. *The Clouded Vision*. Cranbury, N.J.: Associated Univ. Press.

Wheatley, Margaret J. 1992. *Leadership and the New Science*. San Francisco: Berrett-Koehler Publishers.

White, John, ed. 1979. *Kundalini, Evolution and Enlightenment*. New York: Anchor Books.

Williams, Raymond Brady. 2000. Introduction to *The South Asian Religious Diaspora in Britain, Canada, and the United States*, ed. Harold Coward, John R. Hinnells, and Raymond Brady Williams, pt. 3, pp. 213–17. Albany: State Univ. of New York Press.

Winter, Miriam Therese, Adair Lummis, and Allison Stokes. 1994. *Defecting in Place: Women Claiming Responsibility for Their Own Spiritual Lives*. New York: Simon & Schuster.

Woodman, Marion. 1992. *Leaving My Father's House: A Journey to Conscious Femininity*. Boston: Shambhala.

Woodroffe, Sir John. 1929. *Shakti and Shakta*. 3d ed. London: Luzac.

World Sikh News. 1992. "Yogi's crooked crew held in bilking scam." Stockton, Calif. Vol. 8, no. 30, Aug. 21.

Wright, Stuart A. 1987. *Leaving Cults: The Dynamics of Defection*. Washington, D.C.: Society for the Scientific Study of Religion.

Wuthnow, Robert. 1986. "Religious Movements and Counter-Movements in North America." In *New Religious Movements and Rapid Social Change*, ed. James A. Beckford, 1–28. United Nations Educational Scientific and Cultural Organization. New York: Sage Publications/Unesco.

Yinger, J. Milton. 1982. *Countercultures*. New York: Free Press.

"Yoga and the Spiritual Woman." 1983. Course and materials offered at Khalsa Women's Training Camp, July. Author's notes.

Yogananda, Paramahansa. 1946. *Autobiography of a Yogi*. Los Angeles: Self-Realization Fellowship, 1983.

Young, Katherine K. 1994a. Introduction to *Today's Woman in World Religions*, ed. Arvind Sharma, 1–37. Albany: State Univ. of New York Press.

———. 1994b. "Women in Hinduism." In *Today's Woman in World Religions*, ed. Arvind Sharma, 77–135. Albany: State Univ. of New York Press.

Zablocki, Benjamin. 1980. *Alienation and Charisma: A Study of Contemporary American Communes*. New York: Free Press.

Zald, Mayer N., and John D. McCarthy, eds. 1979. *The Dynamics of Social Movements*. Cambridge, England: Winthrop.

Zimmer, Heinrich Robert. 1946. *Myths and Symbols in Indian Art and Civilization*. New York: Pantheon Books.

Index

Bednarowski, Mary Farrell, 296, 334, 337
Benefits of membership in 3HO/Sikh
    Dharma, 10–18, 168, 226–27, 246,
    329–31, 335–37
Bernard, Jessie, 325–26
Bhajan, Yogi: on abuse of women, 129–32;
    addresses to KWTC, xvii–xviii, 7,
    120–29; and adoption of white clothing,
    171–72; and appeal of Tantric yoga to
    counterculture youths, 25; and arranged
    marriages, 184, 185–87, 336; and assess-
    ment of needs of followers, 232; attitude
    toward ex-members, 127–28; biography,
    344–45; as charismatic leader, 231–39,
    331–32; and child-rearing, 193–94; and
    commitment as key to a spiritual life,
    87–88; "Communication, Liberation or
    Condemnation," 67, 122; on competi-
    tion between men and women, 107,
    120, 124; contradictions in portrayal of
    women, 129–36; on creative powers of
    women, 105–6, 128; criticism of within
    the Sikh community, 79–80; criticisms
    of women, 121, 126, 128, 129; on dan-
    gers of leaving 3HO, 87; dependence
    on, 273; and development of a sense of
    security, 119–20; on dress, 109; on drug
    use, 65; and early development of 3HO/
    Sikh Dharma, xiv, xv; and effects of
    behaviors on health, 121, 191; and
    effects of diet on the body, 81–82;
    emphasis on women's dignity, 72; and
    family life, 11, 105–6; and feminine
    modesty, 65; and feminism, 98, 108,
    110, 290; and frame alignment strate-
    gies, 61–66; and future of 3HO, 337,
    338, 339–40; and gender roles, 11–12,
    98, 102–3, 104–5, 108, 119, 127; and
    goddess imagery, 128; and graceful
    womanhood, 102–3, 108, 120–21, 126,
    129, 177, 307; and Guru Ram Das, 133;
    and incorporation of Hindu practices,
    79; and instructions for daily living,
    81–82; and introduction of Sikhism to
    his students, 3, 74–84; and KWTC, xvi;
    and Kundalini yoga, 1–2, 73, 232–33;
    lawsuits against, 127, 215–16; leadership
    role in North American Sikhism, 73, 75,
    77; and leadership structure of 3HO,
    335, 336; and men's psyche 102–3,
    124–25, 130; and merger of yoga and
    Sikhism, 44, 53, 73, 77–78, 79; and
    minimization of the suffering of women,
    131; on modesty in women, 102; and
    need for communication to serve a posi-
    tive purpose, 67, 68–69, 79; and need

for perseverance, 115–16; need for stu-
    dents to elevate and strengthen them-
    selves, 63; and ordination of Sikh
    ministers, 74, 75; personal involvement
    in member's lives, 213, 231–32, 246,
    248–49, 250, 257, 260, 265–66, 273,
    285, 328; personality, xvii, 78, 113,
    115–16, 238–39, 259; and physical
    problems of children as fault of the
    mother, 191; and primacy of spirituality
    in women, 69; and privately expressed
    attitude toward women, 216; and pro-
    jection of the ideal self, 121–22; and
    quantification of gender differences,
    106, 133; and recruitment of 3HO
    members, 155, 165–66; and religious
    tolerance, 279–80; and responsibilities
    of leadership, 133; and role of discipline
    in achieving new identities, 229; role of
    lectures in identity formation, 220–21;
    service to, 120–21, 183; and *shakti*, 2,
    105–6, 129; and *shaktipod*, 87; and Sikh
    Dharma vows, 75–76; and sources of
    women's problems, 106, 107–8, 110,
    129; and Tantric yoga, 2; teaching style,
    133–34; teachings on negativity,
    234–35; teachings regarding marriage,
    65–66, 72, 97–98, 100–101, 102–3,
    124–25, 126–27, 131, 180–81, 187, 188;
    and transition to the New Age, 63–64,
    76–77, 123–24; trips to India, 73–74;
    use of humor, 78–79, 238; use of
    mortification, 219–20, 239, 249, 253,
    257, 273; and use of teachings to bind
    women to 3HO/Sikh Dharma, 134–35;
    and white Tantric yoga, 44–45, 51–52;
    and women as responsible for their
    troubles, 128, 129–31; and women as
    the bulwark of 3HO, 101; and women's
    lives outside of the home, 128–29;
    women's responses to the teachings of,
    135, 325; and women's responsibility for
    men's actions, 124–25, 126, 129–30; and
    women's self-esteem, 99; women's sense
    that he addresses their issues, xviii,
    98–99, 150, 160; yoga classes taught by,
    xvii, 45; and *Yoga Sutras*, 47
Bhakti religion, 27–28
Bhindranwale, Sant Jarnail, 25–26, 43–44
Bibiji. *See* Kaur, Inderjit
Bird, Frederick, 239, 327–28, 331–32
Breath-of-fire (breathing technique), xiii
Bridal imagery in the Guru Granth Sahib,
    32, 292, 295
Bromley, David G., 215, 226, 245, 252, 254,
    260

Brooks, Douglas Renfrew, 48, 50–51
Bruner, Jerome, 12, 16–17
Buddhism, 274–75, 276, 302, 303, 304, 315, 316
Businesses, 3HO: 144, 162, 196, 208–12, 337, 338, 340; and development of collective identity, 144–45; opportunities for women in, 144, 196, 276, 305, 308–9; questionable practices, 211–12, 277–78

C. A. Services Corporation, 211
Canada, Sikhism in, 5, 339, 341–42
Career choices: 3HO businesses, 144, 162, 196, 208–12, 305; non-3HO businesses, 197–98, 210; preparation for, 305
Caste system, 28, 30, 81, 83, 339–40
Central Gurdwara Management Committee, 41
Central Sikh League, 41
Chakras, 49, 50, 51, 306
Chants, xviii, 1, 13
Charismatic leaders: appeal of, 217; efforts to buttress authority, 231–32, 331–32; negative side of, 233, 331–32; role of in 3HO growth, 217, 331–32
Chaupa Singh Rahitnama, 36–37
Chhibbar, Chaupa Singh, 36
Chief Khalsa Diwan, 41
Childbirth, 190
Child rearing: beliefs about, 125, 189–94; children placed with other 3HO families, 222, 248–49, 265–66; children sent to school in India, 192–94, 222, 339; disagreements with leadership on, 222, 248–49, 265–66, 277; and KWTC, 193–94
Chunnis, 13
Code of Manu, 100–101
Cognitive dissonance, 256–57
Common Boundary, 257
Communities, vi
Community life as a reason for joining 3HO, 153–54, 160, 273
Compromise and balance, emphasis on in Indian life, 290
Conger, Jay A., 232, 233
Congress Party, 43
Counterculture: 3HO efforts to counteract, 65–66; attitude toward science, 71; as background of 3HO members, 6, 52–53, 56, 57, 58, 59, 60, 61, 62, 71–72, 85, 123–24, 146–47, 149, 153–54, 155, 164, 167, 170, 232, 295–96, 319, 329, 337; and desire for social change, 64, 65, 70, 85; distrust of

marriage, 65–66, 72; dress, 173; and individualism, 72, 181; and morality, 66, 67, 70; and personal evolution, 170, 214; and religion, 71, 76–77; version of womanhood, 65, 72, 177, 179
Creativity: 3HO and the channeling of, 15; as special power of women, 123–24; Yogi Bhajan's teachings regarding, 105–6, 123
Criminal activities, 211–12

"Dances of Universal Peace," 298
Dasam Granth, 31, 37, 38
Davidman, Lynn, 9
Decision making, intuitive modes of valued by 3HO, 70
Denzin, Norman K., 320
Dependency as a potential problem in 3HO, 233, 315
Desai, Yogi Amrit, 49
Devi, 36, 37–39
Dharmashastras, 100–101
Diet: and 3HO/Sikh Dharma, 4, 13; mono-diets, 81–82, 219; relation of specific foods to particular bodily needs, 81–82, 219; vegetarianism, 4, 76, 79, 81
Disaffiliation: and affiliation with subgroups within 3HO/Sikh Dharma, 254, 255, 260, 270, 278; conditions giving rise to, 244–45, 252, 254–58, 259–61, 267, 273, 277–78, 280–81; degrees of, 254, 262; and efforts to reform 3HO before leaving, 254, 258–61, 278; and identities formed outside 3HO/Sikh Dharma, 254–58, 261; identity issues, 242–43, 247, 259–61, 270–71; and intense seekers, 267–76; and marginalization of members, 256, 260–61, 262, 270, 278; and meditation, 274; organizational view of, 225; and problems with leaders, 253–55, 257, 273, 278, 281; process of, 254, 261; reintegration after, 261–66; responses of members to signs of disaffection; and spouses, 258, 261, 271, 281–82
Divorce, 124, 131, 160, 189, 225, 336
Dress: adoption of white clothing by 3HO members, 3, 81, 109, 171; *bana*, 122, 171–73, 295; and bridal imagery, 295; and counterculture, 173; as form of identity with group, 13, 82, 171–73; and "graceful" appearance, 80, 122, 172; at KWTC, xvii–xviii, 172, 295; Punjabi, 3; and spirituality, 172–73; as a way of projecting the ideal self, 122

Drugs: hallucinatory, 147, 158–59; yoga and meditation as replacement for, 71–72

Durga, 37, 38, 292–93, 295

Dusenbery, Verne A., 64, 71, 79–80, 81, 82–83, 98, 228–29

East-West Cultural Center, Los Angeles, California, 1, 105, 109

Educational backgrounds of 3HO members, 146

Ego: boundaries of, 117, 220, 324, 328; breaking down, 250–51; and Indian personality, 324–25; liberation from, 46, 88; structure of, female, 14

Egotism, and disciplines of Sikhism, 73

Ellis, Albert, 211–12

Ellwood, Robert S., Jr., 322

Embodied spirituality, 13–14, 25, 32, 49, 51, 172, 275, 294, 296, 300, 306–7

Emotionality, disapproval of in 3HO, 67–68

Energy imagery, 64–65

Energy, masculine, 124

Erndl, Kathleen M., 39

Española, New Mexico, xvi, 95, 209–10

Ethical living as a principle of Sikhism, 30

Ethics, situational approach to, 66–69, 70

Ethnography, xix–xx, 320

Evangelical Christians and gender roles, 9

Ex-members: attitude of Yogi Bhajan toward, 127–28; attitude toward leadership of 3HO/Sikh Dharma, 215, 270, 277–78; disillusionment with 3HO, 216–17, 242, 265–66, 277–79; and feelings of betrayal, 252–54, 260–61, 270, 313; former ashram leaders, 209–10, 281–82; lawsuits filed by, 215–16; narratives, 7–8, 9; network of, 301; and rigidity of 3HO organization, 20; role in considerations of disaffected members, 257–58, 262, 270, 278; spirituality of, 264, 271–72, 274–76, 296–304, 330

Family backgrounds of 3HO members, 145–47, 153, 156–58, 160–61, 170

Family life: 3HO community as support for, 12; 3HO placing strains on, 281, 282; and new religious movements, 9–10, 11; role of women in, 106–7, 124, 126–27, 180–81, 187, 197, 241–42, 248, 329

Fascinating Womanhood, 241

Fathers, role of, 125

Feldman, Christina, 303

Feminine ego structure, 3HO practices as a tool for managing and modifying, 14

Feminine modesty, Yogi Bhajan insistence on, 65

Feminine principle: and 3HO women, 294–96, 313–14, 315–16, 324–25, 326–27, 335; and Buddhism, 302–3, 304, 316; and Eastern religions, 289–90; and ex-members, 296, 297–304, 313–14; and Hinduism, 290; perceived denial of in 3HO, 275; and primacy of relationships, 295–96; and Sanatan Sikhism, 38; and Sikhism, 37–39, 291–94, 295–96, 314

Feminine Principle in the Sikh Vision of the Transcendent, The, by Nikki-Guninder Kaur Singh, 291

Feminism: Indian women's critiques of, 290–91; Yogi Bhajan's rejection of, 98, 108, 110, 290

Feminist literature: attitude toward science, 70–71; and dualistic modes of thought, 57–58

Feminist spirituality, 300, 324–25

Feminists: and moral superiority of women, 109–10; and religious organizations, 13; view of womanhood, 177, 178–79

Fenton, John Y., 81

"Five K's," the, 3, 13, 171

Frame alignment: and adoption of new customs, 82, 84; defined, 61; and early history of 3HO, 61–66; and extension of Sikh frameworks, 73; and science, 71; and social and cultural tensions, 64; technology for, 64–65

Frame amplification, 66

Frame bridging, 61

Frame transformation, 65

Framing (and reframing), 61, 64, 65, 73, 75, 127. *See also* frame alignment, frame amplification, frame bridging, motivational framing

Friedman, Lenore, 303

Gandhi, Indira, 5, 26, 42–43, 212

Gandhi, Mahatma, 41

Gardner, Hugh, 75, 76, 88, 97, 233

Gender differences: and grace, 178–79; relief found in acceptance of, 178–79; women's distrust of 3HO attitudes toward, 181; Yogi Bhajan's quantification of, 106; Yogi Bhajan's teachings regarding, 12, 106, 119–20, 135–36

Gender roles: in 3HO ashrams, 97; and 3HO vision of womanhood, 11–12, 306, 307–8, 311–12, 326–27; and binding of women to their leader, 134–35; and the conflict between the individual and society, 15; and the counterculture, 59; as expressions of biological differences, 98; and followers of Bhagwan Shree

Rajneesh, 10; and Hinduism, 100–102, 103–4; and new religious movements, 9–10, 150–51; and Punjabi Sikhism, 4, 6; rewards related to, 226–27; and Sikhism, 32–33

Gill, Pritam Singh, 30

Gitlin, Todd, 57

Gobind Singh, Guru, 30, 31, 32, 33–34, 35, 36, 37, 77, 292–93

God: *bani* as the voice of, 34; consciousness of brought to everyday living, 66, 85–86, 174–76; group consciousness of, 76, 175; need to submit to the inner presence of, 29, 174, 175–76; oneness with as goal of meditation, 1, 3, 29, 175; partial embodiment of in the person of the Guru, 29; *Sadhana* as a means of attaining unity with, 175; self as a channel for, 174–77; Sikh vision of, 3–4, 29; union with as central image in 3HO, 174, 177, 269; yoga as a means to achieve union with, 46–47, 49, 76

Goddess themes: and 3HO gender ideology, 100, 256; appeal to American women, 322; and early civilizations, 99–100; and ex-members, 271–72, 297–304, 316; and feminine spirituality, 300, 314; and Hinduism, 36–39, 99–100, 299–300, 323; and the *gur-bilas*, 36–37; and the Khalsa, 36–37; and Sikhism, 36–39, 323, 334; and Tantra, 47, 48

Golden Temple (India), 3, 14, 25–26, 73, 157, 311, 323

Golden Temple (restaurant, Washington, D.C.), 144, 162, 196, 210

Goldman, Marion S., 10, 145–46

Goldstein, Joseph, 302

Grace of God Movement, 104, 105, 108, 109–10, 128, 306, 309

Graceful womanhood: 3HO women's views of, 103, 135–36, 177–81, 306, 307, 309, 316, 327, 333; description of, 180; and dress, 80, 306; as expression of union with God, 178; as a source of self-esteem, 306, 307, 309, 323, 327; as a tool in relationships, 180–81; Yogi Bhajan's idea of, 65–66, 102–3, 120–21, 306, 316

Granthis, 4

Great Britain, and Punjabi Sikhism, 40, 41, 339–40

Grewal, J. S., 33, 35, 43

Guilt, 325–29, 335

Gurmukhi, 42, 74, 84

Guru, doctrine of the eternal, 34

Guru Granth Sahib, 3, 4, 31, 32–33, 74, 75, 157, 292, 294

Guru Panth, 34

"Guru Paradox, The," by Prabhupati, 264–65

Guru Ram Das Ashram, Los Angeles, California, 74

Gurus: and elevation of the feminine, 31–32; need for guidance of in practicing Tantric, 50–51, 52; partial embodiment of God in, 29; teachings of the, 30–32; worship of living gurus, 34, 40

Hair, 76

Hallucinatory drugs, instrumental in decision to join 3HO, 147

Hargobind, Guru, 32, 36

Health: as 3HO goal, 13; problems as a consequence of bad behavior, 121, 249, 257, 260

Healthy Happy Holy Organization: and achievement of oneness with God, 49; and adoption of Sikh Dharma, 74–77, 81–82; appeal to American women, 6–7; and balancing the many aspects of women's personalities, 14; and benefits attached to membership, 11–18, 322–30; causes of disaffiliation with, 244–45, 246, 252–58, 270, 273, 277–78; and commitment to a spiritual life, 87–88; costs of membership in, 332–34; counseling offered to women, 137; courses offered by, xv, xvi; dangers of leaving, 87, 236, 260–61; described as a dysfunctional family, 242, 258, 271; and development of group consciousness, 76; disillusionment with leadership of, 252, 273, 277–78; educational backgrounds of members, 146; effects of members' maturation on Yogi Bhajan's teachings, 125–29; efforts to reform, 183, 209–10, 254, 258–61, 314, 332; as an emergent form of community, 321; emphasis on emotional control, 67–68; family backgrounds of members, 145–47; and formation of collective identity, 55–56, 63, 73, 76, 81–82, 127–28; and gender differences, 83, 119; gender socialization of women members, 59; goals, vi, 45, 119; growth of individuals in, 329–30; history of, xiv–xv, 25; and increased emphasis on material wealth in the 1970s, 207–8; and individual change as the route to a better world, 91–92, 123–24, 126, 169, 198, 272, 308, 309; initiations, 33; and "keeping up," 88, 244, 335; and kundalini energy, 49; and lawsuit against Yogi Bhajan, 128;

Healthy Happy Holy (cont.)
leadership of, 209–10, 213–14, 215–17, 226, 245, 337, 338; need for members to align their personal lives with 3HO priorities, 63; and need for self-awareness, 177; and need to fight injustice, 69–70; and organizational function of imagery related to merging auras, 52; organizational history, 88–90; organizational rigidity, 331; outlook for the future, 337–43; philosophical bases of the organization, 25; and relationship between self and society, 169–70; and relationship between spirituality and the senses, 13–14; and religious identity, 82–83; rewards of membership in, 226–27, 234, 246, 325–26, 331; role in mediating cultural tensions, 59, 61, 68; role in mediating gendered polarities, 59; role in mediating women's internalized ambivalences, 59; role in ushering in the New Age, 62–64, 76–77; and *sadhana*, 1; seen as North America's only real hope for a spiritual rebirth, 123–24; and self-denial for the community, 72; situational approach to ethics, 66–69; strains on community as members pursued non-3HO careers and education, 210–11; and techniques for building self-esteem, 168–69; "the technology," 64–65; and treatment of ex-members, 87, 236, 247, 260–61, 281–82, 315, 333, 340–41; turnover, 330–31; version of kundalini yoga, 50; view of equality, 82–83; view of reality as transcending all dualism, 16; women's role in the organization, 333–36; Yogi Bhajan's teachings as effort to bind women to the organization, 134–35. *See also* Sikh Dharma
Hershman, Paul, 39
Hewitt, John P., 58, 86, 321–22
Hexham, Irving, 337–38
Hindu Tantric Saktism, 2
Hinduism: and the caste system, 100–101; and the feminine principle, 290, 323; and gender roles, 100–2, 103–4; and goddess themes, 48, 99–100; and identity issues, 324; as a source for 3HO/Sikh Dharma practices, 79, 100, 101, 323; as a source of Sikh beliefs and practices, 13, 27, 28, 29, 36, 40, 101
Hippies and American Values, The, by Timothy Miller, 71–72
Hixon, Lex, 297–98, 299–300
Homeopathy, 154–55, 161–62, 197

Hopcke, Robert H., 284
Human Potential movement, 91
Humor: and *Beads of Truth*, 78–79; and Yogi Bhajan, 79

Identity: and affiliation with 3HO, 151; and 3HO vision of oneness and unity, 16; Indian approaches to, 324; and new religious movements, 18, 322–23; social identity, 86, 88–89; and willingness to experiment, 170–71, 172, 220, 225, 325, 330. *See also* American culture, ego, identity issues
Identity, collective: and 3HO businesses, 144; and adoption of group customs, 82, 84; and adoption of symbols of, 171–72; alignment with individual goals and personalities, 218, 220–21; and communal living, 217–18; and costs to the individual, 332; and gender roles, 135–36; and imagination, 332; linkage of personal identities to the organization, 169, 228, 314, 328; reinforcement of, 127, 228–31
Identity confirmation, 221–23
Identity diffusion and dissolution, 218–20, 230–31
Identity formation: role of images and metaphors in, 84–91; Yogi Bhajan's role in, 220–21, 248, 250
Identity issues: 3HO and new identities, 168–69, 247–48; ambivalence underlying construction of self, 58, 59; and arranged marriages, 248–49; and breaking down of the ego, 250, 251; conflict between career and familial norms, 15; and conflict between family ties and 3HO, 281; conflict between identities inside and outside 3HO, 254–55, 256–58, 260, 332–33, 340–41; conflict between intellect and feeling, 267–69, 271; conflict between self and other's needs, 15; conflict between self-assertion and self-effacement, 15; and conversion to Sikhism, 75; and desire to belong to the group, 171–72, 218–19, 225, 332–33; and dress, 173; and faith in one's intuitive morality, 214, 243, 274–75; gender roles (*see* Gender roles); and the image of the spiritual path, 86, 89–90; and leavers, 263–64, 270, 274–75, 278–79, 301, 314; meditation as a means to resolving, 223, 242–43, 274, 327–28; and personal adaptation of 3HO perspectives and values, 170–71, 221–23, 224, 247–48, 280–81, 314, 325; and primacy

of the spiritual woman, 14, 16, 327; reconstruction of identity after leaving, 263–64, 270–71, 274–75, 301–2, 314, 316, 335; relief from fragmented identities, 14; and search for harmony in interpersonal dealings, 13; and trust, 168

Identity management, 223–24

Identity processes, 169, 218. See also identity confirmation, identity diffusion, identity formation, identity struggles, identity transformation

Identity transformation, role of the teacher in, 235–36, 250

Identity struggles, 223–24, 257, 244–47, 249–50, 270

Identity transformation, 220–21

Imagery, myth, metaphor, 12, 13, 16, 52, 53, 54, 59–60, 65–66, 84–87, 88–90, 92, 169–70, 174, 177, 262, 269, 292, 295, 300, 317–18, 319–22, 328, 343

Immigration of ethnic Sikhs to the United States and Canada, 4–6

India: 3HO children sent to school in, 192–94, 222, 339; and approaches to identity, 324; gender roles in, 101–3; and goddess themes, 99–100; history of the Sikh religion in, 4–5, 6, 25–26, 27–28, 33, 34, 35, 40; and Western-style feminism, 290–91; and women practitioners of Tantra, 50

Individuation and merger, 3HO role in balancing, 14

Information processing simplified by 3HO, 17–18

Insight Meditation Center, Barre, Massachusetts, 302

Institute for the Development of the Harmonious Human Being, 14

Intuition, 214, 309

Jacobs, Janet L., 9, 10, 252, 253, 261, 263–64

Jeffcutt, Paul, 19, 20, 321

Josephs, Stephen, 216, 219, 225

Kabir, 32

Kakar, Sudhir, 324

Kali, 38, 323

Kanter, Rosabeth Moss, 219

Kapany, Narinder Singh, 77–78

Kartarpur, India, 30

Kaufman, Debra Renee, 9

Kaur Khalsa, Inderjit, 11, 104–5, 131, 137, 306

Kaur Khalsa, Krishna, 105

Kaur, Prabhupati, xviii–xxi, 7–8, 9, 17, 54, 68, 104–5, 239–40, 241–43, 258–59, 264, 301–2, 316

Kaur Khalsa, Premka, 80–81, 104–5, 172, 235–36

Kaur, Rani Raj, 293–94, 323

Kaur Khalsa, Shakti Parwha, 105, 118

Kaur Khalsa, Shanti Shanti, 105, 108

Kaur, Simran, 7–9, 19, 213, 214–15, 216, 264, 313–15, 316, 333, 335, 342–43

Keeping up: definitions of, 88, 244; encouragement for, 260

Kent, Stephen A., 60

Khalistan, 43

Khalsa: adopted as last name by 3HO members, 3, 81, 281; and British rule of the Punjab, 40, 41; and ethnic Sikhs, 5, 6, 81; and goddess themes, 36–37; and Guru Gobind Singh, 33–34, 36; origins of, 33–34, 36–38, 40

Khalsa, as last name. See also Kaur

Khalsa, Gurudharm Singh, 339

Khalsa, Gurujot Singh, 211–12

Khalsa, Kirpal Singh, 207–9, 211

Khalsa, Vikram Singh, 259

Khalsa Financial Services, 212

Khalsa International Industries and Trades, xv

Khalsa Women's Training Camp: author's attendance at, 7, 95–96, 111, 114–15, 118–19, 137–39; and children's camps, 193–94; courses offered at, 105, 113, 118, 137; descriptions of, xvi–xviii, 95–96, 111–16; and elaboration of identities, 169; non-members at, 137–38; and personal development, 111, 115–19, 126; purposes of, xvi, 111, 115, 117–19, 126, 134–35, 169; role of service at, 182; sadhana at, 111–12; women's responses to, 116, 117, 118–19; women's responsibilities at, 112–13; yoga at, 111, 112, 115–16; Yogi Bhajan's daily lectures at, 113–14, 115, 119–29; and Yogi Bhajan's teachings on feminine nature, 105–10; and Yogi Bhajan's teachings on gender roles, 105; Yogi Bhajan's use of mortification at, 249, 257, 273

Khande de pahul. See *Amrit*

Kirtan (prayers set to music), xvi, 75, 79

Kishwar, Madhu, 290–91

Kornfield, Jack, 302, 303

Kraybill, Donald, 173

Kripalu, 49

Kundalini energy, 49, 51, 52, 54; and intuition, 67; Sikhism as a means of channeling, 76

Self-awareness and development of new patterns of behavior, 177

Self-esteem/self-respect: and 3HO view of womanhood, 12, 310, 315–16, 329; as benefit of affiliation with 3HO, 11–12, 168, 307, 309–10; and counterculture, 170; encouragement of in women, 99; as a goal of 3HO, 168–69; and graceful womanhood, 179

Self-expression and construction of self, 67–69, 79

Self-improvement: and Khalsa Women's Training Camp, 124; need to maintain commitment to, 69–70, 200

Self-presentation: consequences of negative projections, 123; and ethics, 66–67; goals of, 120–21, 123; and organizational needs, 80, 135, 223; Yogi Bhajan's teachings regarding, 121–23, 126, 307

Sensitivity: heightened by *sadhana*, 176; heightened by wearing *bana*, 172

Sered, Susan Starr, 333–34, 335–37

Service: in ashrams, 183; to the community, 3; conflict between 3HO ideal of and feminism, 181–83, 247; idea of resisted by some 3HO women, 181; ideal of applied to everyday living, 182, 280; at Khalsa Women's Training Camp, 182; in marriage, 183, 188; questions relating to line between service and exploitation, 182; as a road to sainthood, 181; as a Sikh value, 3, 181–82; to the spiritual leader, 120–21, 181; on Yogi Bhajan's staff, 213–14

Shakta Tantra, 48–49

Shakti, 48–49; available to men and women, 103; women as embodiments of, 2, 14, 105–6, 123, 128, 130, 265, 329

Shakti Shoe Corporation, 145

Shaktipod, 223, 249–50, 251, 274

Shanker, Rajkumari, 33

Shapiro, Judith, 15

Shiromani Akali Dal, 41–44, 73–74

Shiromani Gurdwara Prabandhak Committee (SGPC), 41, 73–74, 79–80

Shiva, Vandana, 291, 299

Sikh Dharma: assertiveness of members in the Sikh community, 80–81; calls for changes in, 259–60; composition of, xv; and ethnic Sikhs in North America, 4, 77–78, 79–80, 81–84, 212, 338–39, 340, 341–42; evolution of, 73–84; founding of, xiv–xv; and the image of the spiritual path, 85–88; initiation vows, 75–76; Khalsa Council, 79, 214; as means to

group consciousness of God, 76; ministers ordained at solstice celebrations, 228–29; organizational arrangements, 4, 79, 80; as part of world Sikhism, 4–6, 26; and Punjabi Sikhs, 79–80, 338–39; role of beauty in daily life, 307; role of ministers, 74–75; role of women in administration, 4, 226; role of women in ministry, 4, 74–75, 226, 229; as source of new identities for 3HO members, 75; and spiritual distinctions based on gender or caste, 4; and tithing, 208; urged to abandon patriarchal attitudes, 259; and vision of new order and Khalsa economy, 77; and women as spiritual beings, 69. *See also* Healthy Happy Holy Organization

Sikh Dharma Brotherhood, xiv–xv, 74–75, 79

Sikh Foundation, 77–78

Sikh historiography, 26–27

Sikh independence movement, 43–44

Sikh literature: *gur-bilas*, 36–37

Sikhism: and *amrit*, 3; and the caste system, 4, 34, 81; and celebration of the Mata Devi, 36, 37–38; differences in approaches of westerners and Sikhs to the history of, 26–27, 31; differences with Hinduism, 27, 30, 34, 36; diversity of community of in the United States, 5–6, 81; and ethical living, 30; and the feminine principle, 37–39, 291–94, 295–96; and gender roles, 4, 6, 32–33; and goddess themes, 36–39, 41; Gora Sikhs, 81; Hinduism as a source of beliefs and practices, 13, 27, 28, 29, 37, 38–39, 40, 100–101; history of, 26–44; importance of congregation in, 29, 34; importance of texts in, 31; and Indian independence movement, 41–42; influence of Punjabi folk traditions on, 38–39; initiation ceremonies, 33–34; introduced to Yogi Bhajan's students, 3, 74–84; Islamic influences on, 27; and the Khalsa, 33–34, 35, 37–38, 40, 41; *kirtan*, xvi, 75, 79; as a means of channeling Kundalini energy, 76; and motherhood, 191; and New Age thinking, 76–77; and praxis, 12; and Punjabi politics, 41–44; Punjabi practices, 4; and relation of spirituality to the senses, 14; religious principles, 30; role of music in, xvi, 71, 75, 79; and *sant*-singer tradition, 28–29; and service to others, 181; and use of force in defense of Sikhism, 27, 33, 36; vision of God, 3–4; vision of wholeness, 16, 58, 69, 295, 298; and warrior imagery, 37, 54, 295, 299–300, 310–11, 312; and yoga, 4, 44, 76, 78

Sikhnet, 342

Singh, Bhai Vir, 292, 293–94, 295

Singh, Nikky-Guninder Kaur, 31–32, 37, 38, 97, 132, 291–94, 295–96, 314

Singh, Ranjit, 35, 36, 39

Singh, Sulakan, 35

Singh Sabha movement, 40

Siri Singh Sahib. *See* Bhajan, Yogi

Snow, David, 226

Societal change, individual change as the route to, 91–92, 123–24, 126, 169, 198, 272, 308, 309

Sociocultural contradictions: in American culture, 15–16, 56, 57, 58; in the 1960s and 1970s, 56–58; role of 3HO in mediating, 59, 64–65; role of new religious movements in resolving, 58

Solstice celebrations: as life-changing events, 147, 148, 159–60, 163, 268; as reinforcement of collective identity, 110, 228–31

Sound currents (*nad*), 14, 50, 83, 84, 149, 163

Spangler, David, 263

Spiritual path: appeal of the image of to women, 85–86, 322, 323; danger of losing one's way on, 87, 222–23; definitions of, 85–86, 334–35; harmonizing with career choices, 197–98; as link between public and private selves, 221; and network of spiritual seekers, 262–63, 265; perseverance with regard to, 331; as a reason for joining 3HO, 148–49, 305; role of in Sikh Dharma, 85–88, 306, 310; role of the image of in identity formation, 86, 171, 268–69, 298

Spiritual qualifications not determined by caste standing, 28, 30

Spiritual seekers, network of, 262–63

Spiritual teacher: degree of attachment to as factor in disaffiliation, 261–62, 333; the Goddess as, 297; need for them to practice what they preach, 243, 273; need to surrender to, 235–36, 237, 249, 327; service to, 120–21, 181

Spirituality: and continuing members, 306, 308, 309, 311, 312; development of, 195–96; and ex-members, 264, 271–72, 274–76, 296, 297–304, 330; and Kundalini yoga, 148; and need for harmony in everyday life, 250–51; relation to the

senses, 13–14, 83–84; search for as reason for joining 3HO/Sikh Dharma, 154, 156–57, 158–59, 162, 163–64, 165; and womanhood, 104–10, 121, 308, 309, 315–16, 323, 324–25, 326–27, 328

Stacey, Judith, 9

Stein, Maurice, 321

Stridharma, 100–101, 120–21, 188

Submission to God's will and to the spiritual teacher, 69

Sundari, 16, 293, 295

Sunshine Brass Beds, 208

Sunshine Scents, 208

Sunshine Services, 208

Sword as a Sikh symbol, 295, 299–300

Synchronicity, 284–85

Tantra, 2, 47–53, 59, 103, 264

Tantric Buddhism, 50

Tantric practices, and need for the guidance of a guru, 50–51, 52

Tantric thought, 25, 44–45, 47–48, 243

Tantric yoga, 2, 25, 44–45, 47–49, 51–52, 89, 230

Tat Khalsa, 40, 41

"Technology, the," 64–65

There Are No Accidents: Synchronicity and the Stories of Our Lives, by Robert H. Hopcke, 284

Tibet, 50

Tipton, Steven, 66, 70, 151–52, 214

Tobey, Alan, 64, 229, 230

Trust, 168–69, 342–43

Turbans: adoption of by 3HO members, 3, 81, 171, 172–73; and ethnic Sikhs, 5; role of, 13, 82, 122, 172

Udasis, 35–36, 38, 41

United States, ethnic Sikhs in, 4–6

Upanishads, 45, 47

Van Maanen, John, xx

Varenne, Jean, 46

Vedanta, 30, 35

Vegetarianism, 4, 76, 79, 81, 154

Vipassana, 302, 303

Visions, 210–11, 242, 258–59, 260

Wallis, Roy, 207, 231

Washington Free Community, 167

Weigert, Andrew J., 59

Wessinger, Catherine, 294, 335

White Tantric yoga. *See* Tantric yoga

Wholism as goal of 3HO, 69

Women's camp. *See* Khalsa Women's Training Camp
Women's theologies, 333–34, 335
Woodman, Marion, 326
Wright, Stuart A., 252
Wuthnow, Robert, 207

Yinger, J. Milton, 20
Yoga: as an act of self-denial, 46–47; and ethnic Sikhs, 4; goals of, 44–46, 50; Ma Pa, 298; as a means to alter identity, 84; as a means to experience God, 46, 49; and *sadhana*, xiii; and self-denial, 46–47; as a source of a sense of well-being, 13–14, 148; and spiritual ego, 73

"Yoga and the Spiritual Woman" (women's camp course, 1983), 105;
Yoga classes: as door to involvement in 3HO, 17, 146, 147, 148, 149, 153–54, 157–58, 159, 161, 162, 165, 167, 268; taught by Yogi Bhajan, xvii, 45, 51–52, 165, 238
Yoga sets: said to affect particular bodily organs and glands, 51, 334; to strengthen women, 108, 328
Yoga Sutras, by Patanjali, 45–46
Yogananda, Paramahansa, 45
Yogi Tea Company, 340
Young, Katherine K., 101, 290–91

Zimmer, Heinrich Robert, 319

Graceful Women was designed and typeset on a Macintosh computer system using QuarkXPress software. The body text is set in 10.5/13.5 Janson, and display type is set in Ajile. This book was designed and typeset by Cheryl Carrington and manufactured by Thomson-Shore, Inc.